JUST XML
2ND EDITION

ISBN 0-13-018554-X

90000

9 780130 185549

JUST XML
2ND EDITION

John E. Simpson

PRENTICE HALL PTR
UPPER SADDLE RIVER, NJ 07458
WWW.PHPTR.COM

Library of Congress Cataloging-in-Publication Data

Simpson, John E.
   Just XML / John E. Simpson.—2nd ed.
     p. cm,
   ISBN 0-13-018554-X
   1. XML (Document markup language)   I. Title.

   QA76.76.H94 S57 2000
   005.7'2—dc21

                         00-042791

Editorial/production supervision: *Mary Sudul*
Composition: *FASTpages*
Cover design: *Design Source*
Cover design director: *Jerry Votta*
Manufacturing manager: *Alexis R. Heydt*
Marketing manager: *Bryan Gambrel*
Acquisitions editor: *Paul Petralia*
Editorial Assistant: *Justin Somma*

© 2001 Prentice Hall PTR
Prentice-Hall, Inc.
Upper Saddle River, NJ 07458

The publisher offers discounts on this book when ordered in bulk quantities.
For more information, contact
Corporate Sales Department,
Prentice Hall PTR
One Lake Street
Upper Saddle River, NJ 07458
Phone: 800-382-3419; FAX: 201-236-714
E-mail (Internet): corpsales@prenhall.com

Printed in the United States of America

10 9 8 7 6 5 4 3 2

ISBN 0-13-018554-X

Prentice-Hall International (UK) Limited, *London*
Prentice-Hall of Australia Pty. Limited, *Sydney*
Prentice-Hall Canada Inc., *Toronto*
Prentice-Hall Hispanoamericana, S.A., *Mexico*
Prentice-Hall of India Private Limited, *New Delhi*
Prentice-Hall of Japan, Inc., *Tokyo*
Pearson EducationAsia Pte. Ltd., *Singapore*
Editora Prentice-Hall do Brasil, Ltda., *Rio de Janeiro*

to Toni
(fiery boar to my
once-nervous jackrabbit)

CONTENTS

Preface

Why did I write *Just XML*? It's a fair question. (And I won't even ask you in return to address its obvious flip side: Why are you reading it? I hope to answer that for you in a moment.)

The short answer is that I wrote this book because I work with computers every day and want them to be more useful than they already are. Not just for me, either—every week I meet a hundred-odd people (some of them quite odd, but that's a subject for a different book) who are baffled by the failure of computers to "think" the same way we do.

A longer, more precise answer is that I want the *Internet* to be more useful: When I type a keyword or phrase in a Web search engine, I don't want a list of ten thousand alleged "hits" returned, sorted by a relevance that some machine has calculated based on an algorithm that may or may not have much to do with the documents' actual substance. I want the Internet—and its associated technologies—to be smart about all the information it holds: to *understand* itself, I guess you might say. And I believe that the Extensible Markup Language, or XML, is the surest route to that ideal right now—and the faster it spreads, the faster we'll get there.

Which brings us to a natural corollary: Why, specifically, might you want to read *Just XML* as opposed (or in addition) to a hundred other books on the same topic?

Why *Just XML?*

Let's break that section heading into two separate questions: "Why 'just'?" and "Why XML?" And let's consider the second question first.

Unless you've been in a technological fog for the last five years or so, you already know that the Internet—particularly the part of it called the World Wide Web—has taken the developed world by storm. Everyone from the largest multi-national corporation to the neighborhood butcher lists his or her own *www.com-panyname.com* in the Yellow Pages. It's leached into the daily lives not just of corporate and government entities, but even of everyday people (school-age children have their own home pages).

You may also know that what underlies all the Web's exhilarating breadth of content and style is a simple secret, not exactly a dirty one, but one still capable of shocking innocent newcomers: It's all just *text.*[*] Regular text is bracketed with special strings of other text that instructs a user's browser to render the enclosed matter in some particular style. For example, the tags (as these bracketing strings are called) <em> and </em> say, "Render everything between the opening <em> and the closing </em> in an *emphasized* form." (What "emphasized" means is left up to the browser, but it almost always means italicized.) You don't need any exotic software to create these marked-up text files, although such software is certainly available; all you need is a plain old text editor—such as Windows Note-pad or UNIX vi—and a facility for getting at the <, >, and / keys without breaking your train of thought.

That's all well and good, as my grandmother might have said, but it doesn't go far enough. I'll give you some detailed reasons why in Chapter 1, "Markup Laid Down," but for now, just take it on faith that the Web's established markup language—Hypertext Markup Language, or HTML—fails to establish *meaning* for elements of the documents in which it's written. Furthermore, if you're creating your Web files in Tokyo, you'd better forget about using that nifty new Kanji keyboard: HTML makes easy use of only the characters in the Roman alphabet—letters A through Z and digits 0 through 9. XML easily bests HTML on both counts.

Now about that "Just" in the title….

---

[*]   Well, all right: it's not *all* text. Obvious exceptions include image, sound, and other multimedia files. However, the instructions to the browser about how to display this non-textual information are indeed—like the other 90% of the Web's content—plain old ASCII.

As you'll see, XML shares some of HTML's bloodlines. Many of the folks responsible for getting HTML off the ground, as well as its decades-old parent SGML (Standardized General Markup Language), were involved in the development of the XML standard, too. But both HTML and SGML are different beasts than XML, requiring different mindsets to *use*. I believe that it's not only possible but desirable (if XML is to take off at all) to learn XML without requiring any knowledge at all of its forebears. So you won't find much help here if you're interested primarily in them.

(If you snoop around a bit on the subject of XML, you'll also find copious references elsewhere to Java and other programming languages. That's largely because XML is still so new that many of its adherents are involved in developing the software that will *process* XML, and such folks are naturally concerned with language-specific approaches to handling the new markup style. *Just XML* doesn't have much to say about Java, C++, *et al.*, either.)

So while you're going through this book, put away the wheelbarrows full of knowledge and predispositions you may have acquired about SGML, HTML, and so on. Concentrate on what you want your Web site to say, and on learning how to make it say *that*, uniquely.

Repeat to yourself: Just XML.

Some Things about Me (and what they imply about you)

First, you need to know that I'm not an SGML guru. In fact, before beginning the first edition of this book, I knew virtually nothing at all about it. A friend of mine worked in the late 1980s and early 1990s on a project called EDGAR, an SGML application used by the federal Securities & Exchange Commission; I could tell from the bleary-eyed look in this friend's eyes, and implicit in her e-mail messages, that learning or using SGML was not something to be endeavored casually. Beyond that, I knew nothing except very basic principles (such as that HTML was some kind of SGML derivative).

I have been a computer applications developer (read "programmer") since 1979. Most of my early work was on mainframe computers, and I graduated thence to UNIX-based minis, and eventually to PCs. My first Internet use was in 1991. I built my first Web page in 1994. My "day job" is as an applications developer, mostly using Microsoft Access and Visual Basic 5.0, and I'm the Webmaster for my department's Web site; in my spare time I also maintain the site for Anhinga Press, a publisher of poetry, at *www.anhinga.org*.

Why this dreary recitation of a resumé?

No, I'm not fishing for job offers (I'm quite happy where I am). Really, all I want to do is reassure you that, in my opinion, in order to understand and use XML productively:

- You don't have to know anything at all about SGML; and
- You don't need to know anything at all about HTML (although a general understanding of how it works will help).

In general, I believe that anyone with a basic modicum of intelligence and some simple prior exposure to the Web can understand and use XML. Don't worry about the apparent strangeness of some of its concepts and mechanisms— take one step at a time and you'll do just fine.

Ulterior Motives

All right, I confess: There's more to the "why I wrote this book" than all that noble (however sincere) folderol I mentioned at the outset.

The fact is, although I work all day with computers and the Internet—and think, on the whole, that my life is better because of them—there are times when I'm heartily sick of the things. (Not just when they're not working right, either; sometimes I'm so fed up with just sitting in front of them that I'll drop a favorite, entirely smooth-running game before I even have a chance to figure out the first riddle.)

At such times there's nothing I like better than channel surfing for a movie I've never seen. Even better is a trip to the video-rental store, where I've got some element of control over the selection.

And I'm not talking about recent box-office big hits, either. I mean oddball little films, probably cranked out in black and white in the 1940s through 1960s: the ones featuring casts whose names you can't recall fifteen minutes after they've rolled over the screen (while some corny, likewise forgettable score drones or tootles in the background); the ones whose plots revolve around mysterious creatures from other planets, or unlikely chains of criminal circumstance on our own planet, or men in combat fatigues baring their shallow souls to one another while tinny post-production gunfire whizzes and whines overhead. I mean, in short, B movies.

In thinking about B movies, I realized something wonderful about XML: I can think about B movies a *lot* using XML as a tool for describing them. This would have been nearly impossible to do fully with pure HTML—almost certainly requiring me to write a customized, hard-to-maintain program in Perl or some other Web programming language. It'll be a snap (well, almost a snap!) in XML, though.

So throughout this book, be prepared to think not just about XML, but about low-budget cinema (or at least cinema that frequently *looks* as if it's low-budget) as well.

How *Just XML* Is Organized

This book consists of five main parts or sections:

- **Part 1, XML Basics,** will introduce you to everything you need to know about XML itself. (The "basics" in the title simply means XML as a distinct element apart from its closely-related technologies covered in the remaining parts.) This part will also introduce you to FlixML, a customized XML lingo for communicating information about (yes) B movies.
- **Part 2, XML Linking,** covers XML's tools for hyperlinking documents to one another (or to other parts of the same document) in ways not remotely possible with HTML.
- **Part 3, XML: Doing It in Style,** details the use of Cascading Style Sheets (CSS) and Extensible Stylesheet Language Transformations (XSLT). With these two languages you'll tell browsers how to transform the structure of and display your fully linked XML documents for maximum impact. By the end of this section, you'll know everything you need to create a "database" of your own, using FlixML to describe B movies.
- In **Part 4, Rolling Your Own XML Application,** you'll learn how to develop a Document Type Definition (DTD) for your own purposes, freeing you (should you want to be freed!) forever from thinking that XML is capable of describing only B movies.
- **Part 5, XML Directions,** discusses—and shows examples of—the range of XML-related software available as of this writing. It also covers what's in store for XML-related technologies for the foreseeable future.

Finally, the appendices of *Just XML* will point you to further references—mostly on XML, etc., but also a handful (I'm sorry, just can't help myself) on B movies.

Acknowledgments

Just XML wouldn't have been possible without the generous (and sometimes unknowing) advice and assistance of dozens of participants in the XML Developers mailing list, XML-DEV. In alphabetical order, I'd particularly like to thank: Tim Bray, David Carlisle, James Clark, Steve DeRose, G. Ken Holman, Rick Jelliffe, Michael Kay, Eliot Kimber, Andrew Layman, Chris Maden, Eve Maler, Sean McGrath, David Megginson, Peter Murray-Rust, Paul Prescod, and James Tauber. I doubt that you'll ever know how helpful your postings have been; that said, of course, any errors or omissions in *Just XML* are mine alone.

Although it may seem odd, I'd also like to publicly thank two authors of what are nominally "competing" XML books, neither of whom I've met: Elliotte Rusty Harold, for showing me how to take the subject just seriously enough, and Simon St. Laurent, for showing me how not to take it *too* seriously. I admire both of your books tremendously, for quite different reasons.

Thanks finally to the good people at Prentice Hall/PTR—especially my editor on the first edition, Jeff Pepper, for suggesting the project in the first place, and for his good humor and support over the course of both editions; and Paul Petralia, editor of this edition, for shepherding it to completion when Jeff moved on to his new role as publisher of Prentice Hall/PTR.

PART 1

XML Basics

This section covers everything you need to know about starting to use XML to mark up your documents for meaningful display on the Web. It also introduces you to Just XML's sample application: the B movie guide markup language, FlixML.

Information on linking documents to one another is covered in Part 2, XML Linking, and information on controlling specific display attributes is found in Part 3, XML: Doing It in Style. If you're going to be developing your own customized markup language, such as FlixML, you'll also need at some point to dive into Part 4, Rolling Your Own XML Application. Finally, Part 5, XML Directions, will cover what to expect in the next few years (perhaps even months) from XML-related technology, including the software necessary to support it.

CHAPTER 1

Markup Laid Down

This chapter covers the most basic of basic concepts in any book about displaying information on the Web: What *is* a markup language, and why use one at all? You'll also be introduced to the general characteristics of documents marked up in XML as opposed to other members of its family, and in particular to the ideas that underlie FlixML—this book's customized "language" for describing less-than-blockbuster motion pictures.

If you're familiar with other markup languages, notably HTML, feel free to bound exuberantly over the chapter's first section (Revealing Codes) to the second (The XML Difference), which introduces XML itself.

Revealing Codes

Creating a document via computer was at first no different from creating one with a typewriter: you just pounded away at a keyboard. (Perhaps you began by drafting your words in pencil, then transcribed them into electronic form. I wrote my first book that way, in 1991.)

Even if you're completely new to computers, it should be obvious that the plain old 26 letters of the Roman alphabet (or however many there are in your own language) are inadequate for many purposes. The *meaning* of your words, not just the words themselves, is what is important to your readers. Even if you dress things up with exclamation points and underlining, the most you can hope to communicate in straight, unadorned print is a vague excitement that quickly ceases to hold the reader's attention.

Newspaper and magazine designers have known this for a long time, and augment their plain text with headlines, callouts, and similar devices to emphasize important ideas and to impose a structure to the printed page that would be otherwise lacking.

Shades of meaning

Imagine that you're a late nineteenth-century newspaper publisher. Shortly before election day, you come across a juicy scandal about your biggest competitor, who's running for office. How do you "play" the story?

If you're of the old-fashioned school, you dump the story on the front page with all the other news of the day. It's all set in the same typeface, with only slight variations in size. After all, your words are the important things, right? Responsible readers will read all the news you print, and judge for themselves what's important, right? Well, maybe all that *was* right in earlier times. But with the newspaper industry booming, you know that you've got to do something to catch the eyes of an ever-busier reading public. (It wouldn't hurt if you could stick it to your competitor at the same time.)

So you use all the same words in the story itself. But across the full width of the front page, you shout (with your street-corner newsboys):

Candidate Kane Caught in Love Nest with "Singer"

Ooooh yes. That will get everyone's attention, won't it?

Aside from the size of the type and its placement on the front page, note one other thing about this example (which, by the way, comes from Orson Welles' 1939 classic, *Citizen Kane*[1]): the quotation marks around the last word. A sophisticated reader wouldn't just read the words in the headline; he or she would also catch the added nuance supplied by the punctuation—that the singer in question is really not *much* of a singer.

Those quotation marks (and most other punctuation) are in fact an elementary form of markup. They alter the text, introducing to it a layer of meaning or structure that you can't get from the text alone. Furthermore, in this case, note

---

1.   Decidedly *not* a B movie, although it's got a lot in common with them.

also that the "markup" clearly indicates where the affected text begins and where it ends, and that an opening quotation mark is very similar to, but subtly different from, a closing one. (My sixth-grade teacher called them sixes and nines.)

Markup—whether just in the form of punctuation or on a grander scale, as I'll discuss in a moment—is the simplest way to add layers of meaning to computerized text. But it can do lots of other things, too.

A good illustration of this is the way that the WordPerfect word-processing software keeps track of display styles, fonts, paragraph and document formats, and so on. Yes, now that WYSIWYG displays—fonts, embedded images, all the rest—are universal, WordPerfect does depict a page's visual appearance. But underlying the way the page looks onscreen or on paper, WordPerfect embeds in each document hundreds of bits of information that say, for example, "Begin a left-justified paragraph here, indented a half-inch…beginning here, set the font size to 11 points and italicize it…turn the italicization off here…resume normal font size…end the paragraph here." You can see all these underlying instructions simply by toggling a function key.

Figure 1.1 shows WordPerfect's "reveal codes" window as it depicts a section of the preceding page.

The little pushbutton-like markers within the text can be "edited," after a fashion, by doubleclicking on them. A font marker, for instance, has various attributes (in standard Microsoft Windows terminology, "properties") that can be adjusted through a dialog box that shows a generic sample of how the marked-up text will appear.

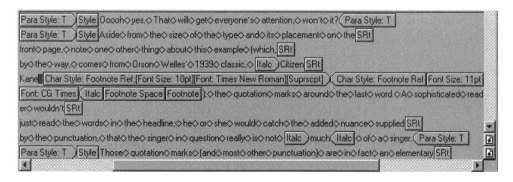

Figure 1.1 WordPerfect (version 7) Reveal Codes window

Simplify, simplify, simplify

WordPerfect and similar word processors provide good examples of markup in general, and how it can be used to fancy-up a document so much that—if you're so inclined—the true meaning of the words themselves can be nearly obscured by the way in which the words are displayed. But there are a few problems with these programs—problems that became especially obvious when the Internet started to take off.

First—and perhaps least obvious—there's a problem for the developers of the specific program (like a word processor). A given piece of code in programming language X will almost never run, unchanged, under a different operating system (sometimes even on simply a different computer) than the one on which it was developed. Different computers differ not only in their underlying hardware, but also in their user interfaces. A fully responsible software vendor therefore must commit to developing a version for the Macintosh, as well as a version for the Apple II, a separate version for older MS-DOS computers, one for Windows 3.x computers, one for Windows 95, one for Windows NT, one for Windows 98, one for generic UNIX, one for Sun's SunOS, one for the Amiga, and so on. It's a nightmare, and at the very least, drives up the cost of *purchasing* software for everyone.

Second, there's a problem for users of these programs' output: Typical word-processing files can be significantly bigger than their contents would appear to warrant. The formatting and other style instructions embedded in such a file, even if invisible to a user of the software, of course take up space of their own. These instructions are in so-called binary form—machine-readable, not human-intelligible. It's possible (and common) to use compression software to reduce the sizes of files needing to be shipped around the Internet, but the specific problem in the case of binary files is that they simply don't compress very well. Depending on its contents, a straight text file might be squeezed to ten percent of its original size; the same contents in a word-processing file format, to no less than forty percent or so.

A final significant problem is for developers of *content*: writers, journalists, corporate public relations staff, and so on. It's one thing to prepare a company newsletter, for example, using Microsoft Word, then e-mail a copy to all the company's employees; after all, the information systems (IS) department requires all company-bought computers to have a copy of Word installed. But what if you want to distribute, say, an electronic sales brochure on the Web? Will all your customers have the same word processor, let alone the same *version* of the same word processor? Can you afford to write off the potential customers who don't?

A possible solution for everyone is just to use plain old text files. That's not a very satisfactory answer, though—it puts us right back to the invention of the printing press.

The technology underlying Web-based documents popularized a wonderfully simple solution all around: include markup with plain text content (just like WordPerfect's Reveal Codes mode), and *put the markup in plain text as well.*

If you think about it, there's one potential danger in this solution, however. Consider this bit of a document marked up in a hypothetical language:

```
BOLDITALICSNowENDITALICSENDBOLD is the time for all. . .
```

In this hypothetical language—let's call it ACML, for All-Caps Markup Language—obviously, the markup is simply expressed in all capital letters. When the ACML browser hits such a string of characters, it knows it must treat the enclosed text differently from "normal" text (and, incidentally, not display the markup with the text). But how do you include content that is itself in all uppercase? If you're writing a story in which a character says, "I cannot BELIEVE you'd be so BOLD. Didn't your mother teach you any manners?" how do you keep the browser from boldfacing the entire second sentence, let alone from choking on the BELIEVE because it doesn't know how to display "believed" text?

There's a simple—though not 100% foolproof—answer to this riddle: You design your markup language so that the presence of markup is signaled by special characters that are very unlikely ever to appear in real content.

The first widely successful, nonproprietary markup language, Standardized General Markup Language (SGML), followed this approach. SGML *tags* (as the markup devices are called) begin and end with angle brackets, the < and > characters respectively. This SGML convention has been carried forward in both of SGML's two popular offspring, HyperText Markup Language (HTML) and now the Extensible Markup Language (XML).

Tags vs. what they tag

The discussion that immediately follows this sidebar speaks specifically of *tags*. In common parlance, you will likely hear the term "tag" used interchangeably with another: "element." We'll see much more about the latter term, throughout *Just XML*, but now might be a good time to give you a quick picture of the differences.

Strictly speaking, a tag is not an element. A *tag* is a physical, typographic "marker" that indicates the presence of an element. An *element* is everything from the opening angle bracket of a start-tag to the closing angle bracket of the end-tag (which might be the same physical tag as the start, if the element is empty). An element may contain other elements (delimited by their own tags), which may contain other elements (and so on), and may also contain text content and other forms of markup.

If you really want to get precise, you might want to be aware of two other terms. An *element type* is the overall class to which a particular *element* belongs; that is, an element is a specific occurrence, in a specific document, of its element type. For example, an XML-based language might include a `paragraph` *element type* that may be used in documents based on that language, whereas a given document may contain one or many `paragraph` *elements.*

The other term—not very widely used, but you may encounter it, usually undefined, on XML mailing lists—is *GI.* This is an abbreviation for *generic identifier*; an element's GI is just its name, the "word" that follows the opening < in the tag.

Strung together, these four terms make up a general-to-specific continuum: element type, element, tag, and GI.

Throughout *Just XML*, I'll use the term "tag" when referring to the actual markup device. There's a formal difference between "element" and "element type" that is important to preserve in some cases, and I'll note those cases when covering them; however, by far most usage on the Internet, even among people who know better, is to use "element" for both. That's the convention I'll follow. I don't expect you to come across "GI" again in these pages.

The rules of the markup game

Here's an HTML version of the above ACML passage:

```
<B><i>Now</I></b> is the time for all. . .
```

Notice the features of the tags in this example:

1. Capitalization is not important at all. This was true of HTML, *but is completely changed in XML.* In XML, if there's a `<boldface>` tag, a reference to a `<BOLDface>` tag won't be recognized as the same thing at all.

2. In this case, there are both *start-tags* and *end-tags*, such as the `<B>` and `</b>`. The only difference between them is that the end tag includes an extra character, a slash (`/`). Again, a difference: Not all HTML tags require an end-tag, while in XML all "normal" tags always come in pairs. (Special allowances are made, as we'll see, for tags that don't need to enclose anything. A good example from HTML is the `<img>` tag for specifying a graphic that's to be inserted inline—all the information is within the tag itself. XML has special provisions for dealing with such so-called empty tags.)

3. The separate tag pairs are *nested*. That is, the "italicize this" markup is fully enclosed within the "bold this" markup. (Actually, that's not always required of HTML documents; browsers can cover for many of a Web-page developer's human failings, such as improper nesting of tags.) In this example, the word "Now" could be just as well specified with italics first, then bold—the order of the nesting (at least in this case) isn't particularly important.

4. Unless you're a supernaturally smooth typist, markup can be a real pain to add to content. Not only is it physically cumbersome to type the < and > symbols, it's also mentally challenging to keep focused on producing the content and not the markup in which it's contained.

The devil in the details

I mentioned above that this convention of "all markup is contained in the special characters < and >" isn't entirely foolproof. It's true that these special characters are seldom used in normal text; it's equally true that they're on the keyboard for a reason—they are *sometimes* used in normal text.

So when a browser encounters a "real" < symbol without a matching >, how does it know not to keep scanning the document all the way to the end, looking for the missing > symbol? There are ways around this dilemma too, and we'll see some of them later in this book. Ultimately, though, it's a real hall of mirrors; you just have to throw up your hands at some point and say, "I don't care about further exceptions to the exceptions to the exceptions."

Do you need to know anything about SGML or HTML to start working with XML immediately? No. Much of the background (historical and technological) will be *useful* for you to know, but none of it is required.

The XML Difference

A markup cartoon

Editorial cartoons use a common convention to help make their metaphors easily grasped by their audience: Any object in the drawing that's not obviously a caricature of a familiar personage, a famous building, or a standard editorial-cartoon symbol (such as donkeys for Democrats, Uncle Sam for the USA, and so on) is *labeled*. I want you now to picture yourself in such a cartoon, an animated one.

You're in the lobby of the Ritz-Markup Hotel, standing before an elevator whose doors part to reveal three passengers. Their gender doesn't matter at all, but let's assume for the sake of illustration that they're men. (Cartoonists do everything for the sake of illustration.) You get on the elevator. And as you usually do, you peek discreetly at the three guys sharing your space.

Passenger #1 is apparently an employee of this tony establishment, the elevator operator. The man has the posture of a drill sergeant and radiates an aura of someone who goes about his business with supreme confidence. You observe that he is dressed immaculately—not in a uniform, as you might expect an elevator operator to be—but in a dark, pin-striped three-piece suit. His vest is made of fine silk; a watch chain runs across the front of it. At least you *thought* it was a watch chain, but then you notice that every time the elevator stops at a floor, the man pulls from the watch pocket of his vest a Swiss army knife and unfolds a different blade, which he then inserts into a slot in the elevator control panel and turns, causing the doors to open, pause, and close. Rather oddly, he has an umbrella hooked over one wrist. (Well, who knows? It *might* rain in an elevator.) There's a sign hanging on this man's chest; it reads "SGML."

Passenger #2 could, in a dim room, be mistaken for the elevator operator. Maybe they're related; they share the same cheekbones, the same eyes, and are about the same height. But there's something just a little off-kilter about this fellow. He's not wearing a suit, for starters, but a sport coat and slacks. He slouches against the back wall of the elevator. He's wearing sunglasses, and his left and right socks are of slightly different shades (although they could be mistaken for identical). He bends down to tie a shoe, giving you a good glance at the sign on his back—"HTML," it reads—and also at the shirt tail inelegantly protruding from beneath the hem of his jacket.

Like the second passenger, the third shares certain of Passenger #1's features, the same eyes and cheekbones. This one—the youngest of the three—

stands as erect as the first, though, and also wears a dark suit. But it's a two-piece, *sans* vest, and consequently he has no Swiss army knife on a chain. No umbrella, either. And unlike passenger #2, there are no shirt tails hanging out, and no untied shoes. At one point on the long ride, passenger #3 removes from his jacket pocket a pair of nail scissors, trims off a jagged edge, then puts the scissors back in his pocket and removes an emery board with which he smoothes the trimmed edge. One separate tool for each separate task. Looking more closely— you really are a snoop—you see that on each of his sleeves is a label: "XML."

Meanwhile, back in the real world...

The differences among SGML, HTML, and XML are like those among the three guys in the elevator.

SGML calls the shots for all three, deciding where they will stop and how they will stop there. SGML is ready for every eventuality it might face, even the most unlikely (the thunderstorm in the elevator car). It is formal, rigorous, precise, and darned near complete.

Second-generation markup—HTML—shares a number of its daddy's features. It's very well-suited for casual purposes. You can bring HTML to a business meeting, but it will always look a bit *déclassé*. The freedom to have loose ends dangling here and there means that HTML can get ready for work a lot faster than either SGML or XML, but it also means that on the way out of the elevator door, things have a tendency to snag.

Finally, XML. Its general form and shape are those of SGML. But unless it's raining, it doesn't bring an umbrella along; and if it needs to attend to some personal grooming, it's got the tool that does exactly that (and no more). Its middle-of-the-road attire means that you can bring it along for just about any business need.

As you'll see in Chapter 2, an XML document doesn't look all that different from its SGML or HTML counterparts. Both the minor differences and more numerous similarities are a direct result of the XML framers' experiences with the two earlier markup languages. From the start, the XML specification has included the following ten design principles; the headings are taken straight from the specification document itself:

XML should be straightforwardly usable over the Internet.

This requirement seems almost to go without saying; of course you'd want a new markup language to be usable on the Internet, particularly the World Wide Web.

But "straightforwardly" adds a subtle extra layer of meaning: like HTML, XML is not rocket science. Furthermore—perhaps less obviously—delivering XML documents does not require any change to the network itself, or to its supporting software and protocols.

XML shall support a wide variety of applications.

Again, this seems like an obvious goal. It marks a radical departure for XML versus its HTML cousin, however. The latter's design supports on its own just a single (albeit powerful) application: Web browsing. All the other stuff that occurs on the Web—Java and ECMAScript, Common Gateway Interface (CGI) forms and database processing, animated images, and audio and video playback—occurs inside simple or exotic add-ons to the core HTML specification itself.

Note that the XML spec does not say *what* other applications will be supported. The XML FAQ, in a favorite burst of encyclopedic whimsy, mentions "music, chemistry, electronics, hill-walking, finance, surfing, petroleum geology, linguistics, cooking, knitting, stellar cartography, history, engineering, rabbit-keeping, mathematics, etc." as possible applications of XML. All of those can be "supported" by HTML as well, of course, but the difficulty is that HTML forces them all into clothing cut from the same fabric.

XML shall be compatible with SGML.

The intention here is to capitalize on the success of SGML. While it has not been trumpeted in the popular media nearly as much (or as loudly) as HTML, SGML is a critical technological weapon in the arsenal of many industries, from newspapers to banking. If XML can take advantage of the embedded base of SGML authors and—especially—software, it will speed the acceptance of the new markup language by those important customers.

Aside from the existing SGML tools and expertise that can be readily adapted to XML, there is much inherent power in SGML that was not carried forward into the HTML specification. In HTML, for example, you can't deviate from the set of element types that are specified for the language. XML's ability to include any element types that a particular purpose requires—the "Extensible" in the name—is a direct descendant of SGML's.

It shall be easy to write programs which process XML documents.

Note that here we're not talking about coding XML documents themselves, but rather about the *programs which process XML documents.* This objective says that the rules of the language should be simple, not just for humans but for machines as well.

Simple examples abound in HTML of how markup languages can be difficult for software to process, while easy for humans to interpret. For example, the "forgivingness" of the HTML specification—or rather of the way in which it's interpreted by Web browsers—allows many elements to be sloppily nested within one another. This is a generous gift to fumble-fingered Webmasters, but can complicate a software developer's life enormously, especially when there are elements within elements within elements: How does the program know when to "turn off" italics that are signified by a `<bold>` tag, which in turn overlaps a particular font specification, which sort of but not quite exactly falls within the scope of a bulleted list item? All the exception handling—the need to deal intelligently with all those dangling shirt tails—can give a programmer fits.

At one time, XML's developers reportedly asserted that writing an XML application program should be at most a "two-week" project for graduate students. This didn't make it into the specification (maybe they floated it among some graduate students, who threatened a walkout), but the philosophy behind that specific target remains very much a part of XML as formally defined.

One important reason why XML programs need to be simple to write lies in the very extensibility of the language. If you've got a particular XML flavor that has been tailored specifically for genealogical records, for example, it would be great to have a "genealogical XML browser" that knows—far more than a generic Web browser could—exactly where on the user's screen to place birthdates, photos of family members, and so on. The requirements for such a browser would be very different from those for a browser of library catalog entries. If you want to encourage the development of such special-purpose browsers, you've got to keep their requirements simple.

The number of optional elements in XML is to be kept to the absolute minimum, ideally zero.

While XML is a direct descendant of SGML (much more so than HTML), it does away with hundreds of optional "features" added to its parent over the course of many years. (One common way of thinking of XML is as "SGML Lite"—or, as one reference says, "SGML⁻" rather than "HTML⁺⁺.")

Note that the "optional features" referred to here are those in the language specification itself. Individual XML document types—the genealogical one I mentioned above, FlixML, the Chemical Markup Language, and so on—can be as baroque and fully featured as their designers desire, including many optional element types *within each document type.*

XML documents should be human-legible and reasonably clear

This, again, is partially a matter of processing efficiency as well as human comfort.

It's important, yes, that you and I be able to read a Triffids.xml file in its "naked," raw-text form, without any fancy software, and figure out what a reviewer of *Day of the Triffids* has to say about the movie, who its cast was, what studio produced it, how likely it is that the Earth would be overrun by hordes of carnivorous ferns, and so on. (If we're writing the review ourselves, it may be equally important to see all the nuts-and-bolts of the markup should the review not "behave" exactly as we'd expected in our FlixML browser.)

But as I mentioned earlier in this chapter, putting not only the content but also the markup itself in plain text form makes the resulting document not only smaller, but more portable across computing platforms. This is a wonderful by-product of using plain text.

The XML design should be prepared quickly

Internet time, they say, is faster than real time. I don't think I've ever heard an estimate of *how much* faster. Even the seven-times-faster of dog years doesn't seem fast enough, though. A new technology crops up for performing Task X, and a week later three or four competitors appear; the next week, there's a new technology for performing the same task, plus Y and Z.

On the Web, what was about to happen was that large enterprises—corporations, banks, the government, and all the rest of the usual suspects—were starting to wonder if they should bail out of the whole standards process. HTML can do quite a bit, especially with the use of browser plug-ins and the like; but the Web was in danger of collapsing under the combined weight of all the things that HTML *can't* do (or do easily), and of all the proprietary software needed to make HTML stand on its head and do the required backflips.

"Quickly" was never defined, but a sense of urgency underlay the preparation of the XML specification. Logistics could have complicated matters further—people working on the spec were widely separated geographically, and most had other commitments to their employers, schools, and so on (to say nothing of their personal lives). Fortunately they all were able to take advantage of advanced technology to communicate with one another, in e-mail, video, and phone conferences. Within about a year of their first "meeting," the next-to-final version of the language spec had been posted on the site of the World Wide Web Consortium. (The consortium, known as the W3C, is an arbiter of specifications and standards for new Internet technologies.) Given the complexities they were dealing with, this was remarkable.

The design of XML shall be formal and concise

Okay, here's this new markup language. Its stated goal is, in brief, to simplify the task of delivering complex content over the Web. How embarrassing it would have been if the design of the new language were more complicated and ambiguous than the language itself!

The XML specification is both formal and concise because it is written in something called Extended Backus-Naur Format, or EBNF. EBNF, a common tool for declaring the syntax of new programming languages, will probably never win any prizes for aesthetic appeal, except among people who appreciate engineering beauty. For example, if you asked a fairly simple question such as, "What's the formal definition of the XML term 'children'?," the spec would answer you as follows:

```
[47] children ::= (choice | seq) ('?' | '*' | '+')?
```

To say that this is alarming doesn't begin to do justice to the term "alarm." But it's undeniably efficient, unambiguous, and yes, even beautiful (in the same way that the interior of Arnold Schwarzenneger's forearm was in *The Terminator*).

Don't panic. *You don't have to know EBNF in order to know XML.* It's true that you can't escape it if you want to read and understand the formal language specification; if you're satisfied with simply using XML, though, you needn't give EBNF a second thought.

(By the way, none of the HTML coders I've ever met knows anything about EBNF. But the HTML spec is written in EBNF, too.)

XML documents shall be easy to create

Like "quickly," "straightforwardly," "legible," and so on, "easy to create" isn't spelled out. But I have to admit that I wouldn't be comfortable if this *wasn't* a goal of XML, no matter how vague the term.

As I mentioned earlier in this chapter, you don't need anything other than a computer to "write XML": no special word processor or other software is required. You can even make do with pencil and paper as long as you either: (a) don't care to actually put your XML online; or (b) have someone else to transcribe your chicken-scratchings into a text file.

Terseness in XML markup is of minimal importance

SGML and HTML both provide for *omitting* markup—particularly end-tags—in some cases. One of the reasons why they permit this is that the resulting documents are shorter and more concise.

The cost of this terseness is often clarity, determining what is intended at a given point where the optional markup might be expected. (It's rather like one of those ancient fortune-tellers trying to predict the future by examining a single entrail.) And the drafters of the XML spec set clarity as one of their guiding principles—hence, this design goal.

Ulterior motives

One of my favorite XML references is the Annotated XML Specification, at:

```
www.xml.com/axml/axml.html
```

Written by Tim Bray, one of the spec's coeditors, this annotated version includes copious notes, explanations, and asides that illuminate the official requirements in often quite wonderful ways.

In discussing the above ten design goals, Bray mentions two other factors that motivated the spec's writers:

Internationalization: "We bent over backward to make XML work properly in all the world's scripts, with a fair degree of success."

The DPH: DPH is an acronym for *Desperate Perl Hacker.* Perl, as you may know, is one of the premier languages for programming the Web (perhaps *the* premier language for that task). As Bray says, the DPH is "the luckless subordinate who is informed that some global change is required in a large, complex document inventory at short notice, and who is able to deliver by applying a scripting facility such as Perl to cleanly-structured data such as XML."

What XML Isn't

First, foremost, and maybe most confusingly, XML is not *a* single markup language.

I know, I know. It's right there in the name, isn't it? "Extensible Markup Language." But despite certain general rules (the requirement that all elements nest properly, the presence of some common conventions such as how to code comments, and so on), there is no single, broadly useful set of markup to learn in order to learn XML. XML is all about *separate markup languages for separate purposes*. This is a huge departure for anyone who has spent the last several years of his or her life memorizing the vagaries of HTML. It's also why most books about XML, including this one, present XML by way of "demonstrators"—customized markup languages (like FlixML) that show the range of things *possible* with XML but don't teach you XML as such, except by example.

Second, XML is not an "all things to all people" solution. HTML will continue to grow, and it will continue to be both more convenient and more flexible for many purposes. You don't need to throw away everything you know (if you do know) about the difference between the effect of HTML's unordered list tag `<ul>` and that of the ordered list tag `<ol>`, for instance.

Third, XML is not in itself a display language. In HTML, tags (and the corresponding elements) generally serve two purposes: they both add structure to documents and imply a certain display style. Paragraphs start on a new line; headings vary in size; bold is, well, bold. In itself, XML is almost exclusively a language not for defining how things look on a screen, but for defining specific content—a language for manipulating the *what* rather than the *how*.

What XML Is

I'll repeat the point from the last paragraph: On its own, XML is a tool for manipulating the *what* rather than the *how*.

It's natural for people who have used the Web at all—heck, even just readers of magazines—to assume the importance of what font sizes and typefaces headings will be displayed in, whether cells in a table will be centered or left-justified, what color the page background will be, and so on.

We've been spoiled by later developments in HTML, though. Originally, for instance, there were no tags for specifying bold or italics text—there were just `<strong>` and `<em>` (for *emphasized*) tags. It was up to a browser vendor to decide what to do with those tags in an HTML document; if they wanted to, they could render all <strong> text in all uppercase letters, and all <em> as underlined. This made page designers crazy: By God, if they *meant* italics, then the browser better not display non-italicized capital letters!

So over time, HTML has drifted into a stew of combined structural and display markup. Most recently, with the introduction of the Cascading Style Sheets standard (CSS1 originally, and since May, 1998, CSS2, with CSS3 in the works as of this writing), a whole mechanism for controlling the *how* has been sort of nailed to the side of the bubbling HTML pot. In the meantime, especially with all the multimedia extensions to Web pages (and the resulting media hoopla), the emphasis on document structure has been lost.

But even if you're an HTML purist who'd die before sullying your pages with font changes, the *structures* possible with that language aren't really sufficient for many advanced (even simple) purposes. They're a least-common-denominator set of structures that could be used in documents of any kind. There's no difference in the *meaning* of the term "paragraph" as it's used on *CNN Interactive* and its meaning on a Web site of academic treatises on the genetic manipulation of the common housefly.[2]

I'll give you another analogy—this one from a different side of computing.

In everyday life I'm an application developer, specifically of small-scale networked databases being used by up to about ten people at a time. One difficulty in designing a new database always is the need to help potential users understand why I don't want to use a spreadsheet to do their work for them, but insist on a real database instead.

First, consider the spreadsheet. Aside from its roots in accounting—the classic row-and-column format of a ledger—every spreadsheet just makes *sense* to people. They're used to seeing printed reports, for example, with one row per "thing" and one column for each of the thing's characteristics.

But then I point out the variety of uses to which they propose to put their data. They don't just want a single report format. They sometimes want to see everything about everything (in which case, a spreadsheet-like layout can indeed

---

2.   There was a profile of Michael Jordan as a celebrity advertising icon a while back in *The New Yorker* magazine. On the face of it, the article has nothing at all to do with XML vs. HTML. But there's a wonderful line by the author (Henry Louis Gates, Jr.) that expresses this quite succinctly: "Different celebrities were repositories of different values and associations: Sigourney Weaver didn't *mean* the same thing as Loni Anderson."

make sense, even if the resulting printout is fifty yards wide and only eight inches deep); more often, they want just to see everything about *one* thing (in which case using a spreadsheet is just crazy). Sometimes they want to highlight a feature that all the things have in common. They don't want to have to type in a lengthy text string more than once. And so on.

It doesn't usually take more than a half-hour of this to convince them.

HTML is like a spreadsheet. Every single HTML document is, basically, the same structure. You can dress it up with colors, fonts, style sheets, or however you want, but it's still the equivalent of a mindless row-and-column design.

XML, by contrast, is like a relational database. The structure is optimized for the particular application. The structure isn't mindless; it's actually mind*ful*.

A truism of Web-page authorship is, "Content is king." The theory is that if you dump rich enough content into a page, the page's value goes up proportionately. But not all truisms are *true*, and the content-is-king theory has in my opinion turned out to be one of the big lies of the technological age—*because HTML lets you emphasize style over substance.*

Ain't no such thing in XML. XML is 100% about content, and how it's structured internally to be most useful.

From the Sublime to the Ridiculous

Well, there's content, and there's content.

Much of the attention paid to XML thus far has been in terms of its potential as a heavyweight application tool. If you're a doctor (we're told repeatedly), you can use XML for maintaining patient records, and then you can make those records accessible and understandable to the patients themselves simply by viewing the data in a "patient's-eye view of his or her records" browser. Corporations can develop intranet databases with `<invoice>`, `<partnumber>`, `<custnumber>`, `<custname>`, and—who knows?—`<warrantyexpirationdate>` tags, and they can easily share those databases with other corporations (such as insurance and service companies).

Yeah, you can do all that stuff with XML. But I don't think you need to be totally serious about it. Commerce, after all, is long, but life is short. You can use XML for almost anything...even a piece of fluff like a B movie database.

Just FlixML

Historically, the Bs—also called "programmers," the implications of which we probably don't want to think about too much—were commonly shown as filler in a bill with more big-ticket films. In an indoor theater, the B might have appeared first, as a warmup for the real feature. In a drive-in theater, it might have been shown second or third, when the audience who had stayed for it was, let's say, less interested in the content of what was on the screen than in the fact that it was dark, and that they were sharing an enclosed, semi-private space with a member of the opposite sex.

By way of analogy, think of the warmup act in a concert.[3] Many in the audience will have no particular reason for hearing the warmup act, may arrive late precisely in order to miss it, or may ignore it if present. But sometimes, even an otherwise dreadful warmup band will come up with an absolute miracle of music-making, one that leaves the headline group's own performance seem pale by comparison.

That happens with B movies, too. Most of them you'll never be poorer for having missed, but many are gems that went unnoticed at the time *because* of their having been paired with blockbusters. They got lost in the shuffle. (And if the A picture was itself a dog, the B was doubly damned.)

Unlike concert warmup acts, a lot of the best B movies are still accessible to us in some way—thanks to television and videotape. But how do we know which ones to go after? How do we tell other enlightened souls about the best ones, in a way that's consistent, complete, reliable, and—ideally—fun?

We use, of course, just FlixML.

The nature of the beast

I'll have much more to say about why FlixML includes the specific things it does (and leaves others out) in Part 4, "Rolling Your Own XML Application." But here are the general areas I want it to cover:

1. The facts: FlixML must be capable of holding as much objective information about a B movie as possible. This stuff is pretty dry—title, year first released, cast, crew, studio, and so on.

---

3.   If you're old enough, you can also think of the "flip side" of old 45-rpm records. This was where the artist or producer dumped a second-tier song to complement the (presumed) hit on the other side. The flip side was also called the B side.

2. The story: This is a little more freeform. A potential viewer of a B film needs to know what it's about.

3. The quality: Not all low-budget movies are created equal, even if they're identical in most of their objective dimensions.

So I've set up FlixML not just to describe a given movie in factual terms, but also to *characterize* it. There are provisions for including reviews (both your own, and those of others—including real critics).

But a markup language for describing movies in general—not just Bs— would cover those same dimensions. What would be the additional features that a B-movie-specific markup language should include?

To answer that question, I've provided for ratings that are both finer-tuned and more subjective, culminating in a single rating on a "B-ness scale." This B-ness figure captures, in a nutshell, how much a film should be considered a true B film, versus a true turkey, an A film that's simply scarred by subpar production values, and so on.

Which brings us to the question: What exactly are the attributes of B movies versus all others?

I've talked to friends about this notion. I know that B movies, like As and Cs, have a director, a cinematographer, and a cast; that they're in black-and-white or color; that they're silent or sound—I know all that. But what are the essential ingredients of a B movie?

Here are some of the things we've come up with:

- Little or no redeeming social, artistic, or intellectual value
- Lukewarm commercial success
- Cheesy or at least obvious "special" effects
- Recycled plot lines
- Don't have sequels (although sequels to some other classifications of movies are themselves often Bs)
- No "name" stars or directors (at least at the time the movie was made)
- TV (and later, videotape) saved them from certain oblivion
- You'll never find a B movie's soundtrack on CD
- There are no parodies of specific B movies
- Not shown on primetime network television
- The men wear suits 24 hours a day, the women dresses, the kids either short pants with suspenders or pinafores
- Nobody ever eats a complete meal

• If you fall asleep during a B movie that is followed by another B movie, and then wake up, it takes you a half-hour to realize you're watching a different movie

(No doubt you can come up with some of your own criteria, but this is a good starting point.)

The key feature that distinguishes a B movie from any other can probably be stated simply like this: It has no *extrinsic* qualities that would make you want to see it. Someone might pass along a word-of-mouth recommendation, but you otherwise probably happened on it by accident. You've read no reviews of it; you don't know any other movies by the same director; and while certain cast members later may have become "stars," you wouldn't have known them at the time. All of a B movie's virtues, if any, are *intrinsic*.

So having a computer handy as you proceed through *Just XML* will be important, of course…just remember to keep the VCR warmed up and ready as well. And your tongue planted firmly in cheek (I know that's where mine will be).

B Alert!

Watch This Space

Throughout *Just XML*, keep your eyes open for a box such as this one.

Each *B Alert!* box will contain a capsule description of a classic B film. I'll include notes on the year the film was released, its plot, and especially why I think it's worth hunting down a copy of the film for your own viewing.

As in most other such, er, artistic pursuits, there will be of course a certain amount of subjectivity at work here. A flick I recommend may well leave you scratching your head, or—who knows?—out-and-out repulsed. (That's always a possibility when looking through films that got lackluster studio support during their making. On the other hand, it's always a possibility when looking through films that *did* receive a lot of TLC and promotional attention from their studios. Go figure.) I'll try at least, though, to make the pitch both clear and encouraging enough for you to make an informed judgment of your own.

A few bits of XML code in *Just XML* describe movies that don't exist. Most of them, though, are real enough. And most of *those* will be honored (if that's not stretching a term too far) with their own *B Alert!* boxes.

One last thing: At my Web site, I've got an XML tutorial, links to XML-related sites, information about B movies, and several examples of FlixML documents both in raw XML format and converted into HTML for viewing. Please stop in; the address is:

```
www.flixml.org
```

CHAPTER 2

Breaking the Ice

$\mathbf{A}$t last, we're ready to proceed beyond the high-level and background information and on into at least some actual details of XML coding.

This chapter deals with the very basics of XML markup. In particular, it introduces the notions of valid and well-formed XML, the document type definition (DTD), and some general principles that apply to markup in XML applications of all kinds. It covers the overall structure of an XML document, and discusses in detail two optional sections of a document, the prolog and "epilog."[4]

How Valid Is It?

If you're developing a Web page in HTML, you know the page is "correct" when it displays what you want, the way you want, in a variety of browsers, at a variety of screen resolutions, and so on. Your HTML authoring software may impose some constraints on you (that a particular start-tag be paired with an end-tag, for instance), and these constraints may be based on the official constraints defined in the HTML specification; but you don't have to be overly concerned with what the constraints are and why they're there.

---

4.   I'll render "epilog" in quotes because the term isn't used at all in the XML spec—
      it seems logical to call it that, but there's no formal recognition of the term.

This book isn't about HTML, though. With the XML specification, we've got a new, more formal definition of correctness that we need to attend to, because the software may not attend to it for you or may impose some constraints that at first glance don't seem to make sense.

Actually there are two kinds of correct XML documents: *valid* ones and *well-formed* ones. We'll be encountering distinctions between the two terms throughout *Just XML*, but it's important that you understand now what they mean in general.

A valid XML document is completely self-describing. Everything you[5] can possibly need to know about the document's structure and contents is contained either within the base document itself, or within certain auxiliary files that are referred to in the base document.

Well-formed documents, on the other hand, contain the bare minimum of what you (or the XML processor) need to know about them. They follow the rules of XML itself but don't need to spell out what their own internal rules are.

The difference between valid and well-formed XML is like the difference between a movie's shooting script and the version of it you see on a theater's screen. In the former, you might find not just dialog, but camera angles, lighting suggestions, and notes on sound effects and music; in the latter, all those specifications are implied, but you don't need to know (and generally *don't* know) about any of them—the thing speaks for itself.

The future isn't quite *now*

One of the first questions often asked by newcomers to XML is, "What does it look like in a browser?" The question comes up, of course, because the bits of an XML document, unlike those of an HTML document, have no inherent display characteristics: The only information in a well-formed document, aside from the content itself, is the document's structure as implied by the nesting of elements within one another, and so on.

One approach adopted by browsers is to display XML documents in outline form—as *trees*—with successively nested layers of content merely indented from their parents. This has been the case with Microsoft's Internet Explorer, version 5 (MSIE5) browsers. The tree of elements appears in the browser window, looking something like a GUI-based operating system's list of directories and files; you click a little "+" sign to expand the tree of elements at that point, and a "-" to collapse it.

---

5.   Especially if "you" are an XML processing application.

> The other approach, currently favored by the Netscape/Mozilla and Opera browsers, is simply to display an XML document's contents *sans* markup as a stream of text—all in the browser's default font, without line breaks or any other adornment of any kind. In a way, this is consistent with the browsers' behavior when processing *any* elements they don't know how to handle. If you want your file's contents to be displayed in a particular way, you can supply a style sheet for doing so. (Style sheets are covered in Part 3.)
>
> It may seem to you that the MSIE5 approach is more sensible. However, it doesn't square with the XML specification, which asserts that XML content has *no* built-in display characteristics. Furthermore, the way MSIE5 achieves its effects is by using a built-in default style sheet...so it's not all *that* much smarter!

The DTD

Chief among the differences between valid and well-formed XML is that valid XML requires the presence of something called a document type definition, or DTD. (The DTD doesn't actually have to appear inside the given valid document; if it doesn't, though, there must be a "pointer" to it.)

What exactly is in a DTD? The contents vary depending on the specific application—FlixML's DTD bears little relation to the one that defines the Microsoft Channel Definition Format (CDF), for example—but the general shape and scope of all DTDs are the same. They include:

- declarations of the **element types** that are used to mark up an application's documents;
- a description of the allowed **structural relationships** among element types—stating, for example, that a `page` element may appear inside a `book` element but not the other way around;
- specification of the **sequence**, if any, in which elements must appear (`preface` must come before `chapter`, for instance);
- lists of the **properties** (called attributes) allowed or required to be applied to the elements (such as `font="serif"` to be used within a hypothetical `<note>` tag); and
- **everything else** it's possible to say about the markup language's grammar.

Wow, you're thinking. That's an awful lot to ask of someone who just wants to prepare, say, a B-movie review. For that reason, most of you will never have to write your own DTDs: You'll simply include in your documents a pointer to the DTD you're using (maybe somewhere out on the Web, or on a local or network drive).

In fact, you can even create a perfectly acceptable XML document without any reference to a DTD at all. Such a document still must follow the general rules of XML documents (such as that elements may not overlap one another's boundaries), but is a *lot* simpler to create.

A document like this—one that does not include a DTD, but otherwise adheres to the common principles of XML—is known as a *well-formed* document.

Well-formed flying

The relationship between the terms *valid* and *well-formed* is that all valid documents are also well-formed. Not all well-formed documents are valid, though!

When I was a kid, one of my favorite pastimes was flying balsa-wood airplanes. These were extremely light-weight constructions, usually rather small and fragile; the fuselage of the plane had slots cut into it, through which you slipped the wings and tailfins. And if you looked closely at the slots, you'd see that they were not just straight cuts, but a little curved, forcing the flexible surface of the wings into a slightly humped shape. This curved shape to the wings was what gave my balsa-wood planes the ability to fly farther than just across a room—they provided *lift.*

Well, these balsa-wood things were certainly airplanes as opposed to boats, dinner plates, or Border collies. They had only some very limited features in common with the Piper Cubs and DC-7s in the New Jersey sky, though—particularly the shape of the wings' surface. They were well-formed (they flew, could spiral, loop, perform Immelman rolls, and so on if you bent the wings and rudder the right way before launching them), but not particularly valid (they couldn't really steer; in particular, they couldn't recover from an impending crash).

So what's the downside? Why not just focus on writing well-formed XML and forget about the DTD and other characteristics of valid documents? The answer is primarily one of control: Many of the things an application program (like an XML editor) is expected do with a valid document are constrained by the DTD. If you write only well-formed documents, you're leaving a large part of this processing up to the least-common-denominator whims of the application program. Don't disregard the usefulness of merely well-formed documents, especially when they're coupled with style sheets as discussed later in this book—but you must accept the loss of control that goes with them.[6]

All of Part 4 discusses the mechanical workings of the DTD and how to build one. For now, the main thing for you to know is that the DTD is the main fence that separates the valid from the well-formed.

External and internal subsets

While the DTD lays down the rules, there's a "back door" available to XML document developers that lets them bend the rules a bit.

For the most part, when you use a DTD you simply use whatever's there. This is the so-called external subset—the one written by the DTD developer, and generally (as the name implies) held in a file external to the XML file itself. However, you can also extend some features of the DTD—even provide an *entire* DTD—in an internal subset. I'll show you an example of this later in the chapter.

XML parsers

Software to process XML is of two general kinds: the software whose results you see on the screen, and the software that tells *that* software how to process the raw XML. Arguably the most important single component of this whole structure is what's known as the *parser.*

Parsing, you may recall from your elementary-school classes in what they used to call "language arts," is the process of reading and classifying a string of characters and words: At one level are nouns, adjectives, verbs, and so on, and at another level are subjects, predicates, prepositional phrases, and the like. All of this analysis helps you to understand the structure of language until its use becomes second nature to you.

---

6. Those of you using HTML should also note that you've been dealing with a DTD all along. The HTML spec has its own DTD that spells out the rules—however flexible and forgiving they might be in HTML's case. One of the signal advantages of XML is that you no longer have to accept someone else's rules of what's allowed.

An XML parser performs this same task for documents marked up in an XML dialect, and passes the results of its analysis downstream both to later steps in the software chain and to you (the author and/or user).

A *validating parser* is one that is DTD-aware. It will know, for instance, that according to FlixML's DTD, there are both `leadcast` and `othercast` element types for marking up cast members' names, and that the `othercast` can't be present unless there's also at least one `leadcast`. Elements in the document that don't conform to the DTD are flagged as incorrect, and if the error(s) are severe enough, any further processing might be halted altogether.

What's the opposite of a validating parser? A *well-formedness parser* might do the trick. ("Well-formedness" is a pretty ugly term, granted. The spec refers to these parsers as *non-validating parsers*, which although formally correct doesn't seem quite accurate—they do *some* "validation," after all, validation in the informal sense of telling you if a document passes some kinds of tests for correctness.) Such parsers, in many cases, needn't make reference to a DTD at all. They simply determine whether a document conforms to general XML principles (such as the proper nesting of elements). Note that if a DTD is available, the well-formedness parser *may* still use it—it just may not come to a screeching halt if the document doesn't conform to the DTD's requirements.

(This isn't to say, by the way, that a DTD is completely useless even if all you're interested in is well-formedness. DTDs can fulfill some quite useful purposes that fall into the category of convenience and consistency, rather than correctness. In order to take advantage of these features, even a well-formedness parser will need to refer to a DTD.)

Regardless whether the parser is checking for validity or well-formedness, it will always perform certain specific jobs. Among these are what might be called "spell-checking" (ensuring that there aren't any unrecognized or inconsistent element names, for example) and the processing of whitespace. Such common "rules of thumb" are covered in the following section.

Rules of Thumb

Before getting into the overall structures common to all XML documents, you need to understand a few things at the "atomic" level. These include tagging conventions, case sensitivity, and the handling of so-called whitespace.

Tags

An XML tag, like those in HTML and SGML, starts with a "left angle bracket" and concludes with a "right angle bracket"—the < and > characters, respectively. Look at the following line of code:

```
<title>He Walked by Night</title>
```

There are two tags in the line (although, per the earlier discussion, there's only one *element*). In practice, tag pairs like this are usually simply referred to as (in this case) "the `<title>` tag." The end tag is implied. Everything between the start and end tags here is *content*; the tags constitute the *markup*. (And the tags plus the content is the element.) All of a document's tags taken together are referred to as its *tagset*.

Some elements don't require any content between start- and end-tags; all that you need to know about their "content" is included, or implied, within the tags themselves. A simple example from HTML is the line-break tag, `<br>`: there's nothing "in" a line break other than the function it performs.

XML departs strongly from HTML in what it requires of such an empty element's markup, though. A basic rule of all XML tags is that they must be paired—text marked up with a given start tag must conclude with an end tag— *or* that a tag must take a special "empty" form. You can, if you want, represent an empty element as a start- and end-tag with no actual content—so a line break would be specified as a `<br>` and `</br>` in succession. Alternatively, you can code an empty element's tag as one that begins with < and ends with /> (note the additional slash), and *has no end tag*. Therefore, if our XML document uses a line-break element type, a line break might be entered in the document as `<br/>`.

Finally, remember—especially if you're coming to XML from HTML—all elements must be perfectly nested within one another. Under this rule, the following code (which would be legal, or at least acceptable, under HTML) will fail when processed by an XML program:

```
<head><title>The BeeHive</head></title>
```

See? The `title` element doesn't reside entirely within the bounds of the `head` element. To correct this error, we'd have to reverse the order of the closing `</head>` and `</title>` tags.

Case sensitivity

HTML is case-*in*sensitive. That is, the HTML `<img>` tag can appear in a document as `<img>`, `<IMG>`, `<iMg>`, and so on. If you're transitioning from HTML to XML, however, you've got to get used to another basic fact of XML life: A hypothetical `<img>` tag and an `<IMG>` tag are *two different tags*. If the document has a DTD, and there's an `img` element type declared in it but no `IMG`, you can't use the latter at all. What's more, even without a DTD, the two corresponding tags "say" different things to the XML processor.

Also note that certain keywords, especially in the DTD itself, must always be capitalized.

Whitespace handling

This is possibly the XML concept most likely to catch you off-guard if you've been using HTML for a while.

Whitespace, if you're new to the idea, is in markup terms anything that separates words or characters (including punctuation) from one another. The following XML fragment includes four kinds of whitespace:

```
<plotsummary>As the title implies,
someone IS killing  the great chefs of Europe...
 </plotsummary>
<mpaarating>NR</mpaarating>
```

- First, and most commonly, there's a blank between each pair of adjacent words.
- Second, there's a *newline* character at the end of the first line, following the comma.
- Third, although it looks like a series of plain old blanks, there's a tab character (probably a typo, if I weren't trying to make a point in this case) between the words "killing" and "the."
- And finally—perhaps most subtly—there's a newline character between the end of the `</plotsummary>` tag and the start of the `<mpaarating>` tag.

Let's contrast the HTML norm with this XML example. In an HTML document, all whitespace is treated the same. The language achieves this simple goal by forcing all whitespace to "mean the same thing": It collapses every occurrence of whitespace into a single space, as though that's what the document's author intended. In practice this is often the case...but not *always*.

In my spare time, I'm the Webmaster for a nonprofit poetry press. Each book in our current catalog has a page of its own on the site, and each such page contains sample poems from the book. If I just let HTML "do its whitespace thing," the pages would be a mess: All lines in a poem would be squashed onto a single line, separated from one another exactly as one word is separated from the next (that is, by a single space) and wrapping down to the next line only when the whole thing got too wide for the browser window. How do I force the browser to display each line as a separate one?

HTML has a number of devices for accomplishing this:

- There's a special `pre` element type that says "display all the enclosed text exactly as entered, preserving all whitespace." One ugly side-effect of using this element, though, is that all the text is rendered in a monospace font (typically Courier or some variant of it).
- If I want to force a line to break at a particular point, I can use the `<br>` tag there. But a twenty-line poem requires `<br>` tags at the end of at least the first nineteen lines—probably all twenty for consistency.
- If I want to insert a *two*-line break, such as the one that appears between stanzas, I can't use two `<br>` tags in succession. Instead, I've got to use the paragraph tag, `<p>`.
- Finally, for poems that have "interesting" spacing *within* the lines, I need to use an HTML convention for representing special characters—the tab, say—which looks like this: `&tab;` (an ampersand, the word `tab`, and a semicolon).

XML simplifies all this. *An XML parser must pass to the application, unchanged, all whitespace in a document.*[7] In an XML document, all whitespace in content is assumed to be significant—that is, intentionally there—unless the downstream application somehow "knows" otherwise. Most XML applications, when they start appearing in force, are likely to default to the same behavior as HTML browsers, with the possible exception that they won't "collapse" newlines. (Even if they don't by default honor newline breaks, however, there's a way to force this behav-

---

7.   Most—maybe all—parsers will also identify whether the given occurrence of whitespace is "significant" or not. *In*significant whitespace in the above example would be the last: the newline between elements. In all other cases, it can't be determined from the document alone whether the whitespace needs to be retained or not.

ior that might be called the xml:space rule. I'll cover it in the next chapter, where we delve into some actual XML code.)

A whitespace parable

In the late 1970s and into the early 1990s, I was an applications developer at AT&T. This was the tail end of the heyday of IBM-compatible mainframes, the universal character set of which was something called EBCDIC (pronounced "ebb-suh-dic"); in EBCDIC, a space was represented in hexadecimal as the number 40, which you could "see" in a file (even though it looked like a true blank when the file was printed) with the aid of special software.

One of the first projects I worked on was a COBOL application. All data used by this system were kept on large reels of tape, and one of the system's primary goals was to ensure that these data were valid. Invalid records were printed on an error report for the system's project manager to annotate and pass back to us for correction.

In our youthful, idealistic quest to give the user complete information, we printed the error records both "normally" and in hexadecimal. The latter format enabled our client to inspect the true contents of certain numeric fields, which appeared like gibberish in the former format. Unfortunately, it also exposed to him the contents of "empty" fields where no data—or blanks—had been entered. We didn't realize this was unfortunate until we met with him soon after coming up with our "solution."

"What's this stuff here?" he asked, pointing at a string of hex 40s.

My project leader answered for us, "Those are blanks. The field is blank."

"They're not blanks. They're 40s."

Several perplexed glances went back and forth around the table of programmers. "Well, yes, they look like 40s," the project leader said, "but that's just the way the computer represents blanks internally—"

"I don't care!" said the client. "Those fields are supposed to be blank—I don't want 40s or anything else in there!"

After a few days' feverish work, we presented the client with a new printout that, of course, displayed all hex 40s as true spaces. The 40s were still there; the guy just couldn't see them. He was blissful, as (in retrospect) we might have expected he'd be.

There's one moral here for application programmers: always give the client what he or she asks for, even if (maybe especially if) you can't deliver what he or she *wants*. There's another moral for authors of XML documents: the whitespace is always there, even if you can't (or choose not to) see it.

Anatomy of an XML Document

At its simplest, an XML document is a systematic set of containers, called *elements*, of what a viewer of the document would consider the actual contents. The containers can contain other containers (as well as actual content), and those containers can contain other containers, and so on; special *empty* containers contain, obviously, nothing at all. Normal elements include a start-tag, some content, and an end-tag; empty elements consist of either a start- and end-tag with no intervening content, or of a simple "empty tag" (for which XML provides a special format).

There are three main pieces of an XML document: the prolog, the root element itself, and—well, call it an *epilog* of miscellaneous items. Only the root is required in a well-formed document; a valid document must include the prolog; and the miscellaneous components dangling at the end of the document are never required.

Remember that the specific *tags* used to mark the boundaries between the root element (where all those containers are) and the two sections that surround it will vary from one XML application to another, so we can't say for certain what these tags will be—except by using examples from a specific application, such as FlixML.

Documents without end

There's some debate about the closing "miscellaneous" section. In some quarters—even among the editors of the XML specification—there's a sense that it was a mistake to include in the spec a provision for an epilog. The reason is precisely that there's no telling what will be in the epilog.

A parser can process a *stream* of XML, which might include more than one physical document. Once the root element of a given document has been parsed, the parser may not be able to tell whether the next bit of markup in the stream belongs to an epilog to the current document, or to the next document altogether.

If you can help it, I'd advise you for now not to use an epilog in your own XML documents. Strictly speaking it's allowed, of course—for now.

The prolog

To repeat: You don't have to include a prolog in an XML document. However, it can provide essential information to an application program (such as a browser)—not just what the document consists of, but also (in limited ways) how to process it. The prolog can also help to explain the document's purpose and scope for human readers, and it uses four basic constructs to do so: the XML declaration, comments, processing instructions, and the document type declaration.

The XML declaration

Here's a sample prolog, indeed the simplest form of the prolog that's possible:

```
<?xml version="1.0"?>
```

The opening `<?` and closing `?>` are standard delimiters in XML for what are usually called *processing instructions*, or PIs. (PIs aren't really part of the document content, but signal to a program that is processing the content that it may need to take some particular course of action.) I'll discuss PIs in greater depth in a moment. For now, note that the above example (formally known as the *XML declaration*) is *not* a PI. It simply uses the same notation, which serves to distinguish the XML declaration from normal elements.

The above XML declaration says to a processing program, "What follows is an XML document, conforming to version 1.0 of the XML specification." If the program is intelligent enough, this declaration will put it into a state in which it knows to process the document according to the rules of that XML version, but to disallow, say, any markup that's acceptable only to a later version (or to any HTML version, for that matter).

Beyond the version number, the XML declaration may also contain an *encoding declaration* and a *standalone document declaration*. You may include either, both, or neither of these components, depending on how complete you want the overall XML declaration to be.

The **encoding declaration** tells the XML program (such as a browser) what character set it needs to be able to deal with to process this document. Are all the characters in the document those of the Western languages—26 letters of the Roman alphabet, digits 0 through 9, basic punctuation and special symbols like ampersands, and so on? Or are special non-Western characters included, such as Japanese or Arabic script? This is one of the potentially most interesting and powerful features of XML—that the tag names and document content do not need to conform to regional character sets (such as US ASCII). The only constraints are the special symbols that distinguish markup from content—that tags need to start with < and end with >, and so on.

Here's a sample XML declaration, including the encoding information:

```
<?xml version="1.0" encoding="UTF-8"?>
```

(The idea of encoding is simple enough, but the details can be rather daunting. Appendix B includes more information, if you're curious.)

The **standalone document declaration** takes a simple yes/no value, which tells an XML processor whether or not the document *and its rules* are completely self-contained. That is, either the DTD for the document is located in some other file, or it's not. (In the latter case, of course, a well-formed XML document doesn't need a DTD at all.) Details about how to specify where to find an external DTD are covered below, in the section of this chapter called "The Document Type Declaration."

Here's a complete XML declaration, with both an encoding declaration and a standalone document declaration:

```
<?xml version="1.0" encoding="UTF-8" standalone="yes"?>
```

Translated, this tells a processing program (or a human reader), that respectively:

- this is an XML document;
- it conforms to the general rules of XML, which are laid down in version 1.0 of the XML specification;
- all characters in this document use the UTF-8 encoding scheme (which is the default, and includes the standard ASCII characters); and
- you don't have to look anywhere other than within the document itself to completely understand the markup and the document structure.

Avoid using a standalone document declaration

A number of warning signs indicate that the standalone document declaration will not last long in the XML spec.

The reasons for this are varied, some quite subtle, but the bottom line is that it's redundant and confusing. As you'll learn in a moment, if you want to use a DTD, you'll say so elsewhere in the prolog, and much more definitely, with the document type declaration. If you don't want to use a DTD, don't include the standalone document declaration.

Comments

Sometimes you'll want to include for human readers of your document a description of a particular section of code, notes on how to use it, and so on. Sometimes you may need to leave the equivalent of a Post-It Note for yourself, for that matter. You can place such comments anywhere in the document, and the prolog is no exception.

Just like HTML comments, XML comments are delimited with <!-- and --> characters, and they can run on for several lines if necessary. You can put anything at all inside a comment except a pair of adjacent hyphens (since that presumably signals to the processing software, "end of comment forthcoming").

We could build up the prolog of our hypothetical XML document with a comment like this:

```
<?xml version="1.0"? encoding="UTF-8" standalone="yes">
<!-- This document contains factoids and opinions about B
movies.
Contents are Copyright © 1998 by John E. Simpson. All
Rights Reserved. <This means you!> -->
```

See? You can dump just about anything in there, including special symbols and even what are otherwise "reserved" XML components such as < and > characters. Because they're enclosed within the open-comment/close-comment delimiters, the XML processor ignores the actual *contents* of comments.

This may tempt you to use comments as a way of temporarily hiding markup that you haven't finished yet, or that you want to get back to later. Succumb to this temptation only if you take the word "temporarily" very seriously: It's almost certain to confuse someone who comes across your document later and believes (understandably) that the stuff in the comment is for *their* attention as opposed to the XML processing program's.

> **Not-so-good comments**
>
> A really dreadful (although convenient) development in HTML has been to use comments as a way of embedding processing scripts (such as ECMAScript and VBScript) in a document. This has been a convenience, because HTML doesn't have any other provision for telling the processor or Web server how to behave at a particular point in the document. But it *really* mucks up a document's source code and can render what you're looking at almost 100% inscrutable. XML explicitly separates a document's content from its processing—the need for scripting is to some extent accounted for by the separate Extensible Stylesheet Language Transformations, or XSLT, specification (covered in Part 3)—so keeping your XML "clean" should never become an issue.
>
> I know, I know—someone somewhere is probably already planning a tool whereby you may twist XML comments to fit some purpose other than "notes to the human reader." There's just one catch—they won't be able to call the result legitimate XML.

Processing instructions (PIs)

We've already seen an example of something that looks like one of these: the XML declaration. Remember, though, that that's not really a PI. The purpose of a true PI is to prepare the application software to handle special sorts of content that aren't covered by XML conventions, or to perform some other non-XML function—even a related but not-quite-XML function like directing the application to a style sheet to be used with this document.

Exactly what goes into a PI depends on the nature of the software that is expected to process the document. For instance, a hypothetical FlixML-aware browser might be expected to handle sound clips such as RealAudio files. Among the characteristics of RealAudio files that the browser might reasonably need to know would be the version of the RealAudio Encoder program that produced the clips, their frequency response, and the bit rate at which they were recorded. A FlixML document intended to be processed by such a browser might include a PI like this:

```
<?realaudio version="5.0" frequency="5.5kHz"
bitrate="16Kbps"?>
```

The word following the opening <? (realaudio, in this case) is called the *target* of the PI. The information following the target simply describes the target's properties *as presented in this document.* (Other documents may of course present quite different properties of the same kind of objects.)

A special consideration: What happens if some *other* application software opens your document? Suppose someone with a generic XML browser opens your file of FlixML reviews and encounters a PI that it doesn't know how to handle?

The answer is—probably—that nothing at all will happen, or perhaps that the generic browser will simply report to the user a message such as, "I don't understand 'realaudio'" and then move on. There's not really any way of telling at this point what the normal behavior of XML application software will be under such circumstances; however, it seems likely that this will be a common enough occurrence that the whole thing will not just shut down or crash.

(A very important sort of PI is the one that links a style sheet to an XML document. I'll cover this PI in Part 3.)

Document type declaration

All right, I know: this is a *really* confusing term—at first glance almost indistinguishable from "document type *definition*" (the DTD covered previously). What may make it even more confusing is that the two terms are related.

I've got a little picture in my head that helps me remember which is which. I think of a person—maybe at a town meeting—*declaring* something, and a different person *defining* the same thing. The first person is making some kind of announcement, stating a simple fact or opinion for everyone else's information. "I'm a neo-Contrarian!" he's announcing, for instance. The second person is more pedantic, more likely to wander off into details for the sake of completeness. This guy is not only giving us a handle by which to refer to him, he's also telling us what the handle means, what each of the ambiguous words in this explanation means, what all the words in the explanation of the explanation mean, and so on. "It's true, I'm a neo-Contrarian," he tells us, "and by that I mean that I'm more likely to disagree with you than not, and by 'disagree' I mean to say that if it's a major issue, I'll take out a contract on your life, and if a minor issue, I'll send you a nasty letter, and one example of a 'major' issue is…" and so on, and so on. (By the time he finishes, the rest of the town meeting attendees—those who haven't fled—are probably rather glassy-eyed.)

A document type *declaration* (sometimes referred to in shorthand as the *doctype* declaration), at its simplest, just specifies what kind of XML document this particular one is—the specific markup language that is used, such as FlixML as opposed to a markup language for manufacturers of snowshoes. This is truly meaningful only if you know what DTD is used for an XML variation, of course, and therefore the document type *declaration* tells the processing software which document type *definition* to use to understand the document. It's as though the first guy in our hypothetical town meeting doesn't just announce that he's a neo-Contrarian, he also adds, "Oh, and if you want to know what we believe, check with Leo over there."

Here's the general syntax of a document type declaration:

```
<!DOCTYPE name externalDTDpointer internalDTDsubset>
```

Of the three pieces that follow the keyword DOCTYPE (note the capitalization, by the way), only *name* is required.

The three components of the document type declaration are as follows:

- The *name* is in general just a label for the document type. Specifically, it identifies the name of the root element. (This makes it easy for a parser to determine where the prolog ends, if there is a prolog, and where the root element begins and ends.) If you've included the optional external DTD reference or declared a root element type in your internal DTD specifications, *name* must match the name of an element declared in the DTD. Without any DTD information at all, a valid doctype declaration might look something like this (although, as I mentioned a moment ago, this doesn't impart much practical information either to software or to human readers):

```
<!DOCTYPE flixinfo>
```

- The *externalDTDpointer* says, "You can find the markup rules to which this document conforms at the following location *outside this document.*" This pointer consists of the keyword SYSTEM, followed by a Uniform Resource Identifier (URI) that indicates where the DTD is located; together these are referred to as the *system ID*. The URI is, for all practical purposes, identical in appearance and function to a Uniform Resource Locator, or URL, which is probably familiar to you from your prior experiences with the Web.[8] The above simple doctype declaration, with a reference to an external DTD, might look like this:

```
<!DOCTYPE flixinfo SYSTEM
"http://www.flixml.org/flixml.dtd">
```

---

8. The general idea is that URLs are only one form of URI, so we should be inclusive, keep an eye cocked on the future, and so on, and drop the term URL. In point of fact, though, as things stand now URLs are the *only* form of URI in anything like common use. In *Just XML* I'll use the terms interchangeably; just understand that they're not formally identical.

A public ID, too

The XML specification allows for the inclusion of a "public ID" as well as the system ID. The notion of a public ID has been carried forward into XML from SGML. It presupposes that the DTD is somehow known to the processing software without having to be located on the Web somewhere; this would be the case with DTDs approved and cataloged by various standards or industry organizations, and perhaps included with commercial XML software in the same way (for example) that standard flow-charting and other symbols are packaged with presentation software.

The XML spec says nothing about what the public ID should or may consist of. Therefore a valid doctype declaration with a public ID might look like this:

```
<!DOCTYPE flixinfo PUBLIC "This is a FlixML
document" SYSTEM [etc.]>
```

This kind of public ID doesn't actually impart much information. For that reason, XML public IDs will probably follow the format of those in SGML. These look at first like system IDs, except that the word SYSTEM is replaced by PUBLIC. On closer inspection, though, the thing that looks like a URL isn't *really* a URL. Here's a sample:

```
<!DOCTYPE flixinfo PUBLIC "-//JohnESimpson//text
flixinfo//EN">
```

The "-" indicates that this document type does not correspond to an official standard (it would be a "+" otherwise); the portion following the first two slashes identifies the "owner"; that following the second two slashes specifies that this is a text document called flixinfo; and the EN identifies the language in which the document is written (English in this case). You can include both a system and a public identifier, like this:

```
<!DOCTYPE flixinfo PUBLIC "-//JohnESimpson//text
flixinfo//EN" SYSTEM "http://www.flixml.org/
flixml.dtd"
```

In practice, it seems likely that most special-purpose DTDs with fairly small audiences and user communities will *not* be identified with a public ID, as it doesn't contribute much beyond whatever you'd find at the system ID URL. Note, though, that system and public IDs are used elsewhere *within* DTDs—in declaring external entities and notations (the latter roughly equivalent to media types)—and in these cases, the public ID can be quite useful.

- The optional *internalDTDsubset* is used instead of or as a supplement to the external DTD. Nearly anything that can be put into an external DTD can appear internally. If a given element or other markup is declared in both the external and internal DTD subsets, the declaration in the internal one takes precedence. As I've mentioned before, we'll be looking at how to build a DTD in Part 4, but for the sake of example here's how a doctype declaration in a FlixML document might specify some markup not covered in the "official" FlixML DTD. Note that the internal DTD information is set off from the rest of the doctype declaration with opening and closing [and] characters, as in this (extremely simple) example:

```
<!DOCTYPE flixinfo SYSTEM
"http://www.flixml.org/flixml/flixml_03.dtd"
[<!ENTITY AIP "American International Pictures">]>
```

(Don't worry for now what this example *means*; again, the details of DTDs are covered in Part 4.)

The root element

If you're not involved in writing your own DTDs, the root element will occupy probably nearly 100% of your attention in preparing XML documents. It's so important, and there is so much to know about what goes in there, that nearly all the details of root element markup have been relegated to Chapter 3.

Even so, in this discussion of a document's structure it's appropriate to talk about some general principles. First and foremost of these is that a single element—a single start-and-end tag pair, and everything between them—contains everything else. This element is the universe in which all of what we'd normally consider the document's real content makes its home.

Fighting over the root element

Let's suppose that you're at a movie theater on a Saturday afternoon in the 1940s. Having bought your ticket, you settle into your seat. The overhead lights go down as the screen illuminates…. Four hours later you emerge, blinking, from the theater's doors, hop on a bus, and ride to your front door. Just in time, too, because dinner's on the table.

> "What movie'd you see this afternoon?" your kid brother asks you, the corner of his mouth smeared with mashed potatoes.
>
> *He really is a pig*, you think, and with a split-second's consideration, you determine to pick a fight. "I didn't just see *one* movie. I saw two. Plus *The March of Time* and a Woody Woodpecker cartoon."
>
> This scene is followed by a certain amount of bickering and parental thunder. But the important thing for our purposes (you were wondering, weren't you?) is that your brother and you have chosen to argue not over something substantive, but over something rather picky (hence the thunder): What was the root element of your time at the theater?
>
> In your brother's terms, you went to the theater to see a movie—the feature. In his frame of reference, you don't go to the movies for all that other stuff. It's outside the root element.
>
> You on the other hand—you're such a romantic—believe, literally for the sake of argument, that you go to the movies for *the whole experience*. Your root element isn't "a movie," it's "an afternoon in a theater."

Normally, in a FlixML document the root element will be `<flixinfo>`. Inside that root is information about one or more B films—but nothing of a FlixML review's true contents, as expressed in this document, exists outside the `<flixinfo>` and `</flixinfo>` start- and end-tags. Here's a complete FlixML root element, albeit not a particularly enlightening one[9]:

```
<flixinfo>
    <title>Ghosts on the Loose</title>
</flixinfo>
```

(Note that throughout *Just XML* I've broken some lines and done some indenting for the purpose of making the examples readable. As I mentioned above in the discussion of whitespace handling, this "prettifying" whitespace will in theory be passed by the parser to whatever downstream software, such as a browser, might actually be processing the XML for display. This downstream software, if it so chose, could ignore the extraneous whitespace in this example, the newlines and tabs, just as if I'd typed everything on one line.)

---

9. It's also not a valid FlixML *document* (although it is well-formed): a valid FlixML document, per the requirements laid out in the DTD, would include several other elements besides flixinfo and title.

Again, there's much more to know about root elements—and especially about what goes in them—than we'll see in this chapter.

The epilog

With the exception of the XML and doctype declarations, what's allowed in a document's epilog of miscellaneous information is exactly what's allowed in the prolog: comments and processing instructions.

It's remotely conceivable that you might need an epilog in a given document. As I mentioned earlier, though, it's not really recommended. Not only might it confuse a parser or other program by obscuring where a given document ends and the next one begins; the whole idea of including "stuff that might be useful for handling this document" *after* the document has been displayed or otherwise processed just doesn't make much sense.

That having been said, there's nothing that FlixML or any other DTD can do to prohibit use of an epilog. That's because it occurs outside the pale of the root element, and "all" a DTD does is declare everything that can happen *inside* the root.

Summary

This chapter covered the basic structure of an XML document, including the three main components: the optional prolog, the root element, and the optional epilog of miscellaneous information. Aside from overall document structure, the chapter also described some general principles of XML markup (tags/elements, case sensitivity, and whitespace handling), and details about the markup that can be found in XML documents of all kinds (especially in the document prolog and epilog).

Chapter 3, "Into the Root," covers general classifications of markup and provides more in-depth examples of the FlixML dialect of XML.

Table 2.1   XML markup covered in this chapter

Markup	Components	Description

`<?xml version`
`encoding`
`standalonedecl?>`
		The XML declaration; part of the (optional) prolog

	`version="version"`	Declares the version of the XML specification to which a document conforms, such as `version="1.0"`
	`encoding="encoding-` `type"`	Specifies the character representation for a document's contents, such as `encoding="UTF-8"` (optional)
	`standalone="yesorno"`	Indicates whether declarations for the markup used in a document appear elsewhere (`standalone="no"`) or not (`standalone="yes"`) (optional)
`<!-- comment -->`		Comments or other text intended primarily for human readers—but not in any case expected to be processed by a parser or other XML software (optional)
`<?target` `piinfo?>`		Processing instructions for non-XML content, such as multimedia or print programs; also used for style sheet linking (optional)

`<!DOCTYPE`
`rootname`
`externalDTDpointer`
`internalDTDsubset>`
		Declares the specific document type of which a document is intended to be an instance (doctype declaration as a whole is optional, but recommended)

Table 2.1   XML markup covered in this chapter (continued)

Markup	Components	Description
	`rootname`	The general name of the document type, and in particular the name of the root element type (required component within a given doctype declaration)

	`externalDTDpointer:`
	`SYSTEM "uri"`
	`PUBLIC "publicID"`
		Gives the Uniform Resource Identifier (URI) for the DTD that declares a document's element types and other markup, and optionally the public identifier for the document type (optional component within a given doctype declaration)

	`internalDTDsubset:` `[markupdecls]`	Declares markup not covered by an external DTD, or overrides declarations that are included in an external DTD (optional component within a given doctype declaration)

Terms defined in this chapter

In addition to those items covered in Table 2.1, this chapter provided the following definitions. They appear here in the order in which they were covered in the text.

valid An XML document is *valid* if its structure and element content is formally declared in a document type definition (DTD) and if the document follows the rules laid out in the DTD.

well-formed An XML document is *well-formed* if using a DTD is not necessary to understanding its structure and element content (perhaps because there's no DTD available for it), but it still complies with general XML principles such as proper element nesting.

document type definition (DTD) A *DTD* formally declares the structure and element content (element types, relationships among different element types, and so on) of a given valid XML document.

parser A *parser* is XML-processing software that: (a) determines whether a document is valid or well-formed; and (b) passes a stream of "correct" XML to a downstream application, such as a browser. If there are problems with the XML code that it is processing, the parser may also take various corrective actions (generating error messages, overriding or ignoring the incorrect code, and so on).

validating/well-formedness ("non-validating") parser A *validating parser* confirms that the XML code accords with the rules laid down in the document's DTD. A *well-formedness parser* (called a *non-validating parser* by the XML specification) may make use of a DTD if one is present, but does not require one. In the latter case, the document's "rules" may be inferred from the nesting structure of the elements in the document.

tag A single piece of XML markup beginning with a left angle bracket and ending with a right angle bracket, such as `<flixinfo>`; a tag is used for marking the beginning or ending of an element. The name of the element is the text enclosed by the opening and closing < and > characters. Unless the corresponding element is empty (see below), tags always must be paired, surrounding the actual content they are meant to mark up; the tag that closes the markup (the end tag) is identical to the tag that begins it (the start tag), with the addition of a slash character. For example, the `<flixinfo>` start tag must be paired with the `</flixinfo>` end tag.

empty element tag Some tags aren't meant to mark up actual content, but rather to signal to the processing software some condition inherent in the tag itself; these are called *empty element tags*. For example, a background sound might be indicated in a document something like this: `<bgsound midifile="thememusic.mid"/>`. Note the presence of the special "`/>`" characters that terminate an empty tag.

whitespace Blank spaces between words, tab characters, and newlines are collectively referred to as *whitespace*. XML parsers pass all whitespace in a document unaltered to downstream applications. (By default, HTML treats every occurrence of whitespace in a document the same way: as if it were a single blank character.)

element Any container in an XML document is an *element*. Elements may contain other elements, processing instructions (PIs), content, and so on. (What a given element *may* contain is established by the DTD, if one is present.)

prolog The (optional) *prolog* is a series of elements that precedes the root element in an XML document. It may include the XML declaration itself, the document type declaration, comments, and PIs.

root element All of an XML document's actual contents are comprised in a single *root element,* including all other elements as well as the text they mark up. The root element is physically positioned between the optional prolog and epilog.

epilog An optional *epilog* of comments and PIs can follow the root element in an XML document.

CHAPTER   3

Into the Root

In Chapter 2, you saw how XML documents are structured in general, and learned about the document prolog and epilog in particular. In this chapter, I'll detail what goes into the real meat of an XML document: the root element. I'll also give you some more details of FlixML, our XML-based B-movie describer, and talk a bit more about B movies in general.

Recall that the root element is the only required portion of a well-formed document. Aside from that, you may need reference to some terms already defined—but if need be, given a basic knowledge of markup principles, you could probably open *Just XML* to this chapter and start reading. (Not that I'm recommending it!)

Naming of Parts

It will be useful for you to get a handle on six terms that encompass, when it comes down to it, all you need to know about what can go into an XML document's root element. One of these terms, the *document type definition* (DTD) was introduced in Chapter 2, and will be covered at length in Part 4. The five remaining terms (some of them touched on earlier) are: *elements, entities* (and the related *entity references*), *comments, processing instructions* (PIs), and *marked sections.*

(Although not part of "core XML," there's a sixth term, *namespaces*, which is critical to using XML in certain more advanced ways, and I'll cover namespaces at the end of this chapter.)

As I've mentioned, a DTD (if one is present) declares many of the components that may or must be present in a given XML document. Even if you aren't going to be involved in developing DTDs, it behooves you to know something about the requirements of the DTD to which you are (at least in theory, ahem) conforming.

If your application does not require a DTD at all—that is, if you're interested in writing merely well-formed XML—you'll need to pay careful attention to what follows. Some of the items covered in this section can't be used at all without a DTD, and some are severely crippled in other respects.

Elements

To call elements the basic building blocks of the markup in an XML document would surely qualify as the understatement of the year. It's possible that an XML document would contain no entities, no comments, no PIs, and no marked sections; but it's impossible to conceive of one without elements. As the name implies, elements are the things that an XML document is truly made of. The rest is window-dressing—powerful, yes, indispensable for many applications, true, but present only at the discretion of the given XML application's designer.

As I mentioned in the preceding chapter, technically speaking, the terms *element* and *tag* aren't synonymous. (The element is the "thing" that's marked up—including the tag itself, and anything that appears between the start and end tags, if it's not an empty element.) But for practical purposes, the terms are interchangeable. When we refer to FlixML's root element, `flixinfo`, we can just as easily refer to the `<flixinfo>` tag.

What's in a tag, then, aside from the enclosing < and > characters?

The name of the thing

First is the name of the element itself. FlixML has elements corresponding to a B movie's title, year of release, cast and crew members, "B-movieness" rating, and so on. In many cases, these elements are simply the names of the things described. For example, the `title` element is used to mark the title of the movie, and the `director` element denotes the name of that particular "crew member."

One thing that might not be obvious about element names is that they are always *tokens*. This term, common outside of programming circles as well as in, has special meaning in the context of programming and other machine-readable text. Wherever it's used, a token is a sign or symbol of something else: A token of affection might be a bouquet or a ring, informing the world (or at least the recipient) something like "This is my beloved"; the presence of a token minority-group member of some organization announces (usually unconvincingly) that this group is open and diverse; and so on.

To this general meaning, the world of computer-processed text adds a requirement of *form*: A token is a single "word." And just as in human language, this sort of "word" is a standalone string of characters; it contains no spaces.

When you're using FlixML to code documents, it makes sense that there would be an element for identifying the lead actress in a movie. But there can't be a `lead female` element, because "lead female" is not a token—it's got a space embedded in it. For that reason, in FlixML terms, a leading lady would have to be identified with a `leadfemale` element if we wanted to do it all in one element name. (Actually, as you'll see, there's one `leadcast` element that may contain `female` as well as `male` elements.)

Even less obvious but also critical is that an XML token is made up of a particular class of characters, collectively referred to as *name characters* (sometimes shortened to the rather inelegant form *Nmchars*). It can't contain any other characters on your keyboard. The valid name characters are the letters of the alphabet[10], the digits 0 through 9, the underscore (_), the hyphen (-), and the period or full stop (.).

Capital follies

One of the trickiest issues about tokenizing text has to do with tags like the aforementioned `<leadfemale>`, those in which two or more "words" are squashed into a single token. The issue is, how to make the component "words" discernible to a human reader if you can't use a space?

One solution is to replace the space with some other legal but nonalphabetic character. Using this solution, our `<leadfemale>` tag could become `<lead_female>`, `<lead-female>`, or `<lead.female>`.

Another solution is to capitalize each component "word" (or at least all of them but the first). In this case, the `<leadfemale>` tag would become `<leadFemale>` or `<LeadFemale>`.

---

10. I am of course using the term "alphabet" loosely here, not just to refer to the letters A through Z. As always, remember that unlike HTML, XML allows just about any non-Roman characters to be used as name characters.

Different solutions to the problem have different virtues, and their own armies of advocates. Personally, I like the mixed-case variant, and use it in my programming work for naming variables; a variable called strQuery, for example, is a string-type variable intended to hold a database query.

All these solutions to the problem require extra effort to *type*, though—all that stabbing at the Shift key—and for that reason, I've named all FlixML elements using strictly lowercase (to distinguish them from XML keywords like DOCTYPE). And in any case, FlixML isn't a particularly complex application; there's not much payoff in agonizing over this issue when the "things being represented" can be fairly unambiguously represented by just a couple of concatenated words.

If your document uses a DTD, remember that this issue will be decided by the DTD's designer, not by you as the author of the document: You won't be able to use *any* elements not declared in the DTD. Even if you're not employing a DTD to validate your document, however—if, that is, your document is simply well-formed—you are still constrained by the no-whitespace/name-characters-only rules for naming elements.

Attributes of the thing

I referred to something like attributes in Chapter 2, particularly in the discussion of the XML declaration:

```
<?xml version="1.0"?>
```

The would-be attribute in this case is version, and it comes with a value— "1.0"—from which it is separated by an equals sign. Technically, though, only *elements*—not the XML declaration, not PIs, not comments, or anything else—can have attributes.

As with the XML declaration, elements *may* (depending on the DTD, if one is present) have attributes. A given attribute in a valid document must itself be one of those declared in the DTD for that element. For instance, the DTD for FlixML has no attribute for identifying the director's date of birth (although it *might*). Therefore, the following is not valid FlixML markup:

```
<director birthdate="06/18/1951">
```

Like element names, attribute names must be tokens, consisting only of name characters; their values may or may not be constrained by the DTD. Among the types of constraints that can be placed on an attribute's value are that it:

- Can contain any text at all.
- Can contain name characters only.
- Must be entered, or is optional.
- Must be one of several discrete values.
- Will assume a default value if none is provided in the document.

Attributes of elements in well-formed documents are not, of course, constrained at all. While this might seem to be an advantage of well-formed over valid XML—it's undeniably convenient—the absence of any rules at all may (and probably will) actually make the document much harder to process in some intelligent way.

Attribute or element?

In the above example of the director's date of birth, the FlixML DTD developer might also have chosen to create a separate *element* for date of birth, rather than assigning it (if indeed I had) as an attribute of the `director` element.

I'll have more to say about this in Part 4. For now, just recognize that it's one of the many decisions that a DTD designer—or even the designer of a simple, well-formed document—has to make.

Built-in attributes

In keeping with two of XML's signature goals, two attributes can be used anywhere, in any element, without being declared by a DTD. These go by the rather odd-looking names `xml:space` and `xml:lang`.

What's odd-looking about them is the colon. That's not a name character, is it? It's actually a signal to the parser and downstream application that this particular attribute applies to elements in the "XML namespace." A *namespace* is an abstract "container" in which all the names for a given content area are presumed to exist—so there's implicitly a "FlixML namespace," I guess you could say, as well as a "script namespace" for dramatic works, a "rabbit-breeding namespace" for documents having to do with rabbit husbandry, and so on. The advantage to using a namespace qualifier like this is that it prevents ambiguities between different documents that use the same name for different things, so that `flixml:director` isn't confused with `playscript:director` and so on. The XML specification reserves the `xml:` qualifier—also variants such as `XML:`, `Xml:`, and the like—for element and attribute names officially declared by it and other XML-related specifications.

(I'll have much more to say about namespaces later in this chapter.)

xml:space

I alluded to the `xml:space` attribute in Chapter 2. There, I mentioned that as Webmaster for a poetry press, I have to come up with some device for preserving the whitespace in a poem's content, regardless of what the downstream application (like a browser) might try to impose on it. (The XML parser itself is supposed to retain all whitespace exactly as it appears in the document, but a browser might assume—as do HTML browsers—that every line break, tab, and sequence of multiple spaces can be "translated" to a single space character.)

So if I were coding a poem for inclusion in an XML document, here's how I'd use the `xml:space` attribute:

```
<poemtext xml:space="preserve">
    I think that I shall never see
        A poem lovely as a tree...
</poemtext>
```

Without the `xml:space` attribute, a browser might attempt to display this as:

```
I think that I shall never see A poem lovely as a tree.
```

Forcing all whitespace to be "simplified" in this way is often exactly what you'd want a browser to do for your content. (Whitespace is, after all, usually for the advantage of the document's author or of some other human who needs to read it.) But it's exactly wrong for special applications like poetry!

The default value for the `xml:space` attribute is—surprise!—`default`. There's no reason to use this except in the context of an element contained within *another* element, the latter of which has an `xml:space="preserve"` attribute; in this case, `xml:space="default"` would serve temporarily (for the life of the contained element) to negate the current `xml:space` setting. (If a light switch is by default in the "off" position, then the only time you need to turn it off explicitly is when it's been turned on.) For example, in the poetry case, some poems include an epigraph—a snippet of text that inspired or is otherwise used to illuminate the poem itself. If the text enclosed in an `epigraph` element was also poetry, there'd be no reason to use an `xml:space` attribute at all—the child would assume the characteristics of the parent (the `poemtext` element). If, however, the epigraph were in *prose*, we might want to tell the application to go ahead and use its default whitespace handling, like this:

```
<poemtext xml:space="preserve">
    <epigraph xml:space="default">
            Joyce Kilmer, who wrote these lines, has a rest
            stop on the NJ Turnpike named after him.
            Ironically, there are no trees at this rest stop!
    </epigraph>
    I think that I shall never see
            A poem lovely as a tree...
</poemtext>
```

xml:lang

The xml:lang attribute is used to specify a language other than the default language for an occurrence of an element and its content.

It's not common for foreign movies to be thought of as B movies, but (except for their native language) many of them *do* share characteristics of English-language Bs. For instance, the great French director François Truffaut's 1960 film, "Shoot the Piano Player," is based on a pulp novel by David Goodis. (The novel was *Down There*, published by Gold Medal in 1956.) It stars Charles Aznavour as famed concert pianist Edouard Saroyan, who changes his name to Charlie Kohler and takes up playing in bars; the *noir*-style plot and character development eventually have him taking up with gangsters, much to his girlfriend's dismay.

Now, this film was also known in English as "Shoot the Pianist"—which, for the sake of our example here, it helps to know is nearly a word-for-word translation of the original French title, *Tirez sur le Pianiste*. In FlixML terms, then, we could represent its various titles like this:

```
<title>Shoot the Piano Player</title>
<title role="alt">Shoot the Pianist</title>
<title role="alt" xml:lang="FR">Tirez sur le
    Pianiste</title>
```

Note that the use of the xml:lang attribute doesn't add anything to the *content* of this entry; you might say, though, that it shades the content a bit. And a sufficiently sophisticated search engine could take advantage of this shading to return, for example, "all movies whose titles or alternate titles are in French."

Like xml:space, xml:lang effectively resets the current value (of the document's language, in this case) for the life of the element in which it appears. And also like xml:space, xml:lang can be applied in successively nested elements; each appearance of the attribute temporarily interrupts the language in which the parent is expressed.

Entities

Here's a common problem in creating even moderate-sized word-processing documents:

Maybe you've got a set of actions you perform over and over. Maybe the document (like the manuscript of *Just XML* I'm working on right now) has to periodically switch back and forth between "smart quotes" (the curly sixes and nines) for plain text, and "straight quotes" (simple small vertical strokes: ") used in code examples. The problem here is that the commands or dialog box selections for performing these actions are buried a couple of levels down in a dialog box or menu; that's an awful lot of keystrokes or mouse clicks to create such an elementary effect, especially if you've got to do it over and over.

Or maybe you need to create *boilerplate* text. This is text—often large chunks of it, extending across whole paragraphs or even pages—that can be bolted into place and reused from one document to another, surrounding text that varies from one document to another. For example, a tenant-landlord rental contract typically looks exactly the same for one property as for another, except that specific words or short phrases (property address, tenant name, and so on) are different.

A given word-processing package might offer more than one way to solve both these problems—shortcut keys, templates, and so on—but one thing that can accomplish both is to use *macros*. These are basically strings of commands, special keystrokes and mouse-clicks, and/or plain text, that are combined into a single, easily accessible "thing" such as a toolbar button. You click on the button and the software runs the macro just as if you had done all that stuff manually.

There are two big advantages to using macros for repeated actions rather than performing them yourself:

- **Convenience:** It takes less time and requires fewer keystrokes and mouse actions to do the same thing.
- **Consistency:** The "thing" that needs to be done over and over will be done the same way every time. Boilerplate text, for instance, will always be spelled, capitalized, punctuated, and so on, exactly the same way whenever it's inserted into the document.

In XML, *entities* perform the same function as macros, and offer the same benefits. They're rather odd-looking beasts; the entity name is immediately preceded by an ampersand, and immediately followed by a semicolon, like this:

```
&entityname;
```

One of the tricks to using entities is that (with a few exceptions, which I'll get to in a moment) they've got to be declared in the document's DTD. Therefore, with those exceptions, a document that lacks a DTD can include *no* entity references.

FlixML's DTD declares several entities for simplifying your markup. One kind, for example, is used for naming distributors from whom you can obtain a copy of a film. To my knowledge, the biggest distributor of movies on tape is Movies Unlimited, based in Philadelphia. To refer to that company in a FlixML review, you might do so like this, taking advantage of one of these entities:

```
<remarks>The "deluxe" version of this film available from
    &MUL; comes with a 60-page shooting script!</remarks>
```

When the parser comes across an entity reference, it *expands* it in-place, and passes the text in its expanded form to the downstream XML application. So in the XML browser, you'd see something like this:

```
The "deluxe" version of this film available from Movies
    Unlimited comes with a 60-page shooting script!
```

Aside from their use as convenient, consistent shortcuts, XML entities offer another significant benefit: They allow easy updating when conditions change. You just change the "expanded version" of the text in the entity declaration, and all references to that entity in any documents that use that DTD will be up-to-date when they are next parsed.

Let's say Movies Unlimited changes its company name sometime in the future to, say, MegaFlixUnlimited, Inc. If the maintainer of the DTD makes a simple change to the `&MUL;` entity declaration, our sample "remarks" element will automatically become:

```
The "deluxe" version of this film available from
MegaFlixUnlimited, Inc. comes with a 60-page
shooting script!
```

Without the use of entities, replacing text like this would be extremely tedious and error-prone—requiring extensive use of a global search-and-replace operation. And if the text to be replaced existed in dozens or thousands of other documents, many of which were maintained by someone else, replacing the text with the current version would probably be impossible. But if all the related documents point to the same DTD somewhere out there on the Web, when that DTD is updated, the change is instantly made.

Entities ≈ Constants

If you've had any exposure to common programming languages, you'll know of an even better analogue than macros for XML's entities: the notion of *constants*.

A constant is a "thing" that you'll be using and reusing many times throughout your program (or in a whole cluster of related programs). Usually constants are declared early in the program's context, in a header or a so-called library, so they'll always be accessible to any program(s) that need to use them.

Here's a typical declaration of a constant (the programming language in this case being Microsoft's Visual Basic):

```
Const strVer = "Version 1.0 (Date:2000/03/01)"
```

The name of the constant—strVer in this case—can be whatever the programmer wants to make it, but is usually chosen to be meaningful in some way. In this case the "str" prefix says that this constant is a *str*ing of characters, and the "Ver" refers to the particular function of this particular string of characters: to declare the version and date of the program. Once it's been declared as a constant, the program's version can then be incorporated anywhere in the application that it's needed: error messages, dialog boxes, as a footer in forms and reports, and so on.

As with constants, which are automatically updated everywhere whenever the program is compiled, entities are expanded everywhere whenever the document is reparsed.

Built-in entities

XML comes with a standard set of entities that aren't required to be declared in a DTD. These are used to sidestep the problem (referred to earlier) of occasionally needing to include in a document's contents characters that have some "special meaning" to an XML parser, and that therefore might trip the parser up. There are five such character entities, as shown in Table 3.1 (note that all five of these can be used in HTML as well):

Table 3.1   Built-in XML character entities

Entity reference	Character name	Character represented
&amp;	ampersand	&
&apos;	apostrophe (single quotation mark)	'
&gt;	greater-than ("left angle bracket")	>
&lt;	less-than ("right angle bracket")	<
&quot;	double quotation mark	"

To use one of the characters from the third column somewhere in your document content, simply insert the corresponding entity reference from the first column into the text.

B Alert!

Targets (1968, Paramount)

1968 was a banner year for Boris Karloff: *Six* of his movies came out then...his *last* six, as it happened. The others were fairly standard, late-in-an-aging-horror-star's-career stuff, but *Targets* jumps out at you.

It's remarkable to me, in particular, in that Karloff plays the role of an aging horror star, Byron Orlok. Orlok has made his last film, he tells his agent; real life is getting too scary for his movies to compete. (*Targets'* plot is based loosely on the story of Charles Whitman, who had recently climbed atop a tower at the University of Texas and fired at passers-by with a high-powered rifle, killing or wounding several.) I can't help wondering how much of Karloff himself went into Orlok's psychology.

Anyway, the agent convinces him to make one final personal appearance before retiring, at a drive-in movie where this last film is the feature. It's getting the full red-carpet treatment; not only Orlok and his agent, but the film-in-the-film's director will also be present. (This director is played by Peter Bogdanovich, the director himself of *Targets*...which was Bogdanovich's *first* feature. All these firsts and lasts are a bit dizzying.)

Meanwhile, on a parallel plot track, there's the story of Bobby Thompson: the classic ex-military guy who hasn't been able to adjust to civilian life. One day, Thompson kills his mother and his wife, then proceeds to the roof of a nearby oil refinery where he takes potshots with a rifle at cars passing on the freeway. This doesn't fully satisfy him—he's too exposed—so he hops in his Mustang convertible and heads (guess where?) to the same drive-in theater where Orlok will be appearing.

The climactic scene takes place after Thompson has worked his way up behind the drive-in screen. He pokes the barrel of the rifle through a hole in the screen and as Orlok's film plays, begins shooting those watching the film, theater workers, basically anyone he can see. A dramatic confrontation between Orlok and Thompson occurs—the killer wheeling madly back and forth between the screen-Orlok and the Orlok-in-the-flesh before him.

Trivia bit: The film's release roughly coincided with Bobby Kennedy's assassination. Paramount rushed to add an antigun prologue to the film in response. (The commercially available videotape doesn't include the prologue, though.)

B movie touch: Have you *ever* seen rooms in a suburban, middle-class home so barren of furniture, wall decor, knick-knacks?

Okay, back to entities. The remarks for this film's FlixML entry might read:

```
<remarks>Bogdanovich&apos;s first feature &amp; one of
Karloff&amp;s last.</remarks>
```

The parser would expand this into the much more readable:

```
Bogdanovich's first feature & one of Karloff's last.
```

The Curse of the Speed Typist

It is possible, even likely, that XML software, like its HTML counterparts, will become more forgiving with the use of literal ampersands, apostrophes, and double quotation marks. These characters—especially the latter two—are awfully common, at least in everyday English use, and much harder to "type without thinking" in their character-entity form than in their literal &, ', and " form.

In the meantime, if you're concerned about it, better to be safe than sorry: Use the character entities rather than the characters themselves (especially for the greater-than and less-than symbols). (Other than < and >, *I'm* not too worried, though; you'll probably find lots of quotation marks and apostrophes in my FlixML examples.)

If an element's contents really do make great use of these special symbols, consider enclosing it in a "marked section," as explained below.

Beyond the keyboard

Depending on what it is that your document has to contain, you may be confronted with the occasional need to include a character or two not represented on your keyboard.

XML's solution for this problem is the same as HTML's: Where you need to insert such a character, insert an unambiguous character entity. These entities, unlike the ones you've seen so far, are *unnamed*, so there's no handy mnemonic token to insert between the opening & and closing ; characters. Instead, you must use a numeric value in the following form:

```
&#value;
```

Note that not only the & and ;, but also the # (pound or hash symbol) are required; for value, you substitute either a decimal or hexadecimal number (the latter requiring that an "x" be placed between the # and value).

The big question you should be asking yourself now is, "How do I know what value to enter?" The answer is that you've got to locate—and probably print out for reference—one of the many lists of ISO (the Organization for International Standards) character sets, and use the values listed therein. There are way too many of these for me to list in *Just XML*, but Table 3.2 shows a small sample (some in decimal, some in hexadecimal):

Table 3.2   Sample ISO special characters

Character/ Symbol	Name	Entity reference
©	copyright symbol	`&#169;`
ç	lowercase c with cedilla	`&#231;`
þ	lowercase Icelandic thorn	`&#254;`
Þ	uppercase Icelandic thorn	`&#222;`
±	plus/minus	`&#xB1;`
ü	lowercase u with umlaut	`&#252;`
≈	"approximately equals" sign	`&#x2245;`

Using the above table, for example, when entering François Truffaut's name in the FlixML entry for *Shoot the Piano Player*, you'd type:

```
<director>Fran&#231;ois Truffaut</director>
```

The variety of special characters you can use is truly dizzying. As for where to find the lists, check the following sites on the Web (Table 3.3):

Table 3.3   ISO special character entity lists

URL	Description/Notes
www.schema.net/entities/	James Tauber's well-organized list (courtesy of Rick Jelliffe) of ISO character sets. (Tauber's XML pages are in general excellent sources of information about all aspects of XML.)
ftp://ftp.unicode.org/Public/ UNIDATA/UnicodeData-Latest.txt	The official Unicode list of all current ISO character representations. To use this list, you need to understand that the first value in each line is the *hexadecimal* value for the character described elsewhere on that line. Therefore, the lowercase c with cedilla (represented in decimal in Table 3.2) would be represented using the hexadecimal value as &x00E7;. While this list is complete and (in theory) always up-to-date, it can be a little overwhelming.

The thoughtful DTD

If you're using a DTD with your XML document, and if the DTD's designer—you, or someone else—has taken into account your possible need to include special character entities in your document, there may be entity *names* available for you, so you don't need to keep a list of the numeric ISO values handy. FlixML's DTD has several such entity names declared; for instance, rather than:

```
<director>Fran&#231;ois Truffaut</director>
```

you can code Truffaut's name as:

```
<director>Fran&ccedilla;ois Truffaut</director>
```

This isn't any easier to type than the number, but it is a bit easier to remember. It's also much more self-documenting than the numeric value, so if you or someone else later needs to read your raw XML code, the intention will be clear.

(By the way, this particular example, the `&ccedilla;` entity, isn't something I can claim credit for. It's actually one of many international standard entities, all of which can be found in the entity sets referred to above. It's also built-in to HTML. One of the points that this illustrates is that it makes little if any difference what entities the outside world "knows about"; in order to use them in an XML document, all entities other than the built-in ones must be declared in a DTD.)

External parsed entities

Aside from merely replacing an entity with a word or phrase, it is also possible to replace an entity with an entire external *document*.[11] This provides a means of logically incorporating one document within another.

As with other entities, this is achieved in part with a DTD. Either the external or internal DTD subset might include a specification such as:

```
<!ENTITY bplate SYSTEM "boilerplate.xml">
```

---

11.   Indeed, there's no requirement that such an external entity even be a "document" in an XML sense. It can be just a lump of undifferentiated text, stored elsewhere other than in the document that refers to it.

Any time a document author wanted to include the contents of the boiler-plate.xml document in the author's own document, he or she could achieve that purpose by inserting:

```
&bplate;
```

at that point. (Once XLink-aware applications are available, as described in Part 2, you'll also be able to use XLinks for including one document within another.)

Note one potential danger of using external entities for this purpose: The "document" that results *may* no longer be valid.

External unparsed entities

I've said repeatedly (and chances are, not for the last time) that XML documents may contain only text. There are two ways, though, for them to *refer to* nontextual content (such as images).

The first way is simply by pointing to this content with a URI, much like HTML points to images in the `<img src="...">` tag (where the URI replaces the "...").

The second, more esoteric approach is to use an external unparsed entity. Accomplishing this, however, is completely dependent on the downstream application's ability to process and interpret *notations*. Use of notations is discussed later in this chapter, in the section headed "Multimedia."

Parameter entities (PEs)

In addition to general entities (like `&amp;` and `&MUL;` in the examples above) and character entities (such as `&#231;` to represent a lowercase c-with-cedilla character), XML provides for a third kind, *parameter entities* (PEs, for short). PEs take a somewhat different form than the other two entity types; more important, you can't use them at all in the root element—only in the document's DTD.

I'll cover parameter entities in the discussion of DTDs in Part 4. For now, be aware that you may see references to the term in other XML resources, and that if you're not developing your own DTDs (or enhancing someone else's), you don't have to be concerned with them at all.

Comments

As in the document prolog and epilog, comments—for clarifying the XML code, providing version information aside from what's in the "real XML," or any other purpose—can appear anywhere in the root element. The rules are the same:

- A comment begins with the characters `<!--` (left angle bracket, exclamation point, two adjacent hyphens, no spaces).
- A comment can span multiple lines in the document.
- A comment ends with the characters `-->` (two adjacent hyphens, right angle bracket, no spaces).
- Anything at all is allowed in a comment, including reserved characters like `<` and `&`, *except* a pair of adjacent hyphens (`--`). (By the way, *any* set of multiple hyphens is disallowed by this rule; you can't use "`---`" either.)
- The parser itself will ignore comments. Depending on the parser, it may or may not pass comments to the downstream processing program. For this reason, be sure that you do not put *anything* in comments that you think the downstream application might actually need.

Here's a comment for a FlixML document:

```
<!-- The B-movie review in this document is copyright
     © 2000 by John E. Simpson. All rights reserved. -->
```

Again, if you want the information (such as the copyright notice in this example) to be available to a downstream application, such as a browser, be sure to include it somewhere else than in a comment.

Processing instructions (PIs)

We also saw these in Chapter 2's discussion of the document prolog and epilog. A PI is some instruction provided either for the parser or for the downstream application's use that has no special meaning in a true document-content sense. For example, maybe you're anticipating that the document will be printed, and you want to force a page break at a particular point. If "what happens to the document" after parsing—the downstream application—recognizes this particular instruction, it will indeed break the page at this point. If the application (for example, a browser) does not recognize the instruction, it will simply ignore it.

You begin a PI with the `<?` characters, and terminate it with `?>`. What goes between those opening and closing characters depends on what the application is expecting—the "command," say, for "force a page break here."

Obviously, this requires some knowledge of the application in question. But we can make up a reasonable example:

Let's suppose that someone is so enamored of the idea of an online B-movie guide that he or she decides to build a FlixML-specific browser. The elements of the document would—as in a typical early XML browser—be displayed in a tree in one pane. Actual contents of the elements would be displayed in a second. And perhaps there's a third, reserved for playing multimedia clips (dialog and/ or actual snippets of film).

Under normal circumstances, our FlixML browser would display whatever content exists in the document, unchanged except for stylistic touches (using cascading style sheets or the XML Stylesheet Language, XSL) like boldface, font changes, and so on. But the browser's developer knows—B movies being what they are—that some of the element content might be too much for users with innocent sensibilities. So the developer has come up with a standard way to tell the browser, "Check the user's preferences and display the following content only if he or she has agreed to be exposed to films with this MPAA rating."

Here's a hypothetical PI that tells the hypothetical FlixML browser to do just that:

```
<?ratingcheck scale="MPAA"?>
```

Another film's FlixML document might specify that the rating check should be against the PICS scale as well as the MPAA rating. Such a document might include this PI:

```
<?ratingcheck scale="MPAA,PICS"?>
```

Either of these PIs provides the application something very close to "content." Indeed, there is a FlixML element, `<mpaarating>`, that seems to do the same thing. But the content (the element) doesn't tell the application what to do—it provides the processing program with no instruction. So (assuming the browser's developer hasn't provided some other way to achieve the same end), it's reasonable that such a PI might in fact be needed.

(One important exception to the "the XML parser doesn't know how to handle a PI" is in the use of *notations* for handling multimedia. See the "Multimedia" section below for details.)

Marked sections

I mentioned previously, in the discussion of character entity references, that it's something of a pain to rely on character entities for things as simple as plain old everyday apostrophes and quotation marks.

Fortunately, there's a way—somewhat ungainly-looking, but it works—to set off a block of text so that you can put anything you want in it. It's called a CDATA marked section, a marked section, or simply CDATA.

> ## To CDATA or to PCDATA?
>
> *CDATA* is SGML- and XML-speak for *character data*, as opposed to "normal" text, which is called *PCDATA* (for *parsed character data*). The latter is processed by the parser (hence the name), which, as you would expect, hiccups every time it comes to a <, a >, and so on.
>
> PCDATA is the default content type for all text in a document. If you're writing an XML document, so goes the logic, you want it to be parsed. In many everyday cases, though, this may not be at all true—especially when the content of a particular element (like `dialog`, in FlixML's case) may be littered with dozens of apostrophes and quotation marks.
>
> So: do you want "normal" in XML terms, or "normal" in real-world terms? Choose your normality.

CDATA sections in an XML document really do stand out to the naked eye. That's because they aren't demarcated by the usual simple angle brackets, but by a special sequence that begins like this:

```
<![CDATA[
```

and ends like this:

```
]]>
```

You may be thinking, "Where in the heck did they come up with *that?*" I wasn't present when the discussion was held, but I think it (or something like it) makes sense. The object, after all, is to come up with some string of characters that: (a) isn't particularly burdensome to type; and (b) will never (well, only in extremely rare cases) appear in "normal" text.

Here's a CDATA section from a FlixML review:

```
<remarks><![CDATA[
    I've seen "Bullwhip" more than once, and
every time, I've cracked up when the heroine says
to the hero:
    "I could never hurt you... I <heavy pause> LOVE
    you!"
There's nothing intrinsically funny about this line.
But there is given the two characters' previous interaction
(the hero has basically usurped the heroine's
authority among her own ranch hands and other
employees, making her look like a fool).]]></remarks>
```

Remember that everything in a CDATA section is passed by the parser, 100% unchanged, to the downstream application. In the above example, there will be a newline after the opening `<![CDATA[`, but not before the closing `]]>`. Furthermore, if you try to use entities in your CDATA section, you'll find that they have *not* been expanded as you expected. This can be a very handy feature for people who are trying to quote XML code, but a real nuisance for anyone who *wants* their entity shortcuts to bloom into the replacement text!

One further note about CDATA sections: The one character sequence they may not include (for obvious reasons) is `]]>`.

Multimedia

Aha. You were wondering if this would show up, weren't you? All this talk of text, text, text may have led you to believe that your beloved Web—with all its GIFs, JPEGs, QuickTime and MPEG animations, VRML worlds, RealAudio recordings, ShockWave presentations, and all the rest—was about to take a giant step backward.

The answer is a qualified "No!" There are as many multimedia features built into basic XML as there are in HTML. The catch is two-fold: There are not yet standard ways of playing or displaying all the bells and whistles (the "I can do it all" XML browser hasn't appeared yet), and XML does indeed put text in the forefront.

Multimedia content "lives" in SGML, XML, and HTML documents only to the extent that it can be described in text form. For example, markup itself can't contain an image; when you use your browser's View Source feature, you don't see any pretty pictures or anything else except text (some of it pretty ugly). All the markup can do is tell the browser where the image is, and hope the browser (or some other helper application that the browser knows about) can handle it.

Some of what follows in this discussion of multimedia content will make reference to DTD coding. Don't panic; the details will be covered in Part 4. Remember that all we're really getting at here is how to incorporate multimedia content in the document.

Notations

In HTML, you tell the browser how to include an image at a particular point using an `img` element. For example:

```
<img src="http://www.XYZCorp.com/logo.gif">
```

The img puts the browser on alert, as it were—"picture coming up!"—and the src attribute, together with its URL value, tells the browser *where the image is* and *what kind of image to expect.* Typically what happens is that the browser determines from the image filename extension whether it knows how to handle the image type. If not (say the filename extension is .zed instead of .gif, .jpg, .png, or other file types the browser recognizes), you get a dialog box that among other options, lets you locate a program on your PC that *can* handle the image type.

For the sake of understanding XML multimedia and other "non-XML" content, though, I want you for a moment to forget about the src attribute and its value. Think instead of the <img> tag, or rather the img element, itself. How does an HTML processor "know" what to do with content identified by the presence of an img element? It "knows" because somewhere deep in the bowels of the system there's an association between the particular syntactic trigger—the <img> tag—and the desired behavior.

This should suggest to you that the proper way to incorporate an image in your XML document is first to *associate a behavior with a particular syntactic trigger.* Such an association is called a *notation,* and is done by way of a declaration in the DTD. (Declaring notations is covered at greater length in Part 4.) All that the notation does is provide a name for the "type of behavior" associated with a particular bit of markup: Do this thing when you encounter this trigger's name, and the other thing when you find this other trigger's name. And when you "use a notation" in your documents you needn't have any idea that you're doing so; they appear as simple attribute values. The connection between a particular value and a particular value is what the notation declaration in the DTD does.

Given, then, that (a) there are no built-in multimedia handlers in XML as there are for (say) HTML's img element, and (b) the DTD designer may create any markup—"syntactic triggers," in the form of notations—that he or she wants, it stands to reason that XML is virtually unlimited in the range of multimedia that it can potentially support.

Just remember that lurking in the word "potentially" lies a "but": For now, few (if any) true-blue XML applications exist that support embedded multimedia *within* the applications themselves.

Namespaces

As you get deeper into XML, you're going to run up against an apparent obstacle. This has to do with occasions—although they may seem rare to you now—when you've got to include bits and pieces of *other* XML vocabularies in your own XML documents.

When would this happen?

There are two good examples you'll encounter in later chapters of *Just XML*: when you're creating XML-enhanced hyperlinks, called XLinks; and when you're using the Extensible Stylesheet Language, or XSL, for transforming and otherwise styling/displaying your XML documents. The problem is that for XLinks, for example, you *must* use certain attributes on certain elements, to inform an XLink-aware processing program that you're establishing an XLink here. And when you're using XSL, the stylesheet is itself an XML document that contains certain reserved elements and attributes from the "XSL vocabulary" *as well as* references to elements and attributes in the vocabulary of whatever document you're transforming your own document into.

The solution to the problem is to identify the "universe of names," or the vocabulary, with which a particular element or attribute is associated, using a prefix on the element or attribute name.

You've already been exposed to two examples of this practice in action, in the names of the `xml:lang` and `xml:space` attributes. By default, any elements or attributes whose names begin with the `xml:` prefix belong to the core XML namespace; you don't need to do anything special to associate that prefix with that vocabulary, and you cannot associate that prefix with any *other* vocabulary. Because there's a prefix to those two names, a given variant of XML, such as FlixML, may include its own attributes called `space` and `lang`, and there will not be any conflict.

But aside from the core XML namespace, how do you associate elements and attributes with a namespace? And once associated with a particular namespace, how do you use such an element or attribute in a document?

Declaring the prefix

The way that namespaces become associated with a document's elements and attributes is with special attributes in the document's root element. These attributes all begin with the letters `xmlns` (for "*XML n*ame*s*pace"), and look like the following (taken from a FlixML document):

```
xmlns:xlink="http://www.w3.org/1999/xlink/namespace/"
```

The portion of the attribute name following the colon—xlink, in this case—identifies a prefix that will be used somewhere in the document, in the name(s) of some elements or attributes.

The portion of this or any other namespace-declaring attribute that looks like a value (following the =, and enclosed in quotation marks) is a little more complicated to explain. Roughly, it translates to something like, "This is a place [a person, an organization, whatever] that has control of this namespace." If you're familiar with Web addresses, you'll recognize the format—it *looks* like a Web address, doesn't it? The complication is that when you're declaring a namespace, the "place that owns the namespace" doesn't really have to be a place. It just has to be *unique within the document* and, in some cases, it must have a particular value.

(For example, XLink-aware applications will be trained to look for the particular namespace attribute value shown above. If you change it to something else, even if it's unique in your document, the XLink won't work.)

You may also declare a *default namespace*, for elements and attributes whose names don't have any prefix at all. The format for this namespace attribute is:

```
xmlns="'address' of default namespace's owner"
```

See? It's basically the same format as above, except that there is no colon and no prefix appended to the xmlns.

Don't panic.[12] In most cases, by far, you as the document author will not have to declare any namespaces; that will have been taken care of by the author of the XML vocabulary—the DTD—that you're working with. (When you get to Chapter 8, on XSLT, you'll have to deal with declaring your namespaces. But by then you'll be an old hand at most of this stuff.)

Using namespaces

There's no particular trick to this; just use the element or attribute name that you're given, including any prefixes.

None of FlixML's elements come from any other namespace. The only attributes that do so are related to XLinks; an element using such an attribute might look like this in a document:

```
<distriblink xlink:href="…" />
```

There *is* no bare-bones, prefix-less href attribute anywhere in FlixML. So it's not even an issue.

---

12.   This may well be *Just XML*'s slogan.

Attribute/Element confusion?

If a given element belongs to a particular namespace, any of its *attributes* from the same namespace don't take a prefix. The only time you need a prefix on an attribute name is when it and its element come from two different namespaces.

Namespace controversy

I'm not going to belabor the issue here, but thought I'd mention it because you may encounter it on XML mailing lists and in XML newsgroups: Namespaces drive a lot of people crazy, and just plain confuse others.

The chief reason they drive people crazy is that they have the potential to make a document unvalidatable. Even if you declare the namespace in your root element, even if you do so correctly and unambiguously, your document may still be rejected by a validating parser if that prefix and that namespace are not also declared in the document's DTD.

The chief reason that they confuse people is that they seem, tantalizingly, to make possible the notion of "merging document types" or some such. It seems sometimes as if this question comes up weekly, even more often. Forget it. As long as you're using DTDs, there's no way to merge document types unless the DTD author wants to do so.

Namespaces solve only one problem, and it's a very simple problem: how to avoid collisions between element and attribute names among vocabularies in the XML universe, where "reserved names" are supposed to be anathema. Don't expect too much from them. Go quietly amid the noise and haste....

Summary

This chapter focused on the contents of an XML document's root element, including five major components: elements, entities, comments, PIs, and marked sections. It also covered, briefly, the use of multimedia content in XML documents.

XML markup covered in this chapter

Unlike Chapter 2, which was able to present XML markup used in *any* document, this chapter was able to present no universally useful markup. That's because the elements that can be used in any given XML document's root vary according to the DTD associated with the document.

However, I *can* present you with a short annotated FlixML document that shows examples of all of the basic components that *may* be present in a root element, and that's what I've done here. The boxed capital letters are cross-referenced in the annotation legend that follows the sample code. (Note that this document doesn't use all FlixML elements—just enough of them to cover the basic building blocks.)

```
<flixinfo> Ⓐ
<title role="main"Ⓑ>Shoot the Piano PlayerⒸ</title>
<title role="alt" xml:lang="FR"Ⓓ>Tirez sur le Pianiste
</title>
<crew>
<director>Fran&#231;Ⓔois Truffaut</director>
</crew>
<plotsummary xml:space="default"Ⓕ>Jaded piano player
changes his name and takes up with gangsters, much to his
girlfriend&apos;Ⓖs chagrin.</plotsummary>
<distributor>&MUL;Ⓗ</distributor>
<dialog><![CDATA[This film doesn't contain the
line, "Play it, Sam" -- but it MIGHT have.]]>Ⓘ</dialog>
</flixinfo> Ⓐ
```

Legend:

Item	Description
Ⓐ	Root element start tag (note end tag at bottom)
Ⓑ	Attribute/value pair
Ⓒ	Text content of `title` element
Ⓓ	`xml:lang` attribute (also note use of `xml:` namespace qualifier)
Ⓔ	Character entity for lowercase c with cedilla; will be expanded by parser to ç
Ⓕ	`xml:space` attribute (also note use of `xml:` namespace qualifier)
Ⓖ	"Built-in" entity (expanded by parser to apostrophe)
Ⓗ	General entity declared in DTD (expanded by parser to `Movies Unlimited`)
Ⓘ	Marked (CDATA) section

Terms defined in this chapter

elements The basic building blocks of an XML document. Each element is a container, whose limits are marked by the presence of tags; its contents can include other elements, straight text, and various kinds of other markup (comments, PIs, and so on). An element may be empty, in which case what it "contains" is inherent in the tag itself.

tokens A single unit of text, separated from other tokens by whitespace. Analogous roughly to a "word."

name characters In XML terms, a *name character* is any of the following: letters (from virtually any language in the world), digits, hyphens, underscores, periods, and colons. Such characters are what can be used in the names of XML elements, attributes, and other key identifiers.

attributes/values Various properties that modify the "meaning" of a given element are specified using *attributes* and their *values*. An attribute is separated from its value with an equals sign (=), and the value is in quotes (single or double). For instance, if a document contains an element reference like `<title role="alt">`, the word "`role`" is an attribute of the element and "`alt`" is the `role` attribute's value.

namespaces A *namespace,* as the term implies, is a sort of abstract cloud in which float names that are related to one another. There's an XML namespace, for instance, and all the XML-specific element and attribute types exist in that namespace. By using the "name of the namespace" as a qualifier on a given element name or attribute, you ensure that you're getting the element *as it is declared in the given namespace.* For instance, as we'll see later in *Just XML*'s section about XML linking, there is an important linking-related attribute, `xlink:type`. The `xlink:` designates the namespace; this makes it possible for the attribute name `type` to have meaning in other contexts, according to other DTDs, and so on.

entities In markup languages that are derived from SGML (like HTML and XML), an *entity* is a special string of name characters (see above) that is used to stand for something else. This makes it possible to insert boilerplate text, special characters that aren't legal using the document's native character set, and so on—even unparsed content—simply by referring to the entity name. If the entity's fully expanded value is declared internally in the DTD, the parser expands the entity reference to its full replacement text before passing the stream of XML to a downstream application. Entity references may also be used to incorporate nontextual content, such as multimedia.

general entities A common form of entity (see above) used in XML documents. References to general entities take the form `&entityname;`, with the `&` and `;` characters required on either side of the entity's name.

character entities A particular type of general entity (see above), whose replacement text is always a single character. Character entity references take the form `&#number;`, where `number` is the decimal or hexadecimal declaration of a special character as provided by ISO, the international standards authority.

external parsed entities You can logically include one XML document (or even simply text) in another using an *external parsed entity*. The entity's declaration in the DTD must include a SYSTEM identifier and the URI of the document to be included; when the parser encounters the entity reference, it substitutes for it the contents of the document at the specified URI.

external unparsed entities Depending on how the DTD is constructed, you can refer to external multimedia content either using a conventional URI (as the HTML `<img...>` tag does) or with an *external unparsed entity*. In either case, the multimedia content won't actually be part of an XML document (which can contain only text); however, using an external unparsed entity also requires the application program to understand notations (see below).

parameter entities *Parameter entities* are a particular type of entity used only within DTDs, not regular XML documents. They're covered at greater length in Part 4.

marked sections (CDATA) Sometimes it's necessary in an XML document to include a block of text that you don't want the parser to process normally, because it contains many characters used to denote the presence of markup (especially < and > characters). You signal the parser not to parse such passages by designating them *marked sections*, which begin with the special character sequence `<![CDATA[` and end with `]]>`. Any text may appear in a CDATA section except the `]]>` sequence.

notations In XML terms, a *notation* is the declaration of a particular content type that is not "understandable" to an XML processor (which can handle only strings of text). Such content types include but are not limited to images, audio, and other multimedia.

XML Linking

Now that Part 1 has prepared you to construct basic XML documents, you're ready to look into establishing links from one part of a document to another, and from one document to another. That's the purpose of this second part of Just XML.

Part 3 will look at ways you can apply various display styles to your XML documents; Part 4, at building document type definitions (DTDs) of your own; and Part 5, at the directions you can expect XML to be headed in the near to mid term.

CHAPTER   **4**

Why XLink?

In your travels around the Internet, you may already have encountered references to something called Metcalfe's Law.[13] It's named after Bob Metcalfe, the inventor of the Ethernet local-area network standard, founder of networking giant 3Com Corporation, and the "law's" formulator.

Roughly stated, Metcalfe's Law says that given a network of n resources, the network's potential value is n-squared. Imagine a simple e-mail network with two users; it therefore has value of 2-squared, or 4 "somethings" (it doesn't matter what the somethings are—let's say each something is $100, for a total of $400). Double the number of users to four and the value doesn't merely double, it *quadruples*—increases from 2^2, or 4 (its original value), to 4^2, or 16. Our little network worth $400 originally is now worth $1600. If you increase the original two users to 10—multiply it by five—the value grows to 10^2 (i.e., 100), or *twenty-five* times the original value. And so on.

Metcalfe's Law is commonly invoked to describe the value—the worth, if you will—of machine or human resources on a computer network. But in the Web universe, we could equally apply it to *documents*. Trying to build a catalog or index to every single resource on the Web is pretty much hopeless, as even the

---

13.   Probably the seminal reference is George Gilder's *Forbes* column, called "Telecosm," which apparently coined the term "Metcalfe's Law." It's at *www.forbes.com/ asap/gilder/telecosm4a.htm*.

most optimistic search engine vendors have discovered; there are by now hundreds of millions of individual documents, and only a relatively small fraction of them are accessible from search engines. So how do you access all that potential hundreds-of-million-squared value?

The answer in XML—as in HTML before it—is with document *linking*.

Linking Basics

Before delving into XML linking conventions, it would be a good idea to get a handle on the practice of hyperlinks as they're used in HTML. If you already know this information, of course, feel free to skip to the later section titled "Trouble in Hyperlinking Paradise."

A short (refresher) course in HTML linking

In HTML, you can have one document point to another by using the so-called "anchor tag," `<a>`. You place this tag in such a way that it surrounds the text or image that you want to link *from*; the `href="url"` attribute specifies a document, or particular point in a document, that you want to link *to*. Here's an example:

```
Looking for an HTML version of the FlixML DTD? You can find it
<a href="http://www.flixml.org/flixml_03_dtd.html>here</a>.
```

The word `here` is bracketed by the `<a>` tag, the `href` attribute of which points to the target's actual location on the Web. That target is expressed as something called a Uniform Resource Locator, or URL.[14] Each URL consists of various parts, some of which are optional depending on the context:

• A service type, represented in the above example as `http://`. The service type identifies the protocol that's used to "bring" the target document from one place to another; other values possible in place of `http` include `ftp`, `gopher`, `news`, and `telnet`. Technically, this is a required URL component, but there are some contexts in which you can omit it. For example, recent versions of most Web browsers let you enter a URL into the browser's "location" field without including a service, in which case the `http://` is

---

14.   As I mentioned earlier, the current preferred term is URI, for Uniform Resource Identifier. For all practical purposes the terms are synonymous.

assumed. Document authors—Webmasters—can omit the service type in the `href` attribute value if the resource being pointed to is located somewhere on the same server as the referencing document.

- The system name, commonly (though not with great precision) called the "server." In our example above, the system name is `www.flixml.org` (the FlixML home page). You can't omit this part of the URL when entering it in a browser window. In an `href` attribute value, you can't omit the system name if you've included the protocol, but you can omit it if you don't include the protocol *and* if the resource being pointed to is on the same system as the document that's pointing to it.

- A pathname to the document, and the document name itself. In our example, the document is found on the path `/flixml_03_dtd.html`. You can omit the path if you've omitted the service type and system name *and* if the resource being linked to is in the same directory as the document that's linking to it. You can omit the document name itself (`flixml_03_dtd.html`, in this case) only if what you're pointing to is within the same document you're pointing from; in this case, you need to provide the next item.[15]

- An optional fragment identifier or location pointer, which shows some precise point in the target document that you want the browser to position itself at. This is signaled in the `href` value by a # (pound, or hash) symbol, and what follows the # must be the name of some location in the target document. For example:

```
You can find the various FlixML entities
<a href="flixml_03_dtd.html#entities">here</a>.
```

Note that in this case, the service type, system name, and path are all omitted, which means that the browser will expect to find the flixml_03_dtd.html document using the `http://` service type, on the same system and path as the referencing document itself is located.

Also note that the text following the # must be placed somewhere in the target document, in an anchor tag that *names* this location accordingly. So

---

15.   You can also omit the pathname *and* the filename if the file to which you're pointing in a link is named index.htm, index.html, or one of a few other variants (depending on the server type). These are default filenames, and will be opened automatically if no specific filename is provided. If these files don't exist at all, the user gets a rather ugly directory listing of *all* the files in that directory.

the flixml_03_dtd.html document is expected to have something like this, somewhere in it:

```
[preceding text, if any]
<a name="entities">Here is some information on the
various entities used in FlixML documents....
```

• Various optional pieces used by CGI and other server-based programs, beginning with ? (question mark) and followed by the various search terms and/or other information used by the program. (These optional components don't concern us.)

Trouble in Hyperlink Paradise

HTML hyperlinking conventions provide wonderful power; the Web wouldn't have taken off without them. But if you can brush the stars out of your eyes for a moment, sit down and think about what they *might* do instead of or in addition to what they already do, you should be able to come up with a number of notable weaknesses.

Each HTML link goes *from* one single point *to* a single other point on the Web.

Let's say that instead of developing a B-movie guide markup language in XML, I'd just decided to put up a general, HTML-based site of information about B movies. On such a site I might include a menu selection—called *Reviews*, say—pointing to a single other page (which I'd also have to build in HTML) where the visitor to my site would find a series of hyperlinks to Roger Ebert's reviews, Joe Bob Briggs' reviews, and a page of review links at the Internet Movie Database site.

Wouldn't it be cool—and a lot less work, for that matter—if when the visitor held his or her mouse cursor over my *Reviews* link, a little menu were to pop up on the screen, presenting those hyperlinks and letting the visitor select then and there which resource to visit, without having to go through a separately-maintained "links to reviews" page on my site?

Each HTML hyperlink retrieves the entire document to which it links.

Many Web pages pretty much stand on their own: Their authors don't place every single paragraph or section on its own page. This makes for simplified document creation and reading on a monitor. It also, unfortunately, means that even if a linking document wants to refer to just a single sentence, phrase, paragraph, section, or whatever, it has to pull the *entire* referenced document across the network.

Note that using a document fragment identifier in the URL—like `#entities` in the example presented a moment ago—merely tells the browser to position that named location at the top of the window, if possible. But the whole document is still retrieved. (There's another significant drawback to using fragment identifiers, which I'll come to in a moment.)

Also note that this shortcoming has a flip side, to wit:

What HTML has put asunder, HTML cannot (easily) join together.

When a document *is* long, many users prefer to click on a "Next page" icon rather than scrolling. In deference to the shape of the browser window and to this preference for mouse clicks, Webmasters may break up a long source document into separate Web pages.

Unfortunately, once you've done this, you've immediately made it difficult (on some servers, impossible) to reassemble the thing into a single document again. And there are reasons why, despite their preferences, users might want that facility from time to time. Printing out all the information on a movie, for example, is terribly wasteful if the cast is listed on one Web page, the plot summary on another, notable dialog on a third, and so on. Cross-referencing the different parts of a scholarly document can be a nightmare when each part is maintained in a discrete unit from the ones it needs to refer to. Comparing a review of one product to another may result in a consumer's buying *neither* if you've forced him or her to toggle back and forth, repeatedly, to compare their features. And so on.

Only one thing can happen when you click on a bit of linked text...

...which is that the browser fills the window with the new document.

Yes, using HTML frames can ameliorate this problem to some extent. Various options of the HTML frame standard let you replace the contents of just a single frame, rather than the entire browser window, or let you open a whole new browser window and fill *that* one with the target document.

But you can't easily—even using frames—*insert* the target document (let alone just a piece of it) into the source document at the point of the link. (Another Web technology, called "server-side includes" or SSIs, can sort of achieve this effect. Server-side includes aren't available on all Web hosting sites, though. Furthermore, they aren't inherently dynamic: they insert the included document or file *always*, not at the user's discretion.)

B Alert!

Detour (1945, PRC Pictures, Inc.)

Shot in six days for almost nothing, *Detour* is a B-movie connoisseur's dream. It's got all the elements of what a lot of people think of when they think "B movie": black-and-white photography, a dark, *film noir* tinge, and (it must be admitted) its share of cheesy production values, a sample of which I'll explain in a moment.

Told for the most part in flashback, with a gritty voice-over narration that makes you feel as though the world is a rotten place indeed, *Detour* is at the start a fairly dull story of a piano player named Al (Tom Neal), who lives in New York City and is engaged to Sue (Claudia Drake), a band singer. Sue gets it into her head that if she really wants to make it big, she's got to go to Hollywood. So off she goes. Some time later, Al decides that he's really got to follow her—he starts out as something of a romantic, see—so off *he* goes. There's one catch: He doesn't have a car, and apparently doesn't have enough money for a train or some other mode of transit. So he sticks out his thumb and hitchhikes.

Through a brief series of misadventures, Al ends up involved with a woman named Vera (Ann Savage). (He'd heard about her from his last ride, a guy who brandishes nail scars on his wrists that make him look more like the victim of a threshing-machine accident than just someone who's had an unhappy run-in with a woman.) They hatch a money-making scheme, but Al ends up killing Vera by accident. (She's talking on the phone in another room; Al yanks on the cord, which strangles her.) The film ends with Al's being arrested for her murder.

As I said, there are some pretty awful bits (no worse than you'd expect in a six-day wonder, though). Al is hitchhiking his way from East to West, for instance, so the filmmakers evidently decided he had to be shown moving physically from right to left. The only problem is that some of the cars he gets rides in were photographed moving from left to right. No money for reshooting, though, so...just flip the negative. The result? The steering wheels in these cars are on the *right* side.

Nonetheless, *Detour* is a wonderful guide to what's sometimes called the dark underbelly of the American soul. In 1946, Hollywood filmmakers were just starting to admit that there *is* such a dark underbelly, and *Detour* helped set the tone.

(Trivia factoid: a 1990 remake of *Detour* featured Tom Neal's son in the role of Al, originally played by his father.)

Using fragment identifiers requires changes to the linked resource.

Let's say I've got a standard HTML-based page of information about *Detour.*

I've found a wonderful essay on the Web, devoted to the movie, part of the *Flicker* site[16] written and maintained by Chad Ossman. I'm particularly fond of his discussion of the *femme fatale* Vera's being to some extent subconsciously *created* by Al—summoned up, as it were, in his voice-over narration with the phrase "There was a woman...." This discussion takes place in Part 4 of Ossman's essay, and there's a separate Web page for each part of the essay; but the particular passage I want is preceded by some stuff that (for purposes of this example) I may not care to distract my own reader with. Of course I could include a fragment identifier in my HTML hyperlink to refer to this particular paragraph, something like this:

```
<a href="http://the-fringe.com/flicker/detour/detour_htbq04.html
    #veracreated">Chad Ossman</a> points out...
```

But where does the #veracreated anchor name come from?

Right: *The linked-to resource's author has to put it there.*

I don't know of *any* Webmasters who insert anchor names into their pages for the convenience of any Webmasters other than themselves!

---

16.   The Flicker home page is at *the-fringe.com/flicker/*.

An HTML hyperlink goes only in one direction.

On the face of it, this isn't terribly significant; in fact, saying that we want bi- or even multidirectional links might seem, well, a little loony. A possible definition of *link*, after all, might be something like, "a pointer from one document to another." Now we're saying we want the link to work *from* the other document *to* this one?

Think of the possibilities, though.

Above, I mentioned Chad Ossman's essay on *Detour.* It's one thing for me to provide a link to that page; someone who's never heard of Ossman or his essay could then easily locate it. Wouldn't it be even nicer if someone who'd found his essay first could somehow, magically, find my *Detour* page as well?

Using HTML hyperlinking, the only way to work this is either to: (a) contact Ossman and ask him to add the link; or (b) use some third-party resource—a "list of links" or portal-type clearinghouse—to which Ossman and I would both provide links. (In the latter case, someone coming to either of our sites would in theory be able to find the other by going through the middleman's service.) Both of these options suffer from the same problem: They require that the "bidirectional" link be maintained by someone else. (Using Option (b) actually compounds the problem by requiring *two* other someones.)

For any HTML hyperlink to work, its originator needs to know something specific about the target's content.

Again, this seems obvious. If you don't know something about the target resource's content, why would you link to it?

It's true that you need to know *something* about the target. After all, if you really knew nothing at all about it, you wouldn't know that it was there to be linked to. But there are many cases in which it might be convenient not to know something about the resource's specific content, but merely to know about its *structure*, in order to link to it. Here are a couple of such scenarios:

• Page 2 of many daily newspapers includes an index to that day's issue, as well as miscellaneous items such as the full weather report, lottery numbers, perhaps a horoscope, and celebrity gossip briefs. Furthermore, the general structure of the page stays exactly the same, year in and year out. (I don't know for certain, but I'd be willing to bet that they get nasty letters from readers whenever they monkey with the layout. Sometimes it seems as though they get nasty letters about everything else, so why would this be an exception?) If you want to link to the day's weather report to the exclusion of everything else, you could simply instruct the browser to retrieve the `weather` element from any given newspaper.

- For a while, I had a VCR that let me "mark" a tape wherever I wanted to. Even if I didn't knowingly use this feature, in fact, whenever I began to record something new, the VCR marked the starting point automatically. The cool thing about this was that when I had a tape (common with the six-hour movies, I could fast-forward or rewind to the beginning of any film (or to any other marked point) simply by telling the VCR to skip n marks. The VCR didn't know anything about the content, it just understood the structure. (Naturally, I no longer have this VCR, so the marks on my old tapes don't mean much anymore.)

Until my Web server can read VHS tapes, of course, this particular example may seem ludicrous. The point is that the analogy holds true for many cases that a Web site *might* want to make use of: Fetch me the Wednesday edition of online newsletter X ("Skip three marks: Sunday, Monday, and Tuesday"), the name of the horse who placed fourth in the sixth race at Belmont ("Skip races one through five, and the win, place, and show horses"), the description of the #2-selling shareware for the week, a patient's current prognosis even though others may be available in the same record, and so on.

In any of these examples, you'd just need to know the general structure of the target resource without knowing anything at all about its specific content. There's no way easily to achieve something like this in HTML.

XML Linking: the Back Story

Roughly paralleling the development of the XML specification itself, a separate (but closely aligned) group was preparing a specification for what was originally called XLL: the XML Linking Language.

XLL was first proposed in August 1997. In March 1998, a new working draft of the specification was issued; this draft split the original unified proposal into three separate documents: a statement of design principles, the XML Linking Language (now called XLink) specification, and a new XML Pointer Language (XPointer) specification. This was the state of affairs for over a year.

By January 2000, though, we saw three further releases of the XLink working draft—and by the time you read this, it should have solidified to full W3C Recommendation status.

Details about XLink and XPointer are covered in Chapters 5 and 6. (The discussion of XPointer, which attained final Recommendation in late 1999, also will cover the related XPath standard used not only in XPointers but also in the XSLT transformation/stylesheet language.) For now, understand simply that XLink and XPointer, taken together, effectively will leapfrog XML linking over the limitations (detailed above) inherent in its simpler HTML counterpart.

All Aboard the Digression Express

The classic metaphor—almost a dead one, by now—for making your way hither and yon on the Web is "surfing."[17] It does have a certain beach-bum kind of charm: tucking your browser under your arm you jog, carefree and tanned, toward the rolling breakers, swim out a bit farther, then get up on your surfboard and cruise back to the beach, laughing (and fighting for balance) all the way.

Aside from its funky, contemporary connotations, though, the notion of *surfing* really doesn't say much about what's actually happening when you move around the Web. When you're watching your browser window, clutching your mouse, you do much more than go out...return...go out to about the same point...come back to about the same point. It's not even particularly sunny on the Web, and God knows the lifeguards aren't much to look at.

Old habits of thought die hard, and I'm not out to smash any cherished romantic icons of point-and-clicking your way around the information sea. But I want you to forget about surfing for a while. Think instead about taking the train to get someplace.

---

17. An even more classic, even deader metaphor for the online world is "the information superhighway." As a general rule of thumb, I think that when a phrase starts showing up in politicians' speeches and acts of legislation, it's time for a new phrase.

> **Modes of transportation**
>
> I know—I could've chosen any of a half-dozen metaphors here instead of trains. But cars and trucks are out (see footnote #17 in this chapter). Buses aren't bad touring vehicles, but they've got almost no romantic connotations at all. Airplanes are certainly more up-to-the-minute than trains, and the network of airline routes could work as an analogy for the Web. Still, airport terminals are among the deadest, least attractive edifices in the world. If I've built a home page for any enterprise, personal or professional, I'd much rather you think of it in terms of, say, Grand Central Station in New York City than as, say, O'Hare Airport in Chicago: as an architecturally appealing destination in its own right, not just a place to shuttle you from one destination to another.

Tracks, stations, tickets to nowhere, derailments

Train travel isn't what it used to be. It's hard to imagine *Murder on the Orient Express* taking place on one of the five-times-daily runs between a given city and one of its suburbs, with dozens of commuters jostling one another in a fight for the same overhead strap. Hitchcock's *Strangers on a Train* is inconceivable in such a setting—you might meet and converse with a stranger, but one of you is probably not an international tennis star with a mucked-up love life, and the other is probably not a scheming heir hoping to bump off his father.

Well, don't think too much about the style or comfort level of taking a train someplace. Think of the *medium* of train travel instead. You can get from anywhere on the network of rails, to anywhere else, and there are thousands of different routes you can take between the two endpoints in your journey. Every now and then you might find a far-flung terminus, somewhere out on a continent's borders, that connects to nothing except the station before it. Rarely, the locomotive jumps the tracks, and even more rarely, it drags the rest of the train with it in a plunge into a gorge.

One-way tickets: HTML linking

All of that sounds to me like the Web of hypertext. There are a couple of exceptions, of course, such as that trains can't cross oceans.

More important for the sake of our discussion about XLinking (you were wondering about that, weren't you?): Although you can start in New York City and get to Cheboygan, Michigan, you might not be able to travel from Cheboygan to New York unless you've done the former trip first. You click on the Grand Central Station link, then on one that takes you to Poughkeepsie, and on a whole series of others that link you across New Jersey, Pennsylvania, Ohio, and on into Michigan. But every one of those terminals in the HTML world is *outbound*. The only reliable way to get back to New York, once you're in Cheboygan, is to use the browser's Back button to retrace your steps. And that works only during the same session; make the mistake of shutting your browser down after stepping off in Cheboygan, and you can forget about setting foot in Grand Central Station (let alone Trenton, Allentown, or Akron) without a completely separate "put me in Grand Central Station" search.[18]

Two-way, three-way, twenty-way tickets: XLinking

XLink won't *require* you to know anything more about creating and using links than you need to know about their HTML counterparts. But if that's the limit of your use, you're missing out on a lot.

With XLink, a properly constructed XML document can become a mini-Grand Central Station in its own right. Each link needn't just carry traffic away from the site; it can also carry traffic *to* the site. What's more, a given link can carry you not just to a single other destination, but to any one of a dozen or more.

As if all that's not enough, with certain advanced XLinking features, you can basically activate the entire document—as if the whole thing constituted the "from" point—enabling you to get someplace else even if you don't know that the someplace else exists.

In short, with XLink (as with so much of the rest of XML), the question really isn't, "Why?" it's "Why *not?*"

---

18.   Of course, you might have bookmarked Grand Central. While that does enable you to get to Grand Central anytime you want, it does *not* mean you can get to Grand Central *from* anywhere else. It's like teleporting. That's cheating in a world limited to train travel. (It's also terribly inconvenient; do you really want to bookmark every page you visit, just so you can get to it whenever you want?)

Summary

This chapter reviewed basic principles behind the idea of Web hyperlinking. It presented a number of arguments to illustrate that as implemented with HTML, hyperlinks don't do all that they *might* do. It wrapped up with an overview of some of the ways that XLinks will help resolve some of the problems inherent in HTML's native hyperlinking feature.

CHAPTER 5

XLink: Getting from Here to There

In Chapter 4, we covered some of the limitations inherent in HTML hyperlinking. One of those limitations was that the HTML `<a href="url">` tag requires that a link be made based on some knowledge of the target resource's content—that simple knowledge of its *structure* doesn't suffice.

One specification related to linking with XML—XPointer—addresses the need for "structure-aware" linking. XPointer and the related XPath specification are, as well, the XML standards for addressing any specific portion of an XML document. You'll learn about XPointer and XPath in Chapter 6. This chapter, on the other hand, deals with the basic XML facility for extending the capabilities of HTML hyperlinks in new, even exotic, ways.

(You can use XLink without XPointer, but not the other way around. That's my real reason for discussing them in this sequence.)

The shifting sands...

The current version of the XLink specification is at:

        www.w3.org/TR/xlink/

Specifically, the version on which this chapter is based is a Working Draft, dated January 19, 2000.

Version 1.0 of the XLink Requirements document, which lays out in general terms what XLink needs to do, is at:

        www.w3.org/TR/NOTE-xlink-req/

Note, by the way, that the W3C itself does not generally use the more common terms "specification" or "standard" to describe its output. When a Working Draft has made its way through the formal process required to become what's called, informally, a specification (as the XML spec did, for example), the status changes from Working Draft to *Recommendation*. (Technically, there are two additional steps, Candidate Recommendation and Proposed Recommendation, which fall between the Working Draft and Recommendation phases.) The term "recommendation" tells us that the W3C is not in the business of *requiring* anything; it *strongly suggests* that vendors and authors abide by the principles of the Consortium (which is, after all, made up of many of those vendors and authors).

In practice, almost no one deviates much from what's laid down in the various W3C pronouncements.[19] This is why most people have come to think of (and describe) these recommendations in more absolute terms, such as specs and standards.

Words, Words

Before getting into the nitty-gritty of XLink syntax and examples, it will help if you know something about the terminology used in the specification. There's a whole section of such terminology in the spec itself; here, I'll compress and/or simplify some things a bit, and elaborate on others. This section of the chapter won't get into specific XLink coding syntax—that will be covered in detail shortly.

Resources

In XLink terms, a *resource* is "a thing that can be involved in a link," *including* the thing that's doing the pointing. In this schematic:

```
X -- > Z
```

x links to z, but both x and z are resources on the link.

---

19. If they do, it's by adding features to them—using the W3C's work as *minimum* requirements. Even so, too much of this "feature bloat" is frowned on by the Web community.

Resources may include, of course, XML documents themselves, but are not limited to them. Other things you can link to with XLink, as with HTML, include other parts of the same document, HTML documents (and specific locations within those documents, if they've been named), images and other multimedia, files for downloading, and so on.

In the first sentence of this section, note the presence of *can be* in the phrase, "a thing that can be involved in a link" (that is, *can be* as opposed to *is*). When something really is a resource on the link (either x or z in the above example), it becomes a special kind of resource, a *participating resource*. All the rest of the Web universe is considered merely potential resources.

XLink provides for a couple of other classifications of link resources. The first, *local* vs. *remote* resources, has to do with the location of the document—indeed, the exact location *in* the document—relative to the point where you're placing the link. That point in that document is the local resource, and the other points (in this document or elsewhere) are all remote resources. In HTML, the "from" end of a link is always in the local document, and the "to" ends can be elsewhere in the same document or somewhere outside it. XLink removes the requirement that a "from" end must be local; you can define XLinks that simply connect multiple remote resources, if that's what you want.

The other classification of link resources, as implied in the preceding paragraph, is the "from" resource vs. the "to." The "from" resource in the example above would be x, and the "to" resource would be z. You may also see these referred to as the source and target, respectively.

Locators

A *locator* is the specific piece of the link's declaration that tells you (or the browser, etc.) where to find the resource to which you're linked. Usually this is a URL, but it can include various other components as well—including an XPointer.

In HTML terms, the locator is the value of the href attribute of an anchor element (a). So in this HTML link:

```
<a href="http://www.imdb.com">
```

the locator is the URL of the Internet Movie Database home page.

Links

A link, says the spec, is a "relationship between two or more resources or portions of resources."

"XLink links"

To be precise, the XLink spec is careful always to refer to the links that *it* deals with as "XLink links." This seems to me unnecessarily awkward; with or without my perception of the phrase, it seems likely that these will come to be known, at least informally, as plain old "XLinks." You won't find the term "XLink links" elsewhere in *Just XML*, but it doesn't hurt to warn you what to expect from the rest of the world.

That word "relationship" adds an abstract air to the definition that tends to obscure what's going on. In practice, *link* is interchangeable with *linking element*: the complete set of XML code that *defines* a given relationship or set of relationships among two or more resources.

In contrast to HTML, which offers only a few very basic types of link[20], XLink offers several additional possibilities. First, XLinks can be *inline* or out-of-line.

You will find an *inline link* in any document that names itself as a local resource. This is like the common HTML anchor tag that includes an `href="url"` attribute: All the information about the link itself, the local resource, and the remote resource is encapsulated in a single element, and that element is colocated, if you will, with the local resource.

Out-of-line links are completely new beasts. The link definition isn't established at a specific point within the document, but elsewhere (to be defined later in this chapter). There is no local resource identified in an out-of-line link; the only resources participating in the link(s) that it defines are "somewhere out there."

Aside from the inline/out-of-line dimension, XLink also provides a simple/extended dimension. *Simple* links are unidirectional, like those in HTML, and can only be expressed using inline link syntax. *Extended* links, on the other hand, can be unidirectional *or* multidirectional (that is, originating from and/or pointing to more than one participating resource), and can be expressed using out-of-

---

20.   Including the `<img>` tag used to link to an image, and the `<link>` tag that connects an HTML document to an external style sheet, as well as the usual `<a>` tag for normal hyperlinks.

line conventions as well as inline (usually the former, however). Extended links are effected by separating the information about the local resource, about the remote resources, and about the link's operation into separate elements, all of them children of the extended linking element itself.

Traversal

To traverse a link is to "make it happen." HTML links are traversed when a user clicks on them; typically, at the moment of the mouse click, the link changes color briefly and then the browser fetches the resource to which the link points.

XLink extends this user-triggered behavior by providing for automatic traversal of links.

Flights of fantasy

You really need to understand something important as we go through this chapter: There's a *lot* of conjecture here.

What we know about links, prior to the XLink variety, comes in the form of standard HTML-based hyperlinks whose behavior is defined, typically, by the interaction of humans and software. A hyperlink shows up on the screen. A user clicks on it. The browser contacts the server to deliver the requested resource. And so on.

XLinks are still way too new for anyone to predict all possible purposes that they'll be used for. They're so different from and more powerful than ordinary hyperlinks that they'll probably turn out to be used in ways that no one can foresee—for instance, establishing links that no human ever needs to be involved with.

In this chapter I'm going to be describing XLink behavior pretty much exclusively in terms of how it might occur in a browser. You'll encounter a virtual amusement park of windows popping open on the screen, menus cascading, messages flashing on the screen...all of which may or may not actually come to pass. If you're reading this chapter a year from the time I wrote it, and you've got some whiz-bang XLink-aware software on your computer, and darn it, *none* of the XLinks are behaving the way Simpson said they should—well, don't assume that you did anything wrong. Also don't assume your software is busted. If anything, blame *me* for going out on a limb and guessing at browser behavior.

That said, I don't think any of these guesses are completely unreasonable!

Arcs

Okay, so let's see—so far we've got a link, that is, two or more resources sharing some sort of relationship. What's missing from this picture?

Right: information about the "relationship" itself. This is all an arc provides. An arc tells the application what the rules are that govern the relationship, for example, "In what direction should this link be traversed?"

Anatomy of an XLink

Remember the classic gotcha of XML as opposed to HTML: If an element hasn't been declared somewhere, either explicitly in the external or the internal subset of the DTD or implicitly using the elements and attributes described in this section, you probably won't be able to make good use of it in your document. (As always, I'll defer an explanation of how to use a DTD to *declare* XLink-type elements, as well as all other kinds, until Part 4.) With HTML, the a element built into the language can be used for creating hyperlinks; but since there are no "built-in elements" in a given XML vocabulary, how do you use an XLink in your documents?

The answer is to use the built-in attributes *in the XLink namespace* on your XLinking elements.

Toeing the line

As always with a namespace prefix, in the following discussion it doesn't *in theory* matter exactly what prefix you use, as long as it's correctly associated with the correct namespace by way of the xmlns: attribute. However, the convention will probably be to use xlink: as the prefix for XLinking elements, and I suggest that you stick close to the likely convention—just in case some software package gets it into its head to mind the prefixes without attending to the xmlns: attribute. (FlixML plays it safe this way: all XLinking attributes are prefixed with xlink:.)

XLinking with reserved attribute names

First, the element in question must include an xmlns: attribute that will be used to tie the reserved attribute names to the XLink namespace. (The namespace, of course, need not be set in the XLink element itself—it may be declared on any element that contains the XLinking element.)

Here's what a basic XLink might look like (assuming the `xmlns:` attribute hasn't already been declared):

```
<reviewlink
    xmlns:xlink="http://www.w3.org/1999/xlink/namespace"
    xlink:type="simple"
    xlink:href="http://www.flixml.org/detour.xml"
    xlink:role="review"
    xlink:title="'Detour' review"
    xlink:show="replace"
    xlink:actuate="onRequest">Detour</reviewlink>
```

In addition to the namespace attribute, the `reviewlink` element here includes six attributes from the XLink namespace. The single word "Detour" constitutes this `reviewlink` element's only content.

Simple XLinks

The example above demonstrated a *simple* XLink. That an XLink is simple is denoted by an `xlink:type="simple"` attribute/value pair. Functionally, it resembles a standard HTML hyperlink in the following respects:

- The link goes from one point in a given document to a point elsewhere (either a separate document or other object, or a different point in the same document).
- The link is unidirectional. In order to reverse the direction and get back to the starting point, you have to depend on the kindness of software (e.g., a browser's "Back" button).
- Everything you need to know about the link is in one place: the document where the link is defined. This sort of XLink is known as an *inline link*. (I'll cover the alternative in the portion of this chapter concerning out-of-line extended links.)
- The target of the link is identified by the value of an `href` attribute.

However, there are also some differences, as encapsulated in the four other attributes: `role`, `title`, `show`, and `actuate`.

In discussing these attributes, I'll use the XLink from above as an example.

Note that one attribute (besides `type`) is always required somewhere if you want to use an XLink of any kind: the `href` attribute. All the others are optional, and some of the optional ones have default values. All characteristics of all attributes can be controlled by the document's DTD, of course, including whether they're optional or required.

Following is information about each of these attributes.

href="*url*"

This required attribute in an XLink element serves exactly the same purpose that it serves in HTML: It provides the location where the remote resource may be found. The URL may include any of the components described in the previous chapter—service type, system name, path and name of the file, and fragment identifier—and they work exactly as they do in an HTML a element's `href` attribute.

Remember that a fragment identifier in HTML is preceded by a # sign, as in:

```
href="somedoc.html#somestartingpoint"
```

This tells the browser to display the target resource's contents starting at the specific location in the resource that is named (with an `<a name="value">` tag) according to whatever follows the # sign: `startingpoint`, in this case.

XML uses the # fragment identifier in the same way. However, if the target resource is itself an XML document, what follows the # sign must be an XPointer. (We'll visit XPointers in Chapter 6.) If the target resource is an HTML document, using a fragment identifier can be expected to work in an XLink exactly as it does under HTML.

role="*value*"

The `role` attribute may or may not be important (even required) in a given case, depending on the type (`simple`, `extended`, and so on). The general idea is to, well, *annotate* the link in some machine-legible way. The range of allowable values for the attribute will probably be established by the DTD developer, for valid XML documents.

Note that for simple XLinks, `role` serves no distinct purpose except perhaps to define "classes" of simple links that you want to process differently somehow, perhaps with a style sheet. However, for more advanced XLinks, `role` is very important; I'll provide more details below, under the discussion of extended links.

title="*value*"

Of the optional `title` attribute, the XLink specification says that it is "used to describe the function of a link's remote resource in a human-readable fashion." Its value might appear in a caption, for instance, when the mouse cursor hovers over the link (like the "tool tips" common in much software, or in the same way that the current Netscape and Microsoft Web browsers display the URL in the status bar when the mouse cursor is placed over a link).

show="*value*"

Here we come to one of the niftier advances of XLink over its HTML counterpart. The `show` attribute, which is optional, tells the application software how to display the retrieved resource—"display" not in terms of what styles or fonts to use, but in terms of *the* display, that is, of the window or other context in which the linking element itself appears.

There are four possible values: `replace` (probably the default when XLink-aware applications start showing up in force), `new`, `embed`, and `undefined`.

- **show="replace"** This works just like the default Web browser behavior when you click on an HTML hyperlink: It fetches the contents of the target resource and (yes—see, you're really getting the hang of this) *replaces* the contents of the current display with the contents of the target.
- **show="new"** Using HTML framing conventions, a Webmaster can tell the browser to open up the target resource in a completely new window. The `show="new"` attribute of an XLink does exactly the same thing.
- **show="embed"** Here's the marvel. This says that when this XLink is traversed, the target resource's contents are to be *inserted* into the linking resource, at the point of the link.

  One area of the *HotWired* Web site[21] used to include a kind of built-in glossary feature called "The Geek." They used this feature in articles on some technical topic, say Dynamic HTML, which might include jargon terms not directly related to the topic at hand, say "cascading style sheets." Where such a term appeared in the text, there appeared a little hotspot labeled "Geek This!"; when you clicked on the hotspot, a paragraph or two of extended description of the term appeared in the text at the point of the

21. HotWired is at *www.hotwired.com*.

"Geek This!" button. (The button itself would then be relabeled, "Remove the Geek.") It didn't replace the surrounding text, it was *inserted*.

The way in which *HotWired* performed this magic isn't particularly important for this discussion, except to say that XLink's `show="embed"` attribute will put the facility into the hands of all the rest of us as well.

- **show="undefined"** This recent addition to the XLink specification seems to have been added to tie up any unforeseen loose ends. The spec says that a processor's behavior is "unconstrained by this specification" if it encounters this value for the `show` attribute—that is to say, the processor may have its own rules for how to handle the situation, but the spec isn't saying what those rules are.

actuate="*value*"

To actuate something is to make it actual—to move it from the realm of the potential into the realm of things that are real and "happening." How this applies to XLink (as it does to HTML, although there's no counterpart to this attribute in HTML) is that until the link is triggered—traversed—it's just sitting there in the document.

The optional `actuate` attribute tells an application, generally, *what the trigger is*. You can use it in any element that describes a *remote* resource. It can take any of three values defined by the spec:

- **actuate="onRequest"** This default value says that the link is traversed whenever the user says, "traverse this link." Normally this will happen in the accustomed manner—the user clicks on a link.
- **actuate="onLoad"** If you use this value, the link traversal occurs without any user intervention at all. This has the potential to be extremely powerful, especially when used in conjunction with `show="embed"`: You can construct entire new documents, on-the-fly, made up of chunks of *other* documents mixed in with your own content.

  (This will introduce some potential copyright and other legal pitfalls. As a general rule of thumb, in XML documents, just as in HTML ones, always attribute the source of any included material. There are also technical issues to be ironed out, such as: When I include another document or document fragment, does the included portion display in the same style—fonts, colors, and so on—as *my* document at that point? And how about if the text I'm embedding also has a `show="embed"`/`actuate="onLoad"` link—and what if that linked resource has such a link, and so on—do they *all* get magically inserted into my document?)

- **`actuate="undefined"`** Like its counterpart for the `show` attribute, this value tells the processor effectively that it's on its own in deciding how to traverse the link.

Well-defined behavior

The XLink spec's authors have taken great pains not to *require* anything of downstream software. The descriptions of the "behavior-related" attributes (`show` and `actuate`), in particular, are carefully worded: The spec says that behaviors are used for signaling the link creator's intentions, without saying how software should react on encountering these attributes.

Therefore, although it might seem reasonable to expect (for example) that `show="embed"` will cause the target resource to appear physically embedded in the linking resource, this isn't necessarily what will happen. A particular XLink-aware application might, say, interpret this in such a way that it pops up the remote resource's contents in a yellow box, in the manner of a Post-It Note.

Also, note that the `show` and `actuate` attributes now have an "undefined" value. Again, this seems to result from a desire by the XLink specification's editors not to force particular behaviors on browsers or other applications. In particular, `show` and `actuate` can actually take *any* value, not just those laid out in the standard; if an XLink-aware processor encounters a value that it doesn't recognize, it is to treat the value the same way as if it had found "undefined" there. This leaves the door open for special-purpose applications to define their own values for these attributes, while at the same time ensuring that the XML document won't be "broken" if processed by another, more generic application.

From the Ground Up (but not too far up)

Let's work through a few examples of basic XLink code. (All of the examples in this section are of *simple* links; extended links will be covered later in the chapter.)

Linking elements in *valid XML documents*

These examples all assume that elements to be used for establishing links have been declared in a DTD. (Remember, too, that if the DTD has not declared valid *attributes* for an element, those attributes can't be used at all in a document based on that DTD.)

The simplest link of all...

...would be the case where the declaration of the linking element has been taken completely out of your hands, via the DTD. A link like this would resemble the following:

```
<homelink>The B-Hive</homelink>
```

In this case, the DTD's designer must have specified values for *all* required attributes of the homelink element, including the all-important xlink:href, as well as any optional attributes deemed necessary.

The simplest *common* link

More likely, the DTD will declare all necessary attributes for linking elements *except* xlink:href. This enables you to use a link in your XML document exactly as you would if you were using HTML instead. The following example assumes that the DTD designer has thoughtfully declared a general-purpose a element for you:

```
Looking for a complete list of Richard Basehart's flicks?
    Find one <a xlink:href=
    "http://us.imdb.com/Name?Basehart,+Richard">here</a>.
```

Probably in this case, the DTD designer would have set xlink:type="simple"—perhaps providing default or required values for one or two of the optional attributes as well—with an eye toward making the general-purpose <a> behave as much as possible like the familiar HTML version of the same element.

Giving the user feedback

An important part of a user interface is letting the user know the purpose of various onscreen gizmos and widgets. Under HTML 4.0, for instance, when you place an image on the page, you can include an `alt="value"` attribute that (in current versions of the major browsers) displays `value` in a tool-tip-style pop-up box whenever the cursor lingers on the image for a couple of seconds.

Assume that in the previous example, the DTD designer declared the `xlink:title` attribute for the XLinking version of the a element. You can then elaborate on the sample a element like this:

```
Looking for a complete list of Richard Basehart's flicks?
    Find one <a xlink:href=
    "http://us.imdb.com/Name?Basehart,+Richard"
    xlink:title="Link to IMDB Filmography">here</a>.
```

Thus, when the user's mouse cursor is placed over the word "here," a little box would pop up at the cursor, displaying the words `Link to IMDB Filmography`.[22]

Linking elements in *well-formed XML documents*

The XLink specification doesn't say that XLink can be used only in valid XML documents (that is, ones conforming to a DTD). Therefore, we can assume that XLink code like the examples in this section might be used (although such code might be *rejected* by application software that doesn't recognize merely well-formed XML, naturally).

A bare-bones well-formed XLink

At a minimum, any XLinking element must provide values for the `xlink:type` and `xlink:href` attributes. So a page of simple XLinks to Web search engines might include code like this:

```
<searchlink xlink:type="simple"
    xlink:href="http://www.hotbot.com">HotBot</searchlink>
<searchlink xlink:type="simple"
    xlink:href="http://www.altavista.com">AltaVista</searchlink>
```

and so on.

---

22. Hypothetical behavior, remember!

More elaborate well-formed XLinks

Any of the attributes used for XLinks in a valid XML document can also be applied in a well-formed document.

For instance, you could expand the above `searchlink` elements to give users feedback about where the links would take them, like this:

```
<searchlink xlink:type="simple"
    xlink:href="http://www.hotbot.com"
    xlink:title="Search HotBot">HotBot</searchlink>
<searchlink xlink:type="simple"
    xlink:href="http://www.altavista.com"
    xlink:title="Search AltaVista">AltaVista</searchlink>
```

Extending Links to a New Plane

The XLink features we've looked at so far have relied on the familiar notion of a *simple* link: one that goes from one resource to another, in one direction only.

Extended links add to this basic functionality the ability to create links among *many* resources, and to establish links that "go both ways."

Breaking the link

The specific device that enables extended links to work their magic is that they separate into multiple elements the information about local resources and information about remote resources. Each extended linking element can have one or more child elements, each of which describes a different local or remote resource or the nature of a linking relationship among the various resources. In simplified form, *sans* attributes, such a link might look schematically like this:

```
<extendedlink [link attributes]>
    <localresource [local resource attributes]/>
    <remoteresource [remote resource1 attributes]/>
    <remoteresource [remote resource2 attributes]/>
    <remoteresource [remote resource3 attributes]/>
    <arcinformation [arc1 attributes]/>
    <arcinformation [arc2 attributes]/>
</extendedlink>
```

The parent element, `extendedlink`, defines a "link" (actually, several different links) among the local resource and (in this case) three separate remote resources, each with its own attributes (`href` and so on). Specifics about the nature of the link(s) among these resources are provided by the two `arcinfor-mation` elements.

In an extended link, naturally enough, the value of the `xlink:type` attribute is `extended`. Subordinate to the `xlink:type="extended"` element are:

- Zero or more `xlink:type="resource"` elements, defining the local resource(s).
- One or more `xlink:type="locator"` elements, defining the resource(s) being linked to.
- Zero or more `xlink:type="arc"` elements, defining the characteristics of the arc—that is, the nature of the relationship—among two or more linked resources.
- Zero or more `xlink:type="title"` elements, providing human-readable labels for the link.

Attributes for extended links

Earlier in this chapter, I described each of the attributes possible in a simple XLink element. One of the pieces of information I didn't get into there was whether the attribute could be used to define local resources, remote resources, or the arc. In a simple link, this isn't an important distinction because such a link combines information about the source and target resources and the arc into a single element *in* the document in question (all of which is what makes it simple!).

With extended links, the relevance of the local vs. remote vs. arc dimension becomes clear. With that in mind, Table 5.1 summarizes the additional attributes used by each of the XLink types named in the preceding section.

Table 5.1   Extended link attributes

Attribute	xlink:type					
	extended	resource	locator	arc	title	none
`xlink:href`			X			?
`xlink:role`	X	X	X			?
`xlink:title`	X	X	X			?
`xlink:show`	X			X		?
`xlink:actuate`	X			X		?
`xlink:to`				X		?
`xlink:from`				X		?

A childless parent

As you can see, a `title`-type XLinking element doesn't take *any* (additional) XLink-specified attributes. We'll see an example of this XLink type later in the chapter.

As for the `xlink:type="none"` option, it's intended for use in situations where an element might be an XLink in some cases but not in others. There aren't any examples of this in FlixML, but a possible place where I could have included this option would be in providing reviews of a film. If the review were internal to the FlixML document, there'd be no need to provide an XLink to it (so `xlink:type` would be none); but if the review were elsewhere, an XLink *would* be required (so `xlink:type` would have one of the other values, probably `simple` or `extended`). Thus the none option allows a single element to perform more than one function, as the need requires.[23]

Most of the attributes in the leftmost column of Table 5.1 were already covered above, in the discussion of simple links. Before getting into how to construct a complete extended link, though, let's look at the two new attributes: `to` and `from`, both of which are applied to `arc`-type elements.

to="*value*"

The `to` attribute (or `xlink:to`, as in Table 5.1, including the XLink namespace prefix) identifies, logically enough, which end of an arc constitutes the "to" end. Its value must equal the value of a `role` attribute supplied for at least one locator (i.e., remote resource) in the same extended link's definition.

from="*value*"

As you might expect, this attribute defines the "from" end of the arc. Surprisingly (to me, anyhow!), the value of the `from` attribute, just like that of the `to` attribute, must equal the value of a `role` attribute for a locator (remote resource) in the extended link's definition: It can *not* match the `role` attribute for a resource (i.e., local resource).

---

23. If you're curious—and why wouldn't you be?—FlixML does provide for both an internal review and XLinks to external ones. Rather than requiring you to choose one or the other, though, FlixML lets you have it both ways, by defining separate element structures for the two kinds of review.

In search of the lost arc

If you're confused by all this business about arcs connecting remote resources to one another, don't worry—the confusion is quite natural. All that's required is an extension of your thinking about what it means to link one thing to another.

Multiple remote resources

First, think about an extended XLink connecting a local resource (A) to more than one remote (B and C).[24] Schematically, this might look something like the following:

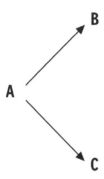

That is, you can get from a single point (resource A, the source) to either of two other points, B or C (the targets).

Bi-directional links

The next logical step is to allow the link(s) to go back the way they came from, as here:

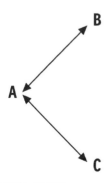

---

24.   Don't worry yet about exactly how this is accomplished, or maybe even what it *means*.

This allows you to return to A from either B or C, without being dependent on some artificial user-interface gizmo like a browser's "Back" button. Resource A now functions sometimes as a source and sometimes as a target.

Linking remote resources to remote resources

Finally, the XLink spec's authors apparently wondered: If your extended XLink already knows what it needs to know in order to hook up to each remote resource, why not provide the ability to connect *them* with one another? For instance:

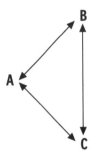

In effect, in such an arrangement there's nothing particularly that distinguishes a given resource from any other—except that the local resource (if one is present) just happens to be where the link is defined.

Armed with (a) Table 5.1, (b) the knowledge that extended links break information about local and remote resources into separate child elements of the extended linking element itself, and (c) our new-found understanding of arcs, we're ready to start examining the coding of extended links.

Coding extended XLinks

One important piece of information missing from Table 5.1 is that aside from the column labeled `extended`, the elements containing the `xlink:type` attributes listed in the other columns are all *subordinate to* the `extended`-type element.

So the first thing you need to know about coding an extended XLink is that—regardless of the specific element names—the XLink will commonly look something like this:

```
<extendedlink>
    <resource/>
    <locator1/>
    <locator2/>
          .  .  .
    <arc1/>
    <arc2/>
          .  .  .
    <title/>
</extendedlink>
```

The specifics may vary from one document type to another—for example, it may be that there's no particular order required, and various subordinate elements may or may not be required[25]—but this is the general rule. There's a "wrapper" extended-type element, within which are multiple empty resource, locator, arc, and/or title elements.

This sort of XLink is called an *inline extended link*. The word "inline" here indicates that all the information you need to know about this extended XLink's constituents is contained in the local resource: the document where the extended link resides. (There's also an *out-of-line extended link*, in which information about the link is kept somewhere other than in the local document. We'll revisit this concept later in this chapter.)

Ch-ch-ch-changes

Earlier versions of the XLink spec provided for inline and out-of-line simple links, as well. The former still exist in the spec's present version: Currently, all simple links are inline.

The current spec is silent on why out-of-line simple links were dropped. I don't *know* the reason(s), but it's likely that no one could explain what it meant to have a link that both contained all its information in the local resource, *and* moved some of that information elsewhere.

---

25. In an extended link, you'll always need to have at least one locator-type element describing a remote resource.

FlixML has one inline extended linking element built into it. It's used for establishing links to information about distributors: where to buy or rent a copy of the film in question.

Let's walk through a hypothetical example. Say you're developing a FlixML document that details information about *Curse of the Undead*. (This is a "vampire Western," whose hero defeats his gun-slinging, blood-sucking opponent using a bullet on the tip of which he's fastened a tiny little wooden cross.[26]) You'd like to include on this page a set of links to Web sites where the (presumably intrigued) visitor to your page can buy a copy of the movie. Here's how you might do so using the `distribextlink` inline extended link element:

```
<distribextlink xlink:type="extended"
    xlink:title="Buy It Online!">
    <distriblink xlink:type="locator"
        xlink:href=
        "http://movie.reel.com/moviepage/12243.html"
        xlink:title="... at Reel.Com"/>
    <distriblink xlink:type="locator"
        xlink:href="http://www.moviesunlimited.com/"
        xlink:title="... at Movies Unlimited"/>
    <distriblink xlink:type="locator"
        xlink:href=
        "http://www.amazon.com/exec/obidos/ASIN/6304119003"
        xlink:title="... at Amazon"/>
    Buy a Copy</distribextlink>
```

(You might be wondering how things would change if you added, say, `xlink:show` and/or `xlink:actuate` attributes to the `distriblink` elements in this example. The answer is that they wouldn't change at all. That's because the FlixML DTD has hard-wired the values of those attributes for the `distriblink` element, to `replace` and `onRequest`, respectively.)

Note that the structure of this link is slightly different from the generic one described a couple of pages back. This one lacks `resource`-, `arc`-, and `title`-type subordinate elements, looking like so:

---

26. Not to be confused with a Japanese "*anime*" film, *Curse of the Undead: Yoma*, more of a ninja-vs.-demons plot. It's also not to be confused with almost any vampire film that is actually entertaining; when you've read the phrase "vampire Western," you know virtually the sole saving grace of *Curse of the Undead*.

```
<extendedlink>
    <locator1/>
    <locator2/>
      .  .  .
</extendedlink>
```

This illustrates a general principle: In an extended link, you always need to define at least one remote resource (represented by `locator`-type elements), but other components—including information about the local resource (that is, `resource`-type elements)—are optional.

So what might happen onscreen when a user interacts with an inline extended link coded as above? No one knows for sure, in the absence of software to demonstrate it; but we can guess it will go something like the following:

First, what the user sees before actually interacting with the link are the words "Buy a Copy." When the mouse cursor moves over these words, a pop-up box displays the value of the `distriblink` element's `xlink:title` attribute, or "Buy It Online!" Then, when the user actually clicks on the words "Buy a Copy" (that is, actuates the link), a pop-up menu appears, looking something like this:

```
... at Reel.Com
... at Movies Unlimited
... at Amazon.com
```

Each item in this menu of links to remote resources has its own `xlink:href` attribute, pointing to the specific resource's URL. Each also has its own `xlink:title` attribute, so that as the mouse cursor slides up or down the list of three distributors, a different pop-up box appears. (The line in the menu that is immediately below the cursor would presumably be highlighted in some way, to make it clear which one the user is currently pointing at.) And when the user clicks on one of the three lines in the pop-up menu, the remote resource at the selected URL is opened.

The lure of the hypothetical

Again, I have to remind you that the state of XLink-aware processing applications is *very* tentative as of this writing. The above scenario, with all its pop-up boxes and menus, represents an expectation (dare I say hope?) rather than a statement of actual software behavior!

I'll try not to interrupt your reading in the balance of this chapter with this caution, but please understand that it applies to later examples as well.

Ruffles and flourishes

The above is a relatively straightforward example of an inline extended link. It's entirely possible that situations will arise in which you want to add adornments to the behavior of such links, though, using some of the optional attributes of linking elements.

In the above example, for instance, maybe you don't want the distributor's page to replace *your* page in the browser's window. The normal default value of the `xlink:show` attribute is `replace`, so that's what would normally happen when the user traverses the link; but you could specify `xlink:show="new"` or `xlink:show="embed"` to force a different behavior instead.

Uses for the `xlink:actuate="onLoad"` attribute in an extended link may seem less obvious. Why, you might wonder, would you want multiple remote resources opened all at once, as soon as the local resource is opened?

But in conjunction with `xlink:show="embed,"` automatic extended link traversal would be useful for assembling whole new "virtual documents" from multiple physical ones. Let's say you've got three separate FlixML documents, each describing a separate *noir*–style B film: *Detour, He Walked by Night,* and *Shoot the Piano Player.* Under normal circumstances, a visitor to your site would want to view information on only one film at a time; but you could offer the visitor a "printer-friendly" document, with a heading something like "Great *Noir* B Flicks"—below which all three documents were strung together, for printing them all at once without having to navigate to and print the three documents separately.

Arcs

The `distribextlink` element and its children, as described above, let you establish links among several resources. This corresponds to the third example, "Linking remote resources to remote resources," in the "In search of the lost arc" section earlier in this chapter. That is, implicitly, with no "rules of the relationship" defined among any resources, they're all assumed to be linked to all others.

To effect multidirectional links in more than this one-size-fits-all manner, you need some way of defining the direction(s) in which you want them to be traversed. And that's when you need an `arc` element, with its `from` and/or `to` attributes.

In order to define an arc, the elements defining the resources to be linked to one another must all have `xlink:role` attributes. In the case of FlixML's `distribextlink` element, in order to create links from the remote resources (the locators) back to the FlixML document itself, we've also got to add a `resource-type` element. So our earlier example will now look like this (differences from the earlier version in boldface; large letters keyed to the discussion below):

```
<distribextlink xlink:type="extended"
    xlink:title="Buy It On-line!">
    <flixmlhome xlink:type="resource"          Ⓐ
        xlink:role="home"
        xlink:title="FlixML Review"/>
    <distriblink xlink:type="locator"
        xlink:href=
        "http://movie.reel.com/moviepage/12243.html"
        xlink:title="... at Reel.Com"
        xlink:role="distrib"/>                 Ⓑ
    <distriblink xlink:type="locator"
        xlink:href="http://www.moviesunlimited.com/"
        xlink:title="... at Movies Unlimited"
        xlink:role="distrib"/>                 Ⓑ
    <distriblink xlink:type="locator"
        xlink:href=
        "http://www.amazon.com/exec/obidos/ASIN/
6304119003"
        xlink:title="... at Amazon"
        xlink:role="distrib"/>                 Ⓑ
    <distribarc xlink:type="arc"               Ⓒ
        xlink:from="home" xlink:to="distrib"/>
    <distribarc xlink:type="arc"               Ⓓ
        xlink:from="distrib" xlink:to="home"/>
    Buy a Copy</distribextlink>
```

Implicitly in this extended link as it was originally coded, arcs went from each remote resource to each of the others. To define a potential traversal back to the local resource as well, I need to provide a "handle" by which the latter can be referred as; that's the purpose of the `<flixmlhome>` resource-type element—particularly its `role` attribute—at Ⓐ.

DTDs as time and code savers

The FlixML DTD includes a number of provisions for making the coding of XLinks easier.

First among these is that it supplies default—and in some cases, *required*—values for many of the XLink-related attributes. So the above looks more complicated than it in fact needs to be; I've included these attributes above solely for the sake of illustration.

> Also note that the elements in this "extended link to film distributors" structure are all named `distrib`-something, *except* the `resource`-type element `flixmlhome`. That's because `flixmlhome` is declared in the DTD as being usable by several extended linking elements, not just `distribextlink`. Considering its default attributes, too, I could have simply coded `flixmlhome` as:
>
> ```
> ```
>
> without altering its "meaning."
>
> If you're lucky, your DTD designer will have built these kinds of shortcuts wherever possible. If you are designing a DTD, your users will be lucky if *you* build these shortcuts.

At Ⓑ, I've added a `role` attribute to each of the individual `locator`-type elements. This will enable the remote resources to be referenced when we construct our arc(s).

At Ⓒ, I've included an `arc`-type element that, translated into English, reads, "Establish a link from every resource marked with a `home` role *to* all resources marked with a `distrib` role." As coded here, this makes explicit the links from the local resource to the three remote ones.

Finally, at Ⓓ, I've set up a link that "goes back"—from each of the resources marked with a `distrib` role to each of those marked with a `home` role.

Although the above example doesn't show it, I could have also established explicit links *among the remote resources.* To do so, I'd just add a third `distribarc` element:

```
<distribarc xlink:type="arc"
      xlink:from="distrib" xlink:to="distrib"/>
```

Note that for this particular example, the ability to connect remote resources may seem silly, especially because all the remote resources have the same `role`. That doesn't have to be the case, though. Let's say some distributors rented movies, some sold them, and some did both. You could then distinguish among them using the following `role` attributes on the various `locator`-type elements, as appropriate:

```
xlink:role="distribrent"
xlink:role="distribsale"
xlink:role="distrib"
```

From that point, of course, it would be easy to establish links only among the renters, and only among the sellers, but not between renters and sellers, by adding these `arc`-type elements to the extended link:

```
<distribarc xlink:type="arc"
    xlink:from="distribrent" xlink:to="distribrent"/>
<distribarc xlink:type="arc"
    xlink:from="distribsale" xlink:to="distribsale"/>
```

Omitting the "from" and/or the "to"

In an `arc`-type element, both the `from` and the `to` attributes are optional. What would omitting one or both of them *mean* in the context of an extended link?

Here's what the current XLink spec says on this issue:

> If no value is supplied for a `from` or `to` attribute, the missing value is interpreted as standing for all the roles supplied on `locator`-type elements in that `extended`-type element.

Therefore, omitting the `from` or `to` attribute is like using a "wildcard" for that attribute. Thus:

```
<distribarc xlink:type="arc"
    xlink:from="distrib"/>
```

(with no `to` specified) tells your XLink processor that you want it to establish implicit links from all resources marked with a `distrib` role *to all other resources with a* `role` *attribute specified*, regardless of what that `role`'s value is. Similarly:

```
<distribarc xlink:type="arc"
    xlink:to="distrib"/>
```

instructs it to establish links *to* all resources with a `distrib` role *from all other resources with a* `role` *attribute specified*, regardless of what that `role`'s value is.

Here's a fragment of a FlixML document. The `<contents>` extended-type XLinking element functions as a "table of contents" into the document; each of its `<section>` children is a `locator`-type element pointing to a particular "chapter" or section of the document, and `<contarc>` is an `arc`-type element. Pay particular attention to the latter as you try to figure out what's going on here:

```
<contents>
    <section xlink:href="#title" />
    <section xlink:href="#cast" />
    <section xlink:href="#director" />
    <section xlink:href="#plotsummary" />
    <contarc/>
</contents>
```

As you can see, the FlixML DTD must have provided default or nonoptional values for all XLink-related attributes except the `xlink:href`s on the `section` elements. As for `contarc`, although you can't see this here, the DTD does not declare any `xlink:from` or `xlink:to` attributes at all—effectively forbidding their use in this case. The net result is that both the `xlink:from` and the `xlink:to` are "wildcarded," and therefore every `section` of a FlixML document that includes a `contarc` element is implicitly linked to every other `section`.

(Note, by the way, that any `locator`-type elements with no `xlink:role` attribute at all will be completely unaffected by any arcs you define; those remote resources will participate only in the normal implicit links. The `section` element's `xlink:role` attribute has a default value, assigned in the DTD, with the result that even if the document author hasn't assigned a `xlink:role`, the extended link acts as if he or she had.)

Titles

Other than to say that `titles` might be used to provide human-readable labels, I haven't said much more about them. What more could there be to say about them?

First, if you're on your toes you will have noticed that there is both a `title` attribute (which can be applied to any type of XLink) and a `title`-type *element.* That is, both of the following might be valid XLinking elements:

```
<link xlink:type="simple" xlink:title="Link to Remote Resource"
    xlink:href="http://www.whereveruwant.com" />
<linktitle xlink:type="title">Link to Remote Resource</linktitle>
```

How might it be useful to have the second form available to you?

First, a `title`-type element (like the second example) will normally be subordinate to one of the other link types; as I mentioned above, in the discussion of Table 5.1, there are no other XLink-related attributes that may be placed on a `title`-type element—so it'd be pretty useless if it were used just by itself.

Second, and more important, creating a `title`-type element gives you some options that using a `title` *attribute* would not. For instance, you can put an `xml:lang` built-in attribute on an element, whereas you can't on an attribute; this attribute could then be used to assign a different title to the link for each of several languages, letting the application select the one appropriate for a given user. A given XML vocabulary might declare other elements to be contained by a `title`-type element, while if the `title` were relegated to an attribute such a nested structure would not be possible. And so on.

FlixML has no `title`-type XLinking elements, but I wanted you to be aware that you may come across a situation in which one might be useful.

Out-of-line extended links

The behavior of browsers and other applications in dealing with inline extended links is fairly easy to guess at, because that behavior will probably correspond closely to our familiar experience with computer-based applications. (Not our experience with Web browsing, however; the pop-up "menu of links" facility in particular is still more or less a novelty.)

Out-of-line extended links are more complex abstractions in that there *is* no local resource defined (at least at a specific point where the link can be actuated). Instead, the remote resources are defined at some common point elsewhere in the document, or even (using what are called external linksets) *outside* the current document. (The latter feature is covered in the next section.)

Consider the example above of the `contents` element. As you saw there, it included multiple `locator`-type children, as well as an `arc`, but no `resource`-type children defining the local resource.

What in the world, you may be excused for wondering, does this mean?

The general idea is that the `contents` element acts (as the element name implies) as a "table of contents" for the document; it defines several remote resources that can be accessed *from anywhere in the document*. The remote resources aren't associated with any particular point within the document—rather, as it were, with the document as a whole.

Before considering how this "table of contents" would actually work in practice, let's look at the rest of this (considerably abbreviated) document:

```
<flixinfo>
    [Above contents element appears here]
    <title id="title"
          role="main">Curse of the Undead</title>
    <cast id="cast">
        [various cast details]
    </cast>
    <crew id="crew">
        [various crew details]
    </crew>
    <plotsummary id="plotsummary">It may be a cliche to
        say that Old West gunslingers (at least in
        Hollywood's classic formulation) were
        bloodthirsty. But in the case of "Curse of the
        Undead" it's literally true...</plotsummary>
</flixinfo>
```

In this case, the *entire document* serves as the "local resource" (although there's no visual cue that this is the case). This might mean, given the right XLink-aware application, that if the user clicks anywhere on the content of the document, he or she will be presented with the menu of extended links, something like this:

```
Title(s)
Cast
Director(s)
Plot Summary
```

From here it behaves the same way as described above, in the example of the links to sources for online purchases of the video. When the user selects one of the remote resources, the page view "jumps" to the corresponding section of the document (as identified by the `xlink:href` attribute, which maps to an `id` attribute assigned to each section).[27]

Peeking into the future

The URLs in this example all include the special # character for addressing a particular location within a document. In this case, because the target document is itself an XML document, what follows the # sign is an *XPointer.* We'll look at XPointers in detail in the next chapter, as I've said. For now, just note the connection between the `xlink:href` attribute of the `locator`-type elements and the `id` attribute of the elements in the body of the document.

Aside from being, well, *cool* in its own right, there's another advantage to using out-of-line extended links like this—one not obvious in this brief example. That is that someone who's come to the page (or a particular section of it) from somewhere outside doesn't even have to know that the extended link is available; they get it "free."

Suppose you're a designer of online games of the old "Adventure" variety. Someone enters your "game" (which conveniently is coded in XML) at a predefined spot (what you'd otherwise call a home page, say), which describes a room in a house. The house has four rooms in it, and from the point of entry,

---

27. Again: There's no XLink-aware software as of this writing, the preceding is speculative, so on and so forth. It *is* reasonable, though. (Not that you doubted that.)

you can proceed to any of those rooms or go "outside" to either of two neighboring houses.

If each house is defined with its own XML document, you can set up the rooms that you can get to in each house using an extended link. (The rooms can be in their own documents apart from the house's, by the way. The above FlixML example simplified the extended link, for purposes of illustration, by placing all remote resources in the same document—but they can be anywhere at all on the Web.) When a user enters a new house all the new rooms are accessible, even if the user doesn't know that they're there. And you also don't have to take up valuable screen real estate by including physically on each house's page a list of all rooms that can be entered—giving you more space for images and the deathless prose that describes the house.

The Twilight Zone: External Linksets

The designers of the XLink spec took the notion of out-of-line extended links one step further: They made it possible to remove all information about a link from any given document that needs to use it, placing it in a completely separate file. XLink accomplishes this using a mechanism called *external linksets.*

This enables several documents, for example, to share a common "menu" of links. (It thereby simplifies maintaining the menu, not incidentally: Add a new link to the external linkset and the new link immediately becomes available to all documents that reference the external linkset.)

Here's a sample external linkset, using FlixML elements. The purpose of the `genrelinkset` element is to link to FlixML documents on other films that share the same genre, or ones like it, as the document in which the element appears:

```
<genrelinkset xlink:type="extended"
    xlink:title="Films in Related Genres"
    xlink:role="xlink:extended-linkset">
    <genrelink
        xlink:type="locator"
        xlink:href="noir.xml"
        xlink:title="Film Noir"/>
    <genrelink
        xlink:type="locator"
        xlink:href="crime.xml"
        xlink:title="Crime Cinema"/>
    <genrelink
        xlink:type="locator"
```

```
            xlink:href="suspense.xml"
            xlink:title="Suspense and Thrillers"/>
</genrelinkset>
```

More terminology

Note that each of the remote resources in this example, identified by the `xlink:type="locator"` attributes, is a special sort of XML document. Each is just a collection of links, called a *linkbase*—basically a "database of links."

There is only one new attribute/value pair for you to notice: `xlink:role="xlink:extended-linkset"`: This identifies the extended link as a *group* of `locator`-type links to one or more linkbases, rather than as an ordinary extended link. (This seems to be the only case in which the XLink spec requires the `xlink:role` attribute to have a particular value, by the way.)

You might understandably be a bit confused by the above example, despite the addition of the new attribute. It certainly looks as though your local document merely has links to three documents, doesn't it? So what's the big deal?

The big deal is that external linksets are treated as special cases by the XLink-aware processing application. When the application encounters an external linkset in an XML document, it immediately attempts to locate the resources named in the child elements whose `xlink:type` attributes have a value of `locator`; each of them is assumed to be a linkbase. When it gets to those linkbases, it looks for any XLinks that *they* contain, and if it finds any, adds the corresponding remote resources to the menu of links available, and so on.

How not to link to the whole XLink universe

There's a special issue to be concerned with when you're using external linksets: What if the linkbases they point to also contain external linksets? Suppose the resources to which those links point are *also* XML documents with external linksets, and so on?

At the very least, you'd risk trying your visitor's patience as the network churned its way through the endless chain of links.

Earlier versions of the XLink spec provided a way to avoid this, using a `steps="n"` attribute. This attribute would take a number as its value, the number indicating how far down the chain to proceed before stopping the search for further extended links. By specifying `steps="2,"` we'd tell the application to go to the indicated resource(s) (that's one step), then to any resources named in external linksets in the indicated resource(s) (that's two steps), and then stop.

But the `steps` attribute has been dropped in recent versions of the spec. Now, it says only that the application is responsible for putting limits on the number of steps to go down the chain.

This means that the unfortunate answer to the question posed by this section is now: You avoid linking to the whole XLink universe by being *careful*.

Summary

In this chapter, you learned about the things that XLink can do for you and how to make it do those things, with various combinations of the attributes of an XLinking element.

For information on which of these attributes may be associated with the various types of XLinking elements, see Table 5.1, presented earlier in the chapter.

Table 5.2   XML markup covered in this chapter

XLinking attribute	Allowable values	Default
`xlink:type`	`simple, extended, locator, arc,` `resource, title, none`	`simple`
`xlink:href`	(`url of remote resource`)	(N/A)
`xlink:role`	(`text`—but must be `extended-linkset` if the element type is `extended` and the link is meant to define an external linkset)	(N/A)
`xlink:title`	(`text`)	(N/A)
`xlink:show`	`replace, new, embed, undefined`	`replace`
`xlink:actuate`	`onRequest, onLoad, undefined`	`onRequest`

Terms defined in this chapter

resource Any object on the Web that may potentially be involved in an XLink is a potential *resource*, including XML documents, HTML documents, images, and so on.

participating resource Any object on the Web that *is* involved in an XLink. Note that in XLink, this means that both the "from end" and the "to end" are participating resources in a given link.

local resource A resource participating in an XLink; specifically, the resource (if there is one) in which the XLink itself exists.

remote resource A resource participating in an XLink; specifically, a resource existing somewhere other than in the local document.

locator A *locator* is essentially a URL—a designator for where on the Web a remote resource can be found.

link A *link*, in XLink parlance, is an element that includes all the information needed to establish a relationship among two or more resources. This includes information about any participating local and remote resources, as well as the rules of the relationships among the resources.

linking element Any element in an XML document with both an `xlink:type` attribute and an `xlink:href` attribute. (Those two attributes need not be explicitly set by the document's author if the DTD establishes defaults for them.)

inline link An *inline link* describes not only the remote resource(s) of an XLink, but also the local one. Omitting properties of the local resource from the link definition makes it an out-of-line link (see below).

out-of-line link Unlike an inline link (see above), the definition of an *out-of-line* link includes *no* information about the local resource.

simple link When a linking element contains information about the local resource, the remote resource, and the link itself in the same element, it's a *simple link*. Contrast this with extended link, below.

extended link In an *extended link*, the link definition is split between parent and child elements. The parent element simply serves to group the children into a single linking structure, and to identify the link as being of the extended type; each `resource`-type child contains information about a local resource; each `locator`-type child contains information about a remote resource; and each `arc`-type child contains information about the nature of the links among the various resources (such as traversal direction).

traversal The act of "making a link happen" is called *traversal*. Until the link is traversed, it's merely a potential link. XLink provides facilities for user-actuated traversal (like HTML), and also for automatically actuated traversal that occurs without user intervention.

arc The rules for traversal among two or more participating resources in an extended XLink are called the *arc*. Arcs may define the direction in which link traversal occurs among the various resources in the link and possibly other information about their relationship(s).

linkbase An external set of links to which an external linkset points is called a *linkbase* (presumably by analogy with "database").

external linkset Not all extended links need to point directly to remote resources; instead, they can point to "catalogs of links," called linkbases, which contain the XLinks to the resources themselves. An extended link that does so is called an *external linkset.*

CHAPTER   6

XPointers and XPath:
The "Where" of XML

The previous chapter, concerning the overall XLink specification, made occasional reference to XPointers, without explaining much at all of what they are for, what they are capable of doing, or how to make them do it.

In this chapter you'll learn what XPointers are and how to use them. You'll also learn about the XPath standard, which specifies how to locate specific parts of an XML document. Understanding XPath is not only critical to understanding XPointers, but also of supreme importance in using the Extensible Stylesheet Language Transformations (XSLT), which will be covered in Chapter 8.

The specs

As with the XLink specification, the one for XPointers is a W3C working draft—that is, a "work in progress" whose final shape and details are subject to change over time. However, the XPointer one is a little further along as of this writing (December, 1999); it's attained a special "last call" status. Basically this means that in the editors' opinion, the spec fulfills their responsibility to produce a complete and unambiguous specification—from here, usually, a W3C standard moves on within a short time to full-blown Recommendation (final) status.

You can find the current XPointer spec online, regardless of its current status, at:

        www.w3.org/TR/xptr

As for XPath, it—like the core XML spec—has attained Recommendation status. It's at:

        www.w3.org/TR/xpath

Note that this chapter, unlike the others in *Just XML*, addresses not primarily one W3C standard, but *two*. Accordingly, and because of the way in which the two standards are related, this chapter is organized a little differently:

- First, I'll cover XPointers in general: why and how to use them.
- Next will come a section describing XPath in detail. While the XPath spec is about the same printed length as the one for XPointers, it is—in my opinion—vastly "weightier" in its impact on the XML world, so this section will be the longest in the chapter.
- Finally, there's a section explaining how the XPointer spec extends what XPath alone can do.

XPointing the Way

XLinks are wonderful enhancements to the larger limitations of HTML hyperlinking. They get you from here to there in various clever—even bizarre—ways. But XLinks alone don't do everything we need for getting around in the XML world.

Why XPointers?

A few chapters ago, I took you on a Digression Express that compared XML hyperlinking to train travel. And that, pretty much, is what XLinking is designed to do: to get you from one destination to another, or many others, and back again.

But to extend the metaphor,[28] that's not really all you need when you go on a trip. You don't just want to arrive at your destination; you want to arrive at a specific point there—it can make a huge difference to your experience if you enter a big city by crossing one bridge instead of another, or by landing at a big regional airport versus a small private field on the outskirts.

The main purpose of XPointers is to extend XLink by making it possible to land at a specific place out of all possible places—to point not only *to* a document, but *into* one.

---

28. Don't worry, I'm not going to be dragging it on much longer. Leave the aspirin— or antidepressant, or whatever drug the phrase "to extend the metaphor" made you reach for—in the bottle. (But [he said, ominously] leave the bottle close at hand.)

Using an XPointer

I reviewed earlier the general form of a URL as it might appear in a Web browser, an HTML <a> tag, or an XLink: the service name (like `http://`), the system/domain/"server" name (e.g., `www.flixml.org`), and the optional path/document name (`/flixml/detour_1.xml`).

In that earlier discussion, I also mentioned the so-called pound (or hash) sign, #, which is used in both HTML hyperlinks and XLinks to denote the start of a "fragment identifier"—that is, a specifier of a *portion* of the overall document being pointed to.

To use an XPointer, you follow the # with the reserved word `xpointer`,[29] an open parenthesis, an XPath-based description of a portion of the document, and a closing parenthesis.

Frills and filigrees

There are also some shortcuts you can use, as well as options that enhance this basic form in different ways. We'll get to them shortly. This format is simply the norm—the starting point.

So a standard XPointer to a portion of the detour_1.xml file would look like the boldface portion of this XLink:

```
http://www.flixml.org/flixml/detour_1.xml#xpointer([XPath
stuff])
```

If the XLink containing this XPointer were itself located in the detour_1.xml file, just as in HTML you could omit everything up to the fragment identifier, like so:

```
#xpointer([XPath stuff])
```

---

29. The `xpointer` portion of an XPointer is called the *scheme*. According to the spec, other schemes are possible—but `xpointer` is the only one the spec defines. For the time being, at least, don't go off and indulge yourself in anything wacky like inventing your own, alternative XPointer scheme.

Shortcut #1: "bare names"

Even if you don't know anything about XPath, you may—depending on your document's DTD, if it has one—still be able to use XPointers. (It may actually be *easier* to do it this way, although it's nowhere near as flexible.)

XML allows for special attributes to be placed on elements, called IDs[30]. As you might guess from the name, an ID is a unique identifier for a given occurrence of that element, in fact of any element, in a given document. By convention, although it's not required, ID-type attributes are also *named* id. In fact, we saw an example of them in use in the last chapter (during the discussion of arcs and extended links):

```
<contents>
    <section xlink:href="#title" />
    <section xlink:href="#cast" />
    <section xlink:href="#director" />
    <section xlink:href="#plotsummary" />
    <contarc/>
</contents>
```

If you peeked into the FlixML DTD, you'd see that every element has an ID-type attribute. The above XPointers (in boldface) are shortcut forms, called *bare names*, of the full XPointer format; each XPointer's value—title, cast, director, and plotsummary–is the value of an ID-type attribute somewhere in the document. (Those are their values *in this document*; they just happen to match the names of the elements in which those attributes appear.) The full format for the first XPointer above would be:

```
<section xlink:href="#xpointer(id('title'))" />
```

(Note that the portion of the XPointer in the outermost pair of parentheses— id('title')–is an XPath expression, albeit a simple one. XPath expressions are covered in much greater detail in the next section.) We can use the bare names form because of the requirement that each ID's value must be unique. Any elements with attributes whose values may not be unique would need to use the full XPointer syntax, addressed with an XPath expression.

---

30. "ID" is pronounced "eye-dee," not like the animal side of human nature in Freudian psychology.

More on IDs

The best thing about IDs, as the XPointer spec mentions, is that they're *robust*. It's hard for an XPointer to be "approximately wrong" if it's based on an ID. If an element with that ID value doesn't exist, the result will be quite obvious: an error message, or a document retrieved from the top, rather than starting with whatever the expected element is. Other means of addressing locations within a document are all subject to subtler forms of errors. For example, consider an XPointer that says, "retrieve the first male cast member's description in this FlixML document." If I or someone else changes the document so that a *different* male cast member is now first, the XPointer may or may not be correct anymore.

As with most things in life, and in XML for that matter, there are also some downsides to using IDs. Chief among these, for now, is that the only way to declare an ID attribute in the first place is via a DTD—which means you can forget about using them if your documents are merely well-formed.

I'll cover how to declare an ID-type attribute in Chapter 9.

Shortcut #2: "child sequences"

An easy way to think of this shortcut is to leave behind—for a moment—the world of popular (or semi-popular) movies, and visit the world of popular (or semi-popular) music; in particular, think of a song (now over twenty years old) by Jimmy Buffett: "Son of a Son of a Sailor." If you were constructing this set of family relationships among three men in the manner of a common computer directory/file system, how would you refer to the youngest person in the chain? Right:

```
/Sailor/Son/Son
```

Each entry occurring after a slash is a child of the entry occurring before the same slash, and `Sailor` is the "root directory."

Now let's expand the family tree a bit. Let's give the middle man a second child, and let's also say we don't care any longer whether we're talking about sons or daughters. How do we refer to the youngest person in the chain?

As a reminder, our hypothetical family tree now looks like this:

1st Generation	2nd Generation	3rd Generation
(Original "Sailor")	Child (original "Son")	Child (Original "Son of a Son")
		Child

So how might we represent the person at the bottom of the tree using our "directory path" notation, especially considering that we don't know anything about genders and assuming that we don't have a unique ID?

One way to do it is like this:

```
/1/1/2
```

That is, for each generation simply use an integer number (separated from "older" and "younger" generations with slashes); the value of the number used represents that person's "birth order" in relation to his or her parent. If our original "Sailor" had had a second child, and that child had four children of his or her own, we could access the "third child of the second child of a sailor" using a notation like this:

```
/1/2/3
```

and so on.

That's how the XPointer "child sequence" shortcut works, too. You need to know what the target document's structure is, but you don't even need to know the element names; you simply need to be able to count children, and children of children, and so on.

A FlixML document, considerably abbreviated, might look roughly like the following:

```
<?xml version="1.0"?>
<!DOCTYPE flixinfo>
<flixinfo>
    <contents>
        <section/>
        <section/>
    </contents>
    <title>. . .</title>
    <genre>
        <primarygenre>. . .</primarygenre>
    </genre>
    <releaseyear>. . .</releaseyear>
    <language>. . .</language>
    <studio>. . .</studio>
    <cast>
        <leadcast>
          <male>
                <castmember>. . .</castmember>
                <role>. . .</role>
          </male>
          <female>
```

```
                    <castmember>. . .</castmember>
                    <role>. . .</role>
            </female>
          </leadcast>
        </cast>
    </flixinfo>
```

As you can see, I've indented the various levels of the element structure—the "family tree," if you will—to make the parent-child relationships plainer.

You may also have noticed that I've omitted all attributes and actual text content of the document. That's because using the child-sequences XPointer shortcut lets you select *only on the basis of elements.* In this hypothetical FlixML document, to XPoint to the last role element in the tree, you'd use a fragment identifier like this, in child-sequence form:

```
#/1/7/1/2/2
```

I guess everyone will have their preferred way of reading this, but the way I work it out in my own head is from right to left: "This XPointer fragment identifier points to the second child (`role`) of the second child (`female`) of the first child (`leadcast`) of the seventh child (`cast`) of the first element (`flixinfo`) in the document."

And now: bare name child sequences

Astute readers will have observed that the child sequence shortcut will always have a "root integer" of 1, since no document can have more or less than one root element.

However, the XPointer spec also allows the bare-name and child-sequence forms to be used together: The first entry in a child sequence, instead of `/1`, may be a bare name—in which case the counting of children starts at the corresponding element, as if *it* were the root element. So if the `leadcast` element in the above document had an ID-type attribute with a value of `leadcastID`, you could combine this information with a child sequence to point to the last `role` element, as here:

```
#leadcastID/2/2
```

I'll leave it up to all readers, astute as well as the other kind, to work out for themselves how this form maps to the purely child-sequence form of the address.

Making XPointers fail-safe

Okay, that's a little misleading. There's pretty much nothing at all you can do to *guarantee* that your XPointers will work in all cases. If you're "XPointing" to a document that no longer exists, the link will be just as dead as a plain old HTML <a> tag pointing to the same location.

Still, you can take advantage of one XPointer feature—with no counterpart in HTML—to make your XLinks at least a *little* more resistant to breakage.

There's apparently no real name for this feature, but it's easily enough described: just chain together the XPointers in the URL from left to right, in your "order of preference"—most preferred to the left, least preferred to the right. The first one that matches something in the target document is treated just as if it were the *only* XPointer in the URL. So something like this:

```
#xpointer([XPath expr1])xpointer([XPath expr2])
```

will cause the processor to try first to locate whatever portion of the document matches the first XPath expression; if it doesn't find a match there, it will try to match on the second XPath expression.

(Note that using this feature requires you to use the full XPointer form—no shortcuts allowed. Also note that it applies only to XPointers; you can't, for example, chain together several complete XLinks in a single URL.)

A few pages back, in discussing the bare-names shortcut, I mentioned that they're a short form for the full XPointer, including XPath expression, `xpointer(id("value"))`. Suppose you knew that for most current FlixML documents, the cast element had an ID-type attribute whose value was `castID`, but in older documents the value tended to be plain old `cast`–and that if a particular document lacked a cast element completely, you'd settle for locating the crew element (with its `crewID` or `crew` ID-type attributes).

The following XPointer would therefore be much less likely to "break" than one that simply pointed to a cast element with a `castID` attribute:

```
#xpointer(id("castID"))xpointer(id("cast"))xpointer(id("crewID"))
xpointer(id("crew"))
```

In the current Web, with no way to specify alternate fragment IDs like this, you're much more likely to encounter a "broken fragment." With XPointers, that risk can be significantly reduced.

B Alert!

He Walked by Night (1948, Eagle-Lion)

Given a superintelligent criminal operating on his own, and the entire Los Angeles Police Department united in a hunt for him, what do you have?

No, you don't have an excerpt from this morning's newspaper. Well, all right, you *might*. But what I'm thinking of is this extremely well-made crime flick, based on a true story and starring Richard Basehart as Davis Morgan, a lowly electronics technician who manages to tie the LAPD in knots.

One night (these things always seem to begin at night), a policeman on his way home from duty interrupts Morgan in the process of breaking into an electronics store. Morgan shoots the officer and manages to elude the police looking for him. He goes home, where he's got a radio tuned to police-band frequencies, and proceeds to shave his mustache in the first of several "disguises." The police interrogate every two-bit crook they can round up in a vain attempt to collar the killer—many of those questioned look no more like Richard Basehart than you or I do—and in the meantime, Morgan embarks on a one-man crime wave, holding up small stores and escaping (hold your breath) by *diving into the Los Angeles storm sewer system.*

A couple of things distinguish the film, aside from the fairly high-caliber writing and cinematography (and the long chase through the sewers).

First, this was apparently one of the first flicks (if not the first) to feature at its center an intelligent, cynical criminal capable not just of eluding the long arm of the law, but of actually *toying* with it.

Second, it was also one of the first to feature the by-now familiar device of forensic technology to help solve a crime. The police don't just take fingerprints and interrogate suspects, they engage in sophisticated ballistics tests. Although they have no idea what their opponent really looks like—he's been wearing different disguises each time he hits a new store—they call in a host of his robbery victims and go through a laborious reconstruction of his face, feature by feature. "Do these eyes look right?" "No, no, they're farther apart than that." "Yes, that's him, that's *him!*"

In a bit part as the forensic wizard is Jack Webb[31], later of television's *Dragnet* series. Reportedly, Webb was so fascinated by the whole tone of this movie—the deadpan cops, the clever criminal, the forensic gadgetry—that he adopted it for use in the series. (This was Basehart's first feature role, by the way.)

Getting around Downtown: XPath

The XPointer syntax rules detailed thus far should be pretty easy to grasp, and they may be suitable for some correspondingly simple applications.

However, they're also pretty inflexible, providing you only a couple ways to get to a particular element matching a particular condition. And you can't get to anything *other* than elements yet: you can't find attributes, PIs, or comments.

It's like being in a big city where the taxis are running all right[32] but all other forms of transportation are broken or nonexistent. You can tell the cabbie what address you need to get to, and he will presumably know how to get there; or you can give him detailed directions consisting only of left and right turns. That's it. If you want to go over or under the street, forget it. If you want to go two and a half blocks instead of two or three, if you want to stop *en route* to wander around a department store on foot for a couple hours, if you want to go to the second house on the street but you don't know the address…well, there are going to be a *lot* of places you can't get to.

The XPath standard is designed to make it virtually impossible *not* to be able to locate some part of a document, no matter how small or insignificant it may be. This will be critical for the success of XPointers, of course, which is why XPath is covered here.

Less obviously, XPath is also of supreme importance to the Extensible Stylesheet Language Transformations (XSLT), to be covered in Chapter 8. That tool's purpose is to enable you to transform and display different parts of an XML document in different ways; if you can't *find* the part you need to transform or display, then what good is the tool?

---

31. This young Jack Webb looks like Eddie Cantor's sardonic kid brother.
32. This doesn't describe the taxi situation in any big cities I'm familiar with.

> **Be Alert!—indeed**
>
> I can't emphasize it enough: If you "get" XPath, you can practically fall asleep during the XSLT chapter. Not quite, but almost.
>
> Unfortunately, that means that you can't afford to drift off here during the coverage of XPath. If you've already been up for twenty hours cramming for finals, trying to get the baby to sleep, or (heaven help you) reading *Just XML*, I advise you to put the book down now and return to it when your head's clear.

A sample document

XPath can be simple, or it can be complicated. A large part of making it the former lies in avoiding generalizations and concentrating on specific examples. With that in mind, here's a sample (partial) FlixML document on *He Walked by Night*, covered in the preceding "B Alert!" (I've here departed from my usual practice of using only fairly short snippets of code as examples. I want to be able to draw on as many combinations of elements, attributes, and so on as I can.)

```
<?xml version="1.0"?>
<!DOCTYPE flixinfo SYSTEM
    "http://www.flixml.org/flixml/flixml_03.dtd">
<?xml:stylesheet type="text/xsl" href="flixml.xsl" ?>
<flixinfo
    author="John E. Simpson" copyright="2000" xml:lang="EN"
    xmlns:xlink="http://www.w3.org/1999/xlink/namespace/">
    <title role="main">He Walked by Night</title>
    <genre>
        <primarygenre>&C;</primarygenre>
    </genre>
    <releaseyear role="initial">1948</releaseyear>
    <language>English</language>
    <studio>Eagle-Lion Films</studio>
    <cast>
        <leadcast>
          <male>
                <castmember id="RBasehart">
                    Richard Basehart</castmember>
                <role>Davis Morgan</role>
          </male>
          <male>
                <castmember>Whit Bissell</castmember>
                <role>Reeves</role>
```

```
        </male>
        <male>
                <castmember>Scott Brady</castmember>
                <role>Sgt. Marty Brennan</role>
        </male>
        <male>
                <castmember>Jack Webb</castmember>
                <role>Lee</role>
        </male>
    </leadcast>
    <othercast>
        <male>
                <castmember>Robert Bice</castmember>
                <role>Detective Steno</role>
        </male>
        <male>
                <castmember>Doyle Manor</castmember>
                <role>Detective</role>
        </male>
        <male>
                <castmember>Bert Moorhouse</castmember>
                <role>Detective</role>
        </male>
        <male>
                <castmember>Steve Pendleton</castmember>
                <role>Detective</role>
        </male>
        <female>
                <castmember>Carlotta Monti</castmember>
                <role>Woman</role>
        </female>
    </othercast>
  </cast>
  <crew>
    <director>Anthony Mann</director>
    <director>Alfred Werker</director>
    <screenwriter>John C. Higgins</screenwriter>
    <screenwriter>Crane Wilbur</screenwriter>
    <cinematog>John Alton</cinematog>
    <sound>Leon S. Becker</sound>
    <sound>Hugh McDowell</sound>
    <editor>Alfred DeGaetano</editor>
    <score>Leonid Raab</score>
    <speceffects>Jack Rabin, George Teague</speceffects>
  </crew>
```

```
<plotsummary>One night (these things always seem to
    begin at night), a policeman on his way home from
    duty interrupts lowly electronics technician
    <maleref
    maleid="RBasehart">Davis Morgan</maleref> in the
    process of breaking into an electronics store.
    Morgan shoots the officer and manages to elude the
    police looking for him. He goes home, where he's
    got a radio tuned to police band frequencies, and
    proceeds to shave his mustache in the first of
    several "disguises."
    <parabreak/>The police interrogate every two-bit
    crook they can round up in a vain attempt to
    collar the killer--many of those questioned look
    no more like Richard Basehart than you or I do--
    and in the meantime, Morgan embarks on a one-man
    crime wave, holding up small stores and escaping
    (hold your breath) by <emph>diving into the Los
    Angeles storm sewer system.</emph>
</plotsummary>
<reviews>
    <flixmlreview>
      <goodreview>
      <!-- Note to self: Don't forget to replace
            placeholder below with REAL review -->
            <reviewtext>(Some text)</reviewtext>
      </goodreview>
    </flixmlreview>
    <otherreview>
      <goodreview>
            <reviewlink
            xlink:href=
            "http://weeklywire.com/filmvault/austin/h/
            hewalkedbynight1.html">The Austin
            Chronicle</reviewlink>
      </goodreview>
      <goodreview>
            <reviewlink
            xlink:href=
            "http://www.kics.bc.ca/~observer/
            link.cgi?http://www.nelson.kics.bc.ca/
            ~observer/columns/movie/walknight.html">The
            Nelson (B.C.) Observer</reviewlink>
      </goodreview>
    </otherreview>
</reviews>
```

```
<distributors>
    <distributor>
      <distribname>Reel.com</distribname>
      <distribextlink>
            <distriblink
                xlink:href="http://www.reel.com/
                movie.asp?MID=4540" />
      </distribextlink>
    </distributor>
</distributors>
<remarks>In a bit part as the forensic wizard Lee is
    Jack Webb, later of television's Dragnet series.
    Reportedly, Webb was so fascinated by the whole
    tone of this movie--the deadpan cops, the clever
    criminal, the forensic gadgetry--that he adopted
    it for use in the series.
     <parabreak/>
    (This was Basehart's first feature role, by the way.)
</remarks>
<mpaarating>NR</mpaarating>
<bees b-ness="&BEE4URL;" b-nesspic="BEE4"/>
</flixinfo>
```

Words and concepts

Like most technical standards, XPath comes with its own share of jargon. Let's take a look at the most important. (Note that some of these terms have cropped up already in *Just XML*, but I've used them informally without defining them.)

node

A node is any discrete "thing" that XPath is able to work with, and XPath can work with seven types of them:

- The document as a whole is contained within a **root** node. This isn't the same thing as the root *element*; the root *node* is an abstract sort of beast, which includes within its scope the document prolog (if any), the root element (and all the elements that the root element contains), and any comments or PIs following the root element.
- There's one **element** node, of course, for each occurrence of an element in a document. For instance, in the sample FlixML document above, there are three `goodreview` element nodes (one subordinate to the `flixmlreview` element, and two subordinate to the `otherreview` element).

- An **attribute** node represents an attribute within some element. The bees element in the above document has two attribute nodes within it (b-ness and b-nesspic). When counting attribute nodes, be sure *not* to count things that look like attributes but aren't, because what they're "in" are not elements. Examples from above are version (in the XML declaration) and type (in the xml:stylesheet PI).
- **Comment** nodes, obviously, correspond to the comments (if any) in the document. The sample document has only one of these, the one beginning, "Note to self."
- For every PI in the source document, there will be one **processing instruction** node. The only PI node in the above appears early in the document; its target is xml:stylesheet. (As I've mentioned, the XML declaration, which looks like a PI, is *not* a PI.)
- There's a **namespace** node for each namespace for a given element. Note in the above that the xlink: namespace is declared in the root element, flixinfo; this means that all the elements contained by that root element also have that namespace node.
- Finally, each block of text constitutes a **text** node. The term "block of text" here refers to character data between tags. For instance, within the remarks element above are two text nodes: one on either side of the <parabreak/> tag.

node-set

As you might guess, a node-set is a group of nodes returned by a single XPath expression.

This concept will be a bit foreign to users and authors of HTML documents. In the HTML Web, when you point to a specific location with a fragment identifier, you point to a single such location. How can you point to more than one? What would it mean to do so, if you could?

Current Web browsers (and pretty much any other software) do not, of course, know anything about XPointers; the standard hasn't been finalized yet, and once it does become final it will take some time to see software that knows about it. But the general idea might be, say, that if your XLink is declared with show="embed" and actuate="onLoad", a single XPointer with a sufficiently general XPath expression could let you automatically embed multiple chunks extracted from the remote resource.

(This will be a much more important and immediately useful concept when we get to Chapter 8. There, where we'll use XPath to decide which portions of the element tree to apply different styles to, the *norm* will be to apply styles to a bunch of different nodes at once—rather than having to single them out and process them one by one.)

context node

Back to our getting-around-town analogy.

Let's say you leave the hotel, bound for a movie theater on the other side of the city. Fortunately, you're with a friend who's got a car—this will be a lot cheaper (assuming you can find free parking) than taking a cab. Unfortunately, this is your friend's first visit to the city; he doesn't know any of the street names. So you've got to direct him one step at a time: "Go one block and turn left. Now three blocks and turn right." And so on.

If instead you'd decided to go to lunch first, then the movie, how would you have directed your friend from the restaurant to the theater?

If your answer to this is, "I'd use exactly the same directions as before!"—and if, of course, the restaurant is not in the hotel where you're staying—I hope your friend is more patient than the norm. Your directions have to be different when you start out from a different place.

That's the idea of an XPath context node. As you "move around" within the document, sometimes within a given XPath expression, you keep changing the point where the following set of directions start.

In the FlixML review of *He Walked by Night*, let's say you're looking to point to the information about Jack Webb. If your starting point is the root node, you've got to get into the `flixinfo` element, then the `cast` element, then the `leadcast` element, and so on until reaching those elements that deal with Jack Webb. If you're already down in the `leadcast` element, the directions will be much shorter. If you're somewhere down within the `crew` or `plotsummary` elements, you've got to go "back up" to a point where you can get to `cast`, then work your way from there down to Webb's information. And so on. Each place you're starting from is a different context node.

Relative vs. absolute addressing

If the element you're trying to get to has an ID-type attribute (like Richard Basehart's information above), you can go right there without worrying about the context node. This sort of "going right there" is referred to as *absolute addressing*.

Knowing the context node is important, for the most part, only when you're using *relative addressing*: "Start at this point, then move in that direction for this distance, then go in that other direction for *this* distance," and so on.

Note though that even if you start out with absolute addressing, when you "go right there" you're still changing the context node. It's like an invisible pointer that moves around with you inside a document—like the insertion point (typically an "I-beam"-shaped mouse cursor) in a word-processing application.

By the way, knowing the context node is much less important when using XPath expressions in an XPointer than it is when using them in XSLT. In an XPointer, the context node will nearly always be the root node. But if you're referring back to this chapter from the one on XSLT, you really do need to pay attention to your context node—it'll be changing literally beneath your feet.

---

location path

A location path is simply the set of instructions in an XPath expression for how to get somewhere in the document, perhaps starting from a given context node. This can be an absolute form, like the XPointers we've already seen that take us to an element with a unique ID (in which case knowing the context node is immaterial); or it can be in a relative form (where knowing the context node is critical). If the latter, it consists of one or more *steps*, separated by slashes (hence the familiar term "path" here).

Coming down to earth: XPath syntax

As the mention of slashes in the preceding paragraph indicates, we're moving from the abstract world of XPath concepts to the concrete world of actually coding an XPath expression.

An XPath expression (to repeat the information from the end of the last section) consists of a location path, in turn consisting of one or more steps (formally called location steps). Each step consists of an *axis*, a *node test*, and a *predicate*, strung together like this:

```
axis::nodetest[predicate]
```

Under certain conditions, one or more of these three components may be absent from the expression. But if both the axis and node test are present, for example, the double-colon (`::`) is required; and if the predicate is present, it must be surrounded by square brackets (`[` and `]`).

The axis

The **axis** (plural *axes*) says in which direction you want to move or "look" in this step from the context node. These directions aren't the familiar up, down, sideways, and back-and-forth; rather they specify how to move within the abstract tree of elements and other nodes in the document. For instance, you can get the "next node" or the "preceding node"; you can get a "child" or "parent" element.

What the axis does, according to the spec, is select a group of *candidates*—nodes that may or may not be the one(s) you're after. (Actually specifying which of the candidates you're actually interested in will be done in the node test and the predicate.)

There are quite a few axes to select from; use whichever one(s) might be appropriate by plugging it into the above syntax, in place of the italicized `axis`:

- `child`: looks "down" the element tree, just one step, from the context node. With the sample `remarks` element as the context node, there's only one candidate along the `child` axis; i.e., the `parabreak` element. If `crew` is the context node, the list of candidates includes both `director` elements, both `screenwriter` elements, `cinematog`, both `sound` elements, `editor`, `score`, and `speceffects`. (This is the default axis, by the way; that information will be important in a moment, when I cover some convenient shortcuts to coding a complete XPath expression.)
- `parent`: as you might guess, looks "up" the element tree a step from the context node. The `parent` axis is therefore a complement to the child—if `B` is a child of `A`, then `A` must be `B`'s parent. Note that every element node in the document has a parent, including the root element (its parent is the root node), but that the root node does not.

Weasel words

The XPath Recommendation plays some apparently arcane games with words and meanings in discussing parent and child nodes. It turns out that there are some exceptions to the statement I just made about hypothetical nodes A and B.

First of these is that if the current node is an attribute, its parent is the element that the attribute "belongs to." But if the current node is an element, looking down the `child` axis will not locate any attributes. Similarly, the parent of a namespace node is the element in which it was declared, while any applicable namespace nodes are *not* children of a given element.

The second bit of waffling is that comments and PIs *are* considered children of any element that happens to contain them, *and* that such an element is not considered to be their parent. (This may seem like common sense rather than waffling; however, the spec does not explicitly say that a comment or PI's parent is its containing element. Note, though, that if a comment or PI is in the document prolog or "epilog," it's considered a child of the root node.)

Text nodes are treated like elements: Their parents are the elements that contain them, and the text nodes are children of those elements. So if you ask for all children of the `remarks` element in our sample document, you get everything between the opening `<remarks>` and the closing `</remarks>` tags—not only the empty `parabreak` element but also all the text.

This business about child text nodes can produce some unexpected situations, which will be resolved in more or less expected ways depending on what software happens to be processing the XPath expression. If you're getting strange results, such as retrieving what looks to you like "too many" text nodes, look especially at the newline characters in your document. In our *He Walked by Night* example, for instance, does the `reviews` element have any text node children? According to the FlixML DTD, there's no character data immediately descended from `reviews`, only other elements. But again, look at the example: Isn't there *something* between the `<reviews>` tag and the `<flixmlreview>` tag? When you get the children of the `reviews` element, do you want to get that "something," or don't you?

- `attribute`: looks at the attributes of the context node. If the `bees` element, down at the end, is the context node, then the `attribute` axis will include two candidate nodes—the `b-ness` and the `b-nesspic` attributes. Obviously—I hope!—if the context node is anything other than an element-type node, inspecting the `attribute` axis will return an empty value.

- `ancestor`: the direction that looks back "up" the tree; doesn't include the context node itself. Let's suppose, using our sample document, that the context node is the `cinematog` element. The `ancestor` axis from that context node will set as possible matches the `crew` element (`cinematog`'s "parent") and the `flixinfo` element (`crew`'s parent), but not `cinematog` itself.

- `ancestor-or-self`: like `ancestor`, but *includes* the context node. Again assuming a context node of `cinematog` in the above document, the `ancestor-or-self node` will produce a list of candidate nodes identical to `ancestor`, but including `cinematog` as well.

- `descendant`: the complement to the `ancestor` axis, this one looks "down" the tree of nodes at children, children of children, and so on; it doesn't include the context node itself. If the context node is the root node of our sample document, looking down the descendant axis will select as possible candidate matches everything in the document except the abstract root node itself—that is, matches the `flixinfo` element and everything it contains, *and* the `xml:stylesheet` PI in the document prolog. When using `descendant`, remember what I just said in the box headed "Weasel words": Since this axis includes children, children of children, and so on, if the context node does not have a child, it won't have any descendants, either; and if a given node is not the child of another node (e.g., an attribute is not the child of the element which sets its value), then it won't appear in the list of descendant candidates.

- `descendant-or-self`: similar to descendant, except that it includes the context node as well as everything below it in the tree that can be a child. For instance, selecting the `descendant-or-self` axis with the root node as the context node will match everything in the document. If `crew` is the context node, the list of candidate nodes will include the `crew` element itself as well as everything between the opening and closing `<crew>` and `</crew>` tags (except, of course, any attributes).

- `following`: tells the XPath processor to look at all nodes "after" the context node. If you were literally reading the sample FlixML document from start to finish, the `crew` element (and its contents), the `plotsummary`, `reviews`, and so on, all occur *after* the cast element, so crew and all the rest would be candidate matches if cast were the context node. However, title, genre, releaseyear, and so on will *not* be candidate matches, because those elements all occur before getting to cast. Also note that if cast is your context node, leadcast and othercast (and their contents) are *not* along the following axis: Although they follow the cast element's start-tag, the following axis requires candidates to follow the context node's *end*-tag. Descendants are therefore never "followers."

- following-sibling: similar to following, but limits the possible matches to the following nodes that share the same parent as the context node. If the context node is cinematog, for example, both editor and plotsummary would be considered following matches—but of those two, only editor is on the following-sibling axis. (That is, both cinematog and editor have the crew parent.) As an aside, comments and PIs—technically not part of the "structured content" that an element may include—will be considered as siblings of any other children of a given node; if an element contains both a comment and another element, for example, the comment and the child element are siblings. In our sample document, if the context node is the comment ("Note to self..."), the reviewtext element ("[Some text]") will match the context node on the following-sibling axis.

- preceding: the "before" counterpart to the following axis's "after." Similarly, along the preceding axis are any nodes that occur before the context node's start (that is, excluding all ancestor, attribute, and namespace nodes). In our FlixML review of *He Walked by Night*, if leadcast is the context node, the nodes along its preceding axis are title, genre, releaseyear, language, and studio–but not cast, which is leadcast's parent (and hence an ancestor).

- preceding-sibling: like preceding, but limited just to those preceding nodes that share the same parent as the context node. The othercast element has one node on its preceding-sibling axis: leadcast. Anything else that occurs physically before othercast is either an ancestor of othercast, or doesn't share its parent (cast).

- namespace: contains all the namespace nodes of the context node. If the context node isn't an element, the set of namespace nodes will be empty. In our sample document, since the xlink: namespace is declared on the root element flixinfo, any element from flixinfo on down in the tree will have the xlink: namespace on its namespace axis. However, if the context node is the comment in the `goodreview` element, looking along the namespace node won't get you anything (even though the comment is also within the scope of the `flixinfo` element that declared the namespace)—a comment node, obviously, not being an element node.

- `self:` contains just the context node itself—no ancestors, descendants, or siblings. This may seem an odd sort of axis to need,[33] but it's a useful tool for constructing an XPath expression within which you need to temporarily move along one of the other axes without resetting the context node. We'll see an example of this below, after covering the rest of the XPath syntax.

The node test

This is where you actually tell your XPath-aware processor "where you want to stop" along the axis you've specified. What you can plug into the basic XPath syntax, in place of the italicized `nodetest`, is one of three things:

- A **name test**: Literally, this tests the names of all candidate nodes along the specified axis. A node with a matching name "makes the cut" and (if there's a predicate) gets passed on for further match processing, or (if there's no predicate) becomes a match with no further processing. For instance, assume the context node is the `crew` element in the example document. If the XPath expression is `child::screenwriter`, an XPath-aware processor will first select everything along the `child` axis (from the first `director` element through the `speceffects` element), and then discard any nodes that are not named `screenwriter`—leaving the two `screenwriter` elements as the only matches. You can use an asterisk here, which means "match anything along this axis, regardless of its name." So if `remarks` is the context node, `following::*` will match the `mpaarating` and `bees` elements.
- One of several **node types** (`comment`, `text`, `processing-instruction`, or `node`) followed by a pair of parentheses: The idea here is that you want to match (as the term "node types" implies) nodes of the specified type on the specified axis, regardless of their names or other characteristics. The XPath expression `descendant::comment()` will (if the context node is the first `goodreview` element or any of its ancestors) match the comment starting

---

33. Kind of like the inspecting-one's-own-navel stereotype of what might be called "meditation professionals."

"Note to self...." The special node type `node()` acts as kind of a wildcard of node types, meaning "I don't care what the node type is along this axis—match 'em all!" So if the context node is the root node, `descendant-or-self::node()` matches *everything*, including the root node itself and the PI in the prolog.

(By the way, the parentheses that follow these node type designators serve a very important purpose: They make it plain that this *is* a node type, not an element of the same name. For example, a construct such as `descendant::node` looks for a descendant of the context node—a descendant *named* node, not a descendant of *type* node. This can produce quite surprising results if you're really after the latter!)

- The literal text `processing-instruction`, followed by a pair of parentheses within which, optionally, you've included a PI target (in quotation marks). There's only one PI in our sample document, but if we wanted to go directly to it from, say, a context node of `distributors`, we could code the XPath expression as (among other options):

```
preceding::processing-instruction("xml:stylesheet")
```

"Among other options"?!?

Yeah. In fact, that's going to be a recurring theme—that there are dozens of XPath routes to almost any piece of an XML document. (The XPaths are many, but the way is one.)

Predicates

What you've learned already about XPath expressions may be sufficient for your needs; the predicate portion of the location path is completely optional. More than likely, though, you'll need to use a predicate to narrow the range of acceptable "targets" more finely than is possible using the axis and node test alone.

Consider the case of the `bees` element in the sample *He Walked by Night* review. It's got two attributes, `b-ness` and `b-nesspic`. Using what you already know, you can construct the following XPointer:

```
#xpointer(/descendant::node()/child::bees)
```

Translated, the XPointer reads (from left to right):

- Set the context node to the root node (`/`).
- Look down the `descendant` axis for a node named `bees`.

So far, so good. But what if we only wanted to select the `bees` element if its `b-ness` attribute had a particular value, otherwise return an empty result? Accomplishing that kind of fine-tuned selection is where you start needing to know about predicates.

As mentioned several pages back, in the generic format for an XPath expression the predicate follows the node test and is enclosed in square brackets. Exactly what goes between those square brackets is one or more "tests," which will yield a true or false result when applied to each node in the currently selected node-set. Each of these "tests" looks like this:

```
something operator somethingelse
```

Of these three components, the simplest to explain (and also the one that will make the purpose of the other two components almost immediately obvious) is *operator*. It is normally:

- an equals sign (`=`).
- a "not equals" sign (`!=`).
- a less-than or greater-than sign (`<` or `>`).
- a less-than-or-equals or greater-than-or-equals sign (`<=` or `>=`).

So, to go back to our example of wanting to select the `b-ness` attribute only if it had a certain value, our new XPointer, complete with predicate, would look like this—note especially the predicate in the square brackets:

```
#xpointer(/descendant::node()/
child::bees[attribute::b-ness="&BEE4URL;"])
```

This adds the following selection criteria to the XPath expression:

- Look down the attribute axis from the current node (`attribute::`).
- Select that node only if it has an attribute named `b-ness`, and then only if the value of that attribute is the expanded form of the `&BEE4URL;` entity (`b-ness="&BEE4URL;"`).

If there is no `bees` element for which this predicate produces a "true" result, then the resulting node-set selected by the XPath expression will be empty—and the XPointer using it won't, in fact, point to anything.

Of entities and XPaths

Be careful using entities like this. If the document where this XPointer appears is not a FlixML document and does not otherwise declare the `BEE4URL` entity, then this XPointer will probably find nothing at all— even if the document being XPointed to has the correct value. (And the local document itself may be rejected as not well-formed.) Just because the document into which you're pointing has some entity declared does *not* mean that the entity will somehow be magically declared in anything that points to that document!

The other entity-related issue to be aware of when dealing with XPath expressions has to do with the special characters < and &. Just as you can't use those characters elsewhere in an XML document without "breaking" its well-formedness, you also can't use them in an XPath expression without fouling up the well-formedness of the document in which the expression appears. The solution here, as elsewhere, is to replace them with the built-in entities `&lt;` and `&amp;`, respectively.

Selecting an element based on its *own value*

The preceding example selected (pointed to, if we're talking about an XPointer) an element based on the value of an attribute. Of course that's not the only approach possible.

As you can see in our sample document, *He Walked by Night* had two directors, Anthony Man and Alfred Werker. You already know that you can select a particular element, like this:

```
/descendant::node()/child::director
```

How do you take that one step further, to get (say) just the `director` element for Anthony Mann? Here's one place where the apparently odd `self::` axis and `node()` node type can come in handy:

```
/descendant::node()/child::director[self::node()="Anthony Mann"]
```

This says to select a director descendant of the root node, regardless of the type of node it is, as long as its value is "Anthony Mann."

Location step shortcuts

A few shortcut methods are available to reduce the complexity of some of these rather ungainly-looking XPath expressions. These are referred to in the XPath spec as the abbreviated syntax.

- An asterisk is a "wildcard" character. If `editor` is the context node, `ancestor::*` selects all ancestors: `crew` and `flixinfo` (as well as the root node) in this case.
- If you omit the axis, by default it will be `child::`. So if `flixinfo` is the context node, coding the predicate as `[releaseyear="1948"]` is identical to coding it as `[child::releaseyear="1948"]`.
- An "at sign," the `@` character, is short for the `attribute::` axis. Therefore `[@b-ness="&BEE4URL;"]` could stand in for the example above, in which we wanted to select the `bees` element depending on the value of its `b-ness` attribute.[34]
- A pair of slashes, `//`, serves the same purpose as `/descendant-or-self::node()/`. To find all screenwriter nodes, you could use the expression `//screenwriter`.
- A single period (or "full stop" character), `.`, is considered identical to `self::node()`.
- *Two* successive periods, `..`, is the abbreviated syntax for `parent::node()`.
- Finally, as we've already seen, a slash all by itself (`/`) represents the "node tree root," or root node.[35]

Given the above shortcuts, the unwieldy XPath expression for selecting the `director` element only if its value is "Anthony Mann" could be considerably shortened, to:

```
//director[.="Anthony Mann"]
```

Big difference, eh? I'll use the abbreviated syntax wherever possible for the remainder of this chapter.

---

34. I don't know for sure how they came up with the `@` sign for this purpose—maybe because "at" is an abbreviated form of "attribute."
35. It seems a little strained to refer to this as an "abbreviated syntax" form; as far as I know there's no *other* way to refer to the root node.

Elaborations on a theme

Again, although you can do quite a bit with XPath using just what I've covered so far, the spec comes with many other ways to achieve the same—or more complex—purposes.

The "union" node-set operator

It's possible that you'll want to combine the results of two entirely different location paths. For example, you might want to get just the lead cast of *He Walked by Night*, plus the two `director` elements, to construct an "important details about this movie" page. The tree of nodes for this document diverges after you get to the root `flixinfo` element, splitting into (among other things) `cast` and `crew` subtrees; as a result you can't simply walk down the tree in one pass to get things from two different branches. Instead, construct both location paths separately, then join them into a single location path with the so-called union operator, a vertical bar or "pipe" symbol: |. In this case, the location path would look something like the following:

```
//leadcast|//director
```

Of course these axis/node test pairs could then be further refined by predicates if you wanted.

Boolean operators in the predicate

The term "Boolean operator" should be familiar to readers who've learned just about any programming language. A Boolean[36] test is a "logical" test—that is, a test to see if a condition is true or false. In this sense, the predicate of an XPath expression is always a Boolean test. A Boolean *operator* is a way of stringing together multiple tests of this kind into a single one. In terms of XPath, you've already (unwittingly) seen some of these in the discussion of predicates: the = sign, `!=`, `>`, and so on. At the time I introduced those symbols I didn't define what went on either side of them, other than to label it `something` and `some-`

---

36. The term "Boolean" comes from the name of the 19th-century English mathematician, George Boole. He didn't have much experience with computers, needless to say, but his contributions to the field of logic had a tremendous impact *on* computers when they finally came along a hundred years later.

`thingelse`. What *those* are can be literal values, like `"Anthony Mann"` in one of our examples; they can also be XPath expressions like `self::node()`.

You can combine these tests using the words `and` and `or` as well as the various other symbols already mentioned.

Suppose you want to select the title of a film only if it was released by Eagle-Lion Films *and* if Anthony Mann was the director, given a context node of `flix-info`. Just include the `and` operator between the two conditions:

```
title[//studio="Eagle-Lion Films" and //director="Anthony Mann"]
```

> **...which also demonstrates:**
>
> ... resetting the context node in a single XPath expression.
>
>   As I mentioned in the text preceding the example, the original context node is `flixinfo`. (That's why it's okay to omit the `child::` axis before `title`.) But within the predicate, we've *reset* the context node to the root node for each expression on either side of the Boolean operator and, with the leading slashes.

So *both* conditions within the predicate need to be true in order to select (or point to) the title node. If we change the `and` to `or`:

```
title[//studio="Eagle-Lion Films" or //director="Anthony Mann"]
```

only one of them must be true in order to select it. If neither condition is true, nothing will be selected.

Expressions on both sides of the operator

I alluded to this under the preceding item, without giving an example of it: You don't have to use a literal value, like `"Anthony Mann"`, in constructing a predicate. Instead, you can use a separate XPath expression.

For instance, we might want to point to the title of a film only if its director was also in the cast. (This isn't true of our sample document, but it might be in the case, say, of a Woody Allen or Kenneth Branagh film.[37]) The XPath expression to do this might look like the following:

---

37. Not that you'd expect to see a B movie by either of *them*. However, it was true of *Targets*, featured in Chapter 3.

```
title[//cast/castmember = //crew/director]
```

Numeric operations

If a particular node's content is numeric, you can add, subtract, multiply, divide, or take the modulus (that is, the remainder when divided by some other number) of its value. I'll hold off showing you an example of this for now, until the section below on numeric functions.

Functions

The notion of a *function* (like that of Boolean operators) will be familiar to those of you who've been exposed to just about any programming language. A function is like one of those crazy mad-scientist machines featured in cartoon parodies of B-grade movies: You put something in at one end, turn a crank or throw a switch, and something totally different comes out the other end. Sometimes you don't have to put anything *in;* just turn it on, and the product rides out on a conveyor belt.

In XPath (as in most programming languages) a function generally looks like this:

```
functionname(input1, input2, input3…)
```

where `functionname` is, obviously, whatever the name of that particular function is, and the various input-type things, called *arguments,* pass data into the "machine" for processing. Many functions may require fewer arguments, or perhaps none at all; the briefest form of a function reference would therefore be:

```
functionname()
```

Most important, functions "return values": something always comes out of a function, like a number or the value true or false.

You use XPath functions in the predicate of an expression (on either the left or right side of an operator). A common example is the position() function, which tells you what the sequence of a particular node is, moving from the context node in the direction of a specified axis. For example:

```
//othercast/*[position()=1]
```

when applied to our sample FlixML document, points us at the first child of the `othercast` node in the document. Loosely translated, it would read, "Starting at the root node, move down the `descendant` axis and get the node named `othercast`, then all of its children; of those, select any whose position is first in the document."

In the more detailed subsections that follow, I'll use these terms to refer to particular kinds of argument(s) passed to a given function:

- *ns*: An XPath expression that represents a group of one or more nodes somewhere in the document. Examples: `child::director`.
- *str*: A sequence of text that is to be treated *as* text, and enclosed in quotation marks. Examples: `"Anthony Mann"`, `"1959"`.
- *obj*: Either a node-set or a string. Examples: `child::director`, `"1959"`.
- *num*: Some value that is numeric, and intended to be operated on that way (as opposed to a string). Examples: `1959` (note absence of enclosing quotation marks), `position()` (which, as in the example above, *returns* a number).

These arguments may be modified below using the following symbols:

- ? (question mark): Argument is optional; if present, can appear only once.
- * (asterisk): Argument is optional; can appear as many times as needed.

If neither of these optionality/repetition symbols is present, the argument must appear once and once only.

Node-set functions

These functions perform some kind of operation on a node-set—selecting a particular node from among a group of them, or returning information about the node-set. Table 6.1 summarizes the node-set functions.

Table 6.1   Node-set functions

Format	Description/Example
`last()`	Returns the number of the last node in the currently selected node-set. Example: `//crew/*[position() = last()]` selects the last child of the `crew` element (the `speceffects` element above).
`position()`	Returns the number of the current node in the selected node-set. Note: `[position()=some number]` as an expression's predicate can be abbreviated as `[some number]`; for example, `[position()=3]` can be shortened to simply `[3]`. Example: See above.

Table 6.1   Node-set functions (continued)

Format	Description/Example
`count(ns)`	Returns the number of nodes in the node-set passed the function. *Example:* Assuming `distributor` is the context node in the above document, `count(distributors)` will return 1.
`id(obj)`	Returns the node with the ID-type attribute whose value equals that of `obj`; if the latter is a string, see the `string()` function below for how the value is converted. *Example:* `id("RBasehart")` returns the first `leadcast/` `male` element.
`local-name(ns?)`	Returns the "local name" (as you might guess) of the argument. As a reminder, the full name of an element is considered to be its expanded name—that is, including the prefix of its namespace, if there is one. The local name is this "full name" with the namespace information omitted. *Example:* There's only one declared namespace in this document—the one for XLink-related markup. Thus, if you use `local-name()` and pass it any non-XLink-related node-set, the function will simply return the first node's name. Doing something like `local-name(//*/` `attribute::xlink:href)` will simply return the string `href`—that is, the expanded name of the first node in the node-set, shorn of its prefix.
`namespace-uri(ns?)`	Returns the URI associated with the argument's namespace, if there is one. *Example:* `namespace-uri(//*@xlink:href)` will return the string `http://www.w3.org/1999/xlink/` `namespace/`, the value of the `xmlns:xlink` attribute that declares the `xlink:` namespace prefix.
`name(ns?)`	Returns the "full name" of an element, including its namespace's prefix (if any). *Example:* Selecting `name(//maleref/@*)` will return the string `maleid`–that is, the full name of the first attribute of the first `maleref` element in the document; since there isn't a namespace prefix on this attribute, none is returned by `name()`.

String functions

This group of functions processes strings in various ways—combining them, selecting portions of them, and so on.

In most cases, you pass the function a string, or several strings; these can be literal string values (like `"Richard Basehart"`) or an XPath expression that produces a string (such as `//castmember[position() = 1]`). In a few cases, you pass a numeric argument to the function, and again this can be either a true number (1, 47, and so on) or an XPath expression that produces a number (like one of those I'll cover below, under "Numeric functions").

Table 6.2 summarizes the use and operation of the string functions. As you can see, there are a couple exceptions to the general rules set forth in the preceding paragraph.

- The `string()` function can take a literal string, a node-set, or no argument at all. If you pass it a string, it behaves as described below; if you pass it a node-set, it behaves as though you had passed it just the first node; and if you pass it nothing at all, it behaves as though you had passed it the context node.
- For both the `string-length()` and the `normalize-space()` functions, the literal-string argument is optional. If you pass one of these functions a string, it behaves as described in Table 6.2; if you pass it nothing it all, it behaves as though you'd converted the context node to a string, and passed it.

N o t h i n g   a c t u a l l y   _changes_
While (again) this won't be news to the programmers among you, functions _do not change_ anything about the original value(s) passed to them as arguments. If anything, they simply return an altered copy of an argument. For example, if you use the normalize-space() function described in Table 6.2, you don't actually strip extraneous whitespace from the argument; you strip it from a _copy_ of the argument, and make the result available for processing.

Table 6.2   String functions

Format	Description/Example
`string(obj?)`	Converts the argument to a string value, which is then returned from the function. *Example:* If the context node is the `female` element, `string(descendant::*)` will return the string `Carlotta Monti`. (This is the only text in any of `female`'s descendant nodes, and it's also the value of the first node—`castmember`—in the passed node-set.)
`concat(str, str, str*)`	Concatenates the various strings passed to it into one big string, which is returned from the function. *Example:* `concat("Mr. ", //male/castmember[2])` returns `Mr. Whit Bissell`—the string "Whit Bissell" is the string value of the second `male` `castmember` element in our sample document.
`starts-with(str, str)`	Is "true" if the first argument starts with the second, otherwise "false". *Example:* `starts-with(//role[1], "Davis")` will return "true" if applied to our sample document.
`contains(str, str)`	Is "true" if the first argument contains the second, otherwise "false". *Example:* You could select all the names in the cast branch of our tree (getting just the cast members' names, not their roles), then test to see if (say) Cary Grant were in this movie, doing something like this: `contains(//castmember/text(), "Cary Grant")`.
`substring(str, num, num?)`	Extracts a portion of the string argument, starting with the position supplied by the first numeric argument, for a length of however many characters are in the third argument (if there is one). *Example:* `substring(//remarks/text()[1], 22, 8)` returns the string `forensic`. (Note that I added the `[1]` predicate to select just the first text node of the `remarks` element. Our sample document's `remarks` contains two text nodes—one before and one after the empty `parabreak` element.)

Table 6.2   String functions (continued)

Format	Description/Example
`substring-before(str, str)`	Returns the portion of the first argument that precedes the value of the second argument. *Example:* `substring-before(//remarks/text(), substring(//remarks/text()[1], 22, 8))` returns the string `In a bit part as the` (including the trailing space). Note that the second argument here makes use of a separate function call; this is all right, as long as the value returned by the function-as-argument is the correct type for the function that's using it.
`substring-after(str, str)`	Returns the portion of the first argument that *follows* the value of the second argument. *Example:* As in the preceding example (the `substring-before()` function), consider the expression `substring-after(//remarks/text()[1],substring-before(//remarks/text()[1], substring(//remarks/text()[1], 22, 8)))`. This passes the result of a string function (the `substring` function in this case) as an argument to a different string function (`substring-before`), and passes the result of *that* function to a third one (`substring-after`). The effect is to return everything in the `remarks` element's first text node *following* the string `In a bit part as the` (including the trailing space) up to the `parabreak` element—that is, the words `forensic` through `use in the series`.
`string-length(str?)`	Returns the number of characters in the argument. *Example:* `string-length(//primarygenre/text())` would return 15. The value of the `primarygenre`'s text node is the entity `&C;`, which when expanded is `Crime/Detective`—a string 15 characters long.

Table 6.2   String functions (continued)

Format	Description/Example
`normalize-space(str?)`	Examines the argument and strips out leading and trailing whitespace in it; also removes extraneous whitespace *within* the argument by replacing two or more occurrences of whitespace with a single space. The value returned by the function is this "stripped" string. This is often done to two strings that you need to compare in the predicate to see if they're equal (perhaps in conjunction with the `translate()` function, described next), when you're not absolutely sure that they have the same number of leading, trailing, and/or internal spaces—normalizing the whitespace in both strings first will guarantee that their spacing is identical. Also useful for ensuring that long text nodes (like `remarks`, `plotsummary`, etc.) don't include extraneous newlines. *Example:* To strip extraneous whitespace from the `plotsummary` element: `normalize-space(//plotsummary/text())`.
`translate(str, str, str)`	Returns the first argument, replacing each occurrence of a character that matches one of the characters in the *second* argument with the character in the corresponding position in the *third* argument. *Example:* Capitalize all vowels in the `title` element: `translate(//title, "aeiou", "AEIOU")` changes the value of our sample film's title to HE WAlkEd by NIght. The function might be read, "Wherever you find an a, replace it with an A; an e, replace it with an E," and so on.

Boolean functions

Each of these functions returns a true/false value, depending on the circumstances that the function detects and, of course, on the value of any arguments passed, the current context node, etc. The functions are summarized in Table 6.3.

Table 6.3   Boolean functions

Format	Description/Example
`boolean(obj)`	Used primarily to test whether or not something "exists." If `obj` is a node-set, the function returns true if and only if the node-set isn't empty; if a string, if and only if the string's length is greater than 0; and if a number, if and only if it is non-zero and a valid number. In all other cases it returns false. *Examples:* Testing to see if the FlixML review in this document contains a bad review of the film: `boolean(//flixmlreview/badreview)` (returns false for this document).
`not(boolean)`	Returns true if the argument passed to it is false, or false if the argument passed to it is true. *Example:* Select the document only if there is *no* bad `flixmlreview` (opposite of preceding condition): `not(boolean(//flixmlreview/badreview))`.
`true()`	Simply returns the value true. Can be useful when you want make your meaning clearer to human readers of your Boolean test. *Example:* Select a document only if there is no bad `flixmlreview` (same as preceding condition): `not(boolean(//flixmlreview/badreview)) = true()`].
`false()`	Simply returns the value false, and (like `true()`, above) useful in situations where you simply want to make your intentions clear.
`lang(str)`	Returns true or false, depending on whether or not the context node has the `xml:lang` value specified in `str`. *Example:* The only `xml:lang` attribute in our sample document is the one on the `flixinfo` root element; because that *is* the root element, all other elements inherit the value of its `xml:lang` attribute, or EN. As a result, `lang("EN")` (or `lang("en")` and so on) will return true for any context node in the document, while `lang("FR")` (or any other language check) will return false.

Numeric functions

The five functions described in Table 6.4 all are intended for processing numeric values in some way. Except for the number() and sum() functions, they take a single numeric argument.

Table 6.4   Numeric functions

Format	Description/Example
number(obj?)	Converts the argument to a number and returns the result. Note that if the argument can't be converted, like when you pass the letter "A" to it, the function returns the string "NaN" (for "not a number"). If no argument is passed, the function operates on the context node. *Example:* To convert the document's copyright year to numeric format, possibly for manipulation by other functions: number(/flixinfo/attribute::copyright).
sum(ns)	Returns the sum of all nodes in the argument. (If you want to simply add numeric values that aren't associated with a node-set, just use the + sign as described below.) Note that you'd generally want to use this only for operating on node-sets that you're confident contain numeric data; otherwise results can be somewhat unpredictable (and probably dependent on the operating system and other software in use at the time of the operation). *Example:* This document (or any FlixML document, for that matter) doesn't really include any node-sets for which you might want to use the sum() function as anything like a practical example. However, sum() might be very useful indeed in an application like billing and invoicing; there, you might use something like sum(//extendedprice) to total up an invoice's amount.
floor(num)	Returns the largest integer that is less than or equal to the argument. *Example:* floor(1.2) returns 1; floor(1.8) also returns 1. floor(-1.2) and floor(-1.8) both return -2.

Table 6.4   Numeric functions (continued)

Format	Description/Example
`ceiling(num)`	Returns the smallest integer that is greater than or equal to the argument. *Example:* `ceiling(1.2)` and `ceiling(1.8)` both return 2, while `ceiling(-1.2)` and `ceiling(-1.8)` both return −1.
`round(num)`	Rounds the argument's value up or down to the nearest integer. The spec says, "If there are two such [integers], then the one that is closest to positive infinity is returned"; this is a quite precise but also possibly confusing way of saying that 1.5 always rounds up to 2, and −1.5 always rounds up to −1. Accurate rounding is somewhat dependent on hardware and operating-system issues; you should test a wide range of possible values to be sure that the round() function will give you the results you want in your application. *Example:* `round(1.2)` returns 1; `round(1.8)` returns 2; `round(1.5)` returns 2; `round(-1.2)` returns −1; `round(-1.8)` returns -2.

Numeric operations

These aren't technically functions as such, but I couldn't reasonably discuss them until having dealt with the various numeric functions. (Don't you love getting little peeks into the dark recesses of the authorial mind?)

There's no particular magic to performing these basic arithmetic operations; you just use the indicated symbol to produce the desired results as summarized in Table 6.5.

Table 6.5   Numeric operations

Operator	Description/Example
`num1 + num2`	Adds two numbers, returning their sum. *Example:* `//*[string-length(self::text()) + number(//releaseyear) > 2000]` would return all element nodes in this document for which the sum of the lengths of their text content and the value of the `releaseyear` element is greater than 2000. Since `releaseyear` is 1948, this should return only those elements whose text content is more than 52 characters long.

Table 6.5 Numeric operations (continued)

Operator	Description/Example
num1 - num2	Subtracts num2 from num1, returning the difference. *Example:* You might want to select a FlixML review only if the year the film was released was no more than 10 years before the FlixML review itself was copyrighted. You could do that using something like `/[number(/flixinfo/attribute::copy-right) -` `number(//releaseyear) &lt;= 10]` (note use of the `&lt;` entity to keep the containing XML document's well-formedness intact). Our sample document wouldn't be selected in this case, because 2000 (the copyright year) minus 1948 (the release year) is 52.
num1 div num2	Divides num1 by num2, returning the quotient. (This is a "floating-point" division, which means that the value returned may include a fractional part. `10 div 4` equals 2.5, not 2 or 3.) *Example:* Was the film's release year a leap year? Find out using an XPath expression like `/[number(//releaseyear) div 4]`.[38]
num1 mod num2	Gets what's called the modulus: divides num1 by num2, returning the *remainder.* This may seem like a rather goofy thing to want to do but it's quite common when you need to take one action for "even somethings" and a completely different action for "odd somethings": If you divide num1 by 2 and there's no remainder, the number is even, otherwise odd. *Example:* Get all the "odd-numbered" lead cast names, starting with the first: `//leadcast/*[position() mod 2 = 1]`.

---

38. Yeah, I know—simply dividing the year by 4 isn't a good enough indicator; you've also got to take into account whether the year is also a century and whether it's evenly divisible by 400. Right, right, right. I had to survive Y2K too, you know.

> **Judicious whitespace**
>
> In general, how you distribute whitespace in the predicate of an XPath expression is not terribly critical (as long as you don't drop any extra spaces *within* any of the keywords, element names, and so on, of course).
>
> You've got to be careful with the numeric operations, though—particularly the minus sign. If the XPath processor sees a string like `-2`, it thinks that it represents literally a numeric value of –2, i.e. "two less than zero"; it does *not* necessarily (or maybe at all) read it as "subtract 2."
>
> The crafters of the XPath spec avoided another potential problem with the slash, typically used as a division symbol (i.e., `100/25` means "100 divided by 25") but with special meaning in an XPath expression (a "path separator," as in `/1/2`). As you can see, they replaced the arithmetical use of the slash with the word `div`.

XPointer Extensions to XPath

Bear in mind that, powerful though it may be, XPath is a specification that's got to serve two masters: XPointer and XSL. One upshot of this is that there will be some things that one of these two standards needs that won't be of interest at all to the other. As a result, each provides a list of "extensions" to XPath—functions or other facilities related to the basic act of locating document fragments and nodes.

For XPointer, these extensions focus largely on providing the ability to locate and extract partial nodes as well as whole ones.

Points and ranges

The idea at first blush seems a bit nutty: allow users and applications to grab any arbitrary chunk of contiguous XML content. Won't that risk fracturing the source document's structure?

Yes, indeed.

On the other hand, there's an important class of applications for which this ability is almost mandatory: selection operations in a graphical user interface (GUI).

Imagine this scenario: You're working on building an XML document with a GUI-based document editor. When you construct an XLink, the editor gives you several options for identifying the URI the XLink is associated with:

- You can simply enter the URI manually, including the fragment identifier or other XPath expression if needed.
- You can open the URI in your XML browser and type a hot-key combination to automatically paste the URI into the document.
- You can go to the URI in your XML browser and, *before* typing the hot-key "copy this URI" keystroke, use the mouse to select a *portion* of the document displayed. The hot key then creates a fragment identifier for you, and pastes the corresponding URI into the document.

It's this third possibility, and ones like it, that seemed to mandate a requirement for XPointer to be able to address partial nodes. For who knows if a user will nice and neatly select a document fragment along element borders—especially if, in a GUI environment, he or she can't even see the markup?

You'll recall that the node test portion of a location path can include the name of a node type: `comment()`, `text()`, `processing-instruction()`, or `node()`. XPointer extends these node types with two new ones, whose purpose will probably be more or less obvious when you see their names: `point()` and `range()`.

Let's start with `range()`. The idea here is that you can identify a start point in the range, and an end point; everything from the one to the other constitutes the range. The `point()` node type is really just a special case of `range()`, where the start and end points are equal.

As a practical matter, it would be wonderful if the XPointer spec provided examples of XPointers that use the two new node types. Unfortunately it does not (XPointer *is* still a working draft, remember). It appears that the use of the two nodes is confined to several new extension functions, such as `range()`, `string-range()`, `start-point()`, `end-point()`, and `here()`. The only examples provided are for the `start-point()` function; they all use a form such as (assuming a FlixML document):

```
start-point(//distributor[3])
```

which locates the very beginning of the third `distributor` element in the document.

We'll probably have to wait for at least one more working-draft iteration of the XPointer standard to see more examples of these functions in use.

One more extension...

Aside from the point-and-range additions to XPath, the one other significant extension is really a simplification.

The assumption is obviously that a very common thing to want to XPoint to is a unique node in a set, or the set of unique nodes in a larger set. Normally you could account for this with the XPath expression `count()=1`. XPointer extends XPath by providing a shorthand version of this expression: `unique()`. You could use this in a predicate as follows:

```
#leadcast//castmember[unique()]
```

In a movie like *Kind Hearts and Coronets*, in which Alec Guiness plays over a half-dozen roles, you might not want his name to be extracted over a half-dozen times—just once. The above construct would enable this to happen.

Summary

In this chapter I explained the relationship between XPointers and XLink, and between XPointers and XPath, and how the three interrelated specifications can be used for locating or extracting specific portions of documents. Detailed coverage of XPath was provided, as was a brief look at some of the proposed XPointer extensions to the XPath standard.

(Also see Tables 6.1 through 6.5 for syntax of XPath expression functions.)

Table 6.6   XPointer-/XPath-related markup covered in this chapter

Item	Description
`#xpointer(XPath expression)`	Basic form of a fragment identifier that includes an XPointer.
`#barename`	Shorthand form of XPointer locating the element with an ID-type attribute whose value is barename in the target resource.
`#xpointer(id('barename'))`	Full form of above bare-name XPointer.
`#/1/7/1/2/2` `#leadcastID/2/2`	Alternate "child sequence" forms of an XPointer to the second child of the second child of the first child of the seventh child of the root element of a sample FlixML document.

Table 6.6   XPointer-/XPath-related markup covered in this chapter (continued)

Item	Description
`#xpointer([ex1])xpointer([ex2])`	An XPointer that, if no match is found for XPath expression `ex1`, attempts to find a match for XPath expression `ex2`.

`axis::nodetest[predicate]`	General form of a location step making up a portion of an XPath expression.
	
	`axis::`: one of `child::` (the default), `parent::`, `attribute::`, `ancestor::`, `ancestor-or-self::`, `descendant::`, `descendant-or-self::`, `following::`, `following-sibling::`, `preceding::`, `preceding-sibling::`, `namespace::`, or `self::`
	
	`nodetest`: either a specific node name, one of several node types (`comment()`, `text()`, `processing-instruction()`, or `node()`), or `processing-instruction("target")`
	
	`predicate`: an XPath expression, function reference, etc., used as a test to further narrow the range of nodes selected by the location step to that point.

`expr1	expr2`	XPath expression which locates *either* XPath expression `expr1` *or* `expr2`.
`[cond1 boolean cond2]`	Expression in the predicate of an XPath location step that tests two conditions. If `boolean` is `and`, both conditions must be true in order for the predicate as a whole to be true; if `boolean` is `or`, either condition alone, if true, will make the predicate as a whole true.

Terms defined in this chapter

bare name An XPointer whose value is simply the value of an element's ID-type attribute (e.g., `#idCast`, where some element in the document has an ID-type attribute with a vale of `idCast`) is called a *bare name*.

child sequence An XPointer constructed of a path of integers, each integer representing an element's position among siblings of the same parent (e.g., `/1/2/6/2`), is a *child sequence*.

node Any single, complete thing that XPath can address is called a *node*. Nodes can be of type root, element, attribute, comment, PI, namespace, or text.

node-set Many times, the result of following an XPath expression is that it locates more than one node. Such an XPath expression is said to return a *node-set*, that is, a group of nodes satisfying the conditions laid out in the expression.

context node As you move from one node to another, how you would get to some other point changes depending on where you are at the moment. This "where you are at the moment" is called the *context node*.

location path The "set of instructions" in an XPath expression for getting somewhere in a document, perhaps starting from the context node and perhaps starting elsewhere in the document, is the *location path*.

axis The *axis* is the portion of the location path that says which "direction" to move, relative to the context node. These directions represent family relationships among nodes, for example child, parent, ancestor, and sibling.

node test The *node test* portion of a location path identifies the specific node, or group of nodes, along the axis that an XPath expression will move along. You can test for nodes with specific names, nodes of particular types (e.g., text, comment), or processing-instruction nodes with particular targets.

predicate A location path's *predicate* is the portion that determines, of all the nodes returned by the node test, which one(s) should actually be considered to match a given XPath expression.

XML:
Doing It in Style

Content is King, says the mantra of Web-site developers: Beauty is only skin deep, and substance will always triumph over style.

The HTML-based Web has rather spoiled both designers and Web surfers, however much they profess to believe the preceding sentence. People want their sites' content to look good. And for good reason: Given two sites clamoring for the attention of the same audience with the same content, the better-looking one will always thrive.

You've already learned, in Part 1 of Just XML, how to build XML documents; and, in Part 2, how to link them to one another. Part 3 covers two approaches to making your documents look the way you want them to look—using (by now it should be needless to say) the FlixML B movie markup language as a "demonstrator."

The next part, Rolling Your Own Application, explains how to build your own DTDs. Part 5, XML Software, covers the current state of XML authoring and viewing tools.

CHAPTER 7

XML and Cascading Style Sheets

The Web, as I guess you should know by now, has been around for only a few years. But in that brief time it's already acquired a standard "official" method for displaying Web-based documents in a wide variety of appealing formats: cascading style sheets, or CSS.

(Note that there is also an XML-specific style specification, called the Extensible Stylesheet Language, or XSL. I'll cover XSL's "transformational" component, XSLT, in Chapter 8.)

The CSS2 specification

Actually, CSS has now gone through *two* iterations as a standard, with a third in the pipeline. And, as with the other Web standards covered in *Just XML*, the CSS2 spec has been the work of the W3C. You can find it online at:

```
www.w3.org/TR/REC-CSS2
```

Although this version was made official in May 1998, nearly two years ago now, not much software yet takes advantage of its more advanced features; however, because it builds on rather than supplants (with minor exceptions) the earlier CSS1 version, the current versions of the two major Web browsers (Netscape Navigator/Communicator 4+ and Microsoft Internet Explorer 4+) should be able to handle most of the basic to midlevel features, and many of the more advanced ones as well. The Opera browser is also quite compliant, and it's expected that both Netscape and MSIE 6 (when and if they come out) will at last show evidence that CSS2, not CSS1, is the current official version.

> CSS2 is a *big* spec, covering many options whose use I won't be able to cover in detail. But if you follow along in this chapter and then get a copy of the CSS2 spec for your own reference, you should be able to extend what you've learned here to the rest of CSS2's functionality.

The Style Problem

Early in this book, we saw a quick survey of the evolution of newspaper layout from solid blocks of text to early 20th-century use of splashy tabloid headlines. That overview appeared as an example of an early form of markup, but it also contained a cruel but undeniable truth: A finite number of audience eyeballs, confronted with a finite but growing number of things to look at, will *always* turn first in the direction of what's more visually "interesting."

(True, they may not stay turned in that direction if the "interestingness" is no more than skin-deep. And it's also true that some of the least visually arresting Web sites, such as Yahoo! and eBay, have always been among the Web's most popular. Both of these observations don't do anything to dilute the central point, which is simply that a given chunk of content expressed as black-on-white text will *never* claim greater initial attention than the same chunk of content expressed, say, as green-on-orange text.)

For the twenty years prior to the appearance of the Web, the amount and breadth of information on the Net was already amazing. But FTP directory listings, gopher and Veronica searches, and Usenet and e-mail messages were, it must be said, less than interesting as purely visual experiences. Graphical user interface (GUI) software developed to handle those kinds of information helped the situation a little, but not much. HTML, with its mix of document-structure elements and what might be called implied styles—heading elements, bulleted lists, and eventually tables and frames, images, browser plug-ins, and so on— attained much of its early success just because Web pages looked so much cooler than the Internet as it had been experienced to that point.

Eventually, the Web started to get so much attention in the media (and among the Internet community itself) that it drew the interest of design professionals who'd been working in other areas: advertisers, typographers, book designers and publishers, video and audio specialists, etc.

The result was probably inevitable. HTML, designed originally as a fairly simple, straightforward tool for displaying online information, began to shudder under the weight of a thousand new stylistic expectations and outright demands.

And now along comes XML...

In some ways, the style problem for XML might seem even worse than for HTML. XML, after all, is *entirely* about content and how to structure it internally. There are no heading elements built into XML itself, and even if a DTD were to create one for a particular application, there's nothing in the XML syntax that can require it to be displayed *as* a heading. It's just part of the element tree, and will therefore be displayed just like any other node in a "pure XML" browser.

But in other (in my opinion, better and more important) ways, the "problem" for XML is no problem at all.

Freedom from display technology

We've already got multiple *media* capable of displaying Web pages.

There are computer monitors, obviously. Perhaps less obviously, users frequently still require that Web pages be printed, and the printed page comes with built-in limitations that don't exist for browser-driven monitors—for instance, page size and margin limits; no scroll bars for accessing content that lies beyond whatever's currently visible; the need to break pages and provide meaningful headers and footers; and the simple inability of many printers to reproduce colors (either exactly as they appear on the monitor, or even at all). Audio-based browsing facilities exist for translating Web documents for access by the visually impaired. And it seems like not a week goes by that some new Web-enabled device isn't announced: telephones, pagers, televisions, hand-held computers and personal information managers (PIMs), and even household appliances.

If everything on the Web is designed for one medium only, *then only that medium will be able to "see" the whole Web as designed.* This is the fundamental problem with HTML as a document markup standard: The elements must perform both content and display functions. Therefore, if the characteristics of the display technology change, a given page can "break" in a host of more or less ugly ways.

By fully separating content from display considerations, XML makes it possible to keep the content stable and simply use whatever style specification is necessary for a given output medium. When a user clicks a "Print This Page" link, for example, we don't want to print the page as viewed on the monitor—instead, we want to restyle it first according to the limits and capabilities of the printed medium, *then* print it.

Demise of the jack-of-all-trades Webmaster

One of HTML's more blue-sky promises has been that content authors don't need to worry about how things look on the finished Web page. "Just supply the content," so goes the theory, "and it can easily be converted to Web format." There's a whole range of software options to support this theory, from more or less simple word-processing-to-HTML converters and filters, on up to full-blown GUI-based "Web page authoring" kits that function, sort of, like word processors (but have ten times as many toolbar buttons and other GUI gizmos).

In actual practice, this hasn't worked out quite as smoothly as promised.

On one hand, content creators who know that their documents are headed for the Web commonly let themselves get all worked up and distracted by the very thing they weren't (supposedly) going to need to worry about. *Should this heading be an H1 or an H2? How's this table going to look? Figure 1 is aligned left; I think I'll make Figure 2 aligned right, and I wonder if I need to reduce the color depth on this GIF...?*

On the other hand, technical and design people who really *do* have responsibility for making Web pages work have to deal with a myriad of almost-but-not-quite-there differences (some subtle, some not) between the way something looks on paper and how it looks onscreen. Hand-coding HTML tags is still something everyone has to do, despite the large market presences of software packages that claim it's a thing of the past.

Again, separating content from style sidesteps a good deal of all this wasted time and productivity. People can focus on what they already know, and forego the obsessions with stuff they don't *need* to know (and in many cases, aren't equipped to know).

Simplified transformations to new styles

When the style and substance of a Web page are one, there's no way to easily *re*style the substance.

The need for doing this can be practical: Something that doesn't "work" (however you define it) when expressed in one style can work when expressed in another. For example, a menu bar across the bottom of every Web page on a site can be a handy bit of consistency when the pages are short, and by "demoting" the interface gadgetry in this way, you simultaneously enhance the importance of the real content. But this device backfires as soon as you start accumulating pages that are longer than a single display window, because newcomers may not know that the menu is there at all unless they scroll to the bottom. Ripping out the menu's HTML code from the bottom of every document and reinserting it at the top is a *very* tedious and error-prone process.

Remaking the look of a site can also be important for subtler aesthetic reasons—even perhaps for *business* reasons: You want people to keep coming back to your site, even if 75% of its content is exactly the same as it was last month. Human senses don't take long to become bored; tap the same spot on a lover's wrist repeatedly, and what was once a charming, even erotic habit becomes first unnoticeable and perhaps eventually even irritating. "Unnoticeability" is one of the worst fates that can happen to a Web site (although perhaps not so bad as when it happens to a lover).

Finally, if content and style are coupled, customizing a Web page for different "views"—either for different classes of users, or for any given user on different visits—is a nightmare. Some of this can be done with relatively advanced technology (cookies, Java applets and applications, server-side databases of user preferences, and the like), but they've all got drawbacks—not the least that they *are* advanced, sufficiently so that their practitioners are but a tiny minority of Web-site developers.[39]

If you've got your Web page's content broken apart from its style, though, it's almost trivial to perform such magic feats as:

- showing someone's bank account number to the account's owner, but hiding it from everyone else;
- reconstituting a page's look on the fly when the user indicates that he or she has moved from a desktop PC with a 19" monitor to a handheld computer with a little-bitty 3" x 5" liquid crystal display; and
- completely reworking your Web site's appearance, from colors and fonts to the placement of navigational aids and important notes.

Simplified markup

If you've ever examined the HTML source code for even a moderately complex Web page, you'll see that lots of elements have lots of attributes whose only pur-

---

39. I don't mean to start a war over the term "developers," which is frequently meant to be synonymous with "programmers." Here I'm using the term in a more general sense: people who develop Web sites at least using plain old HTML, on up through the elite, who are—yes—true programmers.

pose is to specify display characteristics: the body of the page may have a background color and/or image; font styles (including font family, size, and enhancements like bolding and italics) are switched on and off repeatedly; table formatting is nearly an arcane design specialty all its own; image heights, widths, and placement are defined everywhere; odd little bits like "single-pixel transparent GIFs"; and empty table columns or rows are used to position other stuff in the display without containing any content of their own.

Anyone with an interest in the way things look, in short, should be horrified at the appearance of a typical HTML source document. Not only is it cluttered—the lists of attribute/value pairs frequently take up more physical space than the elements, sometimes even the content itself (and takes longer to download, to boot); but in addition, it hinders achieving the real goal of the markup (to illuminate the document's underlying structure).

Take all those display-only attributes out of a document, put them elsewhere, and *voila!*: The markup actually makes sense again.

The Style Sheet Solution

Starting in 1996, the W3C has promulgated a fairly simple way around the content-bound-to-style obstacle: *As much as possible*, place all the formatting instructions for a Web page in a place separate from all the content.

I had to add the qualifying italics in the previous paragraph because, of course, formatting in HTML is always inherent in most of the elements. If an HTML author uses an <h1> tag, his or her intention is plainly to make the heading "more important," visually as well as semantically, than text marked with an <h2> or <h3>–all of them being "more important" (at least visually) than plain old body text.

But with the formatting and other display information maintained in a separate location (called a style sheet), just about any default display characteristics of just about any HTML element type can be *overridden*. You can make your body text larger than your headings; set your page margins to some width other than the limits of the browser window; indent the first lines of paragraphs; position images and other layout elements precisely on the page; display text strings as SMALL CAPS without having to set and reset the font size; and do, in fact, pretty much whatever you want with the look of your pages.

Cascading style sheets

The W3C-approved method for separating form from content is known as cascading style sheets, or CSS. As I mentioned in the box at the beginning of this chapter, the CSS spec is now in its second version, with a third waiting in the wings, but the general principles remain the same:

- Separate the style information *physically* from the content that it's meant to describe; and
- Separate the style information *syntactically* from the constructs used for marking up the document for other purposes.

Physical separation

In an HTML file, you can place the style information, if you want, within the document that it's meant to describe. Even if you decide to do so, though, the style information needs to be at the top of the document to be effective. (Browsers "read" and display HTML documents from top to bottom. If a document contains a formatting instruction for a particular element at line 10, say, and that element appears in the document on any of lines 1 through 9, the element content at that "preformatted" location will have the default appearance, while all subsequent occurrences of the element will follow the instructions provided on line 10.)

More often, formatting instructions are kept in a completely separate file from the document. This not only reinforces the different functions of the two kinds of information, it also enhances the convenience of maintaining them and makes the style information available to *other* documents, so that multiple pages across a site can share the same look.

In the context of an XML document, which is limited strictly to content and structure-defining markup, you will not generally find[40] any style information in the document itself. Instead, *all* the style information resides in a separate file, to which the XML document points with a processing instruction.

---

40. Sorry for the weasel words. There is in fact a standard method for incorporating Extensible Stylesheet Language transformations/formatting within a document. But this is not likely to be used much in practice. Furthermore, there's no way at all to embed CSS styles within an XML document.

Syntactic separation

CSS formatting instructions don't look anything at all like HTML or XML tags. If you were to stumble mistakenly into a style sheet, knowing what you already do about XML, there'd be no doubt that you're not in Kansas anymore.

This is a blessing of sorts with CSS1 and 2—it makes it difficult to accidentally misread style information as regular tags and attributes. It's also something of a curse, however, because to create formatting instructions, you've got to learn a completely new syntax. (The XSL specification, to be covered in Chapter 8, will minimize or eliminate this learning curve: XSL style sheets *are* XML documents.)

About that "cascading"...

What, you may be wondering, is this thing that cascades?

To understand the answer to this question, it will help you to think of who might have a say in how a Web document is (or should be) displayed. There are three parties to this debate, as I guess you could call it; they're shown in the following diagram:

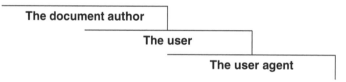

- The document author has a variety of ways to influence the decision of how to display a document. At the most basic, of course, if the document is marked up in HTML, he or she can "require" that it be displayed with a certain background image, that links be displayed in one color and body text in another, and so on. (By using a style sheet, the author has many other options in controlling the display, as we'll see, regardless whether the document is marked up in HTML or in XML.)
- The user is, of course, you or I sitting at our keyboards, mouse fingers all a-twitch. All major browsers come with facilities for applying our own tastes to the way that Web pages display; we can tell the browser to use certain font families as the default, for example, or to suppress image loading, or to use certain colors for page backgrounds. We can tell the browser, in effect, "I don't care what anybody else says, I'm in control here"—even to the point of ignoring *any* style sheet or other formatting instructions.

- Finally, the "user agent" (UA) is the CSS spec's term for what most of us would simply call the browser: the software that acts as our agent in accessing and/or viewing a document. In the absence of any other style information, a UA that plays by the rules of the official HTML specification is expected to apply *default* style behavior to each HTML element type.

The step-like arrangement of these three influences on a document's style provides the most basic *cascade* of decision-making: If a style is specified by an author, use it; otherwise, see if the user has declared any choice in the matter; finally, if the other two don't have anything particular to say about it, let the browser (the UA) apply its default styles. The stylistic decisions, as it were, flow downhill from the author to the user to the browser.

It's not quite this simple in many cases, and the CSS2 spec provides a formula of sorts for determining "who wins" if conflicts occur.

1. Read all available style specifications.

This involves checking to see if, for each element type encountered, either the author or the user has specified a style. If not, use the default style for that element type. If only the author or only the user has specified a style, use that one; if they've both specified a style, "cascade" down to Rule #2.

2. Look for "important" declarations.

CSS1 and 2 provide ways for authors and users to declare, "Even if there's an overriding style specification for this element, don't let *my* specification be overridden." If either the author or user has raised one of these "important" flags, apply that style. If neither has, "cascade" to rule #3.

3. Look for more specific declarations.

Let's say that, assuming no "important" declarations have been made, the author's style for an element type specifies that its content should be displayed in a certain font family. The user, on the other hand, has specified that elements of that type are to be displayed in a totally different font family, using a specific font size and color. The more specific declaration—the user's, in this case—wins.

4. Rank by order received.

All other things being equal (conflicting style specifications are present from the same source—author, user, or agent; they've got the same importance; and they share the same specificity), the last specification "in" is used. For instance, if a style sheet has two conflicting formatting instructions for a heading element type, use the second one. (Note that there can be only one "last one in"; therefore, this rule acts as an absolute tie-breaker.)

Taken together, these four rules act like a stack of gold-miner's sieves. As you shake them all together, fewer and fewer (and smaller and smaller) chunks filter—dare we say, "cascade"?—down to the next level, which catches the very last grains of gold.

Declaring a CSS for XML Documents

To use a CSS to tell a browser how to display an XML document, you've got to tell the browser where to find the style sheet. The way to do this is to include at the top of the XML document a PI with a URL that points to the style sheet; something like this:

```
<?xml-style sheet type="text/css" href="uri_of_stylesheet"?>
```

The `type` specification declares that the document being pointed to contains text, and that the text specifically contains CSS formatting instructions. (Technically, this is known as a MIME-type declaration. MIME is an acronym for the Multi-purpose Internet Mail Extensions standard for Internet content formats.) The `href`, of course, identifies the URL of the style sheet itself.

Basic CSS Syntax

A style sheet consists of one or more *rules*, which as you may expect from the term, lay down the law: Treat *this* element *this* way, and treat *that* element *that* way. A collection of two or more rules is called a *ruleset*. Each rule contains two components, a *selector* and a *property*.

- The rule's selector identifies the *element type* whose content will be affected by the rule.
- Properties, as the term implies, are visual or other characteristics that the selector will have once the rule has been applied. If the selector's contents

are text, for example, the font family, size, and color are all potential properties that can be established with a rule.

Here's the general format of a rule:

```
selectorlist { propertylist }
```

The `selectorlist` is one or more element names, *without* the surrounding angle brackets (< and > characters). Given the FlixML `<releaseyear>` tag, for instance, the selector would be `releaseyear`. If you want the rule to apply to more than one selector, separate them with commas. (More about this later in this chapter, in the section titled "Multiple selectors, same properties.") Note that the list of available selectors will depend on the element types used in a given document (or in the document's DTD, if it's a valid XML document).

The `propertylist` term is, of course, one or more properties that you want to apply to the element type(s) in `selectorlist`. If you need to apply more than one property to `selectorlist`, separate them with semicolons. Note that the characters surrounding `propertylist` are "curly braces," not parentheses or square brackets.

At this point, you also need to know that each property in `propertylist` consists of two parts: the property name and the property's value. These terms are separated from each other by a colon. The list of allowable property names is defined by the CSS specification; under CSS2 there are well over a hundred of them, ranging from the fairly obvious (`background`, `color`, `border`, `font`) to the esoteric (`azimuth`, `marker-offset`, `orphans`, `z-index`). Most of the properties affect the visual display of elements; quite a few of them affect the aural "display" as well, for use in applications like browsers for the visually impaired. Many but not all (or even most) of the allowable values are prescribed, too (such as `top`, `bottom`, `left`, and `right` for the `caption-side` property).

Rules can spill over onto more than one line in the style sheet, but the last character on each line must be either a semicolon or closing brace (`}`).

A caveat, before an example...

Please don't leap to any conclusions about what your current browser will or will not do as you work your way through the following example (and those that follow *it*). Current browser support for CSS might best be described as fair-to-middling. Simply opening an XML document, styled with CSS, in a browser that is advertised by its vendor as both "XML-compliant" and "CSS-compliant" will not at all guarantee that the content will be rendered in the expected form. An excellent resource about browser compliance with CSS, for XML developers as well as HTML developers, is the webreview.com "Master List" at:

```
            www.webreview.com/wr/pub/guides/style/mastergrid.html
    As of this writing, a somewhat more up-to-date reference is RichIn-
    Style.com's "browser bugs" list, which you can find at:
            www.richinstyle.com/bugs/table.html
```

An example

Given the above, the following might be a set of CSS2 rules for displaying FlixML
documents:

```
flixinfo { background-color: yellow }
title { font-family: sans-serif ; font-size: large ;
    background-color: white }
leadcast { font-family: sans-serif ; font-size: medium ;
    display: list-item ;
    list-item-image: url("images/bluemarble.gif") }
plotsummary {font-family: serif ; font-size: medium ;
    display: block }
```

All of which would tell the browser, respectively:

- For each `flixinfo` element, set the overall background to yellow.
- For each `title` element, use a sans serif font, displayed in large size, and set
  the background to white.
- For each `leadcast` element, use a medium-sized sans serif font; display all
  contents of this element in a list form; and mark each list item using the
  "bluemarble.gif" image as a bullet.
- Display each `plotsummary` element as a block of text, wrapping as necessary,
  in a medium serif font.

What happens to nested elements?

This one's easy. Most properties will apply to immediate children of the element
they're applied to, unless any of them provide overriding values. (This is referred
to as *inheritance*.) In this case, the property (or properties) is switched off for the
duration of that child, then returned to whatever was in effect previously.

In the above example, the background color for the `flixinfo` element was
set to yellow. Since `flixinfo` is the root element for a typical FlixML document,
the entire document will have a yellow background—with the exception of any
`title` element(s), where the background will be white.

Also note the rule for the `leadcast` element, whose properties are set in
such a way that any character content will be displayed as a bulleted list item,

using a graphic image (bluemarble.gif) instead of an ordinary bullet. This will force not just the `leadcast` element itself (which has no text content of its own, only subordinate elements) to be bulleted in this way, but its children as well. This might seem reasonable because we might well want the `leadcast/male` and `leadcast/female` descendants to be bulleted. However, there can be a couple of problems with using catch-all style specifications such as this.

First, we might *not* want `male` items and `female` items to be displayed in exactly the same way. Depending on the effects you're trying to achieve, probably a better approach than that used in the example would be *not* to specify an over-all display-type for the main `leadcast` element, just for the individual lists—or to provide overrides for children where you wanted something different.

More Advanced CSS2 Syntax

Of course there are lots of other hoops that CSS2 can jump through than those out-lined in the preceding sections. A sampling of some of these extra tricks follows.

B Alert!

Ms. .45 (1980, Rochelle Films)

A B movie to torture the bleeding heart of any good survivor of the 1960s, *Ms. .45* confronts you with the following dilemma: Knowing what we do about the horrors of loaded guns in the hands of innocents, *why* does it nonetheless make us feel so satisfied every time a sexually assaulted young woman pulls the trigger and bumps off not only her assailant, but over a dozen other men as well? When feminist ideals conflict with a desire for gun control, which should "win"?

While the main title is catchy, the alternative title under which this film was released, *Angel of Vengeance*, sums up the theme better. A shy, mousy, mute seamstress named Thana (Zoe Tamerlis), in New York's garment district, is assaulted one afternoon—not once, but *twice*, by two different strangers. After overcoming the second hoodlum, she takes his gun on stalking rounds of the city, looking for other men on whom to vent her pent-up anger. Many of these roamings occur while she's depositing the body of assailant #2 in various litter receptacles. Over time, our heroine grows ever less shy—culminating in the final scene, a costume party that she attends dressed as a nun (beneath her robes, some *major* undergarments—the .45 of course—tucked in a garter).

> It sounds like a pretty gruesome movie, but in truth it is not. The dismemberment of #2 in Thana's bathroom is implied rather than really shown, and almost none of the many gunshots seems to cause any actual wounds (although the victims stagger, lurch, and heave quite melodramatically). Despite some trademark B-movie touches—pale, washed-out colors by day; murky, impenetrable shadows by night—the film's material, in retrospect, manages to rise above them to make a real social point.
>
> Favorite scene: seamstress readying for party, loading her weapon, kissing bullets one at a time as she inserts them into the magazine.
>
> Key performance: Phil the dog (played by Bogey), who drives his mistress (Thana's neighbor) batty with his ever-yapping curiosity about the contents of Thana's refrigerator.
>
> (You'll note that neither my favorite scene nor the key performance have anything to do with "a real social point." Hey, it *is* a B movie!)

Attribute-specific selectors

Consider this fragment of a FlixML document:

```
<title role="main">Ms. 45</title>
<title role="alt">Angel of Vengeance</title>
```

This pair of `title` elements gives two names by which a particular B movie is known—obviously the main or most common title, and an alternate title by which it is known in a re-release or other editions (such as video).

You can apply different styles for elements such as this when their attributes have specific values, by modifying the *selector* portion of the rule as follows:

```
selector[attrname="value"]
```

So, in the above example, we could place different emphasis on the two kinds of title using rules like these:

```
title[role="main"] { font-size: x-large }
title[role="alt"] { font-size: large }
```

which, of course, displays the main title in very large letters and the alternate title(s) in a somewhat smaller font. In this case, the two titles for *Ms. .45* might appear in the browser like this:

Ms. .45
Angel of Vengeance

"Generating" content for non-content elements

An extremely useful—indeed, almost indispensable—feature of CSS2 for XML style-sheet developers enables you to add text to elements that don't, in themselves, contain any text.

For instance, here is another fragment of a FlixML document for *Ms. .45*:

```
<cast>
    <leadcast>
        <female>Zoe Tamerlis</female>
    </leadcast>
    <othercast>
        <male>Steve Singer</male>
        <male>Jack Thibeau</male>
    </othercast>
</cast>
```

We could, of course, establish different rules for the two types of cast, "lead" and "other," something like this:

```
leadcast { font-family: sans-serif; font-size: x-large }
othercast { font-family: sans-serif; font-size: large }
```

This might result in a display something like the following:

Zoe Tamerlis
Steve Singer
Jack Thibeau

How would someone browsing this document know that the three names displayed above describe the cast, as opposed to crew members? (Note that there's no character content in the `leadcast` and `othercast` elements themselves—only in the child `female` and `male`.)

CSS2 includes a facility called *generated content* that gets us out of this jam; it inserts text into a display just as if the content were physically present in the document. (The inserted content needn't be text, by the way—it can be anything that you want to use as boilerplate. For example, you can automatically insert a logo at the head of each document, by specifying the URL of the logo image.) Here's an example:

```
leadcast:before { content: "Starring: ";
    font-size: large; font-enhancement: underline }
leadcast { font-family: sans-serif; font-size: x-large }
othercast:before { content: "and featuring: ";
    font-size: large; font-enhancement: underline }
othercast { font-family: sans-serif; font-size: large }
```

The ":before" (note the colon) is called a *pseudo-element*, and when used with the content property, it causes the indicated content, in the indicated style, to be inserted *before* each occurrence of the designated element. In our browser, this would be the result of the above:

Starring:
Zoe Tamerlis
and featuring:
Steve Singer
Jack Thibeau

There's also an :after pseudo-element that is used for inserting content *following* the given element. This might be useful in our cast listing by separating the two kinds of cast with a blank line (CSS2 uses the special "escaped" string /A to indicate a newline), as follows:

```
leadcast:before { content: "Starring: ";
    font-size: large; font-enhancement: underline }
leadcast { font-family: sans-serif; font-size: x-large }
leadcast:after { content: "/A" }
othercast:before { content: "and featuring: ";
    font-size: large; font-enhancement: underline }
othercast { font-family: sans-serif; font-size: large }
```

which would look like this in the browser:

Starring:
Zoe Tamerlis

and featuring:
Steve Singer
Jack Thibeau

> **"The paths are many but the way is one"**
>
> Not surprisingly, CSS2—like most Web standards—gives you a variety of tools to accomplish a given task.
>
> The preceding example, adding a blank line following a given element, is one such case. For example, you can alternatively adjust the margin above the `othercast` element to be something greater than the default amount. This would actually be the preferred solution to the indicated problem.
>
> The "add a blank line" example did have one virtue, though: it let me tell you about the "`/A`"!

Hiding element content

Normally, *all* of a document's actual content will be displayed in the browser. There may be cases when you want not to show the content, however. In FlixML's case, for instance, there's an element type that lets you include a video clip. Normally you'd want this clip to be playable, of course—probably using a user-actuated hyperlink. But suppose you wanted to hide it in cases where the film's rating by the Motion Picture Association of America (MPAA) is "NC-17" or "X." (Given the nature of the beast, yes, there are some B movies that fall into these categories.)

If you also know that the `video` element has an `mpaarating` attribute, you could code a ruleset like the following:

```
video[mpaarating="NC-17"]{ visibility: hidden }
video[mpaarating="X"] { visibility: hidden }
```

The special `visible` property (which has allowable values of `visible`, `hidden`, and `collapse`–the latter useful if you want to hide a table row or column) controls whether an element is or is not displayed. If the film's rating matched one of the two proscribed values, the clip would simply be inaccessible.

User interface controls

CSS2 even has a handful of properties that can be used for customizing the user interface when browsing a document, or parts of one. One of these (which you'll probably want to use with care, for reasons I'll go into in a moment) is the `cursor` property. You can give it a value using such reserved words as `crosshair` (which looks like a + sign), `pointer` (the familiar "pointing hand" cursor shape that browsers use to indicate a hyperlink), and `wait` (an hourglass or clock face).

Interestingly, though, you can also designate a custom cursor shape by providing the URL of an image to be used:

```
video { cursor: url("images/camera.cur") }
audio { cursor: url("images/speaker.cur") }
plotsummary { cursor: url("images/book.cur") }
```

This would replace whatever the default cursor is with, respectively, a little movie camera icon when the cursor is over the `videoclip` element; a loudspeaker icon when over the `audioclip` element; and an "open book"-type image whenever somewhere over the contents of the `plotsummary` element.

It's easy to see, though, that doing too much cursor-swapping—at least with images that are outside what the browser is normally equipped to provide—can be overdone. At the very least, there'd be a lag when the new cursor's image is first accessed; users already have to wait awhile to retrieve real content, after all, and I doubt that they'd be greatly charmed by the prospect of a "Contacting site...Reading file..." progress meter in the browser status bar just because they jostled their mouse a bit.

Aural style sheets

The W3C community has a history of concern about Web accessibility by means other than the standard video display computer monitor. In CSS2, one way of addressing this concern yourself is by using special properties that "render" elements audibly rather than visually. Typically, such *aural style sheets* would be used for making a document usable by the blind or visually impaired. (However, note that they can also be used for special-purpose applications such as conference presentations and, as the CSS2 spec suggests, in-car Web browsing systems.)

Hardware considerations

Be aware that nothing in an aural style sheet causes the contents of a document or elements to be heard automatically. Aural style sheets are effective only when the user's "browser"—including the hardware configuration on which it runs—is one that is equipped to handle them. It doesn't do any good to specify the vocal qualities in which text is read aloud, for example, if the user's environment doesn't include a sound card, speakers, and text-to-speech software.

Let's say that we want to make a FlixML document's `dialog` element content (which is used for quoting memorable dialog from a film) capable of being read aloud to this user community. A basic, non-aural rule for the element might be something like this:

```
dialog { font-size: medium }
```

Obviously this has no meaning in an aural context, so we could specify other properties that do make sense, as in:

```
dialog { speak: normal; volume: normal;
    voice-family: cronkite; cue-before: url("intro.au") }
```

This would tell the speech-to-text interpreter to read aloud the content of the `dialog` element, in a normal volume, using the `cronkite` voice family (which is characterized by the CSS2 spec as "a kind of 'audio font'")—and before starting to read it, play an audio cue (perhaps a simple "ding," or maybe even a recording that says something like, "Dialog upcoming!") that a reading is about to begin.

One thing that can trip up current-level text-to-speech converters—which aren't perfect by any means—is that some words simply aren't pronounced the way the software might guess. Obvious examples are acronyms, words in a language other than what the software is tuned to "hear," and proper nouns such as people's names. If there may be confusion on the part of the software, you can instruct it via the aural style sheet to spell out an element's contents, like so:

```
leadcast { cue-before: url("starring.au")
    speak: spell-out pause-after: 2 }
othercast { cue-before: url("featuring.au")
    speak: spell-out pause-after: 2 }
female { cue-before: url("fcast.au")
    voice-family: diana; pause-after: 1 }
male { cue-before: url("mcast.au")
    voice-family: charles; pause-after: 1 }
```

The `spell-out` value of the `speak` property tells the software to "render" the element's content one letter at a time.

There are lots of other options available using aural style sheets: speech rate, azimuth (the point in space where the sound seems to be "coming from"), and so on. I encourage you to explore the aural style sheets section of the CSS2 spec and make use of it to make your XML documents accessible to the broadest possible range of visitors to your Web sites.

CSS2 Shortcuts

After you've used CSS2 for a while, you'll immediately appreciate the availability of some quicker methods to achieve a couple of purposes.

The universal selector

When you want to apply a particular style to *all* elements in the tree, you can use an asterisk (*) as the selector. Note that this can be used as if it were a real element, and so can include an attribute as well, like this:

```
*[role="alt"] { font-family: serif }
```

says to apply this style to *all* elements with a `role` attribute whose value is `alt`.

In fact, to use the universal selector with an attribute/value pair, you can omit the asterisk altogether. The following rule is therefore functionally identical to the above:

```
[role="alt"] { font-family: serif }
```

Shorthand properties

CSS2 assigns many properties that operate on some general classes of "thing." Take, for example, document background styles; you've got these choices:

- `background-color`, to set a color for the background;
- `background-image`, to give the URL of an image to be used for the background;
- `background-repeat`, to specify whether the image (if there is one) is to be "tiled" (that is, repeated across or down the page);
- `background-attachment`, for indicating whether a background image (if there is one) is to remain fixed on the page when the user moves up and down or left and right (by using the scrollbar, arrow keys, and so on); and
- `background-position`, which assigns the positioning of a background image (if there is one).

To specify that a FlixML document's background image is to be tiled, and will scroll with the page as the user moves around on it, you could construct a CSS2 rule like the following:

```
flixinfo {background-image: url("images/beehive.gif");
    background-repeat: repeat;
    background-attachment: scroll }
```

While this works, it's somewhat tedious (hence error-prone) to type, and is also kind of a challenge to read (especially when embedded in a lengthy style sheet). For these reasons, CSS2 provides a number of *shorthand properties* that can be used in place of full property names. As an example, the above rule could alternatively be coded like this:

```
flixinfo {background: url("images/beehive.gif");
    repeat; scroll }
```

The `background` property "stands in for" all the specific properties. Any property values not specified with those of the shorthand property (`background-color` and `background-position`, in this case) assume their default values.

Multiple selectors, same properties

When you want to assign the same properties to two or more selectors, instead of defining separate rules—one per selector—you can combine them in the same rule by combining the separate selectors into a single comma-separated list of selectors.

This example:

```
title, leadcast {font-family: sans-serif, font-size: large }
leadcast {font-color: blue}
```

will display both the `title` element and `leadcast` element with the indicated font characteristics.

Note also in this example that the two rules for the `leadcast` element will be "merged" into a single style, the result of which is to distinguish its display from that of the `title` element by *only* the color. (The `title` element will use the default font color, usually black.)

Elements within elements

While not really a shortcut, there's one other CSS2 option that I wanted to mention here because of its similarity to (and possible confusion with) the "multiple selectors" syntax just described.

As an example, in a FlixML document there are both `leadcast` and `othercast` elements for listing a film's stars and supporting cast, respectively. Both of these elements have the same possible *child* elements: `male`, `female`, and `animal`. Any of these, of course, can be styled using something like the following:

```
male { font: 14pt Helvetica }
```

(Note that font is a shorthand property for font-size, font-family, and so on.) The problem with this is that the rule will apply to all male elements, regardless of whether they're in the lead or supporting casts.

To get around this (assuming, of course, that this effect is not what you're after), as the selector you can specify a list of selectors—without the commas used for multiple selectors—to indicate that you want the rule's properties applied only when the last element in the list exists *within the context of* the elements that precede it in the list. So the ruleset:

```
leadcast male { font: 14pt Helvetica }
othercast male { font: 12pt Helvetica }
```

says to apply one style only to male elements that are descendants of the leadcast element, and a different (smaller, in this case) style to those that are descendants of othercast.

Selector mania

Throughout this chapter, I've only hinted at the variety of options available to you in designating which elements are to receive a given style treatment—the selector portion of a rule. For instance, as the selector you can name an element that *follows* a particular element or is a *child* of it (as opposed to being a descendant); an element over which the user's mouse cursor is currently hovering; or an element with a particular ID value.

By all means, familiarize yourself with the "Selectors" portion (Section 5) of the CSS2 spec. This will minimize many headaches as you strive to customize your documents' look in meaningful[41] ways.

Summary

This chapter introduced you to the concepts of style sheets and why they're so important to XML applications. It covered version 2 of the Cascading Style Sheets (CSS2) specification in some detail.

---

41.   However you want to define that term.

Terms defined in this chapter

user agent The term *user agent*, as used in the CSS2 spec, refers to what we normally think of as a browser. However, it may also be a non-display-type browser, such as a text-to-speech audio unit, a Braille device, and so on. The user agent acts as the user's agent (hence the term) in "reading" Web resources through a CSS2 lens.

cascade The *cascade* (as in the term "cascading style sheets") refers to the hierarchy of "decisions" about how a Web page's components should look—beginning with the style sheet's author, this decision cascades down to the user and, if the user has no preference, then down to the defaults set by the browser (user agent).

rule A CSS2 style specification. It includes a selector and one or more properties (see below).

ruleset All of a style sheet's rules, taken together.

selector That part of a rule that identifies the portions of the document to which a given style is to be applied.

property The part of a rule that identifies the style characteristic(s), such as font size, position on the page, margins and so on, that are to be applied to the rule's selector (see above).

pseudo-element CSS2 identifies several *pseudo-elements*, such as `:before` and `:after`, which can be used to qualify the selector in some way. For example, a selector like `title:before` says that the property specified in this rule is to be applied *before* the `title` element.

aural style sheet A style sheet that describes how an audio-based user agent is to treat a given document's contents.

universal selector To specify that a rule is to apply to all elements in a document, or all elements with a certain attribute/value, use the *universal selector* (an asterisk) in place of the element name portion of the selector.

shorthand properties Many properties address specific facets of the same kind of "thing": the font, the background, and so on. Rather than requiring you to spell out every one of these facets as separate properties in the rule, CSS2 provides *shorthand properties* that let you specify the overall "thing" alone. For instance, the `font-family` and `font-size` properties can be specified separately; or they can be specified all at once with the `font` shorthand property.

CHAPTER 8

Transforming XML with Style: XSL

In the last chapter, you learned why the separation of document content from document style is important. You also learned the basics of using the CSS2 standard for describing display and other style characteristics of an XML document.

As I mentioned in that chapter, one of the drawbacks of using CSS2 as a style mechanism for XML is that its syntax is so foreign to that of XML's own "native tongue." Once you've grown even minimally accustomed to XML markup, all the new rules about using curly braces, colons, semicolons, and commas may feel something like being required to learn Hebrew script in order to publish books in Japanese.

If CSS2 isn't therefore to your taste, you'll be glad to know that you have another option, the Extensible Stylesheet Language (XSL), whose syntax *is* that of XML itself. This chapter covers the basics of using XSL for rendition of your XML documents, and will cover some of the finer nuances as well.

Why XSL(T)?

Before I even give you so much as the location of the current official XSL documents, I want to spend just a little time talking about the reasons why XSL is the way it is.

Style by *transforming*

For the time being—certainly in this chapter, but also in most outside references as well—you'll see the Extensible Stylesheet Language referred to not just as XSL, but as XSL*T*. The extra "T" stands for "Transformations," and the reason for it is that the current, widely accepted standard for "styling" XML is really a standard for turning it into something else.

This notion caused a certain amount of consternation at the time it was first introduced, and for that matter it still does. People were used to CSS2's approach, which is essentially simply to ornament elements and attributes in some way, and the prospect of having to transform XML in order just to display it a certain way was (to put it mildly) distasteful to many observers.

But if you think about it, you *must* transform XML into something else if you want to display it; as I've been hammering away at you, XML is all about structure and content, and doesn't know anything at all about being displayed. Using CSS2 to do so, as in the previous chapter, is kind of like donning a pair of those goofy cardboard red-and-green cellophane eyeglasses to "make things 3-D": You've altered the surface appearance, but what's underneath is still the same old orange-and-blue jumble.[42]

Along comes XSLT. With it, and XSLT-aware software, you can turn any XML document into easily displayable HTML, into "official" XSL formatting objects, indeed into almost any other form of XML, including completely different vocabularies. It's even been used to turn XML documents into less-structured forms of data, like comma-separated-value text files.

Furthermore, XSLT is by no means restricted to turning one form of XML into a completely different one; its effects can be much subtler but just as powerful, by *restructuring* the content of a given document. For instance, although picture captions in a document might always appear in an element following the one for the picture itself, you can use XSLT to "move the captions" so they precede the corresponding picture elements. You can generate an entire table of contents for a document, effectively by displaying the major categories *twice* (i.e., once for the table of contents and once wherever the content is actually located). Such sorts of rearrangement are utterly outside the scope of CSS2.

---

42.   Not that that's not important or desirable in many cases—I'm just saying, philosophically, that it's kind of an inelegant halfway measure.

CSS2, in short, simply makes XML look like something else. XSLT can make it *become* something else.

Separate transforming and display standards

In early 1999, what had previously been one working-draft standard, simply called XSL, split into two. One half became XSLT; the other, still called XSL, specifies a CSS2-compatible set of displayable "things," called formatting objects, which can be used as the output of an XSLT transformation.

There's no particular reason why you *must* hook up an XSL formatting-objects (FO) back end to an XSLT front end, though. Indeed, the most recent working draft of the FO spec is unbelievably long—over 200 pages—leading some people to wonder if any vendors will ever provide software to support it all.

This chapter takes an ostensibly neutral stance on the issue of using XSL FO vs. other types of output—"neutral" in the sense that I'll tell you where to find the FO standard; "ostensibly" in that that will be virtually the last time I mention it.

Where are the specs?

The XSLT specification, which became a full W3C Recommendation in November, 1999, is at:

    www.w3.org/TR/xslt

The XSL FO specification, still (in January 2000) a Working Draft, is at:

    www.w3.org/TR/xsl

Note particularly that the latter retains the plain-old "XSL" designation. This does not make one of the specs a subset of the other, or better than the other, or responsible for the good behavior of the other;[43] in fact they aren't necessarily related at all, except that one (XSLT) can be used to create the other.

---

43. Like the saying goes, "You're not the boss of me!"

Syntax

As I mentioned at the very beginning of this chapter, XSL and XSLT are expressed in "native" XML format, using the familiar syntax of elements, attributes, entities, and so on. This was felt to be desirable because people who'd invested a lot of time, energy, and possibly expense learning all about XML didn't want to turn around and have to learn CSS2's syntax, as well.

I won't detail the XSLT syntax just yet, but there's one potential pitfall to learning it. (And in this case, advanced readers may be at a disadvantage not shared by more basic-level ones.) That is that it's tempting to think that "this XSLT instruction does this," and "this one does the other thing." But XSLT is not a programming language, any more than XML itself (or CSS2, for that matter) is. You don't use XSLT to *do* something; you use it to *describe the desired outcome of some process that* does *do something.* Your XSLT stylesheet requires some software—an XSLT processor—to actually create the output. It's like a recipe that doesn't tell the chef to "beat the mixture in a large bowl with a wooden spoon for five to seven minutes, or until smooth." All it says is, "Prepare a smooth batter," leaving it up to the chef to know (or figure out) a good way to do so.

Differences between CSS2 and XSL

I've already spilled the larger pot of beans on this issue: Unlike CSS2's, XSL's syntax will be more or less accessible to you if you've gotten the hang of regular XML documents. All the familiar < and > characters, attribute-value specifications, and so on have been carried straight through into the style language.

There are other, less immediately obvious (but just as profound) differences between CSS2 and XSL, as well.

Lineage

CSS2 is, of course, a direct descendant of the first version of the cascading style sheets standard, CSS1. CSS1 was made up out of whole cloth, as it were; while the notation is similar to bits and pieces of other computer and text-processing languages, they weren't languages that the great majority of Web developers were likely to have had some familiarity with.

By contrast, XSL began life as a subset of a language known as the Document Style Semantics and Specification Language, or DSSSL.[44] By itself, this isn't particularly significant (I'll bet that almost none, if any, of *Just XML*'s readers "speaks" DSSSL); what *is* significant is that DSSSL is the preferred styling language for SGML documents and is SGML-like in its hierarchical structure. This made it a natural candidate as the "philosophic" parent for XSL. However, DSSSL was not an SGML-based language, but one derived from the Scheme language, which featured copious use of parentheses and no angle brackets. This made DSSSL unsuitable as XSL's *syntactic* parent.

Structure-awareness

In CSS2, a few facilities acknowledge that elements don't exist in a vacuum: they're contained by, and themselves contain, other elements. For instance, as I mentioned toward the end of the previous chapter, it's possible to chain together elements as selectors in such a way as to indicate that a style should be applied to Element B only if it's a descendant of Element A. On the whole, though, CSS2 is notably structure-ignorant; styles apply to *elements*, not to *portions of the element tree*. (That's why it works equally well with XML and HTML.)

XSL reverses this priority, both by implication (XSL style sheets *look like*— indeed, *are*—XML) and by design. Not only can you redesign the appearance of an XML document with XSL; you can also create the effect of having redesigned its structure.

Structure-reordering

Not only does XSL "know about" XML documents' tree structure, it can virtually jump through hoops in rearranging this structure. There's no equivalent at all for this facility in CSS2.

There are a few fairly trivial uses of the ability to restructure an element tree. For instance, given the following FlixML fragment:

```
<castmember maleid="someguyY">Y</castmember>
   . . .
<castmember maleid="someguyX">X</castmember>
```

---

44. Both the name and acronym are a little mind-numbing. I'm very happy to have "XSL" instead of "DSSSL-Lite" or some such. The acronym is pronounced to rhyme with "whistle," by the way.

you could write an XSL transformation to position X's name before Y's in the output. You could turn the `maleid` attributes into elements. And so on.

More powerful, especially in the long run, is XSLT's ability to transform a given XML document into a different XML vocabulary—a different version of the same dialect, or a 100% different dialect altogether. Between the first edition of *Just XML* and this one, FlixML has undergone many changes as I (and, ahem, readers of that edition) found gaps in my understanding of XML; with XSLT, I can easily turn an early-version FlixML document into a current-version one, or vice versa. Furthermore, if you've developed a different XML dialect for describing all movies, not just the Bs—using completely different element and attribute names, tree structure, and so on—we can *exchange* documents with one another by passing them through XSLT filters to convert from one dialect to another.

Sophisticated, quasi-programming features

With CSS2, you have a wide variety of ways to identify which elements will have particular styles applied to them. Yet even if you don't need to restructure the element tree, convert one XML vocabulary to another, and so on, you still (especially if you're a programmer) may be frustrated by CSS2's essential dumbness as a "programming" tool.

Now, don't panic. I'm not going to run off at the mouth, or the keyboard, about arcane topics like C `structs` and Java classes. I'm simply talking about the general kinds of things that you want to accomplish with a program (as opposed to markup)—in particular, specifying looping and if-then-else operations:

- *Looping:* This is the notion that you want to perform some operation *iteratively,* until a given condition is true.
- *If-then-else constructs:* Here, you want to do one thing if a particular condition is true, do something else if another condition is true, and perhaps third, fourth, fifth things if all those other conditions are true.

XSL provides rudimentary forms of both of these kinds of operations, allowing an even greater range of expressiveness and transforming power.

Support for multiple media types

There's no denying that CSS2 does an excellent job formatting content for display on the Web; that is, pretty much by definition, what it was designed to do.

However, CSS2 also frustrates the daylights out of document designers who've cut their teeth on—and continue to need to prepare—documents for *printing*. Wouldn't it be great, these designers wonder, if a formatting language didn't assume that a document would be displayed just on the Web, but might also need to be printed? Or be displayed on a WebTV device instead of a computer monitor? On a "palmtop" device?

This pie-in-the-sky dream is close to being fulfilled with the formatting half of the XSL specification.

Not so fast!

All right, everything's not quite that rosy yet: As of this writing, there's almost no software that can process the "formatting half of the XSL specification."

It's fair to assume, however, that as the XSL formatting language specification calms down into a semblance of its final form, more software will sprout that *does* take advantage of it.

Other Key XSL(T) Concepts

This section will be a discussion partially of terminology, like the ones you've seen in other chapters, and partially of more abstract notions. Having come this far in the book, you know enough about XML that this won't be totally foreign to you. (It won't be totally familiar, either, so don't get cocky just yet.)

Relationship to XPath: nodes

Any XML processing program, presumably, must be capable of handling the individual elements, attributes, PIs, and so on—the document's tree of nodes, as we learned about in Chapter 6 on XPointers and XPath. In XSLT the word "node" assumes nearly as much importance as in XPath.

As a reminder, a *node* (in XSLT terms) is a single, discreet, atomic "thing" capable of being manipulated by an XSLT processor. Each element is a node. Each attribute is a node. Each attribute's *value* is a node. The document itself is a node. And so on. Also important to note is that it's not just the markup that can be manipulated, it's also the text enclosed by the markup. In a FlixML document, the name of the director is actually a separate node from the `director` element node itself.

Under XSLT, XPath expressions are used for singling out those portions of a document that you want to focus on at a particular point. In the XPointer/XPath chapter, I said that if you "got" XPath you could pretty much sleepwalk through *this* chapter. That's an exaggeration; on the other hand, if you didn't get XPath at all there, you will be really at sea here!

Source and result trees

In CSS2, you're using the style language to decorate various portions of the given XML document's tree in various ways. This seems a natural extension of, say, a word processor's style mechanism, with which you can select a word, phrase, or block of text, and apply a format to it so that it looks different from the text adjacent to it.

Under XSLT, though, the "given XML document's tree" is just the starting point. You use XSLT's transformational power to convert this *source tree* into a *result tree*—identical in structure, maybe, but not necessarily so—and it's the result tree that gets "styled."

Keeping the source tree distinct in your head from the result tree, knowing when to talk about the one, and when about the other, is another big part of understanding what's going on in XSLT.

The third tree

It's never really spoken of as such, but aside from the source and result trees there's a *third* one involved in an XSLT operation: the tree of XSLT elements and other nodes in the stylesheet itself.

Linking to an XSLT Style Sheet

In the previous chapter, you saw a PI that could be used in an XML document to associate it with a given CSS2 style sheet. The technique for linking the document to an XSL style sheet is identical, but the particulars vary; use a PI like this, instead:

```
<?xml-stylesheet type="text/xsl" href="uri_of_stylesheet"?>
```

The primary difference between the CSS2 PI and this one is the value of the `type` attribute, which here tells the application that the MIME type of the associated document is text, and in particular an XSL document. Replace `uri_of_stylesheet`, of course, with a URI (relative or absolute) pointing to the stylesheet in question.

Anatomy of an XSL Style Sheet

Like a CSS2 style sheet, a basic XSLT style sheet consists of a series of *template rules* (they're just called "rules" in CSS2), each of which defines a pattern to be matched and corresponding action(s) to perform when a match is found. The patterns represent something to be matched in the source tree, such as element names, attributes, PIs, comments, and so on. The actions, called *templates*, define markup and plain text into which to transform the matching pieces of the source tree.

(The stylesheet may also include bits and pieces of other sorts of things, such as variable declarations, attribute sets, and callable templates, which I'll cover later.)

Bare bones

A typical XSLT document—a stylesheet—looks schematically like this:

```
<xsl:stylesheet [namespace declarations]>
    <xsl:template [match specifications1]>
            [action1]
            [action2]
            . . .
    </xsl:template>
    <xsl:template [match specifications2]>
            [action3]
            . . .
    </xsl:template>
    . . .
</xsl:stylesheet>
```

The nonitalicized portions of text are XSLT keywords—built-in element names, as it were, that any XSLT document would normally include. The italicized portions represent descriptions of specific parts of the source tree to look for, in the case of the `xsl:template` elements with their `match` attributes, and specific actions—creating XML elements, other markup, and/or bare text in the result tree—to take when the processor finds them.

XSLT and Namespaces

Just like XLink, XSLT requires you to intermingle your own XML vocabulary with bits of reserved markup (both elements and attributes, in XSLT's case). In order to do this with XSLT, just as with XLink, you have to tell the downstream application which "universe" each group of elements belongs to—to identify the context in which a given name might mean one thing, vs. other contexts in which it might mean something else. You do this in an XSLT stylesheet with two "built-in" attributes[45] attached to the stylesheet's root element (usually, as I've mentioned, `<xsl:stylesheet>`): `xmlns:xsl=` and `xmlns=`.

Sidestepping confusion

Not to belabor what may be obvious to you, but just in case: The namespace declarations for using XSLT go in the *stylesheet document,* not in the *source document* that you want to transform. The source document's only connection to XSLT—or to CSS2, for that matter—is the `xml-stylesheet` PI.

Given, then, a root element of `<xsl:stylesheet>`, its namespace-declaring attributes would be encoded like this when you're transforming your XML document to, say, well-formed HTML 4.0:

```
xmlns:xsl="http://www.w3.org/TR/XSL/Transform"
xmlns="http://www.w3.org/TR/REC-html40"
```

These attributes are read by an XSLT processor as follows:

- `xmlns:xsl` — This declares that the namespace prefix `xsl:` (the portion of this attribute name following the colon) will refer to elements that come from the universe of elements—the namespace—defined by the W3C XSLT Recommendation, in this example.
- `xmlns` — Note that this is identical to the preceding attribute, except that it lacks the `:xsl`. This means that any elements with *no* namespace prefix belong to the universe of elements declared, in this case, by the W3C

---

45.   They're "built-in" in the sense that a processor that knows about them will accept them.

HTML 4.0 specification. This namespace thus will be the *default namespace* for all unprefixed element names in this stylesheet. Typically these will be the elements that will show up in the result tree, once the source has been transformed.

Given the above, the earlier outline of a typical XSLT document's structure might now look like the following:

```
<xsl:stylesheet
    xmlns:xsl="http://www.w3.org/TR/WD-XSLT"
    xmlns="http://www.w3.org/TR/REC-html40" >
    <xsl:template [match specifications1]>
          [action1]
          [action2]
          . . .
    </xsl:template>
    <xsl:template [match specifications2]>
          [action3]
          . . .
    </xsl:template>
    . . .
</xsl:stylesheet>
```

Every element belonging to the XSLT namespace (its vocabulary) is now prefixed with a unique marker (the `xsl:`) which *says* that's where the element comes from. And any element in the stylesheet with no prefix will be presumed to come from the HTML 4.0 namespace.

Throughout this chapter, I'll use the `xsl:` prefix for all XSLT elements; although this isn't absolutely required, it's consistent with the prefixes used on all elements in the XSLT spec.

Only two namespaces?

As I mentioned in a short box a couple pages back, there are potentially (indeed, usually) *three* namespaces—trees of named nodes—that need to be dealt with in an XSLT transformation: the source tree, the result tree, and the tree of XSLT elements that make up the stylesheet itself. But of these, only two are covered by namespace declarations—the XSLT and result-tree namespaces.

What happened to the source tree? Don't you have to declare *its* namespace, too?

The answer is, "It depends." In a lot of cases, you'll be using XSLT to transform XML from one vocabulary—namespace—to another, such as HTML. In these cases, the source tree's element nodes will not be used in the stylesheet *as* elements. Of course they crop up all over the place in other ways, principally in the values of attributes which represent XPath expressions. But there's no potential for name clashes with these kinds of use...and hence, no need to declare a source-tree namespace.

In other cases, you'll be using XSLT for less radical transformations, such as converting a document from an earlier version of a given XML vocabulary to a newer one. In these cases a source-tree namespace declaration may or may not be necessary, depending on the extent to which the two vocabularies (source and result tree) overlap.

The XSLT element hierarchy

As you can see above, the root element of an XSLT stylesheet is (unsurprisingly) `xsl:stylesheet`. Within that element you may include any of several of what the spec calls "top-level elements." There are a dozen of these, of which by far the most common in most stylesheets will be `xsl:template`. There are others whose purpose is to set various conditions that will be true for the stylesheet as a whole (such as whether or not extraneous whitespace will be stripped), or to define variables and "macro-like" chunks of XSLT code; I'll cover all these top-level elements at least briefly as we wend our way through this chapter.

Beneath the top-level elements, in most cases, are one or more "instruction"-type elements—like `<xsl:apply-templates>` in the above examples—which do much of the heavy lifting in the stylesheet.

Alternative stylesheet forms

The XSLT stylesheets I'll be presenting in this chapter—and, I'd guess, most of the ones you'll encounter elsewhere—are all standalone documents that are linked to documents that want to use them, as I've already described, with an `xml-stylesheet` PI. All of the stylesheets presented here will have `xsl:stylesheet` as their root element.

However, the XSLT spec describes an alternative form that a stylesheet may take.

The idea might be summarized as an "embedded" stylesheet, actually built into an XML document that needs styling or other transformation. This is theoretically similar to the way that you can embed CSS styling instructions in an HTML document. To use such a stylesheet, which you can do only in simple cases, you start with a regular XML document, say a FlixML one. To its elements (`flixinfo`, `leadcast`, and so on) you add various attributes that would normally be associated with reserved XSLT elements.

How might this be useful? It could be quite handy if you were constructing a quick-and-dirty test of how a document might be transformed and/or displayed. It also would likely be simpler for some applications to process, since all the information needed for the transformation/styling is right there, within the very content to be transformed/styled.

On the whole, though, the result is something like a medieval gargoyle that combines characteristics of two fantastic beasts—striking, perhaps even useful, when placed at the top of a Gothic cathedral; but awfully misshapen for common everyday use.[46]

Aesthetic considerations aside, note that most XSLT processing software for now assumes that it will be dealing with a separate, not embedded, stylesheet.

HTML Recap

As I've mentioned, throughout this chapter I'll be using XSLT to transform XML into easily displayable HTML. This presents a potential problem for some readers of *Just XML*, in that one of my goals with the book is not to require readers to know anything about HTML in order to learn XML.

So what I've done in Table 8.1 is to list, briefly, the HTML elements I'll be using here, with brief descriptions of their purposes and foibles. If you already know HTML, of course, feel free to skip this section and go on to the next, "Template Rules."

---

46.   It also reminds me of the old line about a dancing dog in a vaudeville show: What's surprising isn't how well it's done, but that it's done at all.

> **Even if you know HTML…**
>
> Still, there are a few "gotchas" that you may need to be aware of, primarily having to do with HTML as XSLT perceives it. It might not hurt to at least scan Table 8.1.

Table 8.1   HTML tags used in this chapter

Element Type	Parent	Description/Notes
html	(N/A)	The "root element" of an HTML document. Can be preceded by PIs or comments, but browsers are quite happy without them.
head	html	Contains general information about the document, such as the title that will display in the browser's window, various "meta" tags, and so on.
title	head	Content of this element will appear as the title of the browser's window when this page is open.
body	html	The bulk of the page's content goes here—all the text, images, tables, and so on. Typically the next-to-last thing in an HTML document is the closing `</body>` tag—right before the closing `</html>` tag.
hn	body	Creates a heading, whose size depends on the value of n. The largest headings are h1; the next smaller step is h2, then h3, and so on.
p	body, some others	The "paragraph" element used to break long text into shorter sections. Usually displayed by browsers as a blank line between text blocks. Loose HTML rules allow the opening `<p>` tag to be unmatched by a closing `</p>` tag; see further notes about this in the discussion of the `xsl:output` XSLT element, later in this chapter.
br	body, some others	HTML's "newline" character—starts the following text on the next line in the display, but doesn't insert a blank line (as the p element does). Refer to the `xsl:output` discussion for more information.

Table 8.1 HTML tags used in this chapter (continued)

Element Type	Parent	Description/Notes
img	body, some others	This element, as you might guess, is used to display images in a Web page. Has one required attribute, `src`, whose value is the URI of the image in question. This is an empty element that, like , can cause some surprises for someone used to coding plain old HTML. (See the `xsl:output` discussion for more information.)
a	body, many others	An HTML biggie. The "a" stands for "anchor," and the purpose of an anchor element is to *anchor* one end of a hyperlink. There are two main forms: `<a href="…">linking text </a>` is the more familiar of the two; the words `linking text` (in this example) appear in a browser, by default, as blue underlined text; when the user clicks on this text, they're presented with the information located at the URI which appears as the value of the `href` attribute. There's also a less familiar `<a name="…">target</a>` form; this is used to define a specific portion of an HTML document which can be linked to as a fragment identifier. (I covered this form of the `a` element type briefly in Chapters 5 and 6, on XLink/XPointer.) Note that you can make an image "clickable" by enclosing the `<img src="…">` tag within an `<a href="…">…</a>` tag pair.
		Table-defining elements:
table	body	Defines the general size and other characteristics of a table.
tr	table	Defines a table row.
td	tr	Defines a table cell. (The `td` stands for "table data.")
th	tr	Defines a table header, usually at the top of a column; this typically appears in the browser in boldface or some other enhanced font.
		List-defining elements:
ul	body, some others	The start of an unordered (bulleted) list. Generally requires one or more list item (`li`) items beneath it to make any sense.

Table 8.1   HTML tags used in this chapter (continued)

Element Type	Parent	Description/Notes
ol	body, some others	The start of an ordered (numbered) list. Generally requires one or more list item (li) items beneath it to make any sense.
li	ul or ol	A list item, subordinate to an ordered or unordered list element. As displayed by a browser, li elements are preceded by bullets if their parent is an unordered list (ul element), or by ascending numbers if an ordered one (ol element).
Miscellaneous elements:		
i	p and others	Anything between the opening <i> and closing </i> tags will be italicized.
b	p and others	Anything between the opening <b> and closing </b> tags will be boldfaced.
link	head	Used for associating a CSS stylesheet with an HTML document.
hr	body	Inserts a horizontal rule (line) at that point in the document.

(Note that there are many nuances to HTML in general, and these element types in particular, which are not described above, and that the types listed here are only a fraction of all those available to you when constructing an HTML result tree. I simply wanted to be sure you all had the same basic understanding of their use, and how they fit together.)

Template Rules

Here are the steps a typical XSLT processor might take when you run it:[47]

---

47. This is just a generic description; I doubt that any given XSLT processor actually follows this road map exactly. Indeed, the spec makes a point of saying that *it* doesn't care *how* they behave, as long as the result matches what the spec says it should be.

- Read in the stylesheet and parse it, making sure that *it* doesn't have any basic XML syntax errors. Also check it for valid namespace usage, XPath expressions, and so on. Save the stylesheet in memory so you don't need to read it again.
- Read in the source document (like a FlixML review) and parse it, making sure there aren't any basic XML syntax errors and comparing it to the DTD, if there is one, to be sure that the structure is correct for a document of this vocabulary.
- Once you've confirmed there are no errors, return to the source document. Process it from start to finish, top to bottom of the tree, systematically comparing each node—element, attribute, text, comment, and PI—to the stylesheet's instructions. If you find an instruction that matches the node, create the result which the instruction describes. If there are no matching instructions for this node, simply go on to the next one. Repeat until reaching the end of the source document.

We're concerned here (unless we're building an XSLT processor, which most of us are not) only with the last step—the description of what node(s) to match, and the instruction for what to create when and if something in the source tree matches that description.

As I already mentioned, each template rule consists of a *pattern* and an action, called a *template*. Basically, the structure is this:

```
pattern
    template1
       . . .
endpattern
```

There can be more than one *template*, obviously, and in some cases templates can be nested within one another.

The past comes back to haunt

I don't know about most of you, but I first encountered the word "template" when I was a kid, long before seeing or even using my first computer. It was a weird word, I thought—apparently constructed by taking two more familiar words, cramming them into a too-small suitcase, and sitting on the result.

> The occasion on which I encountered this word was some kind of arts-and-crafts project in grade school. We'd been given sheets of heavy paper that had been perforated in the shape of block letters; you could lay the sheet on another piece of paper, on a box, on a soon-to-be-ex-friend's forehead, smear it with poster paint, peel it away, and *voila*—an instant copy.
>
> That's a pretty good metaphor for these XSLT templates, I think. They're really just empty cutouts until the XSLT processor paints them with matching bits of your source document's content.

Here's a simple (almost mindless) template rule for FlixML's `plotsummary` element:

```
<xsl:template match="plotsummary">
    <p><xsl:apply-templates/></p>
</xsl:template>
```

The *pattern* portion of a template rule—represented in this case by the `xsl:template` element's `match` attribute—tells the XSLT processor how to tell whether a particular node matches. Here, we're saying that a node matches if it's an element, and if its name is `plotsummary`.

The *template* portion—the empty `<xsl:apply-templates/>`, here, together with its enclosing `<p>` and `</p>` tags—tells the processor what to create in the result tree when it's found a node in the source tree which matches the pattern.

Given the following snippet of a FlixML document:

```
<plotsummary>The Boys are back at it again in this
sequel to....</plotsummary>
```

the above XSLT would produce this in the result tree:

```
<p>The Boys are back at it again in this
sequel to....</p>
```

See? The XSLT might be translated as:

1. Match any element named `plotsummary`.
2. For each match you find, begin a `p` element in the result tree.
3. Process the children, if any, of the `plotsummary` element (that's what the `xsl:apply-templates` element does). ("Process the children" means see if there any matches among those nodes for other XSLT templates.)
4. Close the `p` element in the result tree.

Conflict resolution

What happens if a node matches more than one template in the stylesheet? Just as with CSS2, there are "tie-breaking" rules in effect for XSLT. These rules provide a natural process of elimination that successively removes otherwise matching templates from consideration, until you're left with only one match.

It's possible that you could end up with two or more matches that can't be further winnowed down. In theory, according to the spec, this is an error; but then it goes on to say that an XSLT processor can either give an error message or resolve the conflict by using the *last* matching template. Assume we've got two template rules for our `plotsummary` element:

```
<xsl:template match="plotsummary">
    <p><xsl:apply-templates/></p>
</xsl:template>
<xsl:template match="plotsummary">
    <p><i><xsl:apply-templates/></i></p>
</xsl:template>
```

Since there's no other indication of how to resolve these exact matches, if the processor doesn't simply throw up its hands and say "I can't decide!" it can use the last one. Result: Our `plotsummary` element's contents will be italicized.

Most conflicts won't be this obvious, thanks to the flexible, many-ways-to-the-same-node nature of XPath expressions. For instance, given that `plotsummary`'s parent element is `flixinfo`, we might encounter a conflict like this:

```
<xsl:template match="plotsummary">
    <p><xsl:apply-templates/></p>
</xsl:template>
<xsl:template match="flixinfo/*">
    <p><i><xsl:apply-templates/></i></p>
</xsl:template>
```

Now, the second matching template of course also applies to all other children of `flixinfo`, and there may be a good reason for doing this—it may not be a mistake in the stylesheet, in other words. But when the XSLT processor comes to a `plotsummary` node, what does it do? Will it select the second template rule in this case, too?

- First, it looks to see which, if either, of the matching template rules has a higher "import precedence" and chooses that one. I'll cover importing stylesheets later; for now, assume that our conflict still exists.

- Next, it looks for a `priority` attribute on the `xsl:template` elements that are causing the conflict. The value of `priority`, if you assign one specifically, is a number (which can be positive, negative, or zero). The highest priority "wins."
- For any of the matching template rules that do *not* have a priority attribute, the processor assigns a default priority. This involves analyzing the XPath expression in the `match` attribute, as follows:
  - The most common XPath expression specifies a particular node name (perhaps with a path leading to the particular name). These rules get assigned a priority of 0.
  - The next most common sort of expression specifies a particular node name *in a particular namespace.* This doesn't apply in this case, but if it did, such a template rule would be assigned priority –0.25.
  - Patterns that just test for specific types of node, without giving a specific name, are assigned a priority of –0.5.
  - Otherwise the default priority is (positive) 0.5.

If you follow this series of steps for our apparently conflicting template rules, above, you find that before the processor gets to the final tie-breaking step (using the rule that was defined last), it will assign default priorities to each template rule. The first rule, whose XPath expression is simply `plotsummary`, is an example of the most common sort of expression—just a node name—so it's given a default priority of 0. The second rule (`flixinfo/*`) is an example of the third sort of pattern—it tests for all children of `flixinfo` but doesn't "name any names." So it gets a default priority of –0.5. Result: The higher-priority rule—0 is higher than –0.5—wins, and our `plotsummary` element will *not* be italicized.

The lesson here is that if some element in your source tree is not being transformed the way you expected, you're probably a victim of this default-priority process. Either make all your XPath expressions specific enough that there are no conflicts, or assign specific priorities greater than 0.5 (the highest that can be set by default) for your specific rules.

> **Everything at once**
>
> Programmers in traditional languages are used to the idea of programs that do first one thing, then another, then another, and so on to the end. The order of instructions in the program is the order in which they're performed.
>
> Not so with XSLT.
>
> The reason is that the source tree controls the order in which things happen; the tree of template rules—"instructions"—in the stylesheet does not. The processor gets one source node, then compares it to all template rules. Then it gets the next node and compares it to all template rules. And so on. In short, *all the "instructions" are under consideration at every node.*
>
> Only two things in a stylesheet depend on the order in which its contents appear. One, as we've just seen, is the possibility that a conflict may be resolved depending on the order of the matching rules ("last one wins"). The second has to do with the order in which stylesheets are imported into one another; I'll be covering importing stylesheets in a moment.

Built-in template rules

If you're so inclined, you can process an XML document with an XSLT stylesheet that looks simply like this:

```
<xsl:stylesheet [namespace-declaring attributes]>
</xsl:stylesheet>
```

The reason you can do this is that an XSLT processor uses a series of *built-in template rules* for handling any node it encounters in the source tree that does not match any of the template rules explicitly provided.

There are three built-in rules, each handling different kinds of nodes.

(Note that you can override any of the built-in rules that follow: Simply retain the match patterns but substitute different templates.)

Root and element nodes with no matching template

If you were coding this template rule explicitly, it would look like the following:

```
<xsl:template match="*|/">
    <xsl:apply-templates />
</xsl:template>
```

The match pattern says when you encounter any element node (`*`) or (`|`) the root node (`/`), then create in the result tree something that matches the template. Since there's nothing in the template except the `xsl:apply-templates` instruction, the template rule processes the first child of the matching node, does nothing with it, then processes the child of that child, and so on. If this were the only built-in rule, then an empty stylesheet would do precisely nothing (after visiting every node in the source tree!).

Text and attribute nodes with no matching template

Luckily, there's a more specific built-in rule that does *more* than nothing when the processor finds an unmatched text or attribute node:

```
<xsl:template match="text()|@*">
    <xsl:value-of select="."/>
</xsl:template>
```

The pattern here says that it will match *any* (that's the `*`) text (`text()`) or attribute (`@`) node. But what's going on in the template itself?

I'll cover the `xsl:value-of` element further, later in this chapter. For now, all you need to know is that it tells the XSLT processor to take some string or other value from the source tree and put it in the result tree; its `select` attribute is kind of a "subexpression" that tells the processor where to find the particular thing in the source tree. So this template tells the processor to take from the source tree the content of the matching node itself (that's the `.` in the `select` attribute's value) and place *it* in the result tree.

The net effect? Any otherwise unmatched text or attribute node that is a child of a node matching the first built-in template will go straight to the result tree. (Reminder: Attributes are not on the `child::` axis from the elements they belong to; this rule alone does not cause the attributes' values to be copied!)

Comment and PI nodes with no matching template

If there are any comments or PIs in the source tree, thanks to the final built-in template rule nothing will be done with them:

```
<xsl:template match="processing-instruction()|comment()"/>
```

As you can see, the `xsl:template` element here (unlike all previous examples) is empty: There *is* no template for creating something in the result tree for comments and PIs in the source tree.

Obvious stylesheet bugs

As I mentioned above in discussing how XSLT processors deal with conflicting match patterns, sometimes it's immediately obvious that things have gone awry—that a particular element, for example, doesn't match *anything* in the stylesheet.

What makes it obvious is this business of built-in template rules. If you're transforming your XML to HTML, for instance, and think your stylesheet accounts for all nodes in the source tree, if you actually miss one then its text content will simply show up in the browser window displayed in the browser's default font at some odd point. If by default all nodes were suppressed, including text ones, then you might not notice a node had been missed until after a visitor to your site (or the content author) pointed out a strange omission—which is much harder to spot than the presence of something simply treated incorrectly.

XSLT Stylesheet Syntax

Okay, so you're now armed with lots of information about the way the XSLT processor will cover for the things you've neglected to do—like match on unique patterns, or assign priorities.

The big question now is: How do you code the things you *don't* neglect to do?

B Alert!

**Carnival of Souls
(1962, Herts-Lion International)**

Timid church organist Mary (Candice Hilligoss) is a passenger in a car run off a bridge by another car in a rollicking, high-spirited race. She emerges from the waters looking about like you'd expect for a young woman in her circumstances in a 1962 movie: her party dress ruined, in fact utterly ghastly. No Wet T-Shirt Night *here*.

Traumatized by the wreck, Mary decides to move away to a town where she knows absolutely no one. Yet her troubles aren't over. On the way, she sees the first of what will turn out to be many ghoulish apparitions: a man in a dark suit, his skin and hair ghostly white, his eyes and mouth those of a zombie. Later, after she's settled in (after a fashion) in a boarding home, she begins to experience terrifying interludes of absolute silence; not only can she not hear anything, but everyone else can neither see nor hear her. Meanwhile she experiences a strange fascination (despite the warnings of the priest who has employed her) with an abandoned amusement park whose days and nights have more music than the merely living might expect. . . .

This is one of the most disquieting horror films ever made, in my opinion—even more so than *Night of the Living Dead* (made six years later). As if Mary's encounters with the dead aren't bizarre enough, her contacts with the living seem scarcely less off-kilter. There's a great moment, just before one of her "episodes," when she wheels her car into a service station to have its transmission looked at. The guy has her pull the car onto the lift and then, naturally (at least naturally for those days), opens the door so she can wait while he works on the car. No, she tells him, she'd like to stay in the car. So he raises it up on the lift. There she sits, perched six to seven feet off the floor, even while the mechanic goes off to attend to other customers. Her being perched there just accents her separation from the world around her; it's not any more claustrophobic than any other scene that occurs in a car, but it sure feels that way.

Reportedly, *Carnival of Souls* cost a mere $30,000 to make; it was shot in Lawrence, Kansas, and in Salt Lake City (the site of the creepy amusement park). Mary's gauche neighbor—the kind of guy you picture wolf-whistling at dames on the street corner—was played by Sidney Berger, a University of Kansas drama teacher at the time.

B-movie moment: the flat cardboard car "window" behind Mary's head as she's driving to her new hometown. Also, my tape of the film (which I bought prerecorded) does *not* display "Carnival of Souls" during the opening credits; instead, it flashes the words "Corridors of Evil" (the movie's alternate title) in a title slide for several seconds There aren't many corridors in the movie, though.

A big example

Here's a full FlixML document describing *Carnival of Souls*. As in the chapter on XPointer/XPath, I've presented a rather lengthy one this time, to give us lots of pattern-matching and tree-transforming possibilities:

```
<?xml version="1.0"?>
<!DOCTYPE flixinfo SYSTEM "http://www.flixml.org/flixml/flixml_03.dtd">
<?xml:stylesheet type="text/XSLT" xlink:href="carnival.XSLT" ?>
<flixinfo author="John E. Simpson" copyright="1999" xml:lang="EN"
 xmlns:xlink="http://www.w3.org/1999/xlink/namespace/">
 <contents>
    <section xlink:title="Cast" xlink:href="castID"/>
    <section xlink:title="Crew" xlink:href="crewID"/>
    <section xlink:title="Plot" xlink:href="plotID"/>
    <section xlink:title="Reviews" xlink:href="revwID"/>
    <section xlink:title="Get It" xlink:href="distribID"/>
    <section xlink:title="Ratings" xlink:href="rateID"/>
 </contents>
 <title role="main">Carnival of Souls</title>
 <title role="alt">Corridors of Evil</title>
 <genre>
    <primarygenre>&T;</primarygenre>
    <othergenre>&H;</othergenre>
 </genre>
 <releaseyear role="initial">1962</releaseyear>
 <language>English</language>
 <studio>Herts-Lion International Corp.</studio>
 <cast id="castID">
    <leadcast>
       <female id="CHilligoss">
          <castmember>Candace Hilligoss</castmember>
          <role>Mary Henry</role></female>
       <female id="FFeist">
          <castmember>Francis Feist</castmember>
          <role>Mrs. Thomas</role></female>
       <male id="SBerger">
          <castmember>Sidney Berger</castmember>
          <role>John Linden</role></male>
       <male id="AEllison">
          <castmember>Art Ellison</castmember>
          <role>The Minister</role></male>
       <male id="SLevitt">
          <castmember>Stan Levitt</castmember>
          <role>Dr. Samuels (psychologist)</role></male>
    </leadcast>
```

```
    <othercast>
       <male>
          <castmember>Tom McGinnis</castmember>
          <role>Boss at the organ factory</role></male>
       <male>
          <castmember>Forbes Caldwell</castmember>
          <role>Laborer at the organ factory</role></male>
       <male>
          <castmember>Dan Palmquist</castmember>
          <role>Service station attendant</role></male>
       <male id="HHervey">
          <castmember>Herk Hervey</castmember>
          <role>Creepy Man</role></male>
    </othercast>
 </cast>
 <crew id="crewID">
    <director>Herk Hervey</director>
    <screenwriter>John Clifford</screenwriter>
    <cinematog>Maurice Prather</cinematog>
    <sound>Ed Down</sound>
    <sound>Don Jessup</sound>
    <editor>Dan Palmquist</editor>
    <editor>Bill de Jarnette</editor>
    <score>Gene Moore</score>
    <makeup>George Corn</makeup>
 </crew>
 <plotsummary id="plotID">Timid church organist
    <femaleref femaleid="CHilligoss">Mary</femaleref> is a
    passenger in a car run off a bridge by another car in a
    rollicking, high-spirited race. She emerges from the waters
    looking about like you'd expect for a young woman in her
    circumstances in a 1962 movie: her party dress ruined, in
    fact utterly ghastly. No Wet T-Shirt Night
    <emph>here</emph>.<parabreak/> Traumatized by the wreck,
    Mary decides to move away from the town, to a town where she
    knows absolutely no one. Yet her troubles aren't over. On
    the way, she sees the first of what will turn out to be many
    ghoulish apparitions: <maleref maleid="HHervey">a
    man</maleref> in a dark suit, his skin and hair ghostly
    white, his eyes and mouth those of a zombie. Later, after
    she's settled in (after a fashion) in a boarding home, she
    begins to experience terrifying interludes of absolute
    silence; not only can she not hear anything, but everyone
    else can neither see nor hear her. Meanwhile she experiences
    a strange fascination (despite the warnings of the priest
    who has employed her) with an abandoned amusement
```

```
    park whose days and nights have more music than the
    merely living might expect....</plotsummary>
<reviews id="revwID">
    <flixmlreview>
        <goodreview>
            <!-- Note to self: Don't forget to replace
            placeholder below with REAL review -->
            <reviewtext>(Some text)</reviewtext>
        </goodreview>
    </flixmlreview>
    <otherreview>
        <goodreview>
            <reviewlink xlink:href="http://www.suntimes.com/ebert/
                ebert_reviews/1989/10/379589.html">Roger
                Ebert</reviewlink>
        </goodreview>
        <goodreview>
            <reviewlink
                xlink:href="http://www.imagesjournal.com/
                issue05/reviews/carnival.htm">Images: A Journal
                of Film and Popular Culture</reviewlink>
        </goodreview>
    </otherreview>
</reviews>
<clips></clips>
<distributors id="distribID">
    <distributor>
        <distribname>&MUL;</distribname>
        <distribextlink>
            <distriblink
                xlink:href="http://www.moviesunlimited.com/
                musite/" />
        </distribextlink>
    </distributor>
    <distributor>
        <distribname>Reel.com</distribname>
        <distribextlink>
            <distriblink xlink:href="http://www.reel.com/
            Content/moviepage.asp?mmid=153" />
        </distribextlink>
    </distributor>
    <distributor>
        <distribname>Amazon.com</distribname>
        <distribextlink>
            <distriblink xlink:href="http://www.amazon.com/
                exec/obidos/ASIN/6303998704" />
```

```
            </distribextlink></distributor>
        <distributor>
            <distribname>&FACETS;</distribname>
            <distribextlink>
                <distriblink xlink:href="http://www.facets.org/" />
            </distribextlink>
        </distributor>
    </distributors>
<dialog>Mary: Thank you for the coffee. It was unsanitary but
    delicious.</dialog>
<remarks>This is one of the most disquieting horror films ever
    made, in my opinion -- even more so than Night of the Living
    Dead (which was made six years later). As if Mary's
    encounters with the dead aren't bizarre enough, her contacts
    with the living seem scarcely less off-kilter.<parabreak/>
    There's a great moment, just before one of her "episodes,"
    when she wheels her car into a service station to have its
    transmission looked at. The guy has her pull the car onto
    the lift and then, naturally (at least naturally for
    those days), opens the door so she can wait while he works
    on the car. No, she tells him, she'd like to stay in the
    car. So he raises it up on the lift.<parabreak/>There she
    sits, perched six to seven feet off the floor, even while
    the mechanic goes off to attend to other customers. Her
    being perched there just accents her separation from the
    world around her; it's not any more claustrophobic than any
    other scene that occurs in a car, but it sure feels that
    way.<parabreak/>Reportedly, Carnival of Souls cost a mere
    $30,000 to make; it was shot in Lawrence, Kansas, and in
    Salt Lake City (the site of the creepy amusement park).
    Mary's gauche neighbor -- the kind of guy you picture
    wolf-whistling at dames on the street corner -- was played
    by Sidney Berger, a University of Kansas drama teacher at
    the time.<parabreak/>B movie moment: the flat cardboard car
    "window" behind Mary's head as she's driving to her new
    hometown. Also, my tape of the film (which I bought
    pre-recorded) does not display "Carnival of Souls" during
    the opening credits; instead, it flashes the words
    "Corridors of Evil" (the movie's alternate title) in a title
    slide for several seconds. There aren't many corridors in
    the movie, though.</remarks>
 <mpaarating id="rateID">NR</mpaarating>
 <bees b-ness="&BEE4URL;"/>
</flixinfo>
```

> **Need a pattern review?**
>
> If you're not sure how to construct a match pattern, you might want to go back to Chapter 6 (XPointer/XPath) for a review. (I'm not going to repeat all that information here, although I'll cover little bits of it.) There are a few XSLT extensions to XPath expression syntax, and we'll see examples of them before reaching the end of this chapter; but for over ninety percent of XSLT match patterns, the syntax is that of XPath.

Templates from the ground up

To start building an XSLT stylesheet for this document (or for any other, for that matter), I recommend you start with just the main xsl:stylesheet element, of course, but also include *explicit* copies of the built-in template rules.

(Why the latter, if they're built-in? Two reasons: First, you want to protect yourself in case the stylesheet should ever be processed by some halfway sort of program that doesn't include the built-ins. Theoretically this won't happen, but you never know. The second and more important reason is that they help make your stylesheet a complete record of everything that it supposedly does. They therefore remind any other human readers of the stylesheet that they exist; and, especially, they remind *you*—so when things don't behave as expected you can slap your forehead and say, "Oh yeah, right, I forgot about those!" Related to the latter is that they can remind you to override them, if necessary, for your particular application.)

So here's our starter, bare-bones stylesheet:

```
<xsl:stylesheet
    xmlns:xsl="http://www.w3.org/1999/XSL/Transform"
    xmlns="http://www.w3.org/TR/REC-html40">
    <!-- Built-in rule for root and element nodes -->
    <xsl:template match="*|/">
        <xsl:apply-templates />
    </xsl:template>
    <!-- Built-in rule for text and attribute nodes -->
    <xsl:template match="text()|@*">
        <xsl:value-of select="."/>
    </xsl:template>
    <!-- Built-in rule for PI and comment nodes -->
    <xsl:template match="processing-instruction()|comment()"/>
</xsl:stylesheet>
```

Note, by the way, that comments appearing in the stylesheet don't get copied to the result tree. (There are, though, a couple of ways to put comments in the result tree, as we'll see.) Also note that the default namespace for any elements in the stylesheet that don't have a namespace prefix will be the HTML version 4.0 namespace; if we wanted to transform our *Carnival of Souls* source tree into some other HTML or XML vocabulary, we'd replace the value of the xmlns attribute with the corresponding URI.

Well-formed stylesheets, too

This is as good a place as any to warn you about something that newcomers sometimes forget: Regardless of what you're transforming your source tree into, your XSLT stylesheet itself is always an XML document. *It must be well-formed.* There are several implications for XSLT stylesheet authors, the most important of which have to do with namespaces, entities, and the balancing of tags.

Namespaces

If any of your source tree's elements or attributes use namespace prefixes, *and* if you reference any of those nodes in your stylesheet, then your stylesheet, too, must declare the namespace prefixes. It won't somehow magically inherit their declarations from the source tree.

In the case of a FlixML document, a number of elements are used for constructing XLinks, and these elements' attributes begin with the xlink: prefix. Therefore we need to add another namespace-declaring attribute to our stylesheet, assuming we will be processing any of the XLinking attributes (which we will!):

```
xmlns:xlink="http://www.w3.org/1999/xlink/namespace/"
```

Entities

Likewise, the XSLT processor doesn't automatically know about any entities that might be referenced in the source tree (other than the built-in ones, like <). So if you need to use any of them, they've got to be declared in an internal DTD subset which precedes the opening <xml:stylesheet...> tag. For instance:[48]

---

48. And yes, I know—you don't yet know how to define an entity or do anything else in a DTD, internal or otherwise. This is just an example.

```
<!DOCTYPE xsl:stylesheet [
<!ENTITY BEE4URL
    "http://www.flixml.org/flixml/images/bee4_0.gif">
]>
```

Starting with the `<!ENTITY` keyword, this is an internal DTD's declaration of an entity that enables you to use the entity reference `&BEE4URL;` in the stylesheet, which would otherwise cause an error even though the entity is already declared in the FlixML DTD.

Balanced tags

Although balancing tags should, by now, be the very first thing that pops into your head when you hear the phrase "well-formed XML," this still seems to be one area most troublesome to XSLT newcomers.

To state the matter once more, as plainly as I can: *The XSLT stylesheet itself must be a well-formed XML document.* Even the element types that are not from the XSLT namespace are considered part of the stylesheet, and so the tags for those element types must be balanced, too.

Several pages back, when discussing template rule conflict resolution, I used a hypothetical rule for the `plotsummary` element; the rule looked like this:

```
<xsl:template match="plotsummary">
    <p><i><xsl:apply-templates/></i></p>
</xsl:template>
```

Its purpose, again, was to transform the `plotsummary` element using HTML's "italics" element. So any text contained by the `<plotsummary>` and `</plotsummary>` tags would look like *this*.

Now imagine a reasonable scenario. It's based on the fact that in a FlixML document, a `plotsummary` element may contain zero or more `emph` elements; any text within an `emph` is meant to be "emphasized" somehow. Someone who fancies himself a clever XSLT stylesheet author[49] might try to do something like the following:

```
<xsl:template match="emph">
    </i><xsl:apply-templates/><i>
</xsl:template>
```

---

49. Not to name any names, of course.

The idea, our Clever Person thinks, is to temporarily shut off the italics in which our plotsummary element is being displayed (that's the `</i>`), display the `emph` element's contents in normal upright text, then turn italics back on (the `<i>` tag) when the `emph` element closes. This would actually work if all the XSLT processor cared about was "turning things on and off" in the result tree.

Unfortunately for Clever Person, on invoking the XSLT processor, he or she learns that the very first thing which happens is that the stylesheet itself is parsed for well-formedness...and flunks the parser's test. The structure of the stylesheet itself is ill-formed, its elements improperly nested, even though the imagined result tree would be fine!

Adding specific template rules

Let's start with something simple—an element whose content we simply want displayed—and add its template rule to the stylesheet. A good candidate for this would be the FlixML `remarks` element; after adding a template rule for it, our stylesheet might look like the following (including the `xlink:` namespace declaration I mentioned earlier):

```
<xsl:stylesheet
    xmlns:xsl="http://www.w3.org/1999/XSL/Transform"
    xmlns:xlink="http://www.w3.org/1999/xlink/namespace/"
    xmlns="http://www.w3.org/TR/REC-html40">
    <!-- Built-in rule for root and element nodes -->
    <xsl:template match="*|/">
        <xsl:apply-templates />
    </xsl:template>
    <!-- Built-in rule for text and attribute nodes -->
    <xsl:template match="text()|@*">
        <xsl:value-of select="."/>
    </xsl:template>
    <!-- Built-in rule for PI and comment nodes -->
    <xsl:template match="processing instruction()|comment()"/>
    <!-- Template rule for remarks element -->
    <xsl:template match="remarks">
        <xsl:value-of select="."/>
    </xsl:template>
</xsl:stylesheet>
```

> **Unstating the obvious**
>
> From here on, I won't repeat the portions of the stylesheet that have already been covered. As I give you further examples, though, bear in mind that all those other portions are still included!

Of course this is already covered by the built-in rule for text and attribute nodes, but it doesn't hurt to make our intentions explicit—for this and any other elements, for that matter.

Putting several things in the result tree at once

Given that we're transforming the FlixML document into HTML, we'll need to create at least a loose HTML structure for the result tree. Looking back at Table 8.1, you should be able to see that an HTML document consists of an outermost `html` element, within which are a single `head` and a single `body` element. Let's put those components into our result tree now.

Remember that in order for the processor to put something into the result tree, it's got to match something in the source tree. Which node in our source tree would we want to be the "trigger" for generating our HTML structure? Right—either the root node, or the root *element* node. (If we generate it from any other element, like `remarks` for example, it might not turn out to be the root of the HTML result tree. Or if we generate it from a match on some node that appears more than once, then the HTML "root" elements will actually appear more than once in the result tree!)

I've seen some stylesheets that generate the root HTML elements from the root node, and some that generate them from the root element node (`flix-info`, in this case). Which is preferable?

If you create the root of your result tree from the root node of your source tree, your result will *always* have the indicated root, regardless of whatever else might be going on in the source tree. For instance, as you know, a document conforming to some DTD does not have to start with the very "uppermost" element type in the tree declared by the DTD—its root element type can be *any* of those declared in the DTD. (It just can't include any branches of the tree outside the scope of whatever element type *is* selected as the root.) In FlixML's case, say, a document author might want to put just the `plotsummary` (and its descendants) in a given document. If the stylesheet generates a root for the result tree when it encounters the root node, then this author's choice will not "break" the stylesheet (or more important, it won't break the result tree).

If, on the other hand, you create the result tree's root only when encountering a *specific* root element node in the source tree, such as flixinfo, you're basically deciding that our hypothetical plotsummary-only document will not be transformed correctly. This sounds like a drawback, and in some cases it is, but it has one important virtue: If the document type is intended *not* to be "sub-typed" like this, then we *want* the stylesheet to be broken, to alert us to the fact that the source tree is incomplete.

The latter is the approach I'll use to create our HTML result tree's root:

```
<xsl:template match="flixinfo">
    <html>
    <head><title>FlixML Review</title></head>
    <body><xsl:apply-templates /></body>
    </html>
</xsl:template>
```

This template rule says, line-by-line:

- Only use this template rule when you find node(s) in the source tree named flixinfo.
- First, open the html element in the result tree.
- Then open in the result tree the head and title elements, insert the literal text "FlixML Review," and then close the title and head elements. This causes the words FlixML Review to be displayed in a browser's title bar when the HTML document is viewed.
- Next, open the body element in the result tree; process all of the flixinfo node's children (the empty xsl:apply-templates element), and close the body element when all child nodes have been processed.
- Close the html element.
- End this template rule (</xsl:template>).

Putting something into the result tree from somewhere else in the source tree

What we've got so far will work fine, but it's a little too, y'know, generic. Bland. Especially that title element in the result tree (and consequently the browser title bar). Since each FlixML review covers a different movie, why don't we put the specific movie's *title* up there, too?

I mentioned earlier that the value of an `xsl:value-of` element's `select` attribute is an XPath expression. Typically, this will be simply ., meaning "insert this element's own content here." But it can be any other XPath expression instead; in this case, we're processing the `flixinfo` element so we need to select (and embed in the result tree) the value of its `title` child. Therefore, our template rule for `flixinfo` would now read:

```
<xsl:template match="flixinfo">
    <html>
    <head>
        <title>FlixML Review:
          <xsl:value-of select="title"/>
        </title>
    </head>
    <body><xsl:apply-templates /></body>
    </html>
</xsl:template>
```

Watching out for loose ends

Our sample FlixML document actually has two `title` elements, one whose value is `Carnival of Souls` and one whose value is `Corridors of Evil`. The above template rule that generates the HTML `title` element works because the value of the `select` attribute actually selects *two* nodes—both movie titles—and converts the first match (in document order) into a string. You'll recall from Chapter 6 that this is normal XPath behavior.

If we wanted to be absolutely sure of getting the main title, not the alternate—regardless of the order in which the elements appear in the source tree—we'd need to make the `select` attribute do a little more work. It helps to know that in the FlixML DTD, the `title` element has a `role` attribute whose default value is `main`; we can use that information to enhance our `xsl:value-of` element like this:

```
<xsl:value-of select="title[@role='main']"/>
```

This way, even if *no* `role` attribute is specified in the source tree, we'll be sure not to get the alternate title. (Of course, if there are more than one main titles explicitly coded or defaulted, we'll still get only the first. And if all the titles have a role attribute explicitly set to something other than `main`, well, *none* will be selected for display in the title bar!)

Status check

If we apply the stylesheet developed so far to our *Carnival of Souls* review by passing both through an XSLT processor, we get the following HTML:

```
<html xmlns:xlink="http://www.w3.org/1999/xlink/namespace/"
xmlns="http://www.w3.org/TR/REC-html40">
<head><title>FlixML Review: Carnival of Souls</title></
head>
<body>
Carnival of Souls
Corridors of Evil
Thriller
Horror
1962
English
Herts-Lion International Corp.
       . . .
NR
</body></html>
```

When you look at this HTML with a Web browser, you see something like
Figure 8.1.

As you can see, this is nowhere near done yet; thanks to our catch-all built-
in rules, all the text nodes are simply displayed, one after another, in the
browser's default style. But as you can also see, the title bar now shows us exactly
what we want.

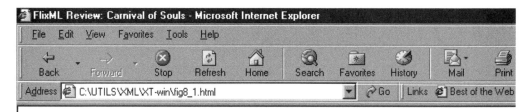

Figure 8.1   First-cut FlixML-to-HTML result

Creating the main result-tree body element

Once past the HTML result tree's `head` node, we can continue to create specific template rules for specific elements and other nodes. These will for the most part follow the general pattern: match the node as specifically as desired, put some text and perhaps HTML markup in the result tree, and include the value of the selected node (as well as, perhaps, other nodes). Because the other elements will be processed as a result of the `flixinfo` template rule's `xsl:apply-templates` element, their resulting "sub-trees" will appear in the final result tree at that point, within the HTML `body` element.

For instance, we probably want to put the film's title(s) in some kind of heading. The following would accomplish this:

```
<xsl:template match="title">
    <h1>Title: <xsl:value-of select="."/></h1>
</xsl:template>
```

It puts the contents of every title into a level-1 (large) HTML heading element, preceded by the word "Title: " as shown in Figure 8.2:

(Aside from the obvious change—the addition of the big headings—also compare Figure 8.2 to Figure 8.1 and notice the subtler change: The two `title` elements no longer appear in the bunched-up list of document content. Adding

Figure 8.2 Adding level-1 headings

a specific template rule for an element's content effectively strips it from consideration by a built-in rule.)

Conditional processing

XSLT comes with two constructs that let you perform a given action if a given condition is true, and possibly one or more actions depending on whether some other conditions are true.

xsl:if

The first of these is the xsl:if element. It has one attribute, test; the value of the test attribute must be some test (obviously) that results in a true or false value.

Say we'd like the XSLT processor to check the author attribute of the flixinfo element. If it has a value, add it to the *end* of the result tree, after all the children of flixinfo have been processed. Here's the new template rule for flixinfo, complete with the xsl:if statement:

```
<xsl:template match="flixinfo">
    <html>
    <head>
        <title>FlixML Review:
          <xsl:value-of select="title"/>
        </title>
    </head>
    <body>
        <xsl:apply-templates />
        <xsl:if test="@author != ''">
          <h4>Review by
                <xsl:value-of select="@author"/>
          </h4>
        </xsl:if>
    </body>
    </html>
</xsl:template>
```

(Note here, incidentally, that the way to test for an empty attribute is just to use a pair of successive quotation marks.)

xsl:choose

The xsl:if element is fine as far as it goes. However, it tests for exactly *one* condition, and never more than one. Often you'll want to test multiple conditions in a single branch of the stylesheet, and in a case like this, coding multiple xsl:ifs can be extremely cumbersome and error-prone. This is a situation made for the `xsl:choose` element.

Actually, what's called "the `xsl:choose` element" consists of a nested structure of elements, of which `xsl:choose` just happens to be the "top." Its general format looks like this:

```
<xsl:choose>
    <xsl:when test="test1">template1</xsl:when>
    <xsl:when test="test2">template2</xsl:when>
    . . .
    <xsl:otherwise>othertemplate</xsl:otherwise>
</xsl:choose>
```

When the XSLT processor encounters an `xsl:choose` element, it drops down into the `xsl:when` tests before building a template. One at a time, it performs each of the tests in the list. When one of the tests yields a "true" result, it builds the corresponding template and drops out of the `xsl:choose` structure. The `xsl:otherwise` element, which is optional, can be used for covering all cases not otherwise tested for, in the event that all tests end up being false.

For example, suppose we don't want a film's *alternate* title(s) displayed in the same large size as its main one(s). Furthermore, for alternate titles we want to use the literal value `a/k/a` (for "also known as") instead of `Title:`. This could be done with two successive `xsl:if` elements; however, any more than that will quickly become cumbersome. So let's use an `xsl:choose`, instead (including an `xsl:otherwise` to trap anything else that would otherwise—as the element's name implies—fall through the cracks); our template rule for the `title` element now looks like this:

```
<xsl:template match="title">
    <xsl:choose>
        <xsl:when test="@role='main'">
            <h1>Title:
            <xsl:value-of select="."/></h1></xsl:when>
        <xsl:when test="@role='alt'">
            <h2>a/k/a:
            <xsl:value-of select="."/></h2></xsl:when>
        <xsl:otherwise>
            <h1>Eh? Some other kind of title:
            <xsl:value-of select="."/></h1></xsl:otherwise>
    </xsl:choose>
</xsl:template>
```

Looping

Many times in the course of processing a source tree whose structure repeats itself over and over, you'll want your stylesheet to do the same thing for each of those repetitions. Happily, there's an XSLT element called `xsl:for-each` that does just that.

As you can see from our sample *Carnival of Souls* document, the links to external reviews might be a good place to look for repeated structure. What we'd like to do is create an unordered list for the `otherreview` branch of the source tree, with each link represented by a separate list item. Here is a template rule to do just that:

```
<xsl:template match="otherreview">
 <ul>
    <xsl:for-each select="goodreview|badreview">
       <li>
          <a href="{reviewlink/@xlink:href}">
             <xsl:value-of select="reviewlink"/>
          </a>
       /li>
    </xsl:for-each>
 </ul>
</xsl:template>
```

The way this works is that when an `otherreview` element is found, XSLT places an unordered-list (`ul`) item into the result tree. Then for each `goodreview` or `badreview` child of `otherreview`, a bulleted list item (`li`) goes into the result tree, the value of which is a hyperlink to the given resource. When the last good or bad review's link is thus transformed, the processing drops out of the `xsl:for-each` loop and goes back to the source tree for the next node outside the `otherreview` structure.

Sorting

It's common to want portions of the result tree to be sorted for display, to make it easier to locate specific information. This is accomplished by placing one or more `xsl:sort` elements in the template rule. (If you use more than one, the effect is that of a "composite key"—that is, the first `xsl:sort` specifies the primary sort key, the second one the secondary key, and so on.) The `xsl:sort` element takes these attributes:

- `select`: Tells the XSLT processor what to sort *on*. For example, if the current template rule is matching on the `distributor` element of our sample document, we might want to sort on its `distribname` child.
- `lang`: As with the built-in `xml:lang` attribute, this specifies for sorting purposes the language in which the sort key is represented. Allowable values match those for `xml:lang`, such as EN, FR, and so on.
- `data-type`: Allowable values `text` (which is the default) and `number`. This may or may not be important to specify; if the sort key is numeric, especially in a format that doesn't include leading zeroes, it will be critical. In the latter case, sorting numbers that range from 1 through 10, with `data-type="number"`, will put them in the expected sequence; if on the other hand you use `data-type="text"` to sort them, the order will be 1, 10, 2, and so on through 9 (because the text string "10" sorts lower than the text string "2").
- `order`: Value `ascending` (the default) or `descending`.
- `case-order`: Can have a value of `upper-first` or `lower-first`. The idea here is that the sort key might have a mixture of upper- and lower-case letters, and that sorting such a key may produce different results depending on whether the letter A (for example) is considered "less than" or "greater than" its lower-case version, a. The default value depends on the language.

Sorting the film's distributors into ascending order might therefore be done using a template rule like the following:

```
<xsl:template match="distributors">
 <table>
   <tr>
     <td>Buy or Rent It</td>
   </tr>
   <xsl:for-each select="distributor">
     <xsl:sort select="distribname"
         lang="EN" data-type="text"
         order="ascending" case-order="lower-first"/>
     <tr>
      <td><b><xsl:value-of select="distribname"/></b></td>
      <xsl:for-each select="distribextlink/distriblink">
        <td>
           <a href="{@xlink:href}">
              <xsl:value-of select="@xlink:href"/>
           </a>
        </td>
```

```
        </xsl:for-each></tr>
      </xsl:for-each>
    </table>
  </xsl:template>
```

Creating "nonliteral" elements and attributes

All the examples I've shown so far have simply used literal values in order to put markup into the result tree. For instance, simply placing <h1> in the template makes the XSLT processor create that element at that point.

However, there are some cases in which you cannot put markup directly into the result tree because doing so would cause the stylesheet to be no longer well-formed. Suppose for example that we had a list of some number of items. The XML document looks like this:

```
<list>
    <item>The first item</item>
    <item>The second item</item>
    <item>The third item</item>
    <item>The last item</item>
</list>
```

So let's say we want to display each of the item elements in successively smaller sizes, using the HTML h1, h2, h3, and so on elements, with the number of the heading corresponding to the item's position in the list. (So the first list item would become an h1, the second an h2, and so on.) The position itself would appear as the first thing on each line, followed by a period and the item element's content itself. The desired outcome would therefore look something like this:

1. The first item
2. The second item
3. The third item
4. The fourth item

One of those clever-but-not-smart kinds of solutions would be to do something like this:

```
<xsl:template match="item">
    <h<xsl:value-of select="position()"/>>
        <xsl:value-of select="position()"/>
        <xsl:value-of select="."/>
    </h<xsl:value-of select="position()"/>>
</xsl:template>
```

Get the idea? Our stylesheet author thinks that what he or she has done is let the stylesheet's logic decide how to size the headings, by creating the hn elements on-the-fly and numbered according to the item's position in the list. As with many such clever ideas, it breaks down in practice: The XSLT processor (actually, the XML parser trying to read the stylesheet in the first place) will choke as soon as it hits that off-the-wall <h< combination.

A couple of XSLT elements can help you out in such a situation.

xsl:element

The xsl:element element, as you might guess, inserts an element into the result tree. The content of the xsl:element's name attribute will become the name of the new element in the result tree. For instance:

```
<xsl:element name="h1">A Level-1 Heading</xsl:element>
```

creates the same result tree as:

```
<h1>A Level-1 Heading</h1>
```

This is particularly handy when you want to *calculate an element name* using some kind of information in the document—like our multiple-sized list, for instance. With xsl:element, you don't need to know in advance the exact name of the element to be created at all!

Here's how to solve the above riddle with xsl:element:

```
<xsl:template match="item">
    <xsl:element name="{concat('h', position())}">
    <xsl:value-of select="position()"/>.
    <xsl:value-of select="."/></xsl:element>
</xsl:template>
```

The real magic here takes place in the <xsl:element> start tag, where the element's name is "calculated," after a fashion, by concatenating a lowercase h and the current item element's position in the list.

Note one thing especially about what's going on there: the curly braces, { and }, surrounding the calculation of the element name. In many cases in XSLT—like the values of the xsl:template match attribute, or the xsl:value-of select attribute—you don't need to do anything special to indicate "perform a calculation here." However, in many other cases—where a literal string value is expected, as with the xsl:element name attribute here—you can't simply dump an XPath or other expression there; the processor would attempt (in this case) to create in the result tree an element literally named concat('h', position())... and would, of course, die as soon as it got to the opening parenthesis. (Element names can't contain punctuation.) The curly braces tell the processor, "perform the calculation shown here, and then place its *result* where indicated."

Another of those oh-by-the-ways...

There's another little glitch you'll encounter, should you actually attempt to create this list+items document and the corresponding stylesheet as shown here, then pass it through an XSLT processor.

I've alluded to this before—that XSLT processors can produce quite surprising results sometimes, due to the presence of "unimportant" newline characters in the source tree that function (at least according to some XSLT processors) as though they were actually text-node children of the elements in which they appear. The list+items document as shown here has a newline after the opening `<list>` tag, plus one after each of the closing `</item>` tags. As a result, the item's positions are not 1, 2, 3, and 4 within their parent, but 2, 4, 6, and 8—the odd-numbered positions are occupied by the newlines, that is, the "text nodes" that are "children" of the various elements.

Moral: Be careful if you're expecting `position()` to produce specific values! If the results are unexpected, go back over both your stylesheet and your source document to be sure that text nodes (particularly the troublesome newlines) are being treated correctly.

---

xsl:attribute

This element works similarly to `xsl:element`—and is used in similar situations. In this case, again, the `name` attribute assigns the attribute's name (which, as with `xsl:element`, can be the result of a calculation). The `xsl:attribute` element's *content* establishes a value for the attribute.

If you're using the `xsl:attribute` element, you must use it immediately after the element (or the `xsl:element` element) to which it applies.

Following are two template rules, one for the `male` element nodes and one for the `maleref` element nodes. (The latter, if any, will appear somewhere in the `plotsummary`.) The first template rule creates an HTML `a` element and gives it a `name` attribute; the value of the `name` attribute will be whatever the value of the `male` element's `id` attribute might be. The second template also creates an `a` element for each `maleref` element, with an `href` attribute; the value of the `href` is the value of the `maleref`'s `maleid` value. See if you can figure out what the effect will be when the created HTML is viewed in a browser, before reading the explanation in the paragraph following the example.

```
<xsl:template match="male">
    <xsl:choose>
        <xsl:when test="@id != ''">
          <a>
                <xsl:attribute name="name">
                    <xsl:value-of select="@id"/>
                </xsl:attribute><xsl:value-of select="."/>
          </a></xsl:when>
        <xsl:otherwise>
          <xsl:value-of select="."/></xsl:otherwise>
    </xsl:choose>
</xsl:template>

<xsl:template match="maleref">
    <a>
        <xsl:attribute name="href">
          <xsl:value-of select="concat('#', @maleid)"/>
        </xsl:attribute><xsl:value-of select="."/>
    </a>
</xsl:template>
```

What's created in the result tree by these two templates are *intra-document hyperlinks*. For every `male` element with an `id` attribute, the first template inserts an `<a name="value of id attribute">` tag at that point in the result tree and goes on to process the `male` element's descendants; otherwise it just processes the descendants. For instance, there's a male cast member named Herk Hervey; this reference will now be "bookmarked" like this:

```
<a name="HHervey">Herk Hervey...</a>
```

As for the `maleref` element, we know that the value of its `maleid` attribute must match the value of some `id` attribute in the document—and if the document author has his head screwed on right, it will be an `id` attribute to a `male` element (hence the attribute's name). The template rule for `maleref` thus creates an `<a href="value of maleid attribute">` tag, *surrounding* the contents of whatever the `maleref` element might be. The result tree node within what used to be the `plotsummary` element in the source tree now looks like this:

```
<a href="#HHervey">a man</a> in a dark suit...
```

So the words `a man` appear in the browser not just as plain text, but as a hyperlink—and when we click on that link, we're taken to the point in the document where the `male` element's reference to Herk Hervey has been transcribed by the first template rule.

Little Funny Bits: "Special" Text

Given the wide variety of hoops that XML is already being called on to jump through, it shouldn't surprise you to learn that XSLT's got a lot of them to pass through as well. Chief among these, to judge from questions posted on XSL(T)-related newsgroups and mailing lists, is the handling of special text: whitespace and entities, in particular.

XSLT provides several mechanisms for dealing with these little funny bits of content.

Using xsl:text to output text

As you know, in general when you want to put something into the result tree, you just put the literal value into the stylesheet and there it is.

This is *not* always the case when it comes to whitespace, for one. XSLT's rules say that if a node consists entirely of whitespace and nothing but whitespace, that node is *stripped*—removed from the tree entirely, not just compressed (as in HTML) into a single space. For instance, you might think that the following HTML-like XML is treated respectably by an XSLT processor:

```
<td>    </td>
```

Shockingly, that's not what happens. You don't create a table cell with four empty spaces in it; you create a table cell with nothing in it at all. *The text node has been completely removed.* This will happen to any text node consisting of nothing but white space, and has implications for anyone who might be depending on text from the source tree being copied over exactly as-is into the result. Is there a way to force XSLT to do so?

Just as with `xml:element` and `xml:attribute`, there's an `xsl:text` element that is very useful in circumstances where you don't want XSLT to do your whitespace-only text nodes the favor of being deleted. The above snippet, using this element instead of just the literal spaces, would then become:

```
<td><xsl:text>    </xsl:text></td>
```

This produces the desired outcome in the result tree:

```
<td>    </td>
```

Output escaping

Another "favor" XSLT does for you is to prevent you from passing troublesome markup-like characters downstream, to some other application. Actually, those quotation marks are unfair; in most cases, this is exactly what you want and need to have happen. Suppose you have something like this in your XML document, either because you put it there or because someone else (including a calculation) did so:

```
<opinion>I like Callard &amp; Bowser candies &lt;
    Snickers</opinion>
```

Of course you couldn't get away with simply using a bare & and < there, or your own XML parser would scream at you for trying to produce ill-formed XML. But suppose what you really want is for the & to be transformed into a true & , and the < into a true <.

The trick to doing this is to *disable output escaping* for the corresponding node in the result tree. You do so by adding to either the xsl:value-of or the xsl:text element a disable-output-escaping attribute, with a value of yes. Using our above example, we might have this:

```
<xsl:template match="opinion">
    <xsl:value-of select="." disable-output-escaping="yes" />
</xsl:template>
```

The result tree coming out of this transformation would be:

```
I like Callard & Bowser candies < Snickers
```

Problem solved!

Really a problem?

Not to belittle anyone else's agonies at the hands of XSLT, but there really *isn't* a problem with XSLT's default handling of these entities. If you don't have a problem with the need for special entities in XML in general, then what XSLT does makes perfect sense.

About the only significant application I can think of where you absolutely must get literal characters into the result tree, and not entities, is where you're using XML to pass *data* to a non-markup sort of application, like a database. To such an application, a & does not even come close to an &.

But otherwise? Relax. Let things that *should be* entities *be* entities.

Marked (CDATA) sections

There's one other approach to solve this problem, incidentally—if you're feeling adventurous, obsessive, determined to prove a point, or a little of all three. That's to wrap what would otherwise be escaped as entities within CDATA sections, hoping to "protect" them. For example:

```
<opinion><![CDATA[I like Callard & Bowser candies
   < Snickers]]></opinion>
```

This may make it easier to create the source tree/document in the first place, but it won't really solve the problem (without also using `disable-output-escaping="yes"`, I mean): The `&` and `<` will still be converted to their entity equivalents in the *result* tree.

And if you think that putting the CDATA section in the template (as opposed to the source tree) will help, well, no. This:

```
<![CDATA[<xsl:value-of select="."/>]]>
```

doesn't come even approximately close. What it produces in the result tree is this:

```
&lt;xsl:value-of select="."/&gt;
```

Controlling the overall form with xsl:output

XSLT is generally thought of as a tool for turning XML into other XML, or perhaps into well-formed HTML. Actually it's more versatile than that: It can turn XML into "loose" HTML (e.g., creating line breaks as plain old <br> tags, without forcing them to be balanced by </br>s that older browsers won't know anything about), or even into non-marked-up text.[50] Dealing with these various forms of text output may require you to know about the top-level `xsl:output` element.

The principal attribute of several that `xsl:output` can take is the `method` attribute, which in turn can take one of three values: `xml`, `html`, or `text`.

(If you don't specify the method, or omit the `xsl:output` element altogether, the XSLT processor figures out which one you want to use. For instance, if the top-level element of your result tree is `html`, then you probably want the

---

50. Yes, it's versatile—but there are some things it can't do, and also some things it's not worth *making* it do.

html output method. But if you want the text method, you *have* to specify it—the processor will choose only between xml and html.)

Note that if you choose method="xml" but fill the result tree with HTML elements, your result tree will probably still be okay when viewed in recent browsers. Older browsers won't "get" all of it, though. The xml method, for instance, will put an empty element tag into the result tree whenever you use the <br> tag in the spreadsheet—typically presenting it as <br/>. Older browsers don't understand this format and may very well simply ignore the tag.

Whitespace behavior with xsl:strip- and xsl:preserve-space

I mentioned above that XSLT, by default, strips whitespace-only text nodes. You can control this behavior in a fairly fine-tuned way using the top-level xsl:strip-space and xsl:preserve-space elements.

Each of these elements takes a single attribute, elements. The value of the elements attribute is a whitespace-delimited[51] list of the elements to which the xsl:strip- or xsl:preserve-space element is meant to apply.

Making Life Easier

After you've finished your first complete XSLT stylesheet using the techniques described so far in this chapter, you could be forgiven for looking back at it and thinking, "Jeez—I repeated myself an awful lot in there…!" Programmers are familiar with shortcuts (like subroutines, functions, and macros) that help them avoid reentering the same code over and over, and some of these techniques have been carried over into XSLT.

Named attribute sets

One of the most common places to find yourself repeating XSLT code over and over is, understandably, where the result tree has some kind of repeated structure—like an HTML table. HTML being what it is, each table is ignorant of the characteristics of all other tables in the same document; within each table, no

---

51. Ironic, isn't it?

row remembers what you said about the other rows; and each table cell in each row is blissfully unaware of the contents and properties of those above, below, and to either side. This means that if you want a bunch of tables to "look alike," more or less, you're going to be doing a lot of duplication of code. And if you ever decide to change the look, you've got to do so in a dozen places or more, exactly the same way.

This is an ideal situation for what are called *named attribute sets*. Basically, each of these is a group of xsl:attribute elements like the ones we've already covered; the group is collected within a single parent element, xsl:attribute-set, which gives the group a name and makes it available for use throughout the stylesheet.

For example, our *Carnival of Souls* FlixML document (for that matter, just about any FlixML document) has a recurring structure to much of its contents: You'll find a group of things, like in the cast or crew, then for each thing there's a name and a title, or a name and a role, and so on. Let's say I want to build HTML tables with identical characteristics for all these structures. Each table will look something like this:

Name of Group (Cast, Crew, etc.)	
Column 1 heading	*Column 2 heading*
Column 1 data	*Column 2 data*
Column 1 data	*Column 2 data*
Column 1 data	*Column 2 data*
Column 1 data	*Column 2 data*

So what I want to do is use the HTML table elements—table, tr, td, and th—consistently for each of these sections of the source tree, and the way I'd do *that* is to repeat the attributes for all of them. Rather than putting all the attributes in every place I want to use them, I put together XSLT code like this (showing just the common table attributes):

```
<xsl:attribute-set name="table-attribs">
    <xsl:attribute name="width">90%</xsl:attribute>
    <xsl:attribute name="cellspacing">3</xsl:attribute>
    <xsl:attribute name="cellpadding">3</xsl:attribute>
    <xsl:attribute name="border">0</xsl:attribute>
</xsl:attribute-set>
```

Then, in a template rule, in order to automatically assign these attributes and their values to a given element in the result tree, I just provide the element with an `xsl:use-attribute-sets` attribute, the value of which is (in this case) `table-attribs`. Like so:

```
<xsl:template match="crew">
    <table xsl:use-attribute-sets="table-attribs">
        <tr>
          <td colspan="2">Crew</td>
        </tr><xsl:apply-templates/>
    </table>
</xsl:template>
```

This not only makes the template rule code cleaner and more concise; it also greatly simplifies making changes later, and keeping those changes consistent.

Named templates

The named attribute sets might have you thinking, yeah, wonderful, but what about common clusters of *elements* that you want to reuse? Is there an `xsl:ele-ments-set` counterpart?

Not quite, but close. What you can do is create a *named template* that can be reused in its entirety, multiple times in a given result tree. To create a named template, just assign it a name with the value of the `name` attribute. The template may or may not have a `match` attribute as well.

As an example of where you might use this, consider a FlixML document (the one above, or any other). Under the `cast` element are two branches of element and text nodes, one headed by the `leadcast` element and one headed by `othercast`. Under each of those are a number of `male` and/or `female` and/or `animal` elements, beneath each of which is exactly one `castmember` and one `role`. This last set of branches might be laid out in a table defined in the result tree, so that it looks something like the following:

Cast member 1	Role 1
Cast member 2	Role 2
Cast member 3	Role 3
Cast member 4 (etc.)	Role 4 (etc.)

Now, the `male` and `female` elements are to be treated exactly the same in this HTML table; regardless of the cast member's gender, here's the basic template we want to create for each row (note the creation of the `name` attribute to the `a` element, by the way, with the value of an `id` attribute, if any, assigned to it):

```
<tr>
    <td>
        <b>
          <a name="{@id}"/>
          <xsl:value-of select="castmember"/>
        </b>
    </td>
    <td>
        <xsl:value-of select="role"/>
    </td>
</tr>
```

It'd be nuts to code this up once for the `male` elements in `leadcast`, once for the `female` elements in `leadcast`, once for the `male` elements in `othercast`, and once for the `female` elements in `othercast`—to say nothing of including cast members from the animal kingdom in the stylesheet as well. Well, maybe not *nuts*—but (to repeat the mantra) it would be a tedious, error-prone, and tricky task to change all the code consistently should the need arise.

To simplify things, we can put this in a named template, as follows:

```
<xsl:template name="casttemp">
    <tr>
        <td>
          <b>
                    <a name="{@id}"/>
                    <xsl:value-of select="castmember"/>
          </b>
        </td>
        <td>
                    <xsl:value-of select="role"/>
        </td>
    </tr>
</xsl:template>
```

And to actually use the named template wherever we need it, we code:

```
<xsl:call-template name="casttemp"/>
```

at that point in the stylesheet. One line in place of 13, every time we need to do the same thing—quite a savings!

There's an even more powerful use of named templates that I'll get to in a moment, under the section on XSLT parameters.

Variables and parameters

All right, let's see…we've saved ourselves some work, some typing, and some future grief by bundling attributes and templates into reusable packets of markup and text. Is there anything else we can do to simplify our stylesheets further?

The one significant bit of business remaining is the XPath expressions, node-sets, strings, and so on that are scattered throughout a typical stylesheet. And fortunately, there's provision in the XSLT spec for saving these, too, in a reusable form—in what's called a variable or parameter.

Either of these things is simply a holding area, as it were, assigned a name by which you can later refer to it. You define a variable like this:

```
<xsl:variable name="varname" select="expression">
    [optional template goes here]
</xsl:variable>
```

and a parameter in the following fashion:

```
<xsl:param name="varname" select="expression">
    [optional template goes here]
</xsl:param>
```

For both, the `select` attribute is optional; if you use it, the `xsl:variable` or `xsl:param` must not have any child nodes (elements or text); and conversely, if you want to define the optional template, you cannot use a `select` attribute.

The most obvious use of these two devices is to hold boilerplate text, like one of those lengthy legal disclaimers at the foot of a page. You define such a string like this:

```
<xsl:variable name="disclaim">
    Not responsible for typographical or other errors.
Information in this review has been prepared by the author
but is not necessarily [blah blah blah]. Void where
prohibited.
</xsl:variable>
```

Then to use it in a template, just insert the variable or parameter name, preceded by a dollar sign. Like this:

```
<p>Legal Notice</p>
<p>$disclaim</p>
```

You can also set a variable or parameter to a node-set, using the `select` attribute. This enables you to reuse information from the source tree over and over, without constantly having to reenter (or copy-and-paste) a given XPath expression. For instance, one piece of information that's used regularly in a FlixML review as displayed is the film's main title. You've already seen (it seems like eons ago, doesn't it?) how to select this from a document; all you need to do to define a variable with this value is to assign this XPath expression to the variable's `select` attribute:

```
<xsl:variable name="titlevar" select="//title[@role='main']"/>
```

This variable can now be used almost anywhere the original expression would normally be used. For instance, as a header to information about where to buy or rent a copy of the movie:

```
<h1>
    Where to Buy or Rent
    "<xsl:value-of select='$titlevar'/>"
</h1>
```

(One place you *can't* use a variable or parameter like this is as the value of an `xsl:template` element's `match` attribute. There, you must use the expression itself.)

So why two elements?

You might reasonably be wondering why there are two XSLT elements which do the same thing. The reason is that they *don't* do the same thing, not really.

When you set a variable's value, it's basically set for the life of the document, within whatever portion of the document the variable is defined in. (For example, if the `xsl:variable` element is a top-level element—a child of `xsl:stylesheet`–the variable's value is "visible" anywhere in the stylesheet. But if it's defined in the confines of some descendant of `xsl:stylesheet`, such as within a template rule, the value is visible only there.)

A parameter, however, can change its value during the course of a stylesheet's processing. Furthermore, it can be given a default value in the event that during the course of processing, no other value is assigned to it. Finally, if the parameter's definition is done in a top-level `xsl:param` element, its value can even be overridden dynamically, by some value passed into the stylesheet from "the outside world."

Using parameters

Within the `crew` portion of a FlixML review, let's say, we want to build a two-column table structured pretty much as we did above for the cast. In the first column will be the person's title—director, cinematographer, whatever—in boldface; in column two will be his or her name.

The catch is that the person's title is not actually part of the review's content. It's implicit, I guess you could say, in the element name. But in some cases the element name just isn't, well, *right* for display purposes: `speceffects`, anyone?

So with a heavy heart, we resign ourselves to code like this—a different (but nearly identical) copy for every title:

```
<xsl:template match="director">
    <tr>
        <td><b>Director</b></td>
        <td><xsl:apply-templates/></td>
    </tr>
</xsl:template>
<xsl:template match="screenwriter">
    <tr>
        <td><b>Screenwriter</b></td>
        <td><xsl:apply-templates/></td>
    </tr>
</xsl:template>
<xsl:template match="cinematog">
    <tr>
        <td><b>Cinematographer</b></td>
        <td><xsl:apply-templates/></td>
    </tr>
</xsl:template>
```

It's not the template match expression that bothers you; it's all that stuff about what's on the table row—between (and including) the `<tr>` and `</tr>` tags. The only thing different is the word in boldface. Isn't there some way to simplify this…?

What we're going to do is define and then use a parameter, *within* a named template:

```
<xsl:template name="crewrow">
    <xsl:param name="crewtitle">[Title]</xsl:param>
    <tr>
        <td><b><xsl:value-of select="$crewtitle"/></b></td>
        <td><xsl:apply-templates/></td>
    </tr>
</xsl:template>
```

254   **Chapter 8 • Transforming XML with Style: XSL**

Then, at each point in the document where we have a row like this, we're going to call the named template instead—and *pass in a value to override the default* (which is [Title] in this case). So our three template rules from above will now look like this:

```
<xsl:template match="director">
    <xsl:call-template name="crewrow">
            <xsl:with-param name="crewtitle">
                    Director
    </xsl:call-template>
</xsl:template>
<xsl:template match="screenwriter">
    <xsl:call-template name="crewrow">
            <xsl:with-param name="crewtitle">
                    Screenwriter
    </xsl:call-template>
<xsl:template match="cinematog">
    <xsl:call-template name="crewrow">
            <xsl:with-param name="crewtitle">
                    Cinematographer
    </xsl:call-template>
</xsl:template>
```

The contents of the three xsl:with-param elements are used to replace the value of the parameter of the indicated name (crewtitle). If the default value is acceptable, you can omit the xsl:with-param element altogether.

Cool, huh?

External Resources

All this chapter so far has kept you confined in a fairly constrained world. In this world are your source document, which provides the source tree; your lone stylesheet, which is applied to the source tree; and your one result tree—probably a file, and in this chapter's case an HTML file in specific.

But the XSLT world is bigger than that. Although it's not yet possible to produce more than one result tree[52], let's look at the other pieces of the transformational puzzle.

---

52. Actually, it *is* possible. But it's not part of the spec, and requires that you use specific XSLT processing software that supports this feature.

Importing and including other stylesheets

Over time, you will probably find yourself repeating things not only within stylesheets, but from one stylesheet to the next. For instance, all the stylesheets you develop may start with the same block of comments and the same explicit built-in rules.

The XSLT specification provides two ways to break that repeated information out into separate modular components that can be combined with others: *importing* and *including*.

Including a stylesheet in another one is the easiest to explain and understand. Basically, the other stylesheet is retrieved and "virtually embedded" in the one you're working with, becoming to all intents and purposes a part of the latter. Nothing about the included stylesheet can be overridden or changed in any way.

Actually causing the include to happen is just about the easiest thing imaginable:

```
<xsl:include href="uri of included stylesheet"/>
```

The included stylesheet must have its own xsl:stylesheet element. Everything between the opening <xsl:stylesheet> and closing </xsl:stylesheet> tags replaces the xsl:include element in the including stylesheet.

The technique for *importing* another stylesheet looks nearly identical:

```
<xsl:import href="uri of included stylesheet"/>
```

However, there are some additional constraints to using xsl:import–and one big feature, vs. xsl:include.

Constraints first:

- All xsl:import elements must appear as the very first children of the xsl:stylesheet element in the importing stylesheet; *no* template rules or other top-level elements (including xsl:include) may precede the xsl:imports.
- The order in which the xsl:import elements occur (assuming there's more than one) is very important. That's because if the imported template rules overlap—match the same nodes—basically, the last matching template rule "wins."

Since the xsl:import elements all occur before the importing stylesheet's own template rules, this second constraint means that the latter may effectively override or modify the effect of template rules established in the imported documents. This is done with a special `xsl:apply-imports` element, which is used like the `xsl:apply-templates` element at each point where you want the information to be included. (The `xsl:import` elements themselves will be at the head of the stylesheet, but their contents aren't actually invoked until you use the `xsl:apply-imports`.)

Accessing multiple source trees

XSLT provides one last but especially nifty bit. It's called an extension function (meaning, an extension to XPath's expression language), so theoretically XSLT processors are free to include or ignore it as they wish; but it's so potentially useful that it's hard to imagine that many will choose the latter.

The problem this extension function addresses is that all the information you need for your result tree may not be available to you in the source tree the stylesheet is currently processing. For example, perhaps you want to include a given director's complete filmography on your FlixML review page; the filmography is available elsewhere, but it's not even in the FlixML vocabulary.

What you do is include, in the XPath expression you're matching or selecting on, code like this:

```
document("uri of other document", node-set?)
```

This looks up the other document, extracts the indicated node-set, and makes it available in the same way as node-sets located in the current source tree.

Even more little funny bits

It's hard to quantify something like this, but I believe that what I've covered in this chapter will be all that *Just XML*'s readers need for over ninety percent of their XSLT work.

Nonetheless, you should be aware that the spec includes a number of other features, in my opinion more or less obscure, that may get you the rest of the way if you run into obstacles. Among these, in no particular order, are:

1. Modes: enable you to selectively use a template rule, depending on the value of a "flag" that you can set and unset as your document is processed.

2. Creating comments and PIs in the result tree, using `xsl:comment` and `xsl:processing-instruction` elements.
3. Using `xsl:copy` to transfer portions of the source tree, unchanged, to the result tree. (Note that `xsl:copy` is supremely important in applications for transforming a source tree to a result tree in the same XML vocabulary, as for instance when you simply need to reorder content.)
4. Defining and using "keys" that function like ID- and IDREF-type attributes for intradocument linking, but don't require declaration of those attributes in a DTD.
5. Creating messages that will (at least in theory) be displayed to a user under circumstances you define; somewhat dependent on the XSLT processor.

I encourage you, if you need facilities such as these, to examine a copy of the XSLT specification. Once again, it can be found at:

`www.w3.org/TR/xslt`

Summary

In this chapter, I explained how to build style sheets based on the proposed Extensible Stylesheet Language Transformations, or XSLT. Examples covered basic features, such as constructing portions of a result tree from portions of the XML document's element tree, on up to more advanced features such as if-then processing, using variables and templates, and sorting portions of the source tree. The chapter concentrated exclusively on the transformational capabilities of XSL, particularly for transforming XML into HTML that can be displayed in any browser.

Table 8.2   XSLT components covered in this chapter

Item	Description
`<?xml-stylesheet type="text/xsl" href="stylesheetURL"?>`	PI in an XML document that specifies an XSL stylesheet to be used for processing the document.
`<xsl:stylesheet>`	Root element of an XSL stylesheet.

Table 8.2 XSLT components covered in this chapter (continued)

Item	Description

`xmlns:xsl="http://www.w3.org/`
`TR/XSL/Transform"`
`xmlns="http://www.w3.org/TR/`
`REC-html40"`
	Namespace declarations for elements in (respectively) the XSLT and HTML 4.0 namespaces; normally placed in the `xsl:stylesheet` element.

`<xsl:template match="match-` `spec">`	Root element for each template rule intended for processing a particular portion of the source tree.
`<xsl:apply-templates>`	Causes the child nodes of the current node in the source tree to be processed.
`priority="priority"`	Attribute that can be placed on an `xsl:template` element to aid in resolving conflicts when more than one template rule matches a given node.
`<xsl:value-of` `select="matchspec"/>`	Places content from the source tree into the result tree at the location of the `xsl:value-of` element.
`<xsl:if test="condition">`	Creates the following template only if `condition` is true.

`<xsl:choose>`
`<xsl:when test="condition">`
`<xsl:otherwise>`
	Creates one of several templates depending on several conditions.

`<xsl:for-each>`	Loops through a portion of the source tree and creates some template for each iteration of the loop.
`<xsl:sort>`	Sorts a portion of the source tree.
`<xsl:attribute name="name">`	Creates an attribute named `name` in the result tree.
`<xsl:element name="name">`	Creates an element named `name` in the result tree.
`<xsl:text>`	Creates a text node in the result tree.

Table 8.2   XSLT components covered in this chapter (continued)

Item	Description
`disable-output-escap-ing="yesorno"`	Attribute to the `xsl:text` or `xsl:value-of` elements, permitting entities such as & and < to be placed in the result tree in their literal form rather than as entity references.
`<xsl:strip-space elements="elementlist>` `<xsl:preserve-space elements="elementlist">`	Specify elements for which whitespace-only nodes should be stripped or preserved, respectively.
`<xsl:output method="method">`	Controls the way in which the XSLT processor treats the result tree as a whole; possible values of `method` are `html`, `xml`, and `text`.
`<xsl:attribute-set name="name">`	Defines a group of attributes that may be placed as a group anywhere in the source tree.
`xsl:use-attribute-sets="name"`	Attribute that may be placed on any element in the result tree; brings in the attribute set named `name` as if its attributes had been applied directly to the element.
`<xsl:template name="name">`	Creates a template rule, named `name`, which may be reused anywhere in the stylesheet.
`<xsl:call-template name="name">`	Brings into the result tree, at the point where placed, the value of the named template named `name`.
`<xsl:variable name="name">`	Defines a variable for later reuse in a stylesheet.
`<xsl:param name="name">`	Defines a parameter for later reuse in a stylesheet.

Table 8.2   XSLT components covered in this chapter (continued)

Item	Description
`$name`	Uses the variable or parameter named `name`.
`<xsl:with-param name="name">`	Used as a child element to `xsl:call-template`, overrides the default value of the parameter named `name`.
`<xsl:include href="uri">`	Includes the stylesheet located at `uri` in the current stylesheet.
`<xsl:import href="uri">`	Imports the stylesheet located at `uri` into the current stylesheet.
`<xsl:apply-imports>`	Processes imported template rule(s) at the point in the stylesheet where the `xsl:apply-imports` element is placed; allows for overriding or modifying some of the imported template.
`document("uri", nodeset?)`	Can be used to select portions of an XML document other than the one currently being processed.

Terms defined in this chapter

In addition to the terms related to specific XSLT markup as summarized in Table 8.2, this chapter also defined the following terms:

DSSSL The Document Style Semantics and Specification Language, or *DSSSL*, is the parent language from which XSLT is derived. Like SGML (for which it is primarily used), DSSSL features a tree-like structure of nested elements and attributes. This makes it possible to easily map styled objects onto portions of the SGML document's element tree.

source tree The tree of nodes (elements, attributes, text, comments, and PIs) that is being "read" by a stylesheet is called the *source tree*. (Compare with *result tree*, below.)

result tree The tree of nodes (elements, attributes, text, comments, and PIs) that is being "written" by a stylesheet, as a result of content and conditions present in the *source tree*, is called the *result tree*.

template rule A *template rule* tests a portion of the source tree; if it finds a match, it creates one or more nodes in the result tree. The result tree's node(s) so created are called the template.

pattern The portion of a template rule that identifies the subset of the source tree for which a template may be created in the result tree.

action The portion of a rule that defines the template to be created when the pattern (see above) matches a node in the source tree.

built-in template rules By default, every XSLT stylesheet, even the most rudimentary, comes with three *built-in template rules* for processing the source tree's content. The three built-in rules cover: the root and element nodes; text and attribute nodes; and comment and PI nodes.

output escaping When an XSLT processor turns literal special characters, such as the ampersand and less-than signs, into entity references such as `&amp;` and `&lt;`, this is referred to as *output escaping*.

whitespace stripping XSLT's default behavior when encountering a whitespace-only node is to completely remove that node; this process is called *whitespace stripping*.

Rolling Your Own XML Application

With your head stuffed with all the information from Parts 1 through 3—XML itself, XLink/XPointer, and styling XML using CSS2 and XSLT—you could be forgiven for wanting a break.

The single big chapter that constitutes all of Part 4 isn't intended primarily as a break, but it will serve that purpose, too, as it leads you through the steps necessary to lay the foundation of an XML application of your own.

The next part of *Just XML*, Part 5, will cover what lies ahead for XML-related technologies.

CHAPTER 9

The XML DTD

Throughout *Just XML,* you've been presented with XML, XLink/ XPointer, CSS2, and XSL examples from a single XML application: FlixML, a markup language for creating full descriptions of B movies.

FlixML is, as things go, a fairly simple XML application. With it, I've hoped to show you that even simple needs, expressed in XML, can be satisfied in powerful and elegant ways. You needn't feel constrained by *my* tastes, though. With XML you can create documents capable of carrying and presenting structured information about, well, *anything.*[53] That's what this chapter is about: rolling your own XML application.

Now, in the event that you're a programmer chomping at the bit to do some real procedural coding, by God, the term "application" here *does not mean "program."* Rather, it's the formal term for what I've generally been referring to as "vocabulary." FlixML is an XML application. There's an XMLized version of HTML, XHTML (which is an XML application), and so on.

---

53. XML's strengths "scale up" well: as your requirements grow, so does the ability of XML to meet them. Beyond a certain point you may wish to consider moving to full-blown SGML, but if so, your experiences with XML will have been indispensable.

Note that we won't be leaving FlixML behind. I don't know what *you* will want to use XML for, and most of the examples of DTD components that I use here will still be FlixML-based. Again, though, just don't kid yourself that FlixML is the be-all and end-all of markup languages!

Where's the spec?

Well, there isn't an "XML DTD specification" as such. It's incorporated in the main XML standard itself, at:

www.w3c.org/TR/REC-xml-19980210

As I mentioned early on in this book, the XML standard is fairly short, only about twenty to thirty pages. Of that total, though, well over half relates to constructing DTDs as opposed to the XML documents that use them. So, if you want the authoritative source for what goes into a DTD and how to express it, that's the place to look.

(Remember though that the spec defines XML in Extended Backus-Naur Form, or EBNF. This is a concise and inscrutable—in roughly equal proportions—language for defining computer languages. It may take you some time to get the hang of it, but if you persist, the effort will pay off!)

Why a DTD?

It's true: You don't need to use a DTD at all. The simple requirements of well-formed XML impose enough structure on your markup that a parser can *infer* a DTD from well-formed code.

Creating and using a DTD to validate your documents, though, offers several advantages over creating documents off the top of your head. Here are some of the most important ones.

Consistency

Things haven't quite gotten to the point where everybody is constructing his or her home page in XML rather than HTML. There isn't any real reason why not, though, once the browsing and other applications catch up to the standards: a home page is a perfect demonstration of a case where we needn't care who uses which element names, what their attributes are, and so on. My home page might use a `jesroot` element as its root, and have (say) `mybio`, `myresume`, and `myinter-`

`ests` children, each with its own unique subtrees—none of which would square with the element names or indeed overall document structure of your or anyone else's home page. Everyone for himself. Liberty, equality, fraternity.

Actually, almost no real XML application would *not* benefit from having a DTD. That's because most documents to be shared over the Web can be classified as members of a family: this one's a press report; that one's an analysis of some important social issue; this other one over here contains Frank Sinatra's discography and some audio samples. . . . Press reports; issue analyses; discographies—see? Families of documents.

With all of us making up our own document structures, element type names, and attribute/value pairs that vary from one page to the next, the scene would get rather messy, to say the least. For me to use an XPointer to display part of your home page, for example, I've got to know what element type names you use. If I hope to build up a page of partial bios of my immediately family without coding them all myself, I've got to know *all* the element types that *all* of them use.

If we all use the same DTD, though, the problem goes away. We can all, literally, be on the same page.

Rigor

This is a value that it seems as a culture we don't heed much any longer—the value of looking before we leap, of not rushing in where angels fear to tread.

I think of myself as a pretty spontaneous kind of guy (I too am a child of the culture, after all). Still, outside of relationships, vacations, choosing pets, dashing with pistol raised into a new Duke Nukem level, and deciding which frozen dinner to eat tonight, it doesn't generally make good sense to just plunge into things without at least some forethought.

Thought before action constitutes the soul of using a DTD. (Even better, if you really want discipline, is the act of *constructing* a DTD.)

XML features requiring a DTD

Some things just can't be done with XML unless there's a DTD (at the very least, an internal subset).

For instance, without a DTD, you can't use any entities. Without entities, forget the prospect of using boilerplate text and single character substitution. And communicating your document's structure to someone else for others to use, either for their own XML documents or for ancillary purposes like linking and style sheets? *Definitely* forget that—or at least, resign yourself to loooong tedious brainstorming sessions.

Getting Started

This is easy advice, glibly stated: *plan ahead*. It's also way too general to be actually useful. Let's take a look at some of the things you need to consider when embarking on your own XML application.

Is there already a DTD you can use?

The prospect of developing a DTD can be simultaneously scary and exciting. It may feel like you're about to enter a forbidden world, whose mysteries are known to but a few. And that alone may be sufficient inducement to do it.

Unless you're really in it for educational purposes, resist the initial temptation. Check around online to see if there's already a DTD for your application, or one very much like it. (There are already some DTD respositories on the Web; see Appendix B for some of them.) Remember that you can extend a DTD in some ways within a document itself, so even if it's not a perfect fit, you may still be able to use an existing one; if necessary, you may be able to contact the DTD's author to ask for features that you *can't* add. Remember, too, that one of the whole points of using a DTD in the first place is to enable documents created by different authors to share the same structures—i.e., interchangeability. Going off on your own works against this goal; maybe there's a *reason* why a given feature is present or absent.

Industry-wide DTDs

It will especially make sense for you to look around if the application you're thinking of building is related to your work. If you're anything from a factory worker to a journalist or a car salesman to a Pope, there's quite likely a consortium somewhere working on the thorny problems common to every business or organization in the same boat as you. Many hands make light(er) work of big jobs like creating a DTD to be used by a thousand similar groups of people, and they've very likely already done your work for you.

> This also applies, by the way, even if your application is *not* work-related. Thinking of developing a DTD to support your tropical fish hobby? Get in touch with other enthusiasts of guppies, anemones, snails, angelfish, and plaster coral-reef and deep-sea-diver ornaments. Pick their brains. Enlist their help—and offer yours!

Your information's structure

Having determined that there's no DTD that already suffices, you *must* think about the structure of the information you want to represent.

Somewhere out there—in an infinite universe, as they say, all things are possible—there may be some kind of information that *can't* be structured. But useful information that resists structure is probably too small-scale to bother developing in the context of a DTD: single words, for instance, and numbers that don't count anything but just sort of drift about in space, unanchored to units of measure. Like that.

Chances are, though, that you can easily rattle off a dozen or more common "kinds of information" that you hope to capture in the XML documents that will eventually be built with your DTD. Here are some of the key things to consider, and a way to organize them once considered.

Relationships between kinds of information

Let's say you're creating a DTD to be used by shipbuilders. You follow my suggestion of the preceding paragraph and write down a list of every kind of "thing" that you need to work with to build a ship:[54] sails and/or engines (oh yeah, and if you've got an engine, you're going to want a propeller, too); rudder; compass and other navigational aids; materials; labor; lumber and/or steel and/or fabric; time; a blueprint or some other drawing—probably more than one, now that you think about it; money; people from whom you buy materials; and then maybe you need more than one person to do all the work. (You may well decide to stop there: The list is starting to grow, you're thinking maybe you should get your shipbuilding buddies together over beer and hammer it out with *them*....)

One thing that tends to leap out at you when you start to build up such a list is that some items are *part of* or *subordinate to* others. There's the category of pre-

---

54. Not a specific ship, but any given ship: the specifics for a given ship will be in the XML document itself, not the DTD.

assembled components—the compass, the anchor, probably the engine and/or sails—and on the other hand is the class of all the things you have to build yourself, using raw materials like wood, fiberglass, plastic, and steel. You'll have contractors come in to do some of the work, and some of them may have subcontractors, and for all this hired help, you'll need names, addresses, phone numbers, etc.

You may be tempted therefore to throw away all the items that represent general *categories* of information and just retain all the details. As with many temptations, on- as well as offline, the proper response is: Don't do it!

Somewhere down the line you'll want to ask questions like, "Tell me everything about all the contractors who worked on Project X." If you've got it all in separate little bits of data with no structure, you'll have to rephrase that question in some laborious manner like, "Tell me the names of all contractors who worked on this project; tell me all their addresses and phone numbers; what work they did and when; how much did they bill me on May 1, June 1, July 1," and so on.

Make up a road map

With your preliminary list of information in hand, sketch out a block diagram of the relationships. Make it a pyramid of boxes, with a tentative name for "the whole thing" in the top box and separate boxes under that for the most general categories beneath it. Figure 9.1 shows a portion of the diagram I first came up with for FlixML.

If possible, build the road map in pencil, or with graphics software like an organization chart builder, or using Post-It Notes or little blocks of paper that you can fasten in place on a background sheet.

The reason? You need to take a close look to determine if the boxes are in the right order, and rearrange them if not. In FlixML I eventually had to decide, for example, if the cast should appear before the crew, where to place the genre, and so on.[55]

---

55. I probably ought to tell you, in case you're the nervous sort, that no XML police will be battering down your door should you choose *not* to prepare a road map before diving in. In fact, as far as I know, no one else even suggests making one up in such a detailed way as I'm describing here. It's just a useful tool to help visualize what we're going to be covering in the next few sections.

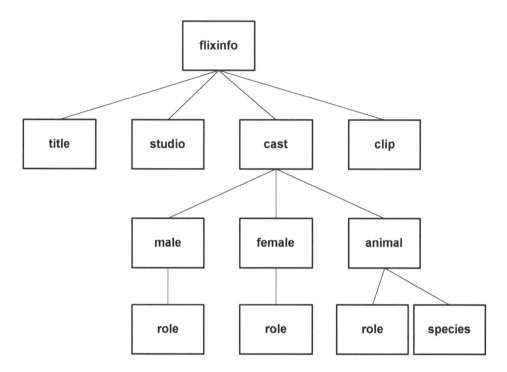

Figure 9.1   Preliminary FlixML road map

Mark items on the road map

What you're going to do next is to indicate on the road map *how many times* each "thing" will probably occur in a given document or project (except the top-level one, of course, which occurs only once). You don't need to keep tabs on *exactly* how many there might be; in fact, you've got only four choices:

- It's optional—might occur in some documents but not in others—but if it's in a document, it will never be there more than once. (This translates to a "**0 or 1**" occurrence. Pencil in a question mark (?) next to these boxes.
- It's optional, and if it's in a given document, it could be there once or more than once—effectively "**0 or more**" times. Add an asterisk (*) next to any box that fits this category.
- It will always be in a document once, but never more than once ("**1 and only 1**" kinds of information). Don't bother marking these boxes in any special way.

• It will always be in a document at least once, and possibly more often—a "**1 or more**" type of occurrence. Next to these boxes, pencil in a plus sign (+).

Figure 9.2 shows you the preliminary FlixML road map of Figure 9.1, with these special markings added.[56]

Now, put the road map aside. You'll need it again in a few minutes, but first you have some more abstract notions to think about.

Ease of use

Wherever possible, you need to consider how easy to use you want and need your DTD to be. Note that the question isn't *whether* you want it to be easy to use, but

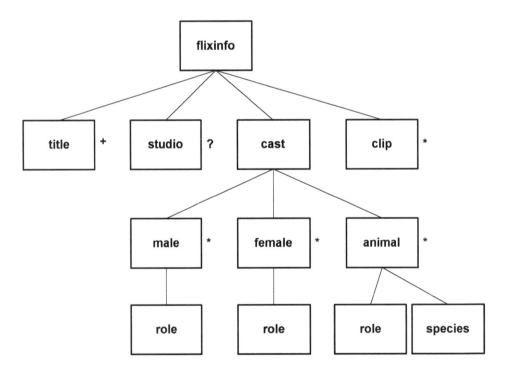

Figure 9.2 FlixML road map (with occurrence labels)

---

56. More experienced readers, especially from the UNIX world, may recognize these special characters: they're used for the same purposes when constructing regular expressions.

how easy. For example, at some point, you're going to be declaring element types that can be used in a YourML document. When others use your DTD, will they have to type unnaturally long or cryptic element names? Is there some way—regardless of what the element names turn out to be—that you can *structure* the names, so that even if they're hard to remember, they're easy for a document author to guess at?

Another ease-of-use consideration is general entities: What possibilities are there for you to declare these, thereby making the document author's job easier (and helping to guarantee consistency, by the way)?

Complete, but not too complete

You'll need to include in your DTD allowances for as many eventualities as possible. You can start by assuming that if something shows up on your preliminary road map, it should probably go into the DTD; don't stop there, though. What have you omitted? Put the road map aside for a day or two and then revisit it. What's missing? What's overdone? Take a look especially at each bottom-level box, those that don't split off into other boxes; have you provided for things like a potential need to emphasize text somewhere *within* each box's contents? If not, do you need to? (If so, of course, add a box for emphasized text.)

On the other hand, don't go overboard. You can fuss with a DTD forever and never get it 100% right—all you'll succeed at is preventing yourself (and everyone else) from ever using the thing to actually construct an XML document (the "don't build an imperfect something until you can build a perfect everything" syndrome).

Remember that you can easily modify the DTD later, especially if you make it available on the Web. Need to add a new element type? Add it to the DTD, and all documents referring to that DTD may now have that element type in their trees as well.

M a y b e   n o t   q u i t e   t h a t   s i m p l e ...

In the preceding paragraph, I skated blithely over the fact that when you make changes to a DTD that's already in use, you risk making the referring XML documents invalid even if they're perfectly compatible with the earlier version. This isn't a way to make friends, even with yourself.

Far better is to publish *versions* of the DTD. New documents that need the new features can simply point to the new DTD, and older documents won't break as long as the earlier version is still around. This is the approach I've taken with FlixML. For the first edition of *Just XML*, I developed the DTD located at:

www.flixml.org/flixml/flixml.dtd

Since then it's gone through several intermediate versions; Version 3 (current as of this edition) is at:

www.flixml.org/flixml/flixml_03.dtd

Documents referring to the first version will still parse correctly; documents needing to take advantage of newer features (and bug fixes!) can point to the later versions instead.

Types of XML Document Content

Think about the XML documents you've already seen. If you mentally throw away the tags, attributes, and other markup, what's left?

Parsed character data

The first and most common thing that's left is plain old text. In XML terms, what's there may not seem particularly significant, but the parser doesn't ignore this document content—indeed, it must read through it to make entity substitutions, collapse whitespace as needed, and so on. It's therefore referred to as *parsed character data*, or in shorthand, #PCDATA. (When you pronounce that, the "#" is silent—just say "pee-see data.")

Nonparsed character data

There may be some stuff that's left after discarding the elements and attributes which you don't *want* the parser to process. If you've got mathematical formulae, for instance, you don't want the parser to hiccup every time it encounters a less-than sign, <, just because it thinks that the < is introducing a new branch of the element tree. If your document is explaining how to create HTML, SGML, or XML documents, you certainly don't want the parser to try validating your examples. And so on.

Such portions of the document are said to contain nonparsed character data, called simply *character data* or CDATA ("see-data").

A confusion of tongues

I know, "character data" seems a woefully inadequate term—at the least, so it would seem, *parsed character data* should be a subset of *character data.* I can't explain this. Sorry.

"Empty data"

When you've discarded all elements and attributes, you'll probably find that *some* content has magically disappeared with them.

For instance, images and other multimedia typically don't "exist" in a document outside the context of an element. In HTML (updated to XML syntax), an image tag might look like this:

```
<img src="images/beehive.gif"/>
```

If you throw away the `<img>` tag, the image goes with it. For many kinds of XML applications, this noncharacter data can be as important as the text—even more important.

Back to the Road Map

Pull out the road map you've got so far. You're going to go back over it and label each box according to its content: `#PCDATA`, `EMPTY`, or `MIXED`–or leave it unlabeled.

Boxes at the bottom: EMPTY or #PCDATA?

The boxes that "contain" no other boxes—they're often the ones all the way out at the furthest reaches of the road map—won't be labeled `MIXED`, so you can ignore that possibility for the moment. So ask yourself: Will these boxes at the ends of the tree contain any text data at all? (In their own right, that is—not as a part of some offspring box's content.)

- If not (i.e., all they contain is *nontext*), label them `EMPTY`.
- If they *do* contain text, they're `#PCDATA`.

> **Missing in action**
>
> You should remember from earlier in this book that some text content in a given document might occur in special "marked sections," so-called CDATA sections, intended to simplify use of special characters like the < and > signs.
>
> There's no special way to signify in a DTD that a given element may include CDATA content; any element that may contain #PCDATA content may have a CDATA section, too.

All other boxes

All the boxes left unlabeled contain at least one other box. They may or may not contain some real data (i.e., text) as well.

- If they do, label them MIXED. (An element type with mixed content is one containing both text—that is, #PCDATA—and other elements.)
- If they don't, don't label them further.

A complete (more or less) road map

Congratulations—you've just done nearly all the real work you need to do in order to build your DTD.

I've tried to use the language carefully while giving you the road map instructions in order not to tip my hand, but you've probably caught on to what's really happening: The road map represents the full element tree of a document coded in YourML. The box at the top—that'll be your root element. All the other elements descend from it, in a series of successively branching and ever-widening pathways until hitting the end of a given branch, where much of the document's true content probably lies. Some blanks will be necessary for you to fill in later (such as attributes, values, and entities), but what's on the road map constitutes perhaps seventy-five percent of the planning.

For the record, Figure 9.3 shows you my preliminary FlixML road map, complete with all the content type labels.

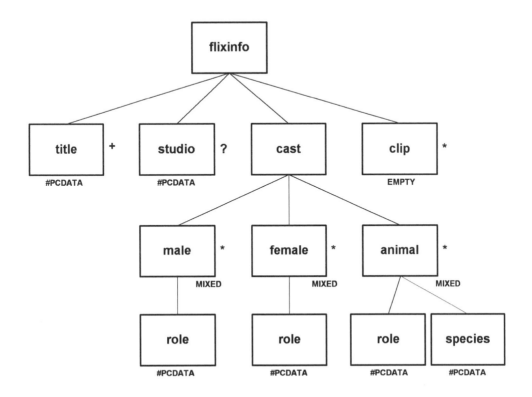

Figure 9.3   FlixML road map (with content types)

Anatomy of a DTD

Before diving into the details of what's inside a DTD, let's take a look at its general characteristics.

Structure

A DTD is (like just about everything else in XML) a text file. It's made up of a series of "statements" of what it is possible to do in a valid XML document using this DTD. Each statement typically takes up a line, although they may extend over many lines if what the thing is trying to say is involved.

In general—with a few exceptions—there's no need to worry about the order of the statements. Parsers need to read in the whole DTD to construct a tree (in their heads, if you will) that matches the expected (potential) element tree of the XML document itself; therefore, if a given element A is to contain elements B and C, you can declare A first, then B, then C, or B and C before A, or use any other order you want.

It's best if you apply *some* reason to the structure, however. This isn't for the good of the parser, which doesn't care; it's for your own good, and the good of any other mere humans who hope to make sense of the DTD. As an example, when I first started working on FlixML, there were only a handful of elements and attributes; the current listing runs to somewhere between eight and ten printed pages (depending on margins, fonts, and so on). That's a lot of haystack to sort through just to find a single needle.

So what order *does* make sense?

You can work from the bottom of your tree up if you want, listing the declarations of all the little-bitty pieces and working your way up to the grand overall piece, the root element. This is better than no structure at all, but only marginally: If there are a lot of leaves on your tree, it will take a much longer time for a human reader to understand the whole picture.

So I recommend starting at the top of the tree, and working your way down a whole branch at a time before moving onto the next branch. If A contains B and C, and B contains D, E, and F, declare A first; then B; then D, E, and F; then C.

A more specific question is where to put the declarations of attributes. Again, you can put them wherever you want—but I think it makes good logical sense to declare each set of attributes immediately after the element that it goes with.

Structural exceptions

In a couple of cases, you may have to declare the characteristics of pieces of a document that don't really belong to any particular branch of the tree—not boxes in their own right, in other words. These are the entities (if any) and notations (if any) that a YourML document may include. I think the logical place to put them in a DTD is at the top, *before* declaring the components of the element tree itself.

Put all the entities together in a single block of "entity-declaring" statements. Put the parameter entities first in this block, which will enable you to use them (if need be) in the general-entity declarations. (I know, you don't yet have any real idea what parameter entities are. We'll get to them later in this chapter.) Follow the parameter entities with the general entities. Remember that whenever a reference to an entity is made in the document (general entities) or in the

DTD (parameter entities), the parser needs to know how to expand it—so be sure to sequence the entity declarations accordingly. If the declaration of Entity X includes a reference to Entity Y, declare Y *first.*

Put all the notation declarations into a single block of statements as well. I'd recommend putting the notations *before* the entities, at the very top of the DTD; this enables them to be used as necessary in the entity declarations.

Structure: summary

So then, the rough outline of what's in your DTD will look like this:

1. Notation declarations
2. Entity declarations
   a) Parameter entities
   b) Character and general entities
3. Element type declarations
   a) Uppermost (usually the root) element type—element declaration first, followed by declarations of any attributes assigned to the this element
   b) Offspring of the uppermost (root) element type, declaring a whole branch at a time—each element declaration followed by declarations of that element's attributes

Appearance

The structure of your DTD will help you (or another human reader) piece together the logical structure of any possible XML document based on it. Its *readability* will also contribute to this understanding.

Use whitespace (which the parser ignores in a DTD) liberally. Line things up, so that all the element names, attribute names, and so on are in the same place as the reader looks up and down the page. Add a blank line after each element's attribute declarations, to separate the whole of an element's specifications from those that surround it.

Finally, don't forget to add *comments* to the DTD. These should at least explain any anomalies or considerations that might not be obvious when reading through the DTD. To the extent possible, they should also be structured the same way for like portions of the DTD: use one standard "comment template" for elements, another for attributes, and so on. Again, the idea is to make using your DTD easy and *unsurprising* for a human reader.

DTD Syntax

The contents of a DTD all follow the same general syntax:

```
<!keyword    keyword-name keyword-name-description>
```

The opening `<!` and the closing `>` are required. The `keyword` must be selected from the list shown in Table 9.1; specific values for `keyword-name` and `keyword-name-description` will vary depending on the XML application for which you're developing a DTD. (The formats of `keyword-name` and `keyword-name-description` are fixed, though; each of the keywords in Table 9.1 has its own section in the rest of this chapter, where you can learn about these required formats.)

Table 9.1   DTD "keywords"

Keyword	Declares:
ELEMENT	An element type that is or may be part of the document's element tree.
ATTLIST	One or more attributes for a given element type.
ENTITY	An entity to be used either in the document itself, or elsewhere in the DTD.
NOTATION	Document content that is outside the scope of the XML standard (e.g., media types).

Informal terminology
The terms "keyword," "keyword-name," and "keyword-name-description" aren't official—certainly not in the way I'm using them here.

Comments

You can—and should—use comments in your DTD just as in an XML document. These can be terrifically helpful in making your intentions plain to a human reader, although they may not mean much (if anything) to a piece of software.

As elsewhere in XML, DTD comments start with a `<!--` sequence and end with `-->`, and may contain anything between those opening and closing characters except a pair of adjacent hyphens (`--`). There's no special standard or even a recommendation (yet) for what form comments in a DTD should take, but it will be most helpful if you structure such comments consistently, using tabs and other whitespace.[57]

Elements

This is the real meat of any XML document. In fact, if you're so inclined you can create a DTD that declares nothing but elements—a DTD without them would be useless.

The declaration of an element looks like this:

```
<!ELEMENT element-name (content-model)>
```

The `element-name` component is, of course, the name of the element. It must start with either a letter or an underscore; beyond the first character it can contain any combination of letters, digits, underscores, hyphens, periods, or colons. You can capitalize all letters, none of them, or a mixture of both. You should however, for consistency's sake, choose some kind of element naming convention, so if you use mixed case in one name, don't make another all caps. Remember the ease of use guidelines as well: Don't make element names too long or too short; make them descriptive of the content they contain.

The parentheses on either side of `content-model` are required, unless the `content-model` consists of only a single item.

But what exactly is `content-model`?

The content model

Simply put, an element's *content model* (as the name suggests) establishes a template into which the content of all occurrences of the element will fit. What you plug into that portion of the element declaration can be as simple as an element name and as complex as two or more element names grouped and subgrouped, any or all of which may have various modifiers applied to them as described in the remainder of this section.

---

57. By the time you read this, the XML Schema spec will probably have attained Recommendation status. This spec defines techniques for expressing the required structure and datatypes of an XML application *in XML form*, rather than in the non-XML syntax used by DTDs. XML Schema does indeed include a specification for the syntax of comments, by way of its `annotation` element.

Referring back to your (or the FlixML) road map, the tree of boxes together with all those little markings outside them provide your content model. They denote:

- **Optionality and occurrence:** Either a box's content is required or it's not. Boxes in the road map labeled with a ? are completely optional; if included, such an element may occur only once within its parent element. If labeled with a *, the element is optional; and if included, may occur one or more times within its parent. If labeled with a +, the element must be present at least once (but possibly more than once) within its parent. If unlabeled with any of these characters, the element must appear once and only once within its parent.
- **Content type:** This element contains parsed character data (#PCDATA), child elements but no real content of its own (unlabeled), or a mixture of content and child elements (MIXED), or it is empty (EMPTY).

The "any content" option

Although I didn't give you this option when stepping you through the road map construction, besides #PCDATA, MIXED, EMPTY, or no label at all, you could also have chosen to label a box ANY. This is a no-holds-barred, anything-goes option, meaning that the given box can contain *any* content type at all: child elements, text, whatever. ANY is kind of like saying, "I want this portion of the element tree to be merely well-formed."

ANY is a useful convenience when you're first preparing a DTD, but in my opinion its overuse makes for a pretty dreadful XML document. It seems to imply that the DTD's designer really hasn't thought through his or her application very thoroughly.

There are also a couple of considerations of element content that *could* be declared on the road map, but will require you to think a bit more about your XML documents' content:

- **Sequence:** Ask yourself as you look over the road map, "Must this box's contents appear in any particular order?" For instance, if you've got a parent "address" box, normally it will contain boxes for street address, city, state or other geographic region, postal code, and country. Do you want to require such child boxes to appear in this order in a document based on this DTD? If the DTD defines a "memo" application, do you want the addressee always to come before the contents, which would always come before the signature?

- **Selection:** Perhaps one of two child elements must be chosen, but not both. Or maybe an element's content can contain either #PCDATA or a child element, but not both.

Special characters can be used to alter what a content model "means"; these special characters (some of which you used in constructing the road map) are summarized in Table 9.2. Note that, especially when using the "content-grouping" parentheses, extremely complex sets of relationships can be built up.

Table 9.2   Special content model modifier characters

Character	Meaning	FlixML Example	Interpretation
Separators between multiple content types			
, (comma between two content types)	*Sequence* of content.	`castmember, role`	`castmember` must appear before `role` in parent element.
| (vertical bar/ pipe between two content types)	*Selection* of content.	`goodreview | badreview`	Parent element contains either `goodreview` or `badreview`.
Content occurrence and optionality			
* (asterisk)	Content occurs *0 or more times.*	`director*`	Parent element does not require a `director` element; if present at all, there can be any number of them.
+ (plus)	Content occurs *1 or more times.*	`title+`	Parent element must have one or more `title` elements.

Table 9.2   Special content model modifier characters (continued)

Character	Meaning	FlixML Example	Interpretation
? (question mark)	Content *optional*; if present, may occur only once.	`plotsummary?`	Parent element may or may not contain a single `plotsummary` element.
(no occurrence symbol)	Content must occur *once and only once*.	`genre`	A `genre` element must be present in the parent.
Content grouping			
( ) (parentheses surrounding two or more content types, separated from one another by commas or vertical bars)	Multiple content types grouped into a single unit.	`(male | female | animal)*`	Parent element may contain any number of `male` or `female` or `animal` child elements, in any order.

Let's put these various modifiers through their paces in some examples.

> **Missing pieces**
>
> If you're still with me, you may have observed that there's no way in an XML DTD to specify that a given element can contain single occurrences of its children elements in any old order.[58] SGML has a connector, the ampersand (&), which is used for just that. For example:
>
>   figure & caption
>
> means, "I don't care what order `figure` and `caption` are in, as long as they're both present." The decision to drop the ampersand option in the move from the SGML spec to the XML spec remains a source of disgruntlement among some SGML aficionados; eliminating it has simplified XML enormously, however (especially the *processing* of XML by parsers and other software).

---

58.   An element can contain multiple occurrences of its children in any order, however—as in the last row of Table 9.2.

> (There's a way to simulate the effect of this unordered content modifier, which I'll mention in a moment.)
>
> Also missing from XML proper is any simple way to specify a particular number of occurrences of a given content type contained by an element, or a minimum/maximum of occurrences. That is, there's no construct like this:
>
> ```
> weekday*7
> ```
>
> to indicate that the weekday element must occur seven times and seven times only. The only way to get around this limitation is to list the recurring content type that many times, and group them, like this:
>
> ```
> (weekday, weekday, weekday, weekday, weekday,
>  weekday, weekday)
> ```
>
> This is a bit clunky for even a moderate number of occurrences; showing, say, that a hypothetical "day" element needs to occur exactly 365 times (let alone *either* 365 *or* 366) would go beyond clunky—probably not worth the trouble.
>
> Both of these limitations may, of course, be addressed in later versions of the XML spec, as well as the XML Schema specification (covered briefly in Part 5).

Simple content models

Most often, the elements at the "leaves" of your element tree will simply contain #PCDATA. An example of such an element is FlixML's role element, whose DTD declaration looks like this:

```
<!ELEMENT role (#PCDATA)>
```

This says that when a FlixML document contains a role element, the only content which that element may contain is parsed character data, or #PCDATA.

In place of the content type, you can also enter an element name. Just one name alone, without any special punctuation, means, "When an element of the type I'm declaring here is present in an XML document, it may contain only one child element whose name I'm also indicating here, and may contain nothing else." (An element which must contain one child and one child only seems a rather limited sort of element, and FlixML doesn't contain such a beast anywhere.)

Even simpler, though not as common, are empty elements—all of whose "content" is *in* the given instance of the element in the document—indeed, actually in the tag itself. FlixML has a few of these, such as the `audio` and `video` elements:

```
<!ELEMENT audio EMPTY>
<!ELEMENT video EMPTY>
```

(Note that the parentheses don't need to appear in an empty element's content model.)

The term "empty" doesn't mean, really, that the element is truly empty; just that there's no start- and end-tag pair required (or if they're present, nothing at all appears between them) in the document. If the above elements didn't require any attributes, any of the following four tags in a FlixML document would be valid:

```
<audio/>
<audio></audio>
<video/>
<video></video>
```

Multiple occurrences of content type

Here's an important, not necessarily obvious, concept: You don't declare how many times an element may occur in the declaration of *that* element; you declare the occurrences in the content model of the *containing* element. This enables a given element (or other content) type to occur a different number of times depending on the context in which it appears.

Suppose you were developing a DTD for a calendar XML application. One of the leaves of the element tree might be a `day` element, whose declaration would be:

```
<!ELEMENT day (#PCDATA)>
```

To include this element as part of a hypothetical `date` element, the latter might be declared as:

```
<!ELEMENT date (month, day, year)>
```

whereas the `daysinmonth` element's declaration would look like this:

```
<!ELEMENT daysinmonth (day+)>
```

FlixML, as it happens, doesn't include any elements that fit this particular scenario. But there are a number of content models in FlixML that use the various "occurrence modifiers" in simple ways, particularly in the case of the root `flixinfo` element (normally the root):

```
<!ELEMENT flixinfo (contents?, title+, genre, releaseyear+,
language*, studio*, cast?, crew?, plotsummary?,
reviews?, clips?, distributors?, dialog?, remarks?,
mpaarating?, bees?)>
```

A complete FlixML document whose root is the `flixinfo` element therefore needs to include *only* a `title`, a `genre`, and a `releaseyear` to be valid (there can be more than one `title` and/or `releaseyear`, per the + signs in the content model). All the rest are optional, although the ones marked with a `?` (`contents`, `cast`, `crew`, `plotsummary`, `reviews`, `clips`, `distributors`, `dialog`, `remarks`, `mpaarating`, and `bees`), if present at all, can occur at most once apiece.

Multiple occurrences of *groups of content type*

Using parentheses to group different parts of the content model, you can declare that different types of content occur a different number of times in that content model. For instance:

```
<!ELEMENT leadcast (male | female | animal)*>
```

Translated, this says that the `leadcast` element can contain any number of `male` *or* `female` *or* `animal` child elements, in any order.

Note, by the way, that it makes a difference where the parentheses and occurrence operators occur. The above example says: "the first child of `leadcast` can be `male`, `female`, or `animal`; the second can be `male`, `female`, or `animal`," and so on. If instead the `leadcast` element were declared this way:

```
<!ELEMENT leadcast (male* | female* | animal*)>
```

which at first glance might seem to produce the same effect,[59] it would actually be saying, "The `leadcast` element can contain any number of `male` child elements, *or* any number of `female`, *or* any number of `animal`." Not the same thing at all!

---

59. Casting back to Mr. G's seventh-grade arithmetic class—what was it?—the distributive principle of multiplication?

The single-occurrence/any order problem

I mentioned this problem earlier—that XML doesn't have an exact equivalent to SGML's & operator for unordered content models.

The commonly recommended solution for this problem is to use the "multiple occurrences of groups of content type" content model, as just described. (That is, separating child elements with the vertical-bar | symbol, grouping them together with parentheses, and appending an asterisk outside the closing parenthesis.) This solution indeed works in most cases; however, it doesn't let you require that there be only *one* occurrence of each child element in any order.

If you absolutely must do this, and must use XML, the only real solution is to move the content that would normally be "&ed together" from the child elements to attributes. Attributes do exactly what you want *if* the child elements are relatively simple, particularly if their own content models specify #PCDATA content only. If their content models are any more complex, you'll have to switch to SGML—or, of course, put up with the limitation in XML.

I'll cover more details on declaring attributes in your DTD in a moment.

Grouped content models are handy in the case of elements, such as FlixML's `plotsummary`, which contain for the most part parsed character data, but *some* of whose parsed character data may need to be treated specially by a style sheet. The `plotsummary` element's declaration looks like this:

```
<!ELEMENT plotsummary (#PCDATA | emph | parabreak | maleref |
femaleref | animalref)*>
```

As a whole, this (which is referred to as a *mixed content model*) says that `plotsummary` may consist of any combination of #PCDATA (text), and/or `emph`, `parabreak`, `maleref`, `femaleref`, and `animalref` elements, in any order. Look particularly at those first two possible subordinate elements. The `emph` elements' contents might be italicized, underlined, or boldfaced by a style sheet; if there is no style sheet, or at least no rule that selects for the `emph` elements, they'd simply be displayed the same way as the rest of `plotsummary`. As for `parabreak`, obviously, it's intended to provide a transition of some kind between one paragraph and the next.

> ### Don't mix meaning and style!
>
> Those last couple sentences were carefully worded: use elements like emph and parabreak (in this case) sparingly in your DTD. Remember that XML is (or is supposed to be!) all about content and meaning, and not at all about style and presentation. An *emphasis* is a sort of nuance of meaning, but it says absolutely nothing about how to communicate (display or present) that nuance. A *paragraph* allows you to group logical units of text together. That either of these is represented in a particular display style is almost an accident of history; they're logical or semantic *necessities*.
>
> Those of you with a particularly twisted streak and previous Web authoring experience might attempt to re-create HTML in XML, with all kinds of "implied style" elements. Please don't do this; all you'll end up with is an XML document with all of HTML's drawbacks built in. If you miss HTML, stick with HTML. (Or better yet, stick with XHTML— the W3C's new XML-compliant version of HTML.)

One important thing to note when declaring your own mixed content models: the #PCDATA must always appear *first* in the content model. That is, the following is incorrect:

```
<!ELEMENT plotsummary (emph | parabreak | #PCDATA | maleref |
femaleref | animalref)*>
```

Why this seemingly arbitrary restriction? It falls under the category of requirements that make life a lot easier for XML-processing programs (and only marginally more difficult for humans).

Baroque castles

FlixML's is actually a fairly simple element tree, which just happens to demonstrate nearly all of XML's capabilities. Your own DTDs may of course be either much simpler or much more complex; you can layer group within group in the content model, some of which occur once, some of which occur more than once, and so on, and the constituent elements and other content types may themselves occur once, several times, and so on, *within* their groups.

However, if you find you're doing a lot of this, it's probably a good sign that you haven't thought hard enough about structuring your information, as I tried to emphasize early in this chapter. Consider a case even so uncomplicated as this:

```
<!ELEMENT product (prodname, version,
      (retailprice, wholesaleprice, acadprice?)+,
      (custname, custPO, qty, date, billto, shipto)*)>
```

This application would almost certainly benefit from moving grouped elements into parent elements in their own right—one called `priceinfo`, say, and one for `invoice` (or whatever). These new parent elements would replace the grouped items in the above declaration of `product`, so it would then resemble the much simpler:

```
<!ELEMENT product (prodname, version,
      priceinfo+, invoice*)>
```

Taking the latter approach basically pushes the details of the document's structure down into lower branches of the element tree: It will probably still contain `retailprice`, `wholesaleprice`, and so on, child elements. But the structure will be much easier for humans (and possibly some programs) to understand; they won't need to "grok" the whole thing at once.

The "attributes vs. separate elements" dilemma

Maybe this is as good a place as any to revisit a question first raised in Chapter 2: What are the pros and cons of putting document content into an element, as opposed to putting it into an attribute?

Here's a sample case: Suppose that you're the designer of the FlixML DTD. You know that you want to keep tabs on the year(s) that a film was released (multiple years meaning that it was rereleased at least once). You've got a couple of choices here:

Option 1: You can create a `releaseyear` element whose content model is strictly #PCDATA; when a document author needs to show that a film was released twice, he or she would code this element something like this:

```
<releaseyear role="initial">1959</releaseyear>
<releaseyear role="alt">1980</releaseyear>
```

Option 2: You can create a `releaseyear` element whose content model is EMPTY. The author would put the `releaseyear` in a "year" attribute. So the sample code above would look like this, instead of the Option 1 version:

```
<releaseyear role="initial" year="1959"/ >
<releaseyear role="alt" year="1980"/ >
```

See the difference? In Option 1, the year information is part of the element's content model. In Option 2, the year information is kept "internally," in an attribute value.

What are the tradeoffs of the two options?

The primary downside of Option 1, of course, is that it's more verbose and more logically complex. Its advantage is that the hierarchical structure may make it more amenable to processing than the flattened "process all of the elements' attributes at the same time" approach enforced by Option 2.

The primary downside of Option 2 is that it *hides real content*. The user's browser may or may not make attribute values visible—a typical Web browser doesn't, for one important example. Of course, you can make any attribute's value "visible" using style sheets to extract and display it; on the other hand, if either the browser doesn't support style sheets *or* the user has turned off the browser's "use style sheets" option (in its Options/Preferences window), the value will remain invisible. If, on still another hand, information is in element content rather than an attribute value, it's *always* visible (unless, yes, suppressed by a style sheet).

So when is Option 2 useful at all? Should you *ever* use attributes?

One reason for using attributes is that they provide a very elementary form of data typing. Your DTD can't declare, for instance, that an attribute "must be a number," but it *can* declare that it must be one of six possible values. There's not even this much data-typing ability in the declarations of elements.

But otherwise, unfortunately, there's no firm rule of thumb. As a guiding principle, anything that is real content probably belongs in an element; anything that is to be used by the machine somehow, rather than directly accessible to a user—URLs are a good example—can safely go in an attribute.

Readers with a sharp eye and an investigative intellect will observe that FlixML sometimes doesn't follow this rule. For instance, why establish a "`role`" attribute for the `title` element? Why not break up `title` into, say, `maintitle` and `alttitle`, without declaring any attribute at all?

I know, I know. Just remember that FlixML has to serve two purposes: to capture information about B movies, *and* to demonstrate XML. Maybe there's an answer there, do you think?

Attributes

Once you've got your elements out of the way, you can proceed to declare attributes for those elements that need them. The declaration of an attribute in a DTD is structured like this:

```
<!ATTLIST elementname attribname attribvalueinfo [...] >
```

The keyword ATTLIST implies that this attribute declaration can include as many attributes as the element (named elementname) requires, and that's also what the [...] means; you can repeat attribname attribvalueinfo as many times as necessary to cover all attributes for the given element.

Let's leave attribvalueinfo undefined for a moment, to look at an example from FlixML.

One FlixML element type, title, can have three attributes, role, xml:lang, and id. The declaration of title itself, and its attribute list, looks like this:

```
<!ELEMENT  title      (#PCDATA)>
<!ATTLIST  title
    role              attribvalueinfo
    xml:lang          attribvalueinfo
    id                attribvalueinfo >
```

This is pretty straightforward. (The various bits of whitespace, by the way—the tabs that force columns of information to align, and the line breaks—don't contribute anything to what these declarations "mean." They're just there to aid readability.)

So what goes into the attribvalueinfo portion?

Attribute values and constraints

When you're building an XML document (as opposed to a DTD), you already know that to use an attribute and its value in a given element, you do so with an attribute/value pair. An example, using the title element type declared above, might look like this:

```
<title role="alt" xml:lang="FR">Tirez sur le
Pianiste</title>
```

This says that the title in question is an alternate title (role="alt") and that the title is in French (xml:lang="FR") rather than the default, which for FlixML is English.

What goes into `attribvalueinfo` is a statement of *what kind of value* can appear after the = sign in an attribute/value pair, within the quotation marks. The constraint can be quite specific ("the value must be *x*"), completely open-ended ("the value can be anything at all"), or somewhere in between. But you do have to specify a constraint of some kind. (As I mentioned in the attributes-vs.-elements discussion, above, this "constraining" ability is one advantage of attributes over elements.)

The format of `attribvalueinfo` is:

```
attribtype attribdefault
```

We'll look at each of those bits of information next.

Attribute types

First you have to ask yourself, "Do I want the attribute's value to be one of a set of specific choices, or do I want the choices constrained in some more general way?"

Table 9.3 lists, with capsule descriptions only, the values that you can use in the `attribtype` portion of the attribute declaration. Detailed explanations of each of these options appear below.

Table 9.3   Attribute types

Keyword	Description
Enumerated attribute type:	
(none—use list of values in place of keyword)	Designates an *enumeration* of allowable attribute values.
String attribute type:	
CDATA	Permits attribute value to contain (almost) any character data.
Tokenized attribute types:	
ID	*Uniquely* identifies an occurrence of an element in the given document.
IDREF and IDREFS	Point to element(s) with a given ID attribute value.
ENTITY and ENTITIES	Name external entities associated with this element.
NMTOKEN and NMTOKENS	Limit attribute values to certain kinds of character data.

Setting specific choices: enumerated type

The `role` attribute of FlixML's `title` element is an example of the "must choose
from a specific list of attribute values" attribute type, also called an *enumerated*
type. The general format is to enclose within parentheses, and separated from
one another by a vertical bar/pipe symbol, a list of all the literal text choices that
the author of the corresponding XML document can use. For instance (including the attribute name itself):

```
role (main | alt)
```

This says that when an author specifies a `role` attribute for the `title` element,
the only allowable values he or she can specify are `main` and `alt`. Both of these
examples would be acceptable:

```
<title role="main">
<title role="alt">
```

but this one would not be:

```
<title role="international">
```

The values in the list must be single "words"—that is, tokens in the sense
that I described in Chapter 2: they can consist of letters, digits, underscores, periods, and colons, and the first character should be an underscore or letter. ("Letter" doesn't mean just those in Western European languages, by the way.)

Note: XML doesn't absolutely forbid it, but you should avoid letting more
than one attribute for a given element have the same value. For instance, assume
that your XML application has a `creature` element, and you want to use
attributes that indicate: (a) whether a given creature is a member of the plant or
animal kingdom; and (b) whether it gets its nourishment primarily from meat,
vegetable matter, or other sources. The attribute list for `creature` (without showing the attribute default information, which we haven't yet covered) might look
like this:

```
<!ATTLIST creature
    type    (vegetable |animal)
    diet    (animal | plant | other) >
```

This is perfectly acceptable in "pure XML" terms. However, SGML-based
software that an author might be using to add a `creature` element *or* that a visitor to the page might be using to learn about this creature will quite possibly
choke when it encounters a case where *both* the `type` and `diet` attributes have a
value of "`animal`."

Special case: NOTATION enumerated type

Your DTD may declare one or more *notations* (described below in the section by that name). If so, you may wish to let the author select from among several notations that may be used as an attribute's value; to do so, prefix the enumeration list with the keyword NOTATION.

FlixML has an audio element that lets an author associate sound clips with his or her FlixML document. The notations in FlixML include several multimedia types, not all of which are for audio formats. Therefore, the attribute list for the audio element looks like this (without the attribute's default):

```
<!ATTLIST  audio
      format NOTATION (wav | au | mid | ra | ram) >
```

The author can therefore construct an audio element that looks something like this:

```
<audio format="wav"...>
```

specifying that this audio clip is in the WAV format. On the other hand, although there's a jpg notation declared in FlixML, the following is *not* valid:

```
<audio format="jpg"...>
```

because jpg is not one of audio's enumerated notation types.

A note on notations

The allowable values for any attribute declared as of type NOTATION, such as wav, au, mid, ra, and ram in the above example, must all be declared in the DTD. You'll learn how to do this when I cover the <!NOTATION> declaration later in this chapter.

Setting general choices I: String type

A string attribute type is pretty much wide open: the value entered by a document's author can contain any character data at all (*except* a less-than/left angle bracket, <). Luckily this is also the simplest attribute type to declare, as in the declaration of the root flixinfo element's author attribute in FlixML:

```
author    CDATA
```

The CDATA keyword says here, as elsewhere in XML, that the value can contain all kinds of weird character combinations—including what looks like "markup." (Note that aside from expanding entity references, the parser won't do anything at all to process an attribute value except pass it to the downstream application. That's why there's no need for a #PCDATA attribute type, too.)

Setting general choices II: ID tokenized type

The syntax for setting an ID attribute type is likewise simple:

```
attribname ID
```

What it *means* to have an attribute like this is a bit involved, though. This and the remaining attribute types are all classified as *tokenized* types, so I want to be sure you understand the significance of that term before getting specifically into the ID type.

You've already encountered the word "token" by itself in *Just XML* (most recently in "Setting specific types," a few paragraphs back). So what does it mean to "tokenize" something? Consider the following string of text:

```
word1 word2     word3
word4
```

On the face of it, it appears that it's already been "tokenized," doesn't it? Actually, no—there's a lot of extraneous whitespace in there. One step in truly tokenizing the string would produce a result like this:

```
word1 word2 word3 word4
```

Specifically what has taken place here is that the whitespace has been *normalized*: Every occurrence of one or more blank, tab, or newline characters has been transformed into a single blank character. What makes an attribute fully tokenized is first, that its whitespace will be normalized this way; and second, that its specific value(s) are taken from a set of discrete *tokens*. It's like a slightly more finely tuned version of the enumerated type: The range of allowable values isn't set explicitly by the DTD, but is relative to some other "pool of candidates" known to the DTD.

In the case of the ID attribute type, the range of allowable values will depend on all the other ID values that occur in the given document.

Let's look at a FlixML example. Beneath both the leadcast and othercast elements are used to identify three "types of cast member": male, female, and animal. If you check the attribute lists for these three child elements, you'll see that they've got attribute lists like this (using male as an example, and excluding the *attribdefault* portion of the declaration, which we haven't covered yet):

```
<!ATTLIST  male
     id     ID >
```

This says that `male` has an attribute named `id`, which is of *type* `ID`–which says specifically that: (a) `id` must be a token; and (b) *the* `id` *attribute's value must be unique among all ID-type attributes in the document* (if an `id` attribute is specified at all, that is). All three "types of cast member" elements also have `id` attributes. So the following fragments of a FlixML document would be valid:

```
<male id="actor1">...
<female id="actor2">...
<animal id="actor3">...
```

while these would not:

```
<male id="actor1">...
<female id="actor2">...
<animal id="actor1">...
```

because the `actor1` value of `id` is not unique across all occurrences of all elements in the document. As you might guess from the term, an `ID` uniquely *identifies* a particular occurrence of some single piece of the element tree.

`ID`s are extremely helpful in applications that make use of XPath expressions to navigate to specific locations within an XML document, such as XPointers and/or style sheets. If you're not certain whether you need to declare `ID` attributes for your elements, it doesn't hurt at all to add them, and liberal use of them can help a lot later on.

(Note: No element type can have more than one `ID`-type attribute.)

More on IDs

I wanted to point out one thing about ID-type attributes that isn't directly related to DTD syntax—more like a question of style.

This has to do with the question of the *name* to give ID attributes. The XML spec says you can call them whatever you want, within the bounds of allowable XML-style names. However, by convention in the SGML world, the name of an ID-type attribute should always itself be "id," or at least contain the string "id" as part of its name (such as empID or fileid to represent an employee or file identifier, respectively). This makes their special nature immediately obvious to a human reader of the document, and for this reason you should follow this convention in developing your own DTDs.

Setting general choices III: IDREF(S) tokenized type

(If you still don't "get" the ID attribute type described above, you'll need to go back and review it until it makes sense. Without knowing what that does, it will be very difficult to understand the IDREF/IDREFS type.)

Recall that the ID attribute type was constrained in this way: The value used by an author must not match any other ID values in the document. The IDREF and IDREFS attribute types stand this constraint on its head: Their values *must* match an ID value somewhere in the document.

Again, let's look at FlixML. As mentioned above, the attribute list for the male element looks like this:

```
<!ATTLIST  male
    id    ID >
```

There's also a maleref element type in FlixML. It can only be used, if at all, somewhere in the content of a plotsummary element, and (per plotsummary's content model) may occur any number of times. Here's the attribute list for maleref:

```
<!ATTLIST  maleref
    maleid IDREF >
```

Now let's consider a FlixML document describing *Targets* (discussed in the "B Alert!" in Chapter 3.) Early in this FlixML document, we might encounter a code fragment like this:

```
<male id="actor1">Boris Karloff</male>
```

and, later on, a plotsummary such as this:

```
<plotsummary><maleref maleid="actor1">Karloff</maleref>
    made a half-dozen movies released in 1968, among them
    Targets - but none of the rest came close to providing
    the suspense that this one introduced to
    the audience....</plotsummary>
```

See? The maleid attribute of the maleref element *points to* a unique ID-type attribute somewhere in the document.

FlixML doesn't contain any examples of the IDREFS (note the plural) attribute type. That type's purpose, though, will be fairly obvious if you think about it a moment: an IDREFS-type attribute *points to* any number of matching ID-type attributes in the document. The value is simply a list of the IDs the author wants to point to, separated from one another with spaces. In theory, for example, it's not too great a stretch to imagine a FlixML `castref` element, with an attribute list such as this:

```
<!ATTLIST  castref
      castids        IDREFS >
```

If the `castref` element were then included in `plotsummary`'s content model, the author could *point to* multiple cast members' information all at once, something like this:

```
<plotsummary>... Watching <castref castids="actor1 actor2">
   Karloff and Bogdanovich</castref> work together as
   actors is great fun, especially when we know that
   <maleref id="actor2">Bogdanovich</maleref> was also
   directing...</plotsummary>
```

The obvious use a processing application might make of these `IDREF`/ `IDREFS` attributes is as a form of internal hyperlinking-*sans*-XLink, as there's a natural "cross-reference" function that they seem to serve.

Setting general choices IV: ENTITY/ENTITIES tokenized type

Here, the constraint is simply that the value of the attribute must match the name of an *external binary* (unparsed) *entity* declared somewhere in the DTD. (An `ENTITY`-type attribute's value must match only one entity name; `ENTITIES`, obviously, can include more than one entity name, separated by spaces.)

Funny little bits

One thing about the ENTITY/ENTITIES attribute type that took a long time for me to get used to: When you actually *use* one of these attributes in a document, you *omit* the opening & and closing ; which you'd normally find in an entity reference to delimit the entity's name.

For instance, suppose the DTD declares an external binary entity called `movie1`, and an attribute, `src`, of a hypothetical `filmclip` element. To reference `movie1` you might expect to see something like:

```
<filmclip src="&movie1;">
```

Not so! Parsers will reject this. Instead, you've got to use (omitting the usual entity-reference punctuation):

```
<filmclip src="movie1">
```

In fact, using *normal* (general) entity references in attributes also comes with a rather bizarre (to me) restriction: A general entity may appear as *part of* an attribute's value, but may not be used as the *complete* value. For instance, suppose you set up an entity called `&flixmlsite;`, whose replacement text is the main URI of the FlixML Web site (`"http://www.flixml.org/"`). Because of this restriction, the following sample XML fragment would be correct:

```
<review src="&flixmlsite;detour_1.xml">
```

but the following would not:

```
<review src="&flixmlsite;">
```

I don't know why this is; perhaps it's got something to do with the way SGML worked, and has been retained for interoperability with SGML applications. Speaking for myself, though, I think it's a little embarrassingly arbitrary.

See the sections on entities and notations later in this chapter for more information about external binary entities.

Setting general choices V: NMTOKEN(S) tokenized type

This attribute type is similar to the plain old CDATA type, but applies an additional constraint: The attribute's value may not contain just any characters, but *only* those characters that can be used to form XML name tokens: letters, digits, underscores, hyphens, periods, and colons. (As always, the term "letters" isn't restricted to the a-z/A-Z range available in Western European languages.)

A rule of thumb when trying to decide whether to use NMTOKEN or CDATA as the attribute type is: If you want (or can anticipate) authors' entering attribute values outside of the valid range for NMTOKEN, use CDATA—otherwise use NMTOKEN.

(Attributes that are expected to contain URLs or file locations are obvious candidates for CDATA, as are those that need to contain internal whitespace. For example, the root flixinfo document has an attribute, author, that identifies the document's author; since this will normally include at least one blank space, the author attribute is of type CDATA.)

The value of a NMTOKENS-type attribute, as you might expect, can include a blank-separated list of tokens.

FlixML is a fairly simple application, as I've mentioned before, and doesn't use NMTOKEN(S)-type attributes to a great extent. (The only exceptions are for various XLink-related attributes.) It's not too hard to think of other cases in which they might be useful, though. A catalog of what used to be called heavenly bodies,[60] for instance, might actually use their international astronomical designations to identify each one with a `name` element; but the `name` element might have a `commonname` attribute, whose type is `NMTOKENS`, whereby the author could enter less precise but more familiar synonyms for the main name itself:

```
<name commonname="Earth earth Terra">X0003.1</name>
```

(I don't know if this is a real example of an "international astronomical designation," or even if such a thing exists. I bet it does, though.)

In this case the `commonname` attribute would have this attribute list (not counting the default value portion of the attribute declaration):

```
<!ATTLIST name
        commonname    NMTOKENS >
```

Of course, if the DTD designer wanted to restrict the author to using only a single token—`Earth` *or* `earth` *or* `Terra`, in this case—he or she would specify an attribute type of `NMTOKEN` (no plural) instead.

Attribute default specification

In addition to declaring each attribute's type, as detailed above, the attribute list also specifies whether and how the parser should supply a default value for the attribute if the document author doesn't use the attribute at all. As with attribute types, what you can enter as the default specification can be summarized in a table—Table 9.4, in this case. I'll provide details on each of the default specifications following the table itself.

Table 9.4   Attribute default specification

Keyword	Description
(*none—DTD author provides explicit default*)	Text value entered is the default if none is supplied by the document author.
`#REQUIRED`	Document author must supply a value.
`#IMPLIED`	Document author need not supply a value.

60.   There's got to be some duller term for them now. Astronomical or celestial objects, maybe.

> **Another reason to validate**
>
> As you read through this section about attribute default specifications, think about one of the consequences of using merely well-formed XML: Unless the document's author explicitly provides an attribute, there's no way for the parser to know that the element in question even *has* such an attribute—and there's no way to provide a default value for any attribute that goes missing.

Explicit default specification

If you as the DTD author know what value you want an attribute to take in the absence of any supplied by the document author, you can simply enter its value (in quotation marks) in the attribute declaration. For example, in FlixML, the title element's role attribute is fully declared as follows:

```
<!ATTLIST  title
     role   (main | alt) "main" >
```

If a FlixML document's author fails to override it with a value of alt (the only other legal choice, given this declaration), the role attribute's value will be "main."

> **Internal inconsistencies?**
>
> Note that in the enumerated content type, the values from which a document author may select are *not* enclosed in quotation marks, but the default selection *is*.

Special case: #FIXED attribute default

In some cases, you may want the DTD to declare the default and *not allow* the document author to override it. This may seem a bit goofy—if you know what the attribute's value *must* be, why bother making it an attribute? Isn't that information "built into" any document that uses that value?

There's one case in which this is a very valuable feature, though:[61] when you don't control the theoretically possible attribute values (because they're declared elsewhere, as with various attributes set by the XLink specification), but

---

61. Not to imply that it might not be very valuable in other cases.

you do want to control the choice(s) made for your particular application. For example, FlixML declares numerous XLink-related elements for which a document author may not override particular attribute values; I wanted the `distrib-link` element type, for instance, always to define an extended link, so its `xlink:type` attribute has a fixed value of `extended`. To use this feature, I declared the `xlink:type` attribute as follows:

```
<!ATTLIST  distriblink
    xlink:type NMTOKEN #FIXED   "extended" >
```

(Note: In this particular example the attribute type is NMTOKEN, but that's not a requirement for declaring a fixed default.)

#REQUIRED default specification

Want to be sure a document's author *always* enters a value for an attribute? Then the `#REQUIRED` keyword is the attribute default specification to use.

A good example of an occasion where you'd want to require that an attribute have a value is in an "empty" element: If it had no attributes, it really *would* be empty.[62] Any DTD that declares an element to be used as containers for images or other multimedia content, for example, will probably want to give it a required `url` or `href` attribute; ditto, elements used in hyperlinking (although these may or may not be empty).

FlixML has a `reviewlink` element, for instance, which is used to point to off-site reviews of a given film by other critics. The attribute list for `reviewlink` looks, in part, like this:

```
<!ATTLIST  reviewlink
    href   CDATA #REQUIRED >
```

Any occurrence of `reviewlink` must therefore include an `href` attribute, such as:

```
According to the <reviewlink
    href="http://www.imdb.com">Internet Movie
    Database</reviewlink>...
```

Take that `href` attribute out of the `reviewlink` element there, and the element will not make much (if any!) sense.

---

62. …except of course for empty elements such as HTML's `<br>` (which inserts a line break but does nothing else), which have no "meaning" apart from the elements' names themselves.

#IMPLIED default specification

This will probably be by far the most common attribute default spec in your DTDs. Translated, it means, "If an author sets a value for this attribute, fine—use that value. If not, it's all right; the value will simply be in a 'not set' state."

FlixML's root `flixinfo` element, among many others in the DTD, has a couple of these "implied" attributes:

```
<!ATTLIST flixinfo
    author      CDATA #IMPLIED
    copyright   CDATA #IMPLIED >
```

If a FlixML author wants to, he or she can thus claim credit for the document. (This may be useful if the document is tied to a style sheet, which could include the information, if present, when the document is displayed.) But it isn't necessary.

Multiple attribute declarations for an element

You may feel that it's easier, more natural, or just "cleaner" to break up attribute lists that declare more than one attribute into separate declarations, one per ATTLIST. Under this theory, the above attribute list for the `flixinfo` element would look like the following:

```
<!ATTLIST flixinfo
    author      CDATA #IMPLIED >
<!ATTLIST flixinfo
    copyright   CDATA #IMPLIED >
```

This will work fine...as long as no attribute is declared twice for a given element. What happens in this case is that the parser discards all declarations for that attribute but the first.

> **XLink element attributes**
>
> We covered XLinking in Part 2 of *Just XML*. Recall from that discussion that an element to be used as an XLink needs to have at least two attributes: the `xlink:type` attribute and the `xlink:href` attribute. Don't forget to declare at least these two attributes for your XLinking elements; it doesn't hurt to declare all the others (`xlink:role`, `xlink:title`, and so on) as well.

You should also be sure to use the `#REQUIRED` default spec for any of those XLinking attributes that you feel to be critical for your application—perhaps even `#FIXED`, so that the application's hyperlinking will function exactly as you want. The FlixML DTD makes liberal use of these options, so that when I want to require (for example) that a particular XLink be used *only* in an extended link group, the FlixML document's author can't override it. Above all, don't forget to include the XLink namespace prefix declaration, `xmlns:xlink`, perhaps even going so far as to make its value fixed. (Some parsers will complain if you do this; others will complain if you try to make it required. Choose your poison!)

Entities

I've mentioned entities throughout *Just XML*. They include the familiar (I hope) *general entities* that function like boilerplate text or a programmer's constants, and the somewhat less familiar but still common *character entities* used to insert special characters (like the c-with-cedilla in "François") into XML character data. They also include entities that may be referred to only in the DTD itself, and the sort of entities whose content lies outside a given document—external entities.

General entities

General entities are those useful gizmos that let you declare shortcuts for long text, boilerplate, and other such substitution.

To declare a general entity, use the following format:

```
<!ENTITY entname replacementtext>
```

The `entname` will be the text that an author uses in the XML document at the point where he or she wants to insert the `replacementtext`. Given this snippet from FlixML's DTD:

```
<!ENTITY  PAR  "Paramount">
```

for instance, an author can code a portion of a FlixML document as follows:

```
... When Targets was released in mid-1968, following
    Robert Kennedy's assassination, &PAR; hastily tacked
    on an anti-gun prologue.
```

The entity reference, `&PAR;`, will be expanded in-place to `Paramount`.

(Note that `entname` in the entity declaration does *not* include the `&` and `;` which enclose the entity name in the XML document, by the way.)

General entities can be used in attribute values just as in regular character data.[63] For instance, if the FlixML `studio` element had a `fundedby` attribute (it doesn't), the following would be a perfectly legal piece of FlixML code:

```
<studio fundedby="Principle funding by &PAR;">&WB;</studio>
```

The `&PAR;` entity would be expanded to `Paramount`, and the `&WB;` entity to `Warner Brothers` (per *its* entity declaration).

Character entities

Character entities are really just a special case of general entities: The entity name is used to place a single special character in the XML document. In this case, the `replacementtext` portion of the entity declaration format I gave above is not usually an actual character, but a numeric value (preceded by a # sign) that maps into one of the ISO tables of character entities; this is useful for including within a document any text that is not part of the document's native character set.

For instance, in the FlixML DTD there's a character-entity declaration for the c-with-cedilla character:

```
<!ENTITY ccedilla   "&#231;">
```

Note that the `replacementtext` in a character entity *must* include both the `&` and the `;` that enclose the numeric value of the character. To give the usual example, in order to include François Truffaut's first name in a FlixML document, the author could use *either*:

```
Fran&ccedilla;ois
```

or:

```
Fran&#231;ois
```

The first choice would be expanded by the parser into the second choice, which would itself be expanded into the special character desired. If the declaration of the `ccedilla` entity didn't include the ampersand and semicolon in `replacementtext`, when the parser expanded it the result would be:

---

63. Yes, they can be used *in* attribute values—but they may not be used *as* attribute values. I griped about this earlier, during the discussion of attribute values.

```
Fran#231ois
```

which, obviously, isn't further expandable into what we really want. (The #231 lacks the opening and closing & and ; which would mark this as an entity requiring further expansion.)

Funny little gotcha

By the way, all the predefined character entities (such as > for the greater-than sign, >) do not, in theory, have to be defined in your own DTD. However, the XML spec says that if you plan to use these references to these entities in a validating context, for "interoperability" (i.e., with SGML processors) you should include their declarations in the DTD.

If you want or need to do this, the spec is unambiguous about how to do so:

```
<!ENTITY lt      "&#38;#60;">
<!ENTITY gt      "&#62;">
<!ENTITY amp     "&#38;#38;">
<!ENTITY apos    "&#39;">
<!ENTITY quot    "&#34;">
```

Note that the declarations of < and & require "double escaping," because < and & are the main individual characters a parser uses to determine a document's well-formedness.

Parameter entities

As your DTD grows ever larger, you'll find yourself using the same bits and pieces over and over. For instance, you may repeat the declarations of attributes for XLink elements—xlink:type, xlink:title, xlink:role, xlink:actuate, and so on—over and over, changing only the element name. Or many of your attribute declarations will, with the exception of the attribute names themselves, be identical, like this:

```
attribname CDATA #IMPLIED
```

Unfortunately, there's no way to use a general entity within a DTD itself; otherwise, you could declare, say, an entity named &attrdefault; with a replacementtext value of "CDATA #IMPLIED."

Fortunately, on the other hand, there *are* parameter entities. These perform the same replacement-text trick that general entities do, except that parameter entities are usable only within the DTD.

The format of a parameter entity declaration is:

```
<!ENTITY % entityname   replacementtext >
```

Note the percent sign (%) that precedes the name, separated from it by a space; this is what tells the parser that this is a parameter and not a general entity. The percent sign is also used in place of an ampersand when you *use* a parameter entity. For instance, given:

```
<!ENTITY % attrdefault "CDATA #IMPLIED">
```

you can declare an attribute list like this:

```
<!ATTLIST flixinfo
    author        %attrdefault;
    copyright     %attrdefault;>
```

Given FlixML's relative simplicity, its DTD makes only limited use of parameter entities. There is indeed an `attrdefault` parameter entity as described above, and an `attrid` parameter entity for ID-type attributes. Attribute default specifications are a common place to encounter parameter entities, because of the frequent repetition of text strings; they can be used pretty much anywhere in the DTD, though, such as in the case of the content models for the `leadcast` and `othercast` elements, which are identical. We could declare a parameter entity for this content model as follows:

```
<!ENTITY % casttypes "(male | female | animal)*"
```

The two element declarations could then be simplified to:

```
<!ELEMENT leadcast %casttypes;>
<!ELEMENT othercast %casttypes;>
```

Be sure to take advantage of parameter entities in your own DTDs; they can save quite a bit of tedious typing.

External parameter entities

The above examples of parameter entities were all *internal* to the DTD in which they were declared and used. A powerful additional option lets you incorporate into your own DTDs entity declarations from files out on the Web somewhere, whether you've created those files or someone else has.

Why would you want to do this? The most obvious example is in the case of all the character entities that some document author *might* want to use. You might be able to anticipate this need, but entering them all yourself would be a nightmare (probably peppered with typos, at the least). All you need to do is find a file that some generous soul has made publicly available, and point to it with an entity declaration and a reference to that entity name, in this format:

```
<!ENTITY % entname SYSTEM "url">
%entname;
```

Optionally, you can include a public identifier as well as the system one, but for most purposes the system identifier followed by the URL will do exactly what you want.

An outstanding resource for such "canned" character-entity files is James Tauber's *schema.net* site.[64] Hyperlinks at that page take you to files (the file extensions are all .pen–for *parameter entities*—and all files were created by Rick Jeliffe) that are coded as lists of SGML/XML character entities; to incorporate the contents of one such file, which declares all the ISO diacritical marks, you could incorporate the following in your DTD:

```
<!ENTITY % isodiacrit SYSTEM
    "http://www.schema.net/public-text/ISOdia.pen">
%isodiacrit;
```

Again, note especially that you not only need to link to the remote file in the entity declaration itself, but also need to *reference* the newly created entity. This causes all the entities declared in the named SYSTEM resource to be automatically available to a document's author just as if they had been declared within your own DTD.

Of course, you could also create such a file of "reusable entity declarations" yourself; you don't have to let someone else do all the work for you. (Obviously, you'd want to do it yourself if your entities were going to be generally useful across several DTDs, rather than just in your own—the *pro bono* principle that makes so much of the Web work.) The contents of the file are simply a bunch of entity declarations, probably annotated with comments just to be sure everyone who might use them understands their purpose. The entities they declare can be general or parameter entities. (See any of the files at Tauber's site for good examples of how to comment a file.)

---

64. Find it at *www.schema.net/entities/*.

Performance anxiety

Because the contents of a remote file, once retrieved, are treated as if they were incorporated into your own DTD, you do have a couple of things to be wary of.

First is the size of these files. Every SYSTEM resource must, of course, be fetched from the Web and then read by the parser; casually peppering your DTDs with an excessive number of such external references can turn the mere parsing of your DTD into a performance drag.

The other thing to be potentially nervous about is that the remote file can itself include an external parameter entity declaration, requiring that *another* remote file be retrieved, and that one can include an external parameter entity declaration, and so on.

The moral of both of these neurosis inducers is that you shouldn't just blindly link to resources that you know nothing about. Look at their contents before adding them (even virtually) to your DTD. If it appears that they'll be overkill, consider simply copying-and-pasting from them into your own *internal* entity declarations.

Unparsed (binary or otherwise) entities

When you compare your DTD to a document that's based on it, you may notice among other things that the DTD declares a number (perhaps a lot) of features that the document doesn't use. Elements, attributes, general and character entities—it can almost make you feel as though you wasted your time adding all those options.

You've learned by now quite a bit about building a DTD, but you're not out of the woods yet. The only things you've learned to declare so far have been the *text* contents that may appear within a document based on your DTD. What about pictures and other non-XML contents? Can you "include" text content which actually resides elsewhere than in the given document instance?

I'll address parts of this question more specifically in the section below on notations. For now, you need to know that you can include in your DTD references to non-XML, even text, content that you want to make available to *any* document based on your DTD. Since you definitely do not want the parser to try to make sense of such content, references to it are made with something called *external* or *unparsed entities.*

In FlixML, it wouldn't make sense to try to anticipate all the audio and video clips that might be used in one particular FlixML document, for one particular B movie's description. What *would* make sense, though, would be to include a standard set of FlixML logos that could be used as the document's author wishes. So assume, then, that I've got little honeybee images, one for each of the possible "B-ness" ratings that summarize, all things considered, how much of a B movie *this* so-called B movie really is. If the bees element indicates 3.5 Bees, for instance, we want a little picture available of three-and-a-half honeybees.

The way to make such a thing possible is to construct an entity declaration that looks similar to a general entity declaration but includes a SYSTEM identifier and the URL where the resource can be found. Additionally, you must include a new keyword: NDATA. Here's the general format of an external binary entity declaration:

```
<!ENTITY entname SYSTEM "url" NDATA notationname >
```

You should be familiar with most of this by now: the entname that a document author can insert into a document where he or she wants to entity to be "inserted," and the url that tells the XML processor where to find the nontext content to be "inserted" into the document at that point.[65] The reference in a document to an external entity can occur only in an attribute value, and it may include neither the & nor the ; used to delimit a standard general entity reference. (Of course, neither of those special characters is actually needed—if the attribute type is already declared of type ENTITY or ENTITIES, the parser already knows to expect an entity name as the attribute value.)

The NDATA keyword is analogous to the CDATA keyword mentioned many times previously: It signals to the parser, "Don't *you* try to make sense of this, parser—leave it up to the downstream application to figure out." The notationname must match the name of a notation (discussed in the next section) which you've declared in your DTD.

Given our three-and-a-half honeybees example, this could be the declaration for the matching image:

```
<!ENTITY bees35
    SYSTEM "http://www.flixml.com/images/bees35.gif"
    NDATA gif >
```

---

65. Not to belabor a point, but again, these entities, text or otherwise, are not actually inserted—an XML document always "contains" nothing but the text and markup in it.

Should a FlixML document's author decide to rate a given film as "3.5 Bees," he or she could add this image using this code:

```
<bees b-nesspic="bees35"/>
```

In order for this to be acceptable to the parser, the `b-nesspic` attribute's type must be of type ENTITY or ENTITIES. Fortunately for this example (ahem), it is.

Notations

I've made reference occasionally in this chapter, and elsewhere, to incorporating multimedia into XML documents. *Notations* declared in the DTD are what makes this possible.

A notation is simply a statement that a particular media type may need to be processed by some program other than the plain old XML-aware software that's handling the DTD and XML document itself. The format is fairly simple:

```
<!NOTATION notationname SYSTEM "programurl" >
```

The `notationname` and `programurl` provide, respectively, a name for a particular media type and the location of a program that's capable of handling files of that media type. For example:

```
<!NOTATION gif SYSTEM
     "file:///C:\MediaUtils\LView\lview.exe" >
```

This tells the XML processor that whenever the `gif` notation name is referred to in an XML document based on this DTD, the reference is to be handled by a program called lview.exe, which can be found at the designated location.

At this point, alarm bells may be ringing for many of you, and ought to be ringing for *all* of you:

- First, there's an implicit assumption in a declaration of an external program like this that the indicated program is even capable of running on the user's system. The lview.exe program mentioned in this example is a Windows and Windows 95 utility; what happens if the visitor to your page is a Macintosh or UNIX user?

- Second, even if you know for certain that the user's system is capable of running and actually *has* the indicated program, how can you know in what directory or folder it's located?

- And third, isn't this a bit, well, *clunky*? Assume that through some magical convergence of lucky breaks, the first two conditions are met. What will happen when a document references a `gif` notation is that the lview.exe program will open *in a separate window* to display the image. Shouldn't the image be somehow made to appear at the point in the document where it's referenced?

There was a time, for the first few years of the Web, when this kind of problem was common. You still encounter it from time to time: You go to a Web page that contains some kind of exotic content, and up pops a box asking you how you want to treat it: Do you want to save the content to a file? Do you want to select a program to handle it? Do you want to be prompted the next time you encounter this media type, or automatically use whatever choice you make here? Do you feel you've answered enough questions already, or would you like to see some more?

Browser plug-ins have eliminated a lot of this clunkiness for standard HTML pages (although you've still got to download and install the plug-in software, of course). The association between media types and the plug-ins to run them is maintained internally by the browser, using a table of Multipurpose Internet Mail Extension (MIME) types that correlate roughly to the notation names you might encounter in an XML document. (Browsers themselves can handle certain basic media types, such as GIF and JPEG images.) This plug-in technology creates the appearance of a single unified Web page with the multimedia objects inside the browser window, even though different portions of the window may be under the control of different programs.

In addition to or in place of the SYSTEM identifier, a notation declaration may provide a PUBLIC identifier for the notation, as in:

```
<!NOTATION jpeg PUBLIC
    "ISO/IEC 10918:1993//NOTATION Digital Compression and
    Coding of Continuous-tone Still Images (JPEG)//EN" >
```

As with other XML features that can take advantage of the PUBLIC identifier option, what follows the keyword PUBLIC is an "official" description of the given resource. And as with those other features, whether an application will actually be able to use this information is still a big question mark.

So unfortunately, we're not quite as far along as we need to be with native XML applications. Until we are, XML's notation-processing mechanism will continue to be hypothetical.

Maybe not that far away, after all

Using notations for multimedia content is a holdover from SGML, where using formal public identifiers to determine "what to do" with a given media type is a long-established tradition.

But then along came the Internet with its own way of doing things: referring to a multimedia resource on the Web by way of a URI, or including a nontext attachment to e-mail by way of the MIME standard. Web browsers and other Internet software come with understanding of external media types built-in.

For this reason, don't be surprised if at some point the W3C replaces the use of notations with one or both of these other standards.

Summary

This chapter detailed how to build your own XML applications, using the medium of the document type definition (DTD). Although the FlixML application provided most of the examples here, if you've read through *Just XML* to this point you now know virtually everything you need to know in order to construct a non-FlixML use of XML, from the ground (the DTD) on up (the documents based on your DTD).

Table 9.5   DTD components covered in this chapter

Item	Description
`<!ELEMENT elementname (content-model) >`	Declares an element and what it may contain.
`<!ATTLIST elementname attribname attribvalueinfo >`	Declares one or more attributes for the given element, including the kind of content that the attribute value may take and default specifications to use in the event no value is provided by the author.
`<!ENTITY entname replacementtext >`	Declares a general entity which can be used in XML documents based on this DTD.
`<!ENTITY % entname replacementtext >`	Declares an internal parameter entity which can be used anywhere in the DTD itself.

Table 9.5   DTD components covered in this chapter (continued)

Item	Description
`<!ENTITY % entname SYSTEM extparamdefsURL >` `%entname;`	Identifies the URL of an external file that contains one or more parameter-entity or other markup declarations, and uses the corresponding `%entname;` entity reference to make all those markup declarations available for use in this DTD just as if they'd been declared locally.
`<!NOTATION notationname SYSTEM programURL >`	Declares a notation and the location of an external program that can handle content of this media type.

This table is merely a summary. Refer to individual tables throughout this chapter for information about the details of each of these items.

Terms defined in this chapter

occurrence/instance An *occurrence* or *instance*, as used in this chapter, refers to the number of times some bit of content may appear in an element's content model.

parsed character data (#PCDATA) Element content consisting of just text that the parser may need to "pay attention to" (e.g., to expand any general entities).

(regular) character data (CDATA) When an element's content or an attribute value consists of text that should *not* be processed by the parser, except for possible entity references, it's called *(regular) character data*, or *CDATA*.

mixed content Elements that may contain both other elements and character data of their own are said to be of *mixed content* or to have *mixed content models*.

content model The *content model* in an element's declaration shows what sort(s) of content it may contain: parsed character data and/or other elements, and if the latter, which elements it may contain, how many times they may occur in the context of this element, and in what order they must appear.

normalized whitespace When an XML parser scans through a document or DTD and converts all occurrences of repeated whitespace into a single blank character, it is said to have *normalized the whitespace* of that document/DTD. You might say it's reduced all whitespace to a lowest common denominator.

general entities Entities used to declare boilerplate or other commonly used text in an XML document.

character entity An entity that stands for a single character that will be expanded by the parser. Characters that can't be represented using a DTD's or document's default character set are commonly represented this way.

parameter entities Entities that are used to declare common or frequently used chunks of DTD code; may be used *only* in a DTD.

external binary (unparsed) entities As flexible and powerful as XML is, it can process on its own *only* text documents. Content that must be dealt with by some outside program other than the XML software itself is declared with *external binary* (or *unparsed*) *entities*.

notation The processing of external binary entities (see above) is specified using *notations* that tell an XML application which outside program to invoke to handle content of a given media type.

PART 5

XML Directions

This final part of *Just XML* covers the things you can expect to see happening with XML and related technologies over the next several months to a year.

Chapter 10 covers the present state of XML software, including tools for processing XSLT, CSS2, and the raw XML itself. In Chapter 11, I'll peer into the crystal ball to give you a sense of where "the whole thing" is headed in the near to mid future.

Although this part concludes the body of *Just XML*, don't forget to take a look at the glossary and appendices which follow to fill in the gaps and direct you to other resources.

XML Software

Computer users are driven by a funny but charming quirk: They like to use software. (Imagine that!) So far, I've avoided mentioning specific packages, and I know this has probably made some of you a bit impatient: "Show me the tools!"

That's the purpose of this chapter, to finally let you see some of the software available to support you as you grow into XML.

State of the Art

As you know by now, even after two years XML is something of a toddler; so it might stand to reason that the software to support it isn't much further along the growth cycle. Yet, a couple of factors have combined to make its blooming much faster than, say, that of its HTML counterpart in the early days of the Web:

- **Experience with SGML:** XML's parent has been around long enough and its adherents are so committed to its root principles that when XML came along, many of the resources—personnel, particularly—that helped SGML succeed were already in place. This isn't to say that all the problems are solved, by any means; most of them *are* familiar ones, though. An SGML parser, for example, needs to recognize the start of a tag as signaled by a left angle bracket, its close by a right angle bracket, and so on. An XML parser needs to do many of the same things. Hence, the considerable body of

SGML-smart software is fairly easy to convert to become XML-smart as well.

- **Experience with (and excitement about) the Web:** By now, users and software developers know what kinds of things the Web *will* and *might be* used for. They know HTML's strengths and weaknesses, and are apt to get quite excited by XML's promise of a better Web. Excitement among users and developers about new technology just about always leads to a rapid burst of new classes of software tools.

- **XML's inherent simplicity:** Although some, on first exposure, look at XML and panic, it's really very simple. If anything, it's complex for *humans*; machines and software are quite adept at handling it, though, thanks to such restrictions as "a start-tag must always be balanced by an end-tag."

- **Community:** HTML was born of enthusiasm initially among a fairly small cadre of academics and scientists, who simply wanted a way to exchange and cross-reference documents on the Internet. By now, of course, there are thousands of developers working on nothing *but* Web-based software. What's more, the tools that many of them are building—often as members of ad hoc, informal teams—are commonly being made available free for use by anyone who wants them.

But we're not out of the woods yet. While a number of vendors (including some industry heavyweights) have taken an active role in developing XML software, the XML toolset is still not as advanced as that for HTML. Many of the products exist only in alpha, beta, or otherwise unsupported versions.

The remainder of this chapter will profile some of these tools, focusing on those that are mature enough to use now and those that are expected to have substantial impact when they *do* mature. Understand that this is nothing remotely like a complete listing; within six months to a year of my writing this chapter, the landscape will have surely changed dramatically.

Sample XML code

In this chapter, I'll use some of the FlixML documents I introduced in earlier chapters. I will also, on occasion, make use of a new FlixML document that looks like the following:

```
<?xml version="1.0"?>
<!DOCTYPE flixinfo SYSTEM "http://www.flixml.org/flixml/
   flixml_03.dtd">
<flixinfo xml:lang="EN"
```

```
xmlns:xlink="http://www.w3.org/1999/xlink/namespace/">
<title role="main">The Laughing Cow</title>
<title role="alt" xml:lang="FR">La Vache Qui Rit</title>
<genre>
<primarygenre>&W;</primarygenre>
<othergenre>&COM;</othergenre>
</genre>
<releaseyear>1959</releaseyear>
<studio>&PAR;</studio>
<cast>
<leadcast>
<male><castmember>Johnny Winthrop</castmember><role>Johnny B</role>
</male>
<male><castmember>Reese B. "High" Noone</castmember><role>"Posse"
  Williams</role></male>
<female><castmember>Joan Torrance</castmember><role>Eva Ramirez</
  role></female>
<animal><castmember>Toto El Toro</castmember><role>Himself</
  role><species>Bull</species>
</animal>
</leadcast>
<!-- Supporting cast list incomplete; videotape version cuts
off end of closing credits. -->
<othercast>
<male><castmember>Thomas Nelson Jackson</castmember><role>Dub</
  role></male>
<male><castmember>Harley da Silva</castmember><role>Chief
Thunder Basket</role></male>
</othercast>
</cast>
<crew>
<director>Jesse Winder</director>
</crew>
<plotsummary>Non-stop laughs and action abound (or were intended to
  abound, maybe) in this surrealistic mix of the Western and comedy
  genres. Sometime cowpoke Johnny B and his slowpoke sidekick Posse
  Williams arrive at the Ramirez Ranch, mistaking it for the much
  larger and considerably more successful REmirez Ranch, which has
  advertised for hands to accompany a cattle drive. At the RAmirez
  Ranch, not only is there no cattle drive planned, but there's
  danged few head of cattle in the first place. In fact, there's
  only a single bovine resident of the ranch: Toto El Toro, playing
  himself in this, his mercifully only Hollywood role.</
  plotsummary>
<bees b-nesspic="BEEHALF"/>
</flixinfo>
```

The chief virtue of this document is its relative brevity; for some of these packages we don't really need to see lengthy documents to get the sense of what's going on.

One difference: The versions of the earlier files that I'm using here lack, for the most part, all the indentation and newlines of the document earlier presented. (This results in documents looking something like the one for *The Laughing Cow.*) The reason for this is that the prettified format makes for easy reading but tricky processing; as I've discussed, XML applications vary in how they handle this whitespace, and with these programs we want to simplify things as much as possible.

XML software categories

I've classified XML software into the following types: parsers, XML document editors, DTD editors and generators, true XML browsers, XML-aware (after a fashion) generic Web browsers, and stylesheet editors. Some of these categories as covered in this chapter are represented by only a single product, some by several. To repeat: Coverage of none of them is exhaustive. Each section will start with a general description of the purpose served by software therein, followed by screen shots and other specifics on selected packages.

XML is sometimes described as what finally gives Java something to chew on. You'll find that many of these tools are therefore Java-based and portable across a range of platforms. Some of them run only on Microsoft's 32-bit Windows systems (Windows 95, 98, and NT), as that of course is where many developers have opted to focus their attention. You should be aware, though, that there exist UNIX-specific and Macintosh-specific XML tools, Perl-based XML tools, Python-based tools, and so on. Check Appendix B for more information, not on specific tools, but on Web sites that are clearinghouses of such information.

Narrow-gauge vision
The products I've chosen to highlight, I've chosen for one common reason: They're all targeted at the same market to which I've been pitching *Just XML*—newcomers to XML, perhaps with some prior knowledge of HTML, probably with little if any exposure to SGML. Such readers probably do not want to spend a lot of money on software yet; they're simply trying to get their feet wet, and to get a handle on what this XML thingum *is*.

Be aware, though, that the range of XML software is much broader, and in some categories deeper, than I'll be painting here. Because of its roots in SGML, a very mature technology by any measure, support for XML is widespread among vendors of SGML and document management products. Such products, however, are aimed at fairly large-scale organizations who demand powerful features available only in software costing hundreds to tens of thousands of dollars. If *you* need that kind of software, rest assured that it's out there for you.

There are also quite a few midlevel shrink-wrapped programs in some of the categories, copies of which cost merely in the hundreds-of-dollars range. I won't have much to say here about these packages either. The emphasis is on free or cheap and, generally, *downloadable.*

Parsers

As I mentioned early on in this book, parsers are what process "raw XML" for use elsewhere. Sometimes the target is simply a pair of human eyeballs; the parser may be used just to confirm that a document is well-formed or valid, or it may be used to generate "pretty-printed" displays of the document's element tree, replete with tabs, newlines, and so on.

By far the most common use of parsers, though, is as a "pre-processor" that passes correct (either well-formed or valid) XML to a downstream application (or to a later portion of a full-blown XML application, for that matter). Any such application must first parse the XML at some point, even if the parsed XML is just saved in a file for reading by the application in batch mode. The process of parsing includes not only verifying that the XML conforms to the spec and to the DTD (if one is present), but also normalizing it in various ways: collapsing extraneous whitespace, for example, and expanding entity references into the text that they represent.

Parsers tend to be command-line programs. Their horsepower is expended on the grunt work of processing a file, and perhaps verifying that external entities and notations exist; they don't require anything like a "user interface." For this reason, only one of the two parsers I discuss below has screen shots to accompany its discussion. For the other, I offer some commentary on a command-line session to show you what happens when a parser is invoked.

Which parser for me?

This is kind of a thorny question, with no simple answer. Not all parsers are created equal; what one parser rejects as unacceptable will often be swallowed without complaint by many others[66]—at the very least, Non-Validating Parser A will perhaps not complain at all if your document is not strictly speaking valid.

The main points of difference tend to be in these areas: speed, size, corporate and language support, and how smart the parser is about handling interfaces between XML documents and the outside world. The outside world in this case includes DTDs, external entities, notations, and other XML documents. If you need to use those facilities, that consideration alone may suffice as a criterion for selecting one parser. Issues of speed and size are beyond the general scope of this book, and as for corporate and language support, what's best for you won't necessarily be best for me or even the person in the next cubicle.

But there's a final issue, which is: What parser does your preferred higher-level application use? This can completely overrule the other considerations; there may be in fact no way to substitute Parser A in a given XML-aware browser, for instance. In general, the question of "Which parser should I use?" is a question for application developers, not for users of XML—who are really interested only in using, not developing, these higher-level programs.

Jeremie Miller's XParse

One of the first questions that an XML newcomer tends to ask is, "Which parser should I use?"—as though you can actually see a parser, interact with it. (It's like selecting what movie you want to go see depending on the manufacturers of the projectors used by various theaters in town.) The truth, however, is that while what parsers do is interesting in a way, they're not the earth-shaking encounters with XML that most people are looking for.

---

66. How many others? That's a tough question; writing a parser is a neat, small-scale project for a talented programmer, even a talented-but-inexperienced one, so a lot of individuals have been attracted to the exercise. One observer of the XML scene once said that he had stopped counting when he reached 200 parsers—and that was in 1998, the year the XML specification became final.

A good example of the simplicity of what parsers do is Jeremie Miller's XParse, a JavaScript-based demonstrator. (Find it at www.jeremie.com/Dev/XML/test/.) Figure 10.1 illustrates the user interface. To the left is a large text area, into which you can copy-and-paste an XML document.[67] To the right is the result of whatever operation you've selected with the radio buttons—"Dynamic Tree" or "Regenerate XML."

As you can also see, the actual information reported by XParse is minimal. Only elements and text content are displayed in the collapsible/expandable tree of folders at the right. For empty elements like bees, here, this is a fatal omis-

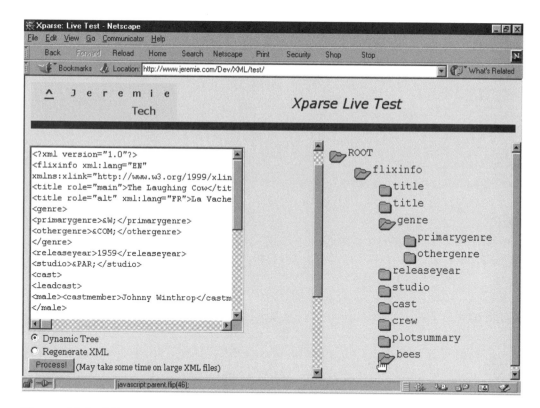

Figure 10.1 XParse JavaScript parser

---

67. There's also an area at the bottom of the page into which you can enter the URI of an XML file on the Web, rather than copying-and-pasting the contents into the text area. However, I've never gotten anything but an error when using the enter-a-URI approach.

sion—all of their content is wrapped up in attributes, which XParse doesn't display at all.

Unlike XParse, most parsers are not meant to operate as standalone programs, except for very limited purposes (such as demonstrations that the parser has been installed correctly). Rather, they're meant to be harnessed to some downstream application that will simply take what the parser produces and stir it together into a medley of more complex features and functions. In fact, in many cases the downstream application will give you a choice of the parser you want to use; in such a case, odds are that you're using a SAX-compliant parser—as discussed next.

SAX

SAX is the simple API for XML; it's not a parser per se, but a "thing" that sits on top of a parser. Let's take a moment to think about what that means.

First there's the term "API," which stands for Application Programming Interface. An API acts as a standard interface—a go-between layer—that mediates between some lower-level function(s) and some higher-level one(s). In terms more appropriate to parsing XML, a higher-level program (what I've been calling by such names as "downstream application") can call any SAX-compliant parser and pass input to it in the same format, regardless of what the parser may be doing internally.

Why would this be important? Primarily because different parsers—even those based on identical specifications, built by roughly equally talented and intelligent developers—can and will often produce different results. If every one of these different programs were to require that it be fed input in a different format, a higher-level program would require a differently-shaped "output pipe" for each one. Having all invocations of the parser in a standard sort of structure means that a higher-order application with a SAX "output pipe" can plug in any SAX-compliant parser of the user's choice. (That choice, of course, being based on which parser will read the DTD and document without choking.)

There's nothing really to demonstrate with SAX, as by itself it simply describes the nature of the communication between parsers and other programs. But it's a very important facility to have been developed.

> ## Eyewitness to history
>
> Like many of you, I suspect, I'm new enough to XML to have missed out on all the excitement when the specification was actually in the works. One of my favorite things about SAX, therefore, was that I could be "present" as it made its way from an idea and out into the world. The gestation and birth process in SAX's case took about two to three months, over the winter of 1997-98.
>
> A group of parser and other program developers on the XML-DEV mailing list were growing concerned about the problem with differently shaped pipes just described. Basically, they put their heads together online and hammered out some (occasionally quite excruciating) differences and how to resolve them. Specifying the SAX interface was the work of David Megginson, at the time an employee of MicroStar and also (not incidentally) the developer of the Ælfred parser, discussed below.
>
> Much of the debate was over my head; it revolved in large part around topics such as the ways in which Java handles exceptions (that is, unexpected events such as errors)—and, as I mentioned earlier, Java isn't a strong suit for me (to put it mildly). Nonetheless it was an exhilarating thing to see happening.
>
> (At this writing in early 2000, Megginson is leading the development of the next level of SAX features, collectively known as SAX 2. To the core SAX features are being added support, for example, for namespaces—intimately wrapped up with the core XML spec, but developed later than it. Of critical importance will be how to add these new features to the interface without "breaking" existing parsers.)
>
> Having watched it happen or not, you'll eventually come to appreciate SAX's development. You may not even "see" the results, ever—and that alone will be a testimonial of sorts: SAX, you might say, will succeed to the extent that it remains invisible.

Ælfred

The Ælfred parser, by MicroStar, is a Java-based, SAX-compliant parser that falls into an interesting crevice: It's a "well-formedness parser" that nonetheless uses a DTD if one is present.

As with most of the Java-based tools here, you invoke Ælfred on the command line by first invoking the Java run-time environment. Most parsers, as we'll see, include a set of command-line options that alter the parser's output in various ways. Ælfred does not, however. Instead, you supply one of four Java class names, each of which produces a corresponding output stream.

For example, in Session 10.1 you see the results of using the EventDemo class, which logs basically everything that Ælfred has encountered and does during parsing—a wonderful educational tool if you're interested in what happens during a typical parser's execution.

(I've abbreviated the listing in Session 10.1 to eliminate a lot of repetitious output. Once you've seen one "Resolving entity," you've seen 'em all.)

Session 10.1   Ælfred

```
C:\>java EventDemo laughcow.xml Ⓐ
Start document  Ⓑ
Resolving entity: pubid=null, sysid=file:/C:/UTILS/XML/Aelfred/
  laughcow.xml  Ⓒ
Starting external entity:    Ⓓ
file:/C:/UTILS/XML/Aelfred/laughcow.xml
Resolving entity: pubid=null, sysid=http://www.flixml.org/flixml/
  flixml_03.dtd
Starting external entity:  http://www.flixml.org/flixml/
  flixml_03.dtd  Ⓔ
Ending external entity:  http://www.flixml.org/flixml/
  flixml_03.dtd
Doctype declaration:  flixinfo, pubid=null, sysid=http://
  www.flixml.org/flixml/flixml_03.dtd  Ⓕ
Attribute:  name=xml:lang, value=EN (specified)
Attribute:  name=xmlns:xlink, value=http://www.w3.org/1999/xlink/
  namespace/ (specified)
Attribute:  name=copyright, value=null (defaulted)
Attribute:  name=author, value=null (defaulted)
Attribute:  name=id, value=null (defaulted)
Start element:  name=flixinfo
Ignorable whitespace:  "\n"  Ⓖ
Attribute:  name=role, value=main (specified)  Ⓗ
Attribute:  name=xml:lang, value=EN (defaulted)
Attribute:  name=id, value=null (defaulted)
Start element:  name=title
Character data:  "The Laughing Cow"
End element:  title
Ignorable whitespace:  "\n"
Attribute:  name=role, value=alt (specified)
Attribute:  name=xml:lang, value=FR (specified)
Attribute:  name=id, value=null (defaulted)
Start element:  name=title
```

Session 10.1 Ælfred (continued)

```
Character data:  "La Vache Qui Rit"
End element:  title
Ignorable whitespace:  "\n"
Attribute:  name=id, value=null (defaulted)
Start element:  name=genre
Ignorable whitespace:  "\n"
Attribute:  name=id, value=null (defaulted)
Start element:  name=primarygenre
Character data:  "Western"   Ⓘ
End element:  primarygenre
Ignorable whitespace:  "\n"
Attribute:  name=id, value=null (defaulted)
Start element:  name=othergenre
Character data:  "Comedy"
End element:  othergenre
Ignorable whitespace:  "\n"
End element:  genre
 .  .  .
Ignorable whitespace:  "\n"
Attribute:  name=b-nesspic, value=BEEHALF (specified)
Attribute:  name=b-ness, value=null (defaulted)
Attribute:  name=id, value=null (defaulted)
Start element:  name=bees   Ⓙ
End element:  bees
Ignorable whitespace:  "\n"
End element:  flixinfo
Ending external entity:
file:/C:/UTILS/XML/Aelfred/laughcow.xml   Ⓚ
End document   Ⓛ
```

Notes on this session:

Ⓐ This is the command line that invokes Ælfred's EventDemo Java class, which (as you can see by scanning through the session listing) records all the "events" fired during the course of execution.

Ⓑ The "Start document" event just signifies, "All right, I've accepted the command-line arguments and am actually beginning the parse."

Ⓒ The "Resolving entity" lines mean that Ælfred is confirming that external files referred to in this parse actually exist at the specified URLs. They do not have anything to do with "external entities" in the sense of external binary entities.

Ⓓ Ælfred is opening the laughcow.xml file.

Ⓔ What's come before this is the handling of the document's prolog (in laughcow.xml's case, just the document type declaration). Here Ælfred signals that it's actually embarking on processing the element tree of the source document, beginning with reading the DTD. The flixml_03.dtd file mentioned here appears to have passed muster with Ælfred—note that following this line, Ælfred indicates it's done with the DTD. If the DTD itself were in error, line Ⓔ would be followed by error messages and, depending on the severity of the error, further processing might continue or stop altogether.

Ⓕ This begins the processing of the root `flixinfo` element. Note that Ælfred's events present the element's attributes first (they are, after all, in the start-tag), followed by its content.

Ⓖ Some whitespace in a document is "ignorable": it doesn't fall within element content, but between two elements. The `<flixinfo>` start tag (its presence noted on the preceding line) is followed immediately by a newline between it and the `title` element—hence this event.

Ⓗ When an attribute's value is specified in the source document, Ælfred makes note of it this way.

Ⓘ Note that in the source laughcow.xml document, the genres (Western and comedy, the primary and other genre, respectively) are actually represented by general entities. When this "character data encountered" event fires, however, each entity has already been expanded. There doesn't seem to be an "expand entity" event (although we know it must have happened).

Ⓙ Just because the `bees` element is empty doesn't mean it's dispensed with in one step; note that the "start element" and "end element" events are two separate events.

Ⓚ Ælfred has reached the end of laughcow.xml.

Ⓛ Ælfred is through processing laughcow.xml.

This stream of "events" illustrates one key principle of all SAX parsers: they are event-based. As the parser makes its way from beginning to end of a document, it reports what it's finding. Some information must be retained for later use (like entity declarations, if the parser handles them); the rest is simply reported to the outside world, usually another application program, and then forgotten.

Document Editors

If you're authoring or revising an XML source document, there's no need for any special whiz-bang fancy software. Just open up UNIX vi, Windows Notepad, or any other general-purpose text processing program and start flailing away at the keys. (In a structured way, of course.)

Still, that can be a tricky endeavor:·

- If a document is to be valid as well as well-formed, you've got to keep flipping through the DTD to find out the names of elements, what order they've got to appear in, whether or not their attributes are required, whether there are any entities you can use and in what contexts, and so on.
- As veteran HTML hand-coders know, it's painfully easy to omit a closing angle bracket or a full end-tag. You can spend an hour or so creating a complex document, only to have it fail to parse properly because the parser couldn't find an element's end-tag (or because the end-tag was misspelled, which amounts to the same thing).

Automated XML document editors circumvent these problems (or at least ameliorate them to some extent); in addition, many of them are packaged in attractive GUI "wrappers" so you don't need to worry about being all thumbs. In time, they may come to include advanced features such as checking the validity of XLinks and XPointers, or providing stylesheet-aware preview modes for seeing how the document will look when displayed.

We're not quite that far along the turnpike yet, but here's a sampling of a couple of the products available to date.

WordPerfect

What? A word processor as XML editor?

Yes indeed. Way back at the beginning of *Just XML*, I talked about WordPerfect's "Reveal Codes" feature that has always functioned as a rudimentary sort of balanced markup. Recent versions of the software take this a step further, by supporting SGML and XML.

The way this is handled in the most recent version, WordPerfect 9, is that you first define an XML "project." A project is basically a standard word-processing template based on a DTD. The result looks something like Figure 10.2 when using the FlixML DTD to create a new document. Note at the top left the dropdown list in which the word flixinfo occurs; this is normally the location where you'd expect to see a word-processing document's "style" appear—proof that we're now operating inside a template.

Down the left side of the window is where the list of currently available elements will appear; a large window to the right is where the document tree will be displayed, and where the user adds text (#PCDATA) content to elements that will accept it. The pop-up "Edit Attributes" dialog allows you to change the values of attributes declared for the currently selected element.

WordPerfect will also validate the document at any time. You control the extent to which you want the validation to take place by way of a separate dialog, as shown in Figure 10.3.

(The notion of "optional validation steps" rather flies in the face of the term "validation," at least as the latter term is used in the XML spec—almost blasphemous. Either a document is valid, or it's merely well-formed; there shouldn't be any such thing as "validated except for entity declarations," for example, or "valid throughout the last fifty percent." Nonetheless, this is undeniably useful when you're first developing a document and simply want to deal with one or another potential problem area at a time.)

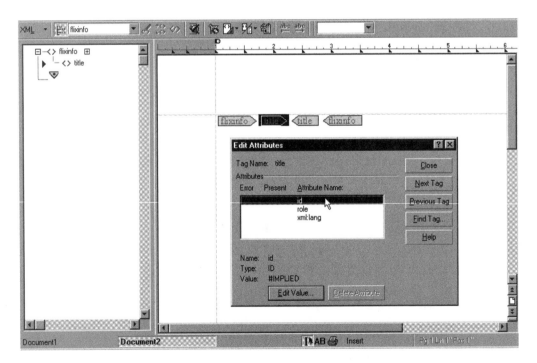

Figure 10.2   WordPerfect 9 XML document editor

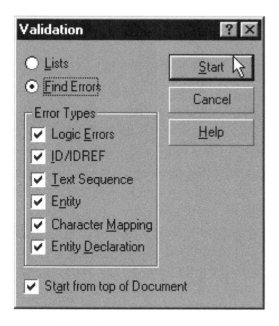

Figure 10.3 Validation options with WordPerfect

As you might guess, working with a GUI-based editor like WordPerfect is largely a matter of clicking on some gizmos, doubleclicking on others, and dragging-and-dropping still others. For example, as in Figure 10.4, you insert an entity reference where desired by scrolling through a list of available entities, selecting the one you want, and clicking the Insert button in a dialog box. Note that when you select the entity, WordPerfect tells you in the lower left corner what its value is.

(By the way, in the list of radio buttons at the top of the box, notice the one labeled "Specific Character Data (SDATA)." SDATA is not valid with XML; it's a type of entity usable only under full-blown SGML.)

All is not perfect in WordPerfect, however. Figure 10.5 illustrates what happens when you try to insert an xml:stylesheet PI. Presumably the problem here is that the WordPerfect XML parser either is not namespace-aware or (more likely) simply is being a little too hard-nosed about the XML spec's statement that the namespace prefix xml: is "reserved."

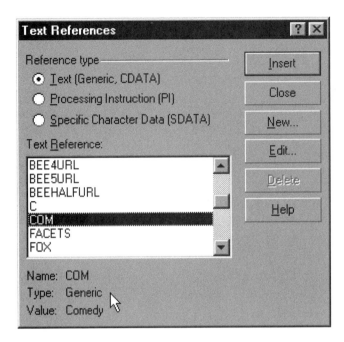

Figure 10.4   Adding entity references in WordPerfect 9

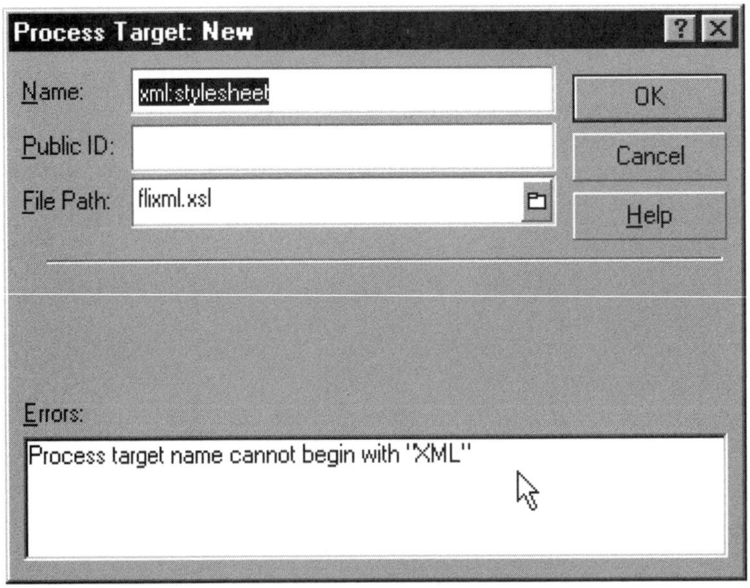

Figure 10.5   Misinterpretation of the XML spec? (WordPerfect 9)

Xeena

Xeena (pronounced "zee-na," accent on the first syllable), from IBM, is just one of that company's many Java-based XML products. It functions similarly to Word-Perfect 9, shown in the preceding section.

Figure 10.6 shows what you see when you first create a new document based on a particular DTD (in this case, the FlixML DTD). You can circumvent this prompt by specifying on the command line what the document's root element will be; normally, of course, you'd want it to be `flixinfo`.

As you add elements to the element tree in the upper right pane, you can also edit their attributes directly (rather than in a separate dialog, as with Word-Perfect 9) in the lower left corner, as Figure 10.7 shows. Note that if the associated DTD declares valid or default values for an attribute, they will show up in a little drop-down list such as the one (EN) for `xml:lang` in this case.

Also as you can see in Figure 10.7, the upper left portion of the window is occupied by a list of elements that fit somewhere within the content model of the element currently selected in the document tree (`flixinfo`, here) displayed in the large area at the upper right. To add one of these elements as a child of the currently selected element, right-click on it in the list of elements, as shown in Figure 10.8. The pop-up menu allows you to add the element as a child, or to replace the currently selected element.

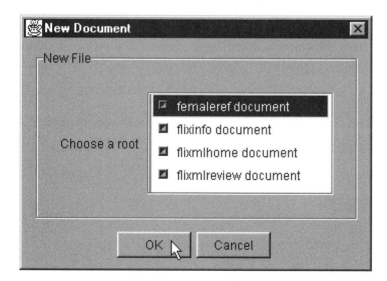

Figure 10.6   Selecting a new document's root element with Xeena

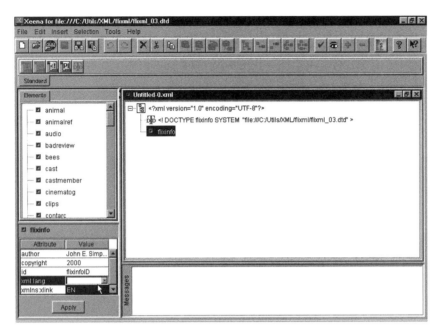

Figure 10.7   Editing attribute values in Xeena

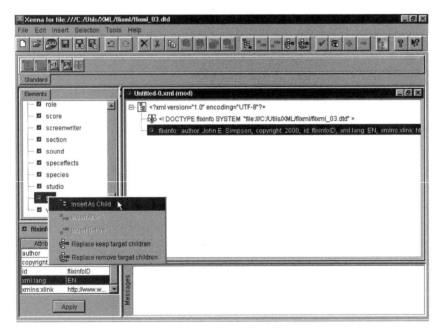

Figure 10.8   Inserting a child element with Xeena

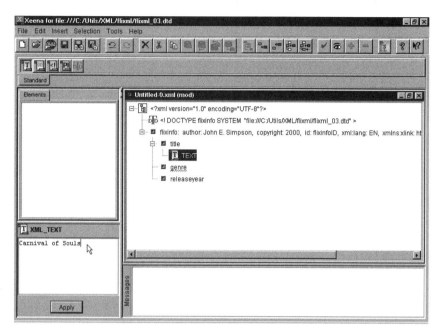

Figure 10.9 Adding #PCDATA (text) content with Xeena

To insert a text node—that is, #PCDATA content—just select the parent element and click the toolbar button at the upper left labeled with a large capital "T." As you can see in Figure 10.9, this replaces the attribute list for the currently selected element, at the lower left, with a box labeled "XML TEXT." Here you just enter whatever text content you need (including entity references, if needed). There's a separate toolbar button for inserting a marked (CDATA) section, if that's appropriate.

Of course as you continue to edit a document—or, as in Figure 10.10, have loaded a complete one to start with—you'd want the list of valid elements to change, depending on the element you've selected in the upper right pane. Figure 10.10 shows the contents element selected; the list of elements at the upper left has changed to include only those elements that are descended from contents.

Note by the way the use of the pop-up "tool tip"-style messages. In Figure 10.10, as you can see, when the mouse cursor hovers over an element the message displays the element's content model.

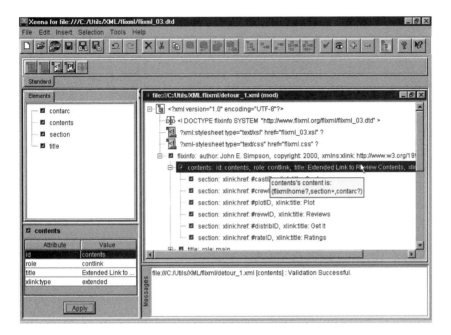

Figure 10.10   A complete FlixML document, ready for editing in Xeena

What do I use?

Since publication of Just XML's first edition, I've been asked on a number of occasions what XML editor I use.

Uh, well….

The fact is, I don't use an editor designed specifically for dealing with XML. What I use is a "programmer's editor," called UltraEdit-32, which is also useful for editing CSS and XSLT stylesheets, HTML, Perl scripts, and so on. What I like about UltraEdit-32 is that you can make it "vocabulary-aware"; it doesn't really follow a DTD—it depends on you to know about all the content models and so on—but will display known tags in customizable colors, making the markup stand out from the actual content. (This is a feature employed by other programmer's editors, by the way.)

Using one tool like this for several different kinds of work means, of course, that I've only got to remember how to deal with one interface. Anything that helps one's memory by the time you get to be my age is worth considering.

DTD Editors/Generators

Let's face it: setting out to develop a new DTD is not something you may be looking forward to—not having survived the rigors of Chapter 9.

The planning that I describe in Chapter 9 is necessary and unavoidable, and it enables you to think (and think, and think) about your pet subject much more than you thought you'd ever have a chance to. No, the real problem in developing a DTD is the actual physical process of coding it. In my opinion, it's far more excruciating than coding XML by hand: all that bizarre punctuation, the need to keep close tabs on things (such as entities and IDREF attributes) that refer to other things.... So it stands to reason that tools to automate the process would have a natural market.

Not much has been done about this problem so far, though. Here are a couple of possibilities.

XML Spy

Sitting on the fence between an XML editor and a DTD editor is XML Spy, from Icon Information Systems, now in its third version. It includes facilities for editing both sorts of structure.

Figure 10.11 shows XML Spy's DTD-editing mode. Two of the three small panes on the left are not used when editing the DTD. At the bottom, on the left, are available parameter entities that can be used in the DTD. To the right is the DTD itself; as you can see, when elements are expanded (as with the `contents` element here) both their content models and their attribute lists are visible.

For comparison with Xeena, you might want to take a look at Figure 10.12—depicting XML Spy editing the same detour_1.xml file that I showed you in Figure 10.10, during the discussion of Xeena.

XML Spy and Xeena both demonstrate the advantages of using a GUI-based program for document and DTD editing: Not only are they simple for just about anyone to use, they also make it virtually impossible to mistype important text such as element and attribute names, or to violate other central XML tenets such as the proper nesting of elements. I seriously doubt that any software ever written (or to be written) can be perfect, but the GUI approach is hard to fault in an XML editor.[68]

---

68. ...unless, of course, you (like me) just prefer to key things in rather than to key in some things (text content, attribute values) and point-and-click others.

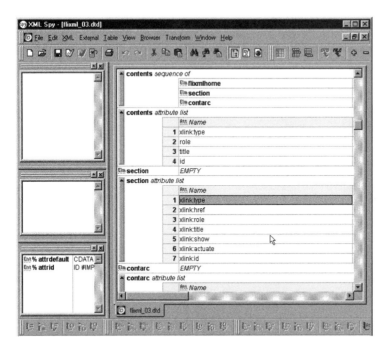

Figure 10.11   Editing a DTD with XML Spy

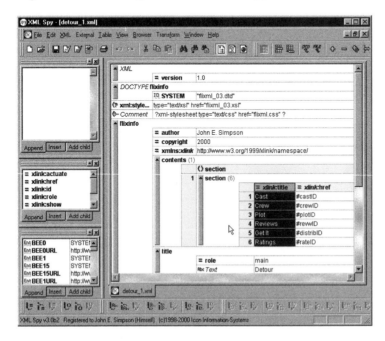

Figure 10.12   Editing a DTD with XML Spy

DTDGenerator

The DTD editing features of XML Spy and similar programs certainly make it hard to goof up when building a document type. Not everyone wants a drill sergeant breathing down his or her neck, though.

A somewhat more casual method of creating a DTD is represented by DTD-Generator, written by Michael Kay of ICL: Feed the program a well-formed XML document, and DTDGenerator will attempt to create a DTD to which the document would conform. Why "casual"? Maybe that's overstating the case a bit; you do still have to be somewhat mindful of what you're doing. But after you've sweat bullets over your first DTD editing experience, DTDGenerator is undeniably a breath of fresh air.

The program, which is written in Java, is actually a simple demonstration application for a complete package called SAXON. (I'll talk more about SAXON below, in the coverage of XSLT processors.)

To run DTDGenerator, you use this command line:

```
java DTDGenerator inputfile >outputfile
```

For `inputfile`, supply the name of your well-formed XML document. (If it's not well-formed, of course, the parser will tell you so.) Use the optional `>outputfile` command-line argument to tell DTDGenerator the name of the file to which you want it to write its output—the generated DTD.

Making life simple

Unless you're using SAXON for other purposes, such as XSLT processing, I recommend that instead of downloading and running it locally, you use the nifty "DTDGenerator FrontEnd," developed by Paul Tchistopolskii and available online at:

```
www.pault.com/Xmltube/dtdgen.html
```

All you do is click on the "Browse..." button in the window and select the XML file on which you want to base your DTD; then click on the "Generate DTD!" button. This runs a Perl script that invokes DTDGenerator and presents its output in another window; from there you can simply copy-and-paste it into your DTD. There are a few restrictions, such as that the XML document cannot refer to any external entities; on the whole, though, this "FrontEnd" makes a simple process even simpler.

I'll show you the output of a sample DTDGenerator session in a moment. First, I want to show you the XML document I'm using. It's a modified version of the laughcow.xml file I mentioned earlier in this chapter; for the most part, I've made the modifications to demonstrate certain features of DTDGenerator. As usual, the square-blocked letters are keyed to the annotation that follows. Here's the customized laughcow.xml:

```
<!DOCTYPE flixinfo [     Ⓐ
<!ENTITY W "Western">
<!ENTITY COM "Comedy">
<!ENTITY PAR "Paramount">
<!ENTITY BEE0 "NO Bees">
]>
<flixinfo>
<title role="main">The Laughing Cow</title>
<title role="alt" xml:lang="FR">La Vache Qui Rit</title>
<genre>
<primarygenre>&W;</primarygenre>
<othergenre>&COM;</othergenre>
<othergenre>Romance</othergenre>     Ⓑ
<genrelinkgroup xlink:type="extended" xlink:title="Other Films in
   This Genre:">     Ⓒ
<genrelink xink:type="locator"
xlink:href="http://www.flixml.org/gowest.xml"
xlink:title="Go West, Young Man"/>
<genrelink xlink:type="locator"
xlink:href="http://www.flixml.org/trighappy.xml"
xlink:title="Trigger Happy"/>
<genrelink xlink:type="locator"
xlink:href="http://www.flixml.org/mesamess.xml"
xlink:title="Mesa Mess"/>
</genrelinkgroup>
</genre>
<releaseyear role="main">1959</releaseyear>
<releaseyear role="alt">1962</releaseyear>
<studio>&PAR;</studio>
<cast>
<leadcast>
<male>Johnny Winthrop<role>Johnny B</role></male>
<male>Reese B. "High" Noone<role>"Posse" Williams</role></male>
<female>Joan Torrance<role>Eva Ramirez</role></female>
<animal>Toto El Toro<role>Himself</role><species>Bull</species></
   animal>
</leadcast>
```

```
<othercast>    D
<male>Larry Winder<role>Doc</role></male>
<female>Rosalind Puerto<role>Miss Eva</role></female>
</othercast>
</cast>
<crew>
<director>Jesse Winder</director>
</crew>
<plotsummary>Non-stop laughs and action abound (or were intended
   to abound, maybe) in this surrealistic mix of the Western and
   comedy genres. Sometime cowpoke Johnny B and his slowpoke
   sidekick Posse Williams arrive at the Torrance Ranch, mistaking
   it for the much larger and considerably more successful
   Torrence Ranch, which has advertised for hands to  accompany a
   cattle drive. At the <emph>TorrAnce</emph> E Ranch, not only
   is no cattle drive planned, but there's danged few head of
   cattle. In fact, there's only a single bovine resident of the
   ranch: Total El Toro, playing himself in this, his mercifully
   only appearance.</plotsummary>
<bees>&BEE0;</bees>
</flixinfo>
```

Now, the notes on this document:

A Since DTDGenerator's purpose is to *create* a DTD, you don't need a document type declaration at all. However, if the document in question contains any general entities, you'll have to declare them in an internal subset, as shown here.

B In addition to the `primarygenre` and `othergenre` elements that appear in the normal laughcow.xml document, this one contains a second `othergenre`. This was a test to see what DTDGenerator would guess to be the content model of the parent `genre` element.

C The `genrelinkgroup` XLinking element, with its children `genrelink` elements, is a fairly complex structure (at least as far as FlixML is concerned)—note especially all the attributes here and in the children elements.

D According to the real FlixML DTD, `leadcast` and `othercast` have exactly the same content models: optional `male`, `female`, and `animal` elements, in any order. Here in this document, while sticking to what I know is the correct structure, I've set up an `othercast` element (with `male` and `female` children, but no animal) in addition to laughcow.xml's usual `leadcast`. This, again, is a matter of curiosity: What will DTDGenerator do?

Ⓔ The emph element isn't used in the normal laughcow.xml file. I've added it here to determine if DTDGenerator will successfully identify the plotsummary element's mixed-content model.

DTDGenerator's output is shown in Session 10.2; annotations follow. Note that for the session listing reproduced here I've stripped out the extra newlines that DTDGenerator inserts between each element's declaration. You may wish to compare this automatically generated DTD with the true FlixML DTD in Appendix A.

Session 10.2   DTDGenerator's DTD created from laughcow.xml

```
<!ELEMENT animal ( #PCDATA | role | species )* >    Ⓐ
<!ELEMENT bees ( #PCDATA ) >
<!ELEMENT cast ( leadcast, othercast ) >
<!ELEMENT crew ( director ) >
<!ELEMENT director ( #PCDATA ) >
<!ELEMENT emph ( #PCDATA ) >
<!ELEMENT female ( #PCDATA | role )* >
<!ELEMENT flixinfo ( title+, genre, releaseyear+, studio, cast,
crew, plotsummary, bees ) >    Ⓑ
<!ELEMENT genre ( primarygenre, othergenre+, genrelinkgroup ) >
<!ELEMENT genrelink EMPTY >    Ⓒ
<!ATTLIST genrelink xlink:href CDATA #REQUIRED >
<!ATTLIST genrelink xlink:title CDATA #IMPLIED >
<!ATTLIST genrelink xlink:type NMTOKEN #IMPLIED >
<!ELEMENT genrelinkgroup ( genrelink+ ) >
<!ATTLIST genrelinkgroup xlink:title CDATA #REQUIRED >
<!ATTLIST genrelinkgroup xlink:type NMTOKEN #REQUIRED >
<!ELEMENT leadcast ( male+, female, animal ) >    Ⓓ
<!ELEMENT male ( #PCDATA | role )* >
<!ELEMENT othercast ( male, female ) >    Ⓓ
<!ELEMENT othergenre ( #PCDATA ) >
<!ELEMENT plotsummary ( #PCDATA | emph )* >
<!ELEMENT primarygenre ( #PCDATA ) >
<!ELEMENT releaseyear ( #PCDATA ) >
<!ATTLIST releaseyear role NMTOKEN #REQUIRED >
<!ELEMENT role ( #PCDATA ) >
<!ELEMENT species ( #PCDATA ) >
<!ELEMENT studio ( #PCDATA ) >
<!ELEMENT title ( #PCDATA ) >
<!ATTLIST title role NMTOKEN #REQUIRED >    Ⓔ
<!ATTLIST title xml:lang NMTOKEN #IMPLIED >
```

Notes on this session:

Ⓐ Why does the `animal` element come first, even though in the source document it's buried somewhere in the middle? Look down the list of elements for the answer: DTDGenerator maintains a list of elements that appear in the document, not in the order of appearance, but rather in alphabetic order—`animal`, `bees`, `cast`, `crew`, `director`, and so on. We don't know, but can probably guess, that the reason for this is that it needs to retain (and easily look up) a list of element names for later use.

Ⓑ For the root `flixinfo` element, however—actually, for any element whose content model contains other elements—the content model is specified in order of appearance. Content models can, of course, specify a sequence of child elements, and it's reasonable to assume that the order in which they appear in the source document is the order in which they *should* appear. Note that `flixinfo`'s generated content model specifies *sequence* (by separating the child elements with commas) rather than *optionality* (using the pipe, or |, character). This is one area that may require hand-tweaking of the generated DTD.

Ⓒ DTDGenerator has correctly determined that `genrelink` is an empty element. Attributes are listed immediately after the element to which they apply, each attribute in its own ATTLIST declaration; attributes appear in alphabetical order within the elements to which they apply, presumably for the same reason as the attributes themselves.

Ⓓ The `leadcast` and `othercast` elements' content models don't precisely match here, although they do in FlixML's DTD. Again, this fact isn't really surprising; DTDGenerator can't build its output based on anything it doesn't know about—such as the optional `animal` element in othercast, which simply doesn't appear in this FlixML document.

Ⓔ For these attributes of the `title` element, note that DTDGenerator has declared `role` to be #REQUIRED, and `xml:lang` to be #IMPLIED. How did it figure this out? Look back at the laughcow.xml source file: both instances of `title` come with a `role` attribute, but only one has an `xml:lang` attribute. So the program guesses that the former is required and that the latter is not. Compare this guess with the one made for the attributes of the `genrelink` element (note Ⓒ, above); all occurrences of this element *in the source document* include all three attributes, hence the assumption that all three attributes must be #REQUIRED.

DTDGenerator does have its limits. Mostly these are attributable, as in a few cases noted above, to the simple impossibility of determining on the basis of a single document instance all possible structures that *may* be legal; the most that can be said is what appears to be legal according to *this* document's structure. On the whole, though, it's a great idea, cleanly implemented. And it's potentially a real time- and stress-saver: It's quite simple to work with model XML files, fine-tuning them till they seem complete, and then running a fairly all-encompassing one through DTDGenerator to produce a first-cut DTD.[69]

Style Sheet Tools

As with DTDs, one of the main problems with creating your own style sheets is that they're so *different* from the rest of what you do with your XML application. Even though XSLT uses XML syntax and structure, it's a rather far cry from knowing and understanding your XML application itself to knowing and under-standing the intricacies of construction and style rules.

So it's good to see that products are emerging to simplify this task. I'll look at two of these tools here.

HomeSite Style Editor

Allaire's HomeSite editor is widely used by hand-coders of HTML for its intelli-gent design and for the nice balance it strikes—GUI-based, but not too GUI-based. In recent versions, Allaire has bundled with HomeSite a separate Style Editor package for creating and maintaining CSS style sheets.

The Style Editor assumes that you're using it for style sheets to be used with regular HTML, as you can see in Figure 10.13. Down the left side are arrayed a set of standard selectors for HTML. To its right are the stock list of CSS proper-ties.

For XML use, the first thing you'll probably want to do is remove all the HTML-specific selectors and add those relevant to your own vocabulary (such as FlixML). In Figure 10.14, I've started this process for a new FlixML stylesheet—adding a `title` element selector and beginning to designate its font properties.

The box at the bottom left corner of the window is a preview pane, showing you the currently selected style *in* the style you've designated for it. (In this case, since we're just starting out, the `title` selector has no special display proper-ties.) To the right of the preview pane is the actual CSS2 code that will be saved

---

69.   Actually, it's so simple that I wish I'd had DTDGenerator handy when I first started working on FlixML.

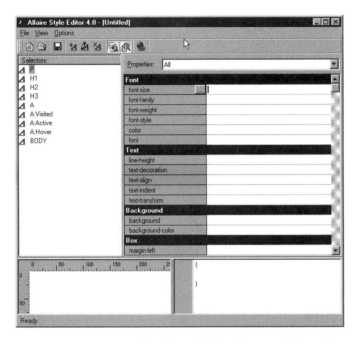

Figure 10.13 HomeSite Style Editor (new stylesheet)

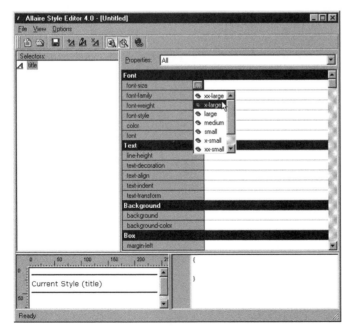

Figure 10.14 Selecting font properties (Allaire Style Editor)

when you save the style sheet. (If you're so inclined, you can edit the code here manually.) Note that the drop-down box in the list of style properties lets you select only standard CSS properties—nothing so specific as 24pt (for 24-point type). However, instead of selecting from the drop-down, you can manually enter a specific size. In Figure 10.15, you can see this effect.

The .primary selector (currently selected in the top left pane), as you can see, will be displayed in 24-point bold type on a 26-point-high line; its font will be Verdana if available, then Helvetica, then Univers, or finally the browser's generic sans serif font. The preview pane at the bottom shows how this selector will actually look when displayed, including the teal background (invisible in this screen shot, but you can see it specified in the code-view window on the right).

Excelon Stylus

A recent addition to the style sheet-editing toolkit is this little marvel from Excelon (formerly Object Designs).

Why do I say "marvel"? Because, frankly, I wondered if such a thing would ever be possible: an XSLT style sheet editor that shows you pretty much everything you'd want to know about your style sheet's effects.

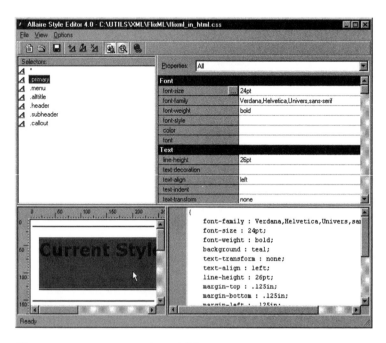

Figure 10.15   A complete CSS stylesheet, viewed in Allaire's Style Editor

When you first start up Stylus, you're prompted to select from somewhere on your system a style sheet and/or an XML document. Figure 10.16 is typical of the screen you'd see next.

There are three panes to the default Stylus window:

- At the top left is the XML document itself (a FlixML document, in this case). The contents of this pane (and the others, for that matter) are color-coded to make markup stand out from text content.
- At the top right is the HTML code—the result tree—resulting from the transformation of the XML source by your style sheet...
- ...which is shown in the bottom pane.

In that bottom pane is just a single template, for a single match pattern (the distributors element, in this case). If the template is named, its name will appear in the gray area at the top right of the pane (as will any mode or priority settings you may have assigned it).

I kind of jumped over it without further comment, but the second bullet above included something very interesting (and possibly very limiting): the information that Stylus is intended for use *only* in transforming XML to HTML.

Figure 10.16 Stylus main editing window

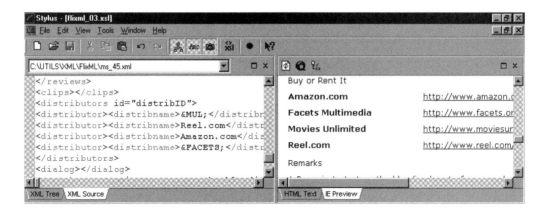

Figure 10.17   Stylus "IE5 Preview" feature

A further sign of this is that the top right pane, where your results are displayed, includes an "IE Preview" tab. If you click on this tab, you see, as in Figure 10.17, how the transformed page itself will actually look in a browser. (I've trimmed off the stylesheet template display for this screen shot, and also scrolled the document itself, in the left pane, so you can see the relationship between what the browser will see and what's actually in the document.)

There's one little hitch in Stylus that you'll uncover if you actually try to use the above XML code, by the way: Its parser does not read the external DTD subset. Accordingly, I had to include an internal subset declaring the &MUL; and &FACETS; entities that are referenced above.

The other thing I've learned about Stylus has to do with the IE5 preview pane. The XSLT style sheet loaded above actually includes, in its template for the root element, a link to a CSS style sheet. (You can see this CSS stylesheet link at the top right of Figure 10.16.) The preview pane does not take this CSS style sheet into consideration when displaying the result tree. We'll see in a moment how this portion should look.

Style Sheet Processors

Someday, probably sooner rather than later in the grand, geologic scheme of things, we'll have browsers capable of reading raw XML as transformed by XSLT style sheets also present on the user's machine—similar perhaps to Stylus's preview pane. Until that happy day, we'll need this class of tool: standalone style sheet processors.

There's nothing really to show you, alas. "All" that these programs do is apply an XSLT style sheet to a source document, transforming it to a result tree or document. (That's not by any means to belittle what it is they do, which is quite amazing!)

You can run a typical XSLT processor in a couple of different ways: as a plain old program run at an operating system command line, or as a more dynamic process executed by a Web server. Option 1 is simple but dull; for every document you want transformed, you run the processor over, and over, and over, generating a succession of corresponding result documents—probably HTML—which can then be displayed by a browser or dealt with by some other application. Despite its dullness, this—because of its simplicity—is currently the favored approach used by many.

Option 2 is a bit snazzier, but also a bit more complicated. Here you hitch up one of these style sheet processors to a server and run it as a Java servlet, a Perl- or Python-based CGI program, or whatever. When a visitor to your Web site requests an XML document, rather than passing the document through directly (as it does an HTML document, for instance) the server feeds it through the servlet (etc.)—whose output (not the original source tree) is what the user actually experiences.

A number of large corporations have developed XSLT processors. Oracle, for example, has developed one, as has IBM. (The latter's product, LotusXSL, was donated to the Apache Project's open-source XML effort.) But a quick review of the archives of the XSL-List mailing list will probably reflect that most developers are currently using one or both of two smaller-scale efforts: James Clark's XT and Michael Kay's SAXON.

XT

It's hard to do XML for any length of time without running across James Clark's name. Among other things, he developed the expat XML processor (later adopted by the Mozilla browser project to support their own XML efforts), and he has edited a number of W3C specs—notably both XPath and XSLT. It is of course this latter role that makes XT what it is.

Basically, it's a Java application (also available as a Win32 executable) that takes up to three command-line arguments: the name of the XML document, the name of the XSLT style sheet, and the name of the resulting document. XT chugs through the first, applying the templates in the second to produce the third.

Because its author is James Clark, XT tends to be considered the "standard" by which other XSLT processors are measured. Does your XSLT processor produce a different result tree than XT does? Chances are then that your XSLT processor is wrong. It's not perfect—although its "flaws" fall under the heading of officially-blessed XSLT features not yet implemented, rather than things done wrong. It just comes awfully close.[70]

SAXON

You've encountered SAXON once before in this chapter; the DTDGenerator mentioned above is one of its sample applications.

SAXON, developed by Michael Kay, is much more than DTDGenerator, though. (It even has its own support and discussion mailing list.) Lately, it's also become tremendously popular as a result of its XSLT processing capabilities. (SAXON, like XT, is written in Java; it also is available as something called "SAXON Lite," a Win32 executable just for its XSLT processing.)

The chief reason for SAXON's popularity, in my opinion, is the way in which its author participates openly in discussion and contributes willingly to extending the reach of XSLT."

"Horrors!"

"Extending" XML and related standards is a tricky area. On the one hand, extensibility is built-in, you might say, as a core value of the technology; on the other hand, you're not supposed to come up with off-the-wall proprietary extensions that bend the rules laid out in the specs.

The approach to extensibility taken in SAXON and similar products is generally welcomed: The extensions are developed and discussed in a fishbowl as it were, with lots of people chiming in (and—this is the Internet, after all—occasionally complaining). Extensions developed in this manner have a way of showing up in later standards.

---

70. As of this writing, I used XT for generating all HTML-from-FlixML documents at www.flixml.org.

For instance, one area of XSLT that routinely tortures those who try to follow the spec religiously is that there's no easy way to group data. You can sort it, sure, but you still end up with potential duplication in the result tree. In Mike Myers' *Austin Powers* films, he plays more than one role; ideally, transforming a FlixML document to HTML would turn the multiple identical `castmember` elements of the former into a single "group header" in the latter. You can do this, but it requires jumping through hoops to determine if this is the first or a later occurrence of the element, and transforming the source tree accordingly.

SAXON adds a grouping construction that makes this easy. With it, you can create a template rule like the following:

```
<saxon:group select="attribute" group-by="section">
  <xsl:sort select="section"/>
  <section name="{section}">
    <saxon:item>
      <attribute name="{@name}"/>
    </saxon:item>
  </section>
</saxon:group>
```

This effectively both sorts and groups the source tree. (Note, by the way, the element names specifically in the SAXON namespace.)

XML-ized Generic Web Browsers

Other than creating and styling (or transforming) XML documents, the first thing most people want to know when they first learn about the new markup language is whether they can *browse* XML, just like they do with HTML. The answer is a qualified "yes"—we're getting close, just not quite there yet.

Microsoft Internet Explorer 5 (IE5)

When Microsoft first announced the availability of Version 5 of their Internet Explorer browser, the XML community was, well, *excited*. The reason: the claim that MSIE5 would be able to view XML documents directly.

In a way the notion was almost, well, bizarre. As I've mentioned many times, XML has no inherent display characteristics; so how, then, would IE5 "know" how to display a FlixML document, for example? The answer to the riddle is that although individual elements don't have intrinsic display characteristics, there's an *implicit* display in any XML document's structure. This structure will be familiar to users of most operating systems with a graphical user interface—it's just like a "directory tree."

(In fact, you've already seen something like it in this chapter: Jeremie Miller's XParse JavaScript-based parser.)

IE5 has both a parser and an XSLT processor built into it (as well as a default XSLT style sheet, for that matter); and—in keeping with the usual tendency by Microsoft to push the envelope of what's allowed under the term "standard"—it behaves in ways accessible in no other way than through the proprietary Microsoft interface. Figure 10.18 shows you how a FlixML review looks, by default, when opened in IE5.

As you can see, the document appears as a collapsible/expandable tree; click on a plus sign to expand that node, on a minus sign to collapse it.

Also note in Figure 10.18 that I had to comment out the `xml:stylesheet` PI. I didn't do this just for the sake of simplifying the example; I had to do it

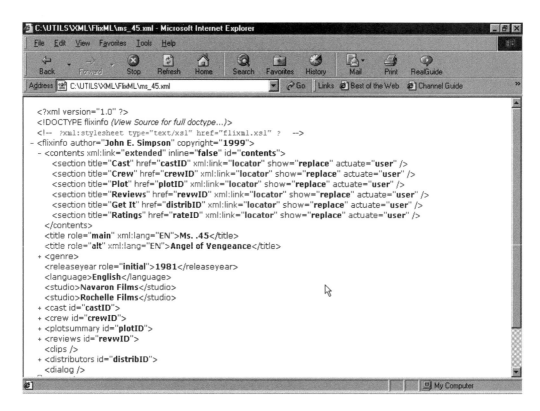

Figure 10.18   Microsoft IE5 browser default display

because the version of XSLT supported by IE5 at the moment is over a year old—indeed, from the time before there was a separate transformational component split off from the main XSL spec. So if it doesn't support XSLT, what choices do we have other than the default shrinking/expanding element tree?

Figure 10.19 shows one such option.

It's not very attractive, but it makes a couple of points.

First, this is the same document as viewed above—using a CSS2 style sheet instead of an XSLT one. It's great to be able to style some things directly this way; however, because IE5 doesn't yet support the full CSS2 standard, some features (particularly generated content) don't work at all. It'd be nice to show something like:

Title: Ms. .45
Alternate Title: Angel of Vengeance

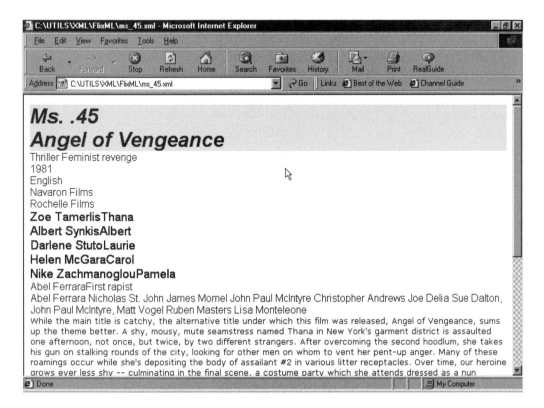

Figure 10.19   IE5 display of FlixML document (CSS2 only)

But because the words "Title:" and "Angel of Vengeance" aren't in the source document, without the ability to generate them they can't appear in the browser.

The second point—subtler—is that the day is close, tantalizingly close.

Now look at Figure 10.20.

What I've done here is first run the Ms. .45 review through an XSLT processor (XT, in this case) to simply produce an HTML document; it's this HTML document, not the raw XML, that Figure 10.20 depicts (as you can see from the file name in the little "Address" window at the top left).

Of course I could take it even further, by including in the result tree of the generated HTML a link to a CSS style sheet. The result of that step appears in Figure 10.21.

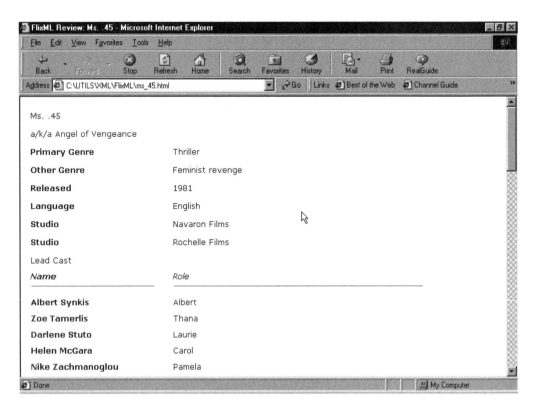

Figure 10.20 *Ms. .45* review, post-XSLT (in IE5 browser)

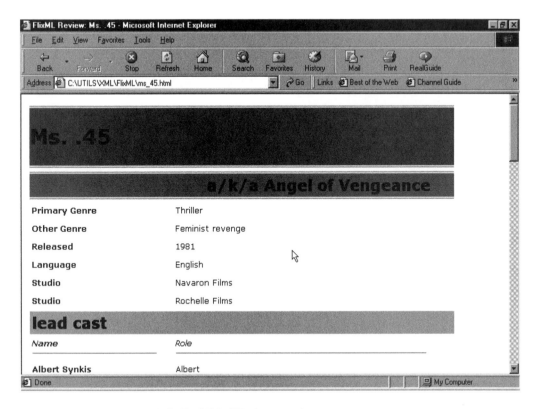

Figure 10.21   FlixML+XSLT+CSS (IE5 browser)

While you can't see it in this black-and-white screen shot, the various shaded bands going across the screen appear in colors—in fact, the CSS2 style sheet used here is the same one I loaded into the HomeSite Style Editor, above.

Mozilla/Netscape 5

Microsoft has pretty much had the browser-innovation market to themselves for the last few years, but there are signs that situation's about to end. On the not-so-far-off horizon, at last, is the first full production release of the Netscape open-source browser, code named Mozilla.

Let's start by showing Mozilla's presentation of the *Ms. .45* review in Figure 10.22. Aside from the browser's default font, this is pretty much the same view we saw in Figure 10.20, above, and for the same reason: It's really an HTML document, transformed from the XML sans CSS styling.

Figure 10.22   Ms. .45 review, post-XSLT (Mozilla browser)

Next, also for comparison purposes, is Figure 10.23—the Mozilla counter-part to the full-blown, post-XSLT, including-CSS view of IE5 that appeared as Figure 10.21.

But now we come to Figure 10.24, which shows what happens when you simply try to open an XML file in Mozilla directly, with no intervening XSLT step at all.

Right: Ugly. There is no "default style sheet" in Mozilla, as there is in IE5. So the result is that all the content is simply run-together, with the tags hidden. (The Mozilla team has XSLT support on its agenda, and this will likely include some sort of default display when it's available.)

XUL: XML in action in Mozilla

The Mozilla project has undertaken something very interesting—not earth-shattering, but interesting. This is the XML-based User Interface Language, or XUL. (I've also seen XUL spelled out as the "Extensible User Interface Lan-

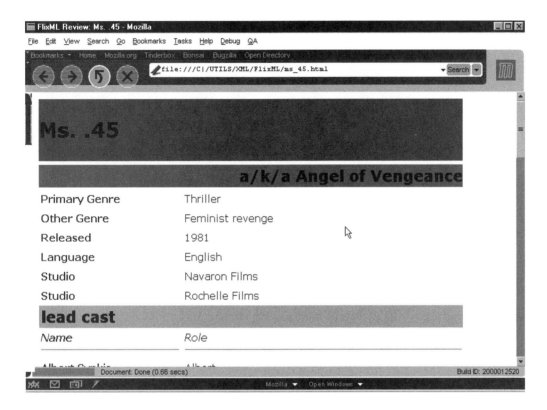

Figure 10.23   FlixML+XSLT+CSS (Mozilla browser)

guage"; however, the former expansion is the one appearing on the Mozilla Web site.)

Basically, XUL is an XML vocabulary for describing the various "widgets" and gizmos that you interact with in a GUI environment. For instance, a typical browser window has pushbuttons, menus, clickable non-button images, and so on. XUL encapsulates all of this so-called chrome into a set of XML element types. These element types are used, in general, to describe the function and purpose of the given widget; its appearance is more carefully calibrated controlled by an accompanying CSS style sheet. In the so-called M13 build of Mozilla, there are over 170 .xul files (.xul being the file name extension for XUL interface descriptions).

In theory this will allow tremendous customization of the user interface—akin to the idea of "skins" in such software as MP3 players. It remains to be seen

Figure 10.24 "Straight XML" in Mozilla browser

how much users actually take advantage of this, as the XUL tagset is not for the faint of heart!

Summary

This chapter covered a broad range of XML software currently available, including parsers, document editors, DTD editors, browsers, and stylesheet tools. The list of tools covered was not exhaustive—in particular, there wasn't any discussion of large-scale toolsets like those that have grown up around SGML and been converted to being XML-aware.

Most important, this chapter should have left you with the sense that it's all coming together for XML. You are a computer user, after all, and what's a computer user (even an XML-savvy one) without software?

CHAPTER 11

Whither XML?

$\mathbf{N}$ow that you know as much about the present state of XML as I do, you may be wondering what's coming up in the future. How much of what you've learned will be applicable in a year? What *new* things will you need to learn?

This chapter will examine three major directions in which XML-related technology is headed: the ever-changing state of the official specifications; XML and databases; and where *you* should be headed.

Upcoming XML Specifications

Bear in mind as you read this section that the W3C does *not* publish for public consumption any kind of ongoing record of its deliberations. Things may be whispered in the halls, as it were, but a great deal of what follows in this section must be speculative.

The W3C divides its work up among working groups, each of which is devoted to a specific subject. In their currently published calendar of upcoming events, four working groups are named: Core XML; XML Schema; XML Linking; and XML Query.

Core XML Working Group

This group seems to have the most varied menu of things on the plate at the moment. They include the preparation of Proposed Recommendations for:

Canonicalizing XML

Yeah; what a mouthful. You can kind of get at what's involved if you think of the phrase (common among academics, especially of the literary sort) "the canon." In academic circles, "the canon" is an overarching term for the ultimate works on a subject—the authorities. The plays of Shakespeare, for example, are considered canonical works of literature. *Canonical XML* tackles a thorny, almost philosophical question: How can we know for sure that two documents are "equal" or not? You've seen some signs of this question in *Just XML*, when I discussed normalizing whitespace; reducing all whitespace in two documents to the least common denominator, as it were, is just one step (a simple one) in canonicalizing it—making it a "reference" (authoritative, unambiguous) version. Expanding all entity references is another.

XML Fragment Interchange

Likewise, you've been unknowingly exposed to this subject already. Let's say you're building an XLink to incorporate some portion of a remote resource within the local. The Fragment Interchange specification will help answer the question, "What does the local resource 'know' about the retrieved content?" For example, does it know the style in which the content is presented? Does it know what its parent element is? Does it know how to deal with a non-well-formed chunk of the remote resource?

XML Information Set

If you browse through this specification you'll probably be left scratching your head; it's one of the most abstract in a family of documents where the gene for abstraction is clearly dominant.

InfoSet, as this spec is called, attempts to nail down, as unambiguously as possible, *what an XML processor is required to report.* Of course you can read the core XML 1.0 Recommendation to get a feel for this, but there are enough gray areas—especially among theoreticians, implementors of software, and developers of XML-related standards outside core XML itself—that a strong need was perceived to "define the atoms," as it were, that make the physics and chemistry of XML work. In order to accomplish this goal, the InfoSet defines the specific units of information that a processor can pass to a downstream application.

Personally, I'd be surprised if someone told me that I needed to understand the Information Set in order to understand XML; the same is probably true of you. On the other hand, given its clear importance to XML's theoretical infrastructure, there's also no denying that it will have some impact on all of us. I think of the InfoSet spec as that hypothetical butterfly, flapping its wings in China; whether I ever see the butterfly or not, let alone how well I "understand" it, someday, somewhere, a breeze will ruffle my hair and I'll say, "Huh—what the heck was *that?*"

XML Linking: XLink/XPointer

Current plans are for these specs to attain Proposed Recommendation status in "early 2000." There's no way of knowing what form the final specs will take, of course; but given the number of Working Drafts and the length of time involved, chances are probably good that they won't be too different from what I've discussed here.

XML Query

The idea here is that you should be able to "ask a question" about an XML document in some standardized way, and get a reasonable answer. The analogy is to the Structured Query Language (SQL) of relational databases. The specifics will vary depending on whether the database in question is loaded with inventory and parts data, stock quotes, news headlines, B-movie reviews, or whatever; but the *form* of the query should be consistent. This working group plans to continue with its design work in 2000—no specific timetable for deliverables at this date.

XML Schema

Another hot topic is how DTDs might be improved if the information they conveyed were represented in XML form. This Working Draft is already enormous, and like that of XSL and XSLT has been broken into two chunks: a standard for representing structures, and a standard for representing datatypes. (Lots of people want the latter, especially—the ability to assert, for instance, that this element or attribute must contain a date, a floating-point number, a text string no more than twenty characters long, and so on.) The Working Group's target is to have a Candidate Recommendation available sometime in the spring of 2000.

XSL Formatting Objects

I discussed this briefly[71] in Chapter 8. At the moment, this Working Draft is pretty big—my printed copy runs to over 200 pages. It covers an incredible range of formatting characteristics, from the obvious (e.g., font sizes, margins) to the more arcane (kerning, first-page displays vs. all others). Generally speaking, you'll know that someone is talking about this spec when their code examples include elements and/or attributes whose names are prefixed `fo:`, indicating that the names are in the XSL-FO namespace. No timetable has been published for further releases of this spec, to my knowledge.

Document Object Model (DOM)

The DOM specification (like SAX, not really a software product in itself but an API—a specification for how software products may communicate with one another) has implications not just for XML but for HTML as well. We're already seeing new applications take advantage of this standard.

What the DOM does is give an application a standard way to manipulate chunks of an XML or HTML document as a unit. These chunks don't necessarily have a precise physical counterpart in the document itself; for example, from a complete FlixML document you can extract in a single bite "all the `male` elements," regardless of whether they're physically located in a `leadcast` or `othercast` context. (This sounds rather like the XPath node-set concept—not coincidentally.) It enables manipulation of not just XML units, but pieces of related things like HTML, CSS, and ranges. Furthermore, the DOM allows adding, changing, and deleting these chunks—it's not a "read-only" spec.

The DOM Level 1 Recommendation was released in fall, 1998. DOM Level 2 advanced to "Last Call" status in fall, 1999, and may well have been approved as a Recommendation by the time you read this.

XML and Data

To someone who's come from the database world to XML, tying XML in some way to databases seems like a natural fit. There's a lot of activity, both official and unofficial, in this area.

---

71.   To say the least.

RDF

The Resource Description Framework (RDF) is a proposal to give to XML the same kind of "metadata" facilities available to HTML—only (need I add?) better. For starters, HTML's `<meta>` tag is about as unstructured as HTML itself; RDF, on the other hand, will itself be expressed in XML syntax.

Metadata is *data about data*. Some simple examples, given a particular XML document: Who wrote it? Is it copyrighted? May it be quoted from? When was it created, and when last modified? Is its content suitable for viewing by five-year-olds? None of this information has anything to do with the subject matter of whatever markup language the document uses—indeed, it could well be considered potentially applicable across all documents. If I'm doing a doctoral dissertation on the works of John Updike, I don't want to have to know one markup language to grab all his novels, one for all his short stories, one for his poetry, and yet another for his essays and other nonfiction: I just want to say something on the order of, "Get me all documents authored by Updike."

The implications of this will be far-reaching, especially in the area of searching the Web. Obviously XML itself—with meaning embedded in document structure—will go a long way to help. Data *about* the millions of XML documents to come will take us the rest of the way.

But on the downside...

The RDF "model and syntax specification" has been out since February, 1999. In that time, while it has gotten quite a bit of attention in some circles, by and large it has been met with what might politely be called a resounding silence.

Why is this, given its potential usefulness?

Part of it is the namespace bugaboo; if you're going to include "RDF elements" in your documents, then of course you've got to allow for the RDF namespace declaration—and/or include those elements in your own DTD.

I'm no expert, but I think it's probably got a lot more to do with human nature—in particular, the disinclination to *explain* what you're doing, as opposed to simply doing it. The bane of corporate MIS departments has always been the failure of programmers to comment their code; on a larger scale, "Shoot first and ask questions [let alone provide answers] later" is practically a religious tenet in contemporary society. This is a difficult but nevertheless heartbreaking fact of life.

> In any case, if you can spare a few hours of rigorous intellectual exercise, I encourage you to obtain and read and *think about* the RDF spec, and maybe even adopt it in your own application. You can find the spec at:
>
> `www.w3.org/TR/1999/REC-rdf-syntax-19990222/`

XML Vocabularies

As even a dumb-as-dirt forecaster could have predicted two years ago, in this area there has been no slacking off at all in XML activity. You may recall the quote from the XML FAQ in the beginning of this book—that potential applications for XML included "music, chemistry, electronics, hill-walking, finance, surfing, petroleum geology, linguistics, cooking, knitting, stellar cartography, history, engineering, rabbit-keeping, mathematics, etc." I wouldn't be at all surprised to find that those have all crossed over from the realm of the potential to the world of the real, and I suspect that we'll see ever more as the collection of standards matures.

Here's a summary of a couple of interesting emerging vocabularies.

SVG: Scalable Vector Graphics

As you may know, by far most images on the Web are so-called bitmap images: GIF, JPEG, a smattering of PNGs. The format of such files represents a given image as an assemblage of closely-packed dots, which the human eye and brain work together to recognize *as* a picture by filling in the gaps, as it were, between one dot and another.

At once more sophisticated and simpler are *vector* graphics. The quintessential vector graphic application is computer-aided drafting, or CAD: Each side of a rectangle, let's say, is represented not by a series of dots that all happen to have the same X or Y coordinates, but by an "instruction" to the device rendering the image: "Draw a straight line from point (X1, Y1) to point (X2, Y2)." The effect of this is to make vector graphics, unlike bitmaps, virtually immune to changes in the output medium. If you shrink a bitmap, you give it a severe case of the "jaggies"; shrink a vector image and it's simply a smaller picture. What's more, typically the components of a vector image are manipulable as distinct entities—you move a line; you drag a point connected to two lines. In a bitmap, there is no such thing as a line: It's all just *dots*.

How best to represent a vector image's instructions in some universally acceptable way has been the Holy Grail (well, one of them) for graphics vendors and users. Solutions tend to cover a fairly small range, from fully proprietary (like the CAD vendors') to marginally so (like PostScript).

And then along comes XML. Because of what you now know about XML, you can probably see where this might be headed: Maybe you'd have one element structure representing points, each point being tagged with its own ID-type attribute; and then there'd be a line, its from and to ends associated with points by way of an IDREF....

SVG is a lot more complex than this, providing descriptors not just of points and lines but of polygons and other geometric shapes, surfaces, colors, animations—almost the whole of what you'd want to do with a graphic. SVG documents are almost overwhelming; I recently saw one that, when viewed, depicted a drawing of a boat: The document itself was *thirteen pages long*. Looked at another way, though, it was only about 75,000 bytes in size, including all that markup. That's a *lot* smaller than an equivalent bitmap image.

XBEL: XML Bookmark Exchange Language

What's one of the most annoying practical problems of working with the Web? Yeah, yeah—the sluggish downloads. That almost goes without saying. But the one that will continue to drive me really nuts long after I finally have a zippy broadband connection, I'm sure, is that the three browsers I use regularly all have different formats and file structures for remembering visited Web sites: bookmarks.

A team made up of participants in the Python XML Special Interest Group were apparently bugged by this, too. In any case, they decided to do something about it, and XBEL was the result.

"Python"?

I've dropped mention of Python in a couple of other places in *Just XML*. It's a programming language that's grown up, as it were, with the Web. One of the chief characteristics of Python—at least for programmers—is that it's *fun* to use.

In some ways XBEL is almost the opposite of FlixML. The FlixML DTD is pages long, its purpose almost completely of no consequence (except, I hope, to have helped teach you XML without putting you to sleep). The XBEL DTD, by contrast, takes barely a page (once you strip out the comments) to do something guaranteed to put a smile on the face of any cross-platform Web user.

To my knowledge only one browser uses the native XBEL format, the not-exactly-a-household-word Grail browser, which runs on platforms that support Python. I don't of course have any idea if *future* browsers will take advantage of it; on the other hand, with our XSLT toolkit tucked in a back pocket, how hard can it be to generate browser-specific bookmarks from a generic XBEL (dare I say it) linkbase?

Whither *You?*

I don't know what's going on in your head now. I don't know if you're roundly fed up with all things XML, excited beyond words, or depressed at the prospect of leaving *Just XML* behind. Maybe you're just hungry.[72]

But here's what I see in your XML future:

You won't be able to escape it.

Where to go from here

That last line about not being able to escape XML was pretty glib. If anything, the choice will be less a matter of avoiding XML than a matter of what to do next.

"It depends," of course. (Didn't you used to hate it when adults answered your most angst-ridden questions with that phrase?) If you're a Web developer, you'll want to focus on some applications and tools; a network administrator, on others; a college professor or student, on still others.

I do have a special request, though.

Don't lose touch with your light side. Yeah, nearly all of us have to work, alas. Some of us will be lucky enough to work with XML. Computers and Internet technology in general will continue to become ever more interwoven with our daily lives. But I've always thought that technology that doesn't help us be

---

72.   I don't know—at the moment, I can kind of sympathize with all four points of view.

(and become more) human isn't technology worth investing in…and if you're not laughing *more* as a result of technology, well, it's just not helping you become more human!

Please let me know how you're doing—not just with XML, nor even with FlixML, but with B movies, too (or whatever else you conjure up as your ideal XML application). You can always reach me at simpson@flixml.org. I'll be the one slouched on the sofa, absorbed in some black-and-white or washed-out color melodrama on the tube. And (you better believe it) laughing.

APPENDICES

The FlixML Files

This appendix has everything you need to know about FlixML, as incorporated in its DTD. There are also a sample FlixML review and an XSLT stylesheet to transform it to HTML, as well as a CSS2 stylesheet for displaying the resulting HTML. All are also available on-line, at:

```
http://www.flixml.org/flixml
```

The FlixML DTD (Version 3.0)

Yes, it's true: Writing a book about any subject is no proof that you know everything there is to know about it. So the FlixML DTD has gone through several changes—some significant, some not so much—in the year and a half since publication of *Just XML*'s first edition.

A complete version history and conditions of use are included in a block of comments at the head of the DTD at the above Web address; I've omitted these comments in this printed version.

```
<!--
 FlixML DTD (Version 3.0)
-->

<!-- ********** NOTATIONS ********** -->
<!-- ********** NOTATIONS ********** -->
<!-- ********** NOTATIONS ********** -->

<!NOTATION au    SYSTEM "utils/mplayer.exe">
<!NOTATION wav   SYSTEM "utils/mplayer.exe">
<!NOTATION ra    SYSTEM "utils/mplayer.exe">
<!NOTATION ram   SYSTEM "utils/mplayer.exe">
<!NOTATION voc   SYSTEM "utils/mplayer.exe">
<!NOTATION mid   SYSTEM "utils/mplayer.exe">
<!NOTATION mov   SYSTEM "utils/mplayer.exe">
<!NOTATION qtw   SYSTEM "utils/mplayer.exe">
<!NOTATION mpg   SYSTEM "utils/mplayer.exe">
<!NOTATION mpeg  SYSTEM "utils/mplayer.exe">
<!NOTATION gif   SYSTEM "utils/lview.exe">
<!NOTATION jpg   SYSTEM "utils/lview.exe">
<!NOTATION jpeg  SYSTEM "utils/lview.exe">
<!NOTATION png   SYSTEM "utils/lview.exe">

<!-- ********** ENTITIES ********** -->
<!-- ********** ENTITIES ********** -->
<!-- ********** ENTITIES ********** -->

<!-- Parameter entities for use elsewhere in the DTD -->
    <!ENTITY % attrdefault "CDATA #IMPLIED" >
    <!ENTITY % attrid "ID #IMPLIED" >

<!-- General entities for use anywhere -->
    <!ENTITY ccedilla "&#231;">

<!-- Genre entities -->
    <!ENTITY W   "Western">
    <!ENTITY C   "Crime/Detective">
    <!ENTITY R   "Romance">
    <!ENTITY WAR "War/Battlefield">
    <!ENTITY COM "Comedy">
    <!ENTITY H   "Horror">
    <!ENTITY SF  "Science Fiction">
    <!ENTITY T   "Thriller">

<!-- Studio entities -->
```

```
<!ENTITY WB  "Warner Brothers">
    <!ENTITY PAR "Paramount">
    <!ENTITY MGM "Metro/Goldwyn/Mayer">
    <!ENTITY FOX "20th Century Fox">

<!-- Common (nay, overused) reviewer ratings entities -->
    <!ENTITY  twothumb "Two thumbs up!">

<!-- Distributor entities -->
    <!ENTITY MUL    "Movies Unlimited">
    <!ENTITY FACETS "Facets Multimedia, Inc.">
    <!ENTITY VAULT  "Video Vault">

<!-- "B-ness" ratings URLs (for styling images via XSL) -->
    <!ENTITY BEE5URL
"http://www.flixml.org/flixml/images/bees5_0.gif">
    <!ENTITY BEE45URL
"http://www.flixml.org/flixml/images/bees4_5.gif">
    <!ENTITY BEE4URL
"http://www.flixml.org/flixml/images/bees4_0.gif">
    <!ENTITY BEE35URL
"http://www.flixml.org/flixml/images/bees3_5.gif">
    <!ENTITY BEE3URL
"http://www.flixml.org/flixml/images/bees3_0.gif">
    <!ENTITY BEE25URL
"http://www.flixml.org/flixml/images/bees2_5.gif">
    <!ENTITY BEE2URL
"http://www.flixml.org/flixml/images/bees2_0.gif">
    <!ENTITY BEE15URL
"http://www.flixml.org/flixml/images/bees1_5.gif">
    <!ENTITY BEE1URL
"http://www.flixml.org/flixml/images/bees1_0.gif">
    <!ENTITY BEEHALFURL
"http://www.flixml.org/flixml/images/bees0_5.gif">
    <!ENTITY BEE0URL
"http://www.flixml.org/flixml/images/bees0_0.gif">

<!-- "B-ness" ratings entities -->
    <!ENTITY BEE5
        SYSTEM "http://www.flixml.org/flixml/images/bees5_0.gif"
        NDATA gif>
    <!ENTITY BEE45
        SYSTEM "http://www.flixml.org/flixml/images/bees4_5.gif"
        NDATA gif>
```

```
<!ENTITY BEE4
        SYSTEM "http://www.flixml.org/flixml/images/bees4_0.gif"
        NDATA gif>
    <!ENTITY BEE35
        SYSTEM "http://www.flixml.org/flixml/images/bees3_5.gif"
        NDATA gif>
    <!ENTITY BEE3
        SYSTEM "http://www.flixml.org/flixml/images/bees3_0.gif"
        NDATA gif>
    <!ENTITY BEE25
        SYSTEM "http://www.flixml.org/flixml/images/bees2_5.gif"
        NDATA gif>
    <!ENTITY BEE2
        SYSTEM "http://www.flixml.org/flixml/images/bees2_0.gif"
        NDATA gif>
    <!ENTITY BEE15
        SYSTEM "http://www.flixml.org/flixml/images/bees1_5.gif"
        NDATA gif>
    <!ENTITY BEE1
        SYSTEM "http://www.flixml.org/flixml/images/bees1_0.gif"
        NDATA gif>
    <!ENTITY BEEHALF
        SYSTEM "http://www.flixml.org/flixml/images/bees0_5.gif"
        NDATA gif>
    <!ENTITY BEE0
        SYSTEM "http://www.flixml.org/flixml/images/bees0_0.gif"
        NDATA gif>

<!-- ********** DOCUMENT CONTENT MODEL ********** -->
<!-- ********** DOCUMENT CONTENT MODEL ********** -->
<!-- ********** DOCUMENT CONTENT MODEL ********** -->

<!ELEMENT       flixinfo
                (contents?,
                title+,
                genre,
                releaseyear,
                language*,
                studio*,
                cast?,
                crew?,
                plotsummary?,
                reviews?,
                clips?,
                distributors?,
```

```
                    dialog?,
                    remarks?,
                    mpaarating?,
                    bees?)>
<!ATTLIST          flixinfo
    author         %attrdefault;
    copyright      %attrdefault;
    id             %attrid;
    xmlns:xlink CDATA #REQUIRED
    xml:lang       NMTOKEN "EN" >

<!ELEMENT          contents (flixmlhome?, section+, contarc?) >
<!ATTLIST          contents
    xlink:type     NMTOKEN #FIXED "extended"
    role           %attrdefault;
    title          %attrdefault;
    id             NMTOKEN #FIXED "contents">

<!ELEMENT          section EMPTY >
<!ATTLIST          section
    xlink:type     NMTOKEN #FIXED "locator"
    xlink:href     CDATA    #REQUIRED
    xlink:role     CDATA "section"
    xlink:title    %attrdefault;
    xlink:show     NMTOKEN #FIXED "replace"
    xlink:actuate NMTOKEN #FIXED "user"
    xlink:id       %attrid;>

<!ELEMENT          contarc EMPTY >
<!ATTLIST          contarc
    xlink:type     NMTOKEN #FIXED "arc"
    xlink:show     NMTOKEN #FIXED "replace"
    xlink:actuate NMTOKEN #FIXED "onRequest">

<!ELEMENT          title (#PCDATA) >
<!ATTLIST          title
    role           (main | alt) "main"
    xml:lang       NMTOKEN "EN"
    id             %attrid;>

<!ELEMENT          genre (primarygenre,
                    othergenre*,
                    genrelinkset?) >
<!ATTLIST          genre
    id             %attrid;>
```

```
<!ELEMENT      primarygenre (#PCDATA) >
<!ATTLIST      primarygenre
    id         %attrid;>

<!ELEMENT      othergenre (#PCDATA) >
<!ATTLIST      othergenre
    id         %attrid;>

<!ELEMENT      genrelinkset (genrelink+)>
<!ATTLIST      genrelinkset
    xlink:type    NMTOKEN #FIXED "extended"
    xlink:title   CDATA   #REQUIRED
    xlink:show    NMTOKEN #FIXED "replace"
    xlink:actuate NMTOKEN #FIXED "onRequest"
    xlink:role    CDATA   #FIXED "extended-linkset">

<!ELEMENT      genrelink EMPTY>
<!ATTLIST      genrelink
    xlink:type  NMTOKEN #FIXED "locator"
    xlink:href  CDATA #REQUIRED
    xlink:title CDATA #REQUIRED>

<!ELEMENT      releaseyear (#PCDATA) >
<!ATTLIST      releaseyear
    role       (initial | alt) #IMPLIED
    id         %attrid;>

<!ELEMENT      language (#PCDATA) >
<!ATTLIST      language
    id         %attrid;>

<!ELEMENT      studio (#PCDATA) >
<!ATTLIST      studio
    id         %attrid;>

<!ELEMENT      cast (leadcast, othercast?) >
<!ATTLIST      cast
    id         %attrid;>

<!ELEMENT      leadcast (male | female | animal)* >
<!ATTLIST      leadcast
    id         %attrid;>
```

```
<!ELEMENT      othercast (male | female | animal)* >
<!ATTLIST      othercast
    id         %attrid;>

<!ELEMENT      male (castmember, role)* >
<!ATTLIST      male
    id         %attrid;>

<!ELEMENT      female (castmember, role)* >
<!ATTLIST      female
    id         %attrid;>

<!ELEMENT      animal (castmember, role, species)* >
<!ATTLIST      animal
    id         %attrid;>

<!ELEMENT      castmember (#PCDATA) >
<!ATTLIST      castmember
    id         %attrid;>

<!ELEMENT      role (#PCDATA) >
<!ATTLIST      role
    id         %attrid;>

<!ELEMENT      species (#PCDATA) >
<!ATTLIST      species
    id         %attrid;>

<!ELEMENT      crew (director*,
               screenwriter*,
               cinematog*,
               sound*,
               editor*,
               score?,
               speceffects*,
               proddesigner*,
               makeup*,
               costumer*) >
<!ATTLIST      crew
    id         %attrid;>

<!ELEMENT      director (#PCDATA) >
<!ATTLIST      director
    id         %attrid;>
```

```
<!ELEMENT       screenwriter (#PCDATA) >
<!ATTLIST       screenwriter
    id          %attrid;>

<!ELEMENT       cinematog (#PCDATA) >
<!ATTLIST       cinematog
    id          %attrid;>

<!ELEMENT       sound (#PCDATA) >
<!ATTLIST       sound
    id          %attrid;>

<!ELEMENT       editor (#PCDATA) >
<!ATTLIST       editor
    id          %attrid;>

<!ELEMENT       score (#PCDATA) >
<!ATTLIST       score
    id          %attrid;>

<!ELEMENT       speceffects (#PCDATA) >
<!ATTLIST       speceffects
    id          %attrid;>

<!ELEMENT       proddesigner (#PCDATA) >
<!ATTLIST       proddesigner
    id          %attrid;>

<!ELEMENT       makeup (#PCDATA) >
<!ATTLIST       makeup
    id          %attrid;>

<!ELEMENT       costumer (#PCDATA) >
<!ATTLIST       costumer
    id          %attrid;>

<!ELEMENT       plotsummary (#PCDATA | emph | parabreak |
    maleref | femaleref | animalref)* >
<!ATTLIST       plotsummary
    id          %attrid;>

<!ELEMENT       emph (#PCDATA) >

<!ELEMENT       maleref (#PCDATA) >
<!ATTLIST       maleref
```

```
        maleid        IDREF #REQUIRED>

<!ELEMENT          femaleref (#PCDATA) >
<!ATTLIST          femaleref
    femaleid       IDREF #REQUIRED>

<!ELEMENT          animalref (#PCDATA) >
<!ATTLIST          animalref
    animalid       IDREF #REQUIRED>

<!ELEMENT          reviews (flixmlreview, otherreview*) >
<!ATTLIST          reviews
    id             %attrid;>

<!ELEMENT          flixmlreview (goodreview | badreview) >
<!ATTLIST          flixmlreview
    id             %attrid;>

<!ELEMENT          otherreview (goodreview | badreview)* >
<!ATTLIST          otherreview
    id             %attrid;>

<!ELEMENT          goodreview ((reviewtext | reviewlink),
reviewrating?) >
<!ATTLIST          goodreview
    id             %attrid;>

<!ELEMENT          badreview ((reviewtext | reviewlink),
reviewrating?) >
<!ATTLIST          badreview
    id             %attrid;>

<!ELEMENT          reviewtext (#PCDATA | emph | parabreak)* >
<!ATTLIST          reviewtext
    id             %attrid;>

<!ELEMENT          reviewlink    (#PCDATA) >
<!ATTLIST          reviewlink
    xlink:type     NMTOKEN #FIXED "simple"
    xlink:href     CDATA   #REQUIRED
    xlink:role     %attrdefault;
    xlink:title    %attrdefault;
    xlink:show     (new | replace | embed) "new"
    xlink:actuate  (user | auto) "user">
```

```
<!ELEMENT        reviewrating   (#PCDATA) >
<!ATTLIST        reviewrating
    id           %attrid;>

<!ELEMENT        clips      (video*, audio*) >
<!ATTLIST        clips
    id           %attrid;>

<!ELEMENT        audio       EMPTY >
<!ATTLIST        audio
    format       NOTATION (wav|au|mid|ra|ram) "wav"
    id           %attrid;>

<!ELEMENT        video EMPTY >
<!ATTLIST        video
    mpaarating   (Unrated | G | PG | PG-13 | R | NC-17 | X
    | Unknown) "Unknown"
    format       NOTATION (mov|qtw|mpg|mpeg) "mov"
    id           %attrid;>


<!ELEMENT        distributors (distributor)+ >
<!ATTLIST        distributors
    id           %attrid;>

<!ELEMENT        distributor (distribname, distribextlink)* >
<!ATTLIST        distributor
    id           %attrid;>

<!ELEMENT        distribname (#PCDATA) >
<!ATTLIST        distribname
    id           %attrid;>

<!ELEMENT        distribextlink (flixmlhome?, distriblink+,
distribarc*) >
<!ATTLIST        distribextlink
    xlink:type   NMTOKEN #FIXED "extended"
    xlink:title %attrdefault;
    id           %attrid;>

<!ELEMENT        flixmlhome EMPTY >
<!ATTLIST        flixmlhome
    xlink:type   NMTOKEN #FIXED "resource"
    xlink:role   NMTOKEN #FIXED "home"
    xlink:title CDATA   #FIXED "FlixML Review" >
```

```
<!ELEMENT     distriblink EMPTY >
<!ATTLIST     distriblink
    xlink:type   NMTOKEN #FIXED "locator"
    xlink:href   CDATA #REQUIRED
    xlink:role   NMTOKEN #IMPLIED
    xlink:title  %attrdefault;
    id           %attrid;>

<!ELEMENT     distribarc EMPTY>
<!ATTLIST     distribarc
    xlink:type    NMTOKEN #FIXED "arc"
    xlink:show    NMTOKEN #FIXED "replace"
    xlink:actuate NMTOKEN #FIXED "onRequest"
    xlink:from    NMTOKEN #IMPLIED
    xlink:to      NMTOKEN #IMPLIED >

<!ELEMENT     dialog (#PCDATA) >
<!ATTLIST     dialog
    id           %attrid;>

<!ELEMENT     remarks (#PCDATA | parabreak)* >
<!ATTLIST     remarks
    id           %attrid;>

<!ELEMENT     parabreak EMPTY >

<!ELEMENT     mpaarating (#PCDATA) >
<!ATTLIST     mpaarating
    id           %attrid;>

<!ELEMENT     bees EMPTY >
<!ATTLIST     bees
    b-ness       %attrdefault;
    b-nesspic    ENTITY #IMPLIED
    id           %attrid;>
```

Sample FlixML Review

I've included what are currently the most complete of these—for *Carnival of Souls* and *Detour*. I haven't prettied them up with indentations, for the obvious reason—they're meant to be *processed*, and consequently the less extraneous whitespace, the better.

carnival_of_souls.xml

```
<?xml version="1.0"?>
<!DOCTYPE flixinfo SYSTEM "http://www.flixml.org/flixml/
  flixml_03.dtd">
<?xml-stylesheet type="text/xsl" xlink:href="flixml2.xsl" ?>
<flixinfo author="John E. Simpson" copyright="1999" xml:lang="EN"
xmlns:xlink="http://www.w3.org/1999/xlink/namespace/">
<contents>
<section xlink:title="Cast" xlink:href="castID"/>
<section xlink:title="Crew" xlink:href="crewID"/>
<section xlink:title="Plot" xlink:href="plotID"/>
<section xlink:title="Reviews" xlink:href="revwID"/>
<section xlink:title="Get It" xlink:href="distribID"/>
<section xlink:title="Ratings" xlink:href="rateID"/>
</contents>
<title role="main">Carnival of Souls</title>
<title role="alt">Corridors of Evil</title>
<genre>
<primarygenre>&T;</primarygenre>
<othergenre>&H;</othergenre>
</genre>
<releaseyear role="initial">1962</releaseyear>
<language>English</language>
<studio>Herts-Lion International Corp.</studio>
<cast id="castID">
<leadcast>
<female id="CHilligoss"><castmember>Candace
Hilligoss</castmember><role>Mary Henry</role></female>
<female id="FFeist"><castmember>Francis Feist</
  castmember><role>Mrs. Thomas</role></female>
<male id="SBerger"><castmember>Sidney Berger</
  castmember><role>John Linden</role></male>
<male id="AEllison"><castmember>Art Ellison</castmember><role>The
  Minister</role></male>
<male id="SLevitt"><castmember>Stan Levitt</castmember><role>Dr.
  Samuels (psychologist)</role></male>
</leadcast>
<othercast>
<male><castmember>Tom McGinnis</castmember><role>Boss at the
organ factory</role></male>
<male><castmember>Forbes Caldwell</castmember><role>Laborer at
  the organ factory</role></male>
<male><castmember>Dan Palmquist</castmember><role>Service station
  attendant</role></male>
```

```
<male id="HHervey"><castmember>Herk Hervey</
  castmember><role>Creepy Man</role></male>
</othercast>
</cast>
<crew id="crewID">
<director>Herk Hervey</director>
<screenwriter>John Clifford</screenwriter>
<cinematog>Maurice Prather</cinematog>
<sound>Ed Down</sound>
<sound>Don Jessup</sound>
<editor>Dan Palmquist</editor>
<editor>Bill de Jarnette</editor>
<score>Gene Moore</score>
<speceffects></speceffects>
<proddesigner></proddesigner>
<makeup>George Corn</makeup>
<costumer></costumer>
</crew>
<plotsummary id="plotID">Timid church organist <femaleref
  femaleid="CHilligoss">Mary</femaleref> is a passenger in a car
  run off a bridge by another car in a rollicking, high-spirited
  race. She emerges from the waters looking about like you'd
  expect for a young woman in her circumstances in a 1962 movie:
  her party dress ruined, in fact utterly ghastly. No Wet T-Shirt
  Night <emph>here</emph>.<parabreak/>Traumatized by the wreck,
  Mary decides to move away from the town, to a town where she
  knows absolutely no one. Yet her troubles aren't over. On the
  way, she sees the first of what will turn out to be many
  ghoulish apparitions: <maleref maleid="HHervey">a man</maleref>
  in a dark suit, his skin and hair ghostly white, his eyes and
  mouth those of a zombie. Later, after she's settled in (after a
  fashion) in a boarding home, she begins to experience
  terrifying interludes of absolute silence; not only can she not
  hear anything, but everyone else can neither see nor hear her.
  Meanwhile she experiences a strange fascination (despite the
  warnings of the priest who has employed her) with an abandoned
  amusement park whose days and nights have more music than the
  merely living might expect....</plotsummary>
<reviews id="revwID">
<flixmlreview>
<goodreview>
<!-- Note to self: Don't forget to replace placeholder
below with REAL review -->
<reviewtext>(Some text)</reviewtext>
</goodreview>
```

```
</flixmlreview>
<otherreview>
<goodreview>
<reviewlink xlink:href=
"http://www.suntimes.com/ebert/ebert_reviews/1989/10/379589.html"
>Roger Ebert</reviewlink>
</goodreview>
<goodreview>
<reviewlink xlink:href=
"http://www.imagesjournal.com/issue05/reviews/carnival.htm">
Images: A Journal of Film and Popular Culture</reviewlink>
</goodreview>
</otherreview>
</reviews>
<clips></clips>
<distributors id="distribID">
<distributor><distribname>&MUL;</distribname><distribextlink>
<distriblink xlink:href="http://www.moviesunlimited.com/musite/">
</distriblink></distribextlink></distributor>
<distributor><distribname>Reel.com</distribname><distribextlink>
<distriblink xlink:href=
"http://www.reel.com/Content/moviepage.asp?mmid=153">
</distriblink></distribextlink></distributor>
<distributor><distribname>Amazon.com</distribname>
<distribextlink><distriblink xlink:href="http://www.amazon.com/
  exec/obidos/ASIN/6303998704">
</distriblink></distribextlink></distributor>
<distributor><distribname>&FACETS;</distribname><distribextlink>
<distriblink xlink:href="http://www.facets.org/"></distriblink>
</distribextlink></distributor>
</distributors>
<dialog>Mary: Thank you for the coffee. It was unsanitary but
delicious.</dialog>
<remarks>This is one of the most disquieting horror films ever
  made, in my opinion -- even more so than Night of the Living
  Dead (which was made six years later). As if Mary's encounters
  with the dead aren't bizarre enough, her contacts with the
  living seem scarcely less off-kilter.<parabreak/>There's a
  great moment, just before one of her "episodes," when she
  wheels her car into a service station to have its transmission
  looked at. The guy has her pull the car onto the lift and then,
  naturally (at least naturally for those days), opens the door
  so she can wait while he works on the car. No, she tells him,
  she'd like to stay in the car. So he raises it up on the
  lift.<parabreak/>There she sits, perched six to seven feet off
```

the floor, even while the mechanic goes off to attend to other customers. Her being perched there just accents her separation from the world around her; it's not any more claustrophobic than any other scene that occurs in a car, but it sure feels that way.<parabreak/>Reportedly, Carnival of Souls cost a mere $30,000 to make; it was shot in Lawrence, Kansas, and in Salt Lake City (the site of the creepy amusement park). Mary's gauche neighbor -- the kind of guy you picture wolf-whistling at dames on the street corner -- was played by Sidney Berger, a University of Kansas drama teacher at the time.<parabreak/>B movie moment: the flat cardboard car "window" behind Mary's head as she's driving to her new hometown. Also, my tape of the film (which I bought pre-recorded) does not display "Carnival of Souls" during the opening credits; instead, it flashes the words "Corridors of Evil" (the movie's alternate title) in a title slide for several seconds. There aren't many corridors in the movie, though.</remarks>
<mpaarating id="rateID">NR</mpaarating>
<bees b-ness="&BEE4URL;"/>
</flixinfo>

detour.xml

```
<?xml version="1.0"?>
<!DOCTYPE flixinfo SYSTEM "http://www.flixml.org/flixml/
  flixml_03.dtd">
<?xml-stylesheet type="text/xsl" href="flixml.xsl" ?>
<flixinfo author="John E. Simpson" copyright="2000"
  xmlns:xlink="http://www.w3.org/1999/xlink/namespace/">
<contents>
<section xlink:title="Cast" xlink:href="#castID"/>
<section xlink:title="Crew" xlink:href="#crewID"/>
<section xlink:title="Plot" xlink:href="#plotID"/>
<section xlink:title="Reviews" xlink:href="#revwID"/>
<section xlink:title="Get It" xlink:href="#distribID"/>
<section xlink:title="Ratings" xlink:href="#rateID"/>
</contents>
<title role="main">Detour</title>
<genre>
<primarygenre>Crime/Detective</primarygenre>
</genre>
<releaseyear role="initial">1945</releaseyear>
<language>English</language>
```

```
<studio>PRC (Producers Releasing Corporation)</studio>
<cast id="castID">
<leadcast>
<male id="TNeal"><castmember>Tom Neal</castmember><role>Al
Roberts</role></male>
<female id="ASavage"><castmember>Ann Savage</
  castmember><role>Vera</role></female>
</leadcast>
<othercast>
<male id="EMcDonald"><castmember>Edmund McDonald</
  castmember><role>Charles Haskell, Jr.</role></male>
<male id="TRyan"><castmember>Tim Ryan</castmember><role>Guy at
  diner</role></male>
<male><castmember>Don Brodie</castmember><role>Used-car
salesman</role></male>
<female id="CDrake"><castmember>Claudia Drake</
  castmember><role>Sue Harvey</role></female>
<female><castmember>Esther Howard</castmember><role>Holly</
  role></female></othercast>
</cast>
<crew id="crewID">
<director>Edgar G. Ulmer</director>
<screenwriter>Martin Goldsmith (adapted from his novel)</
  screenwriter>
<cinematog>Benjamin H. Kline</cinematog>
<sound>Max Hutchinson</sound>
<editor>George McGuire</editor>
<score>Erdody</score>
<speceffects></speceffects>
<proddesigner>Glenn P. Thompson</proddesigner>
<makeup>Bud Westmore</makeup>
<costumer>Mona Barry</costumer>
</crew>
<plotsummary id="plotID">The plot revolves around a guy
<maleref maleid="TNeal">Al</maleref>, who's a piano player in an
  act with his fiancee <femaleref femaleid="CDrake">Sue</
  femaleref>, a night-club singer in Manhattan. Seeking her
  fortune, Sue decides to move to California. Al stays behind for
  a while, but eventually comes to feel he's got to follow her to
  the Golden State.
<parabreak/>
There's one problem: He doesn't have a car. So he makes up his
  mind to hitchhike across the country. His last ride is with a
  guy named <maleref maleid="EMcDonald">Haskell</maleref> who
  tells him a horrific story of a woman he met, a real tigress
```

```
    (as they used to say) -- for proof, he rolls up his sleeves to
    show Al the scars her nails left on his arms. ("You know, there
    oughta be a law against dames with claws," Haskell says.)
<parabreak/>
Weirdly (but this is a B film, after all), Haskell dies while
    Al's in the car. (He gets out in a rainstorm, slips and hits
    his head on a rock.) Al panics, thinking that he may somehow be
    implicated in killing the poor man; he drags the body into the
    desert and hides it where it won't be found. Then (also
    weirdly) he <emph>assumes the dead man's identity</emph> --
    takes his wallet and car, and drives off.
<parabreak/>
On the way, he picks up a hitchhiker of his own -- a woman named
    <femaleref femaleid="ASavage">Vera</femaleref>. Guess which
    woman she is? Right: the dame with claws.
<parabreak/>
(I won't spoil your enjoyment of Detour by giving you further
    plot details at this point. All in good time, all in good
    time.)
</plotsummary>
<reviews id="revwID">
<flixmlreview>
<goodreview>
<reviewtext>A knockout of a B film, especially if you like your
    Bs cool, noir, and cheesy.<parabreak/>Now, don't think "cheesy"
    in the sense of unwatchable -- "Detour" is indeed quite
    watchable. When I say "Cheesy" I mean just that it
    <emph>looks</emph> and <emph>sounds</emph> cheesy.</reviewtext>
<reviewrating></reviewrating>
</goodreview>
</flixmlreview>
<otherreview>
<goodreview>
<reviewlink xlink:href="http://the-fringe.com/flicker/detour/
    index.html">Chad Ossman's Complete "Detour" analysis</
    reviewlink>
</goodreview>
<goodreview>
<reviewlink xlink:href="http://us.imdb.com/
    TUrls?COM+Detour+(1945)">
Internet Movie Database page of "Detour" links</reviewlink>
</goodreview>
<goodreview>
<reviewlink xlink:href="http://www.amesev.net/movies/reviews/
    detour.html">
```

```
William Shriver's/Ames Iowa - At the Movies "Detour"
review</reviewlink>
</goodreview>
</otherreview>
</reviews>
<clips></clips>
<distributors id="distribID">
<distributor><distribname>&MUL;</distribname><distribextlink>
<distriblink xlink:href="http://www.moviesunlimited.com/musite/">
</distriblink></distribextlink></distributor>
<distributor><distribname>Reel.com</distribname><distribextlink>
<distriblink xlink:href=
"http://www.reel.com/Content/moviepage.asp?mmid=4026">
</distriblink></distribextlink></distributor>
<distributor><distribname>Amazon.com</distribname>
<distribextlink><distriblink xlink:href=
"http://www.amazon.com/exec/obidos/ASIN/6303038743">
</distriblink></distribextlink></distributor>
<distributor><distribname>&FACETS;</distribname><distribextlink>
<distriblink xlink:href="http://www.facets.org/"></distriblink>
</distribextlink></distributor>
</distributors>
<dialog>Al: That's life. Whichever way you turn, Fate sticks out
   a foot to trip you.</dialog>
<remarks>This is a great, but inarguably B-grade, film. The
   black-and-white Detour was written and directed by Edgar G.
   Ulmer, and shot in six days on an extremely limited budget. It
   looks it, too. But Detour really is a classic, and set the
   noir-style template of disillusion and cruel fate that marked
   many later postwar films.</remarks>
<mpaarating id="rateID">NR</mpaarating>
<bees b-ness="&BEE4URL;" b-nesspic="BEE4"/>
</flixinfo>
```

XSLT Stylesheet

The stylesheet shown here isn't the only one I've used for transforming FlixML reviews to HTML. But it does show the widest range of XSLT syntax, including named templates, attribute sets, and so on.

flixml.xsl

```
<xsl:stylesheet version "1.0"
    xmlns:xsl="http://www.w3.org/1999/XSL/Transform"
    xmlns="http://www.w3.org/TR/REC-html40"
    xmlns:xlink="http://www.w3.org/1999/xlink/namespace/">

<xsl:output method="html"/>

<xsl:variable name="title" select="//title[@role='main']"/>

<xsl:template match="flixinfo">
    <html>
    <head><title>FlixML Review: <xsl:value-of
        select="title"/></title>
    <link rel="stylesheet" type="text/css"
        href="flixml_in_html.css"></link>
    </head>
    <body>
        <xsl:apply-templates/>
    </body>
    </html>
</xsl:template>

<xsl:attribute-set name="table-attribs">
    <xsl:attribute name="width">90%</xsl:attribute>
    <xsl:attribute name="cellspacing">3</xsl:attribute>
    <xsl:attribute name="cellpadding">3</xsl:attribute>
    <xsl:attribute name="border">0</xsl:attribute>
</xsl:attribute-set>

<xsl:attribute-set name="td-attribs-col1">
    <xsl:attribute name="width">200</xsl:attribute>
</xsl:attribute-set>

<xsl:attribute-set name="td-attribs-col2">
    <xsl:attribute name="width">400</xsl:attribute>
</xsl:attribute-set>

<xsl:template name="casttemp">
    <tr>
        <td xsl:use-attribute-sets="td-attribs-col1"><b>
        <a name="{@id}"/><xsl:value-of
            select="castmember"/></b></td>
```

```
            <td xsl:use-attribute-sets="td-attribs-col2">
                 <xsl:value-of select="role"/></td>
      </tr>
</xsl:template>


<xsl:template match="title[@role='main']">
    <table xsl:use-attribute-sets="table-attribs"><tr>
    <td class="primary"><xsl:apply-templates/></td></tr></table>
</xsl:template>

<xsl:template match="title[@role='alt']">
    <table xsl:use-attribute-sets="table-attribs">
         <tr>
              <td class="alttitle">a/k/a
                    <xsl:apply-templates/></td></tr></table>
</xsl:template>

<xsl:template match="bees">
    <table xsl:use-attribute-sets="table-attribs">
         <tr><td class="header">B-ness
              Rating</td></tr><tr><td>
              <img src="{@b-ness}" border="0" />
              <xsl:apply-templates/></td></tr></table>
</xsl:template>

<xsl:template match="primarygenre">
    <table xsl:use-attribute-sets="table-attribs">
    <tr><td xsl:use-attribute-sets="td-attribs-col1">
    <b>Primary Genre</b></td>
    <td xsl:use-attribute-sets="td-attribs-col2">
    <xsl:apply-templates/></td></tr></table>
</xsl:template>

<xsl:template match="othergenre">
    <table xsl:use-attribute-sets="table-attribs">
    <tr>
         <td xsl:use-attribute-sets="td-attribs-col1">
              <b>Other Genre</b></td>
         <td xsl:use-attribute-sets="td-attribs-col2">
              <xsl:apply-templates/></td></tr></table>
</xsl:template>

<xsl:template match="releaseyear">
```

```
    <table xsl:use-attribute-sets="table-attribs">
    <tr>
            <td xsl:use-attribute-sets="td-attribs-col1">
                    <b>Released</b></td>
            <td xsl:use-attribute-sets="td-attribs-col2">
                    <xsl:apply-templates/></td></tr></table>
</xsl:template>

<xsl:template match="language">
    <table xsl:use-attribute-sets="table-attribs">
    <tr>
            <td xsl:use-attribute-sets="td-attribs-col1">
                    <b>Language</b></td>
            <td xsl:use-attribute-sets="td-attribs-col2">
                    <xsl:apply-templates/></td></tr></table>
</xsl:template>

<xsl:template match="studio">
    <table xsl:use-attribute-sets="table-attribs">
    <tr>
            <td xsl:use-attribute-sets="td-attribs-col1">
                    <b>Studio</b></td>
            <td xsl:use-attribute-sets="td-attribs-col2">
                    <xsl:apply-templates/></td></tr></table>
</xsl:template>

<xsl:template match="cast">
    <table xsl:use-attribute-sets="table-attribs">
            <tr><xsl:apply-templates/></tr></table>
</xsl:template>

<xsl:template match="cast/leadcast">
    <table xsl:use-attribute-sets="table-attribs">
            <tr><td colspan="2" class="header">Lead Cast</td></tr>
            <tr>
                    <td xsl:use-attribute-sets="td-attribs-col1">
                            <b><i>Name</i></b><hr size="1"/></td>
                    <td xsl:use-attribute-sets="td-attribs-col2">
                            <i>Role</i><hr size="1"/></td></tr>
            <xsl:for-each select="male | female">
                    <xsl:call-template name="casttemp"/>
            </xsl:for-each>
    </table>
</xsl:template>
```

```
<xsl:template match="cast/othercast">
    <table xsl:use-attribute-sets="table-attribs">
            <tr>
                    <td colspan="2" class="header">Supporting
  Cast</td>
            </tr>
            <tr>
                    <td xsl:use-attribute-sets="td-attribs-col1">
                            <b><i>Name</i></b><hr size="1"/></td>
                    <td xsl:use-attribute-sets="td-attribs-col2">
                            <i>Role</i><hr size="1"/></td></tr>
                    <xsl:for-each select="male | female">
                            <xsl:call-template name="casttemp"/>
                    </xsl:for-each>
    </table>
</xsl:template>

<xsl:template match="crew">
    <table xsl:use-attribute-sets="table-attribs">
            <tr><td colspan="2" class="header">Crew</td></tr>
    <xsl:apply-templates/></table>
</xsl:template>

<xsl:template name="crewrow">
    <xsl:param name="crewtitle">[Title]</xsl:param>
    <tr>
            <td xsl:use-attribute-sets="td-attribs-col1">
                    <b><xsl:value-of select="$crewtitle"/></b></td>
            <td xsl:use-attribute-sets="td-attribs-col2">
                    <xsl:apply-templates/></td></tr>
</xsl:template>

<xsl:template match="director">
    <xsl:call-template name="crewrow">
            <xsl:with-param name="crewtitle">Director
                    </xsl:with-param>
    </xsl:call-template>
</xsl:template>

<xsl:template match="screenwriter">
    <xsl:call-template name="crewrow">
            <xsl:with-param name="crewtitle">Screenwriter
                    </xsl:with-param>
    </xsl:call-template>
</xsl:template>
```

```
<xsl:template match="cinematog">
    <xsl:call-template name="crewrow">
        <xsl:with-param name="crewtitle">Cinematographer
            </xsl:with-param>
    </xsl:call-template>
</xsl:template>

<xsl:template match="sound">
    <xsl:call-template name="crewrow">
        <xsl:with-param name="crewtitle">Sound
            </xsl:with-param>
    </xsl:call-template>
</xsl:template>

<xsl:template match="editor">
    <xsl:call-template name="crewrow">
        <xsl:with-param name="crewtitle">Editor
            </xsl:with-param>
    </xsl:call-template>
</xsl:template>

<xsl:template match="score">
    <xsl:call-template name="crewrow">
        <xsl:with-param name="crewtitle">Score
            </xsl:with-param>
    </xsl:call-template>
</xsl:template>

<xsl:template match="speceffects">
    <xsl:call-template name="crewrow">
        <xsl:with-param name="crewtitle">Special Effects
            </xsl:with-param>
    </xsl:call-template>
</xsl:template>

<xsl:template match="proddesigner">
    <xsl:call-template name="crewrow">
        <xsl:with-param name="crewtitle">Production Design
            </xsl:with-param>
    </xsl:call-template>
</xsl:template>

<xsl:template match="makeup">
    <xsl:call-template name="crewrow">
        <xsl:with-param name="crewtitle">Makeup
```

```
                        </xsl:with-param>
    </xsl:call-template>
</xsl:template>

<xsl:template match="costumer">
    <xsl:call-template name="crewrow">
            <xsl:with-param name="crewtitle">Costumes
                </xsl:with-param>
    </xsl:call-template>
</xsl:template>

<xsl:template match="plotsummary">
    <table xsl:use-attribute-sets="table-attribs">
            <tr>
                    <td class="header">The Plot</td></tr>
            <tr>
                    <td><xsl:apply-templates/></td></tr>
    </table>
</xsl:template>

<xsl:template match="maleref">
            <a href="#{@maleid}"><xsl:apply-templates/></a>
</xsl:template>

<xsl:template match="femaleref">
            <a href="#{@femaleid}"><xsl:apply-templates/></a>
</xsl:template>

<xsl:template match="parabreak">
    <p></p><xsl:apply-templates/>
</xsl:template>

<xsl:template match="emph">
    <em><xsl:apply-templates/></em>
</xsl:template>

<xsl:template match="otherreview">
    <table xsl:use-attribute-sets="table-attribs">
    <tr><td class="header">External Reviews</td></tr></table>
    <ul>
    <xsl:for-each select="goodreview|badreview">
            <li><a href="{reviewlink/@xlink:href}">
                    <xsl:value-of select="reviewlink"/></a></li>
    </xsl:for-each>
    </ul>
```

```
</xsl:template>

<xsl:template match="distributors">
    <table xsl:use-attribute-sets="table-attribs">
            <tr>
                    <td class="header" colspan="2">Buy or Rent
                        "<xsl:value-of select="$title"/>"</td></tr>
                    <xsl:for-each select="distributor">
                        <xsl:sort select="distribname"/>
                    <tr>
                    <td xsl:use-attribute-sets="td-attribs-col1"
                            valign="top">
                            <b><xsl:value-of
   select="distribname"/></b>
                    </td>
                    <xsl:for-each select="distribextlink/
   distriblink">
                            <td xsl:use-attribute-sets="td-attribs-
   col2"
                                    valign="top"><a
   href="{@xlink:href}">
                                    <xsl:value-of
   select="@xlink:href"/>
                                    </a></td>
                    </xsl:for-each></tr>
            </xsl:for-each>
    </table>
</xsl:template>

<xsl:template match="remarks">
    <table xsl:use-attribute-sets="table-attribs">
    <tr><td class="header">Remarks</td></tr>
    <tr><td><xsl:apply-templates/></td></tr></table>
</xsl:template>

<xsl:template match="mpaarating">
    <table xsl:use-attribute-sets="table-attribs">
            <tr><td class="header">MPAA Rating</td></tr>
            <tr><td><xsl:apply-templates/></td></tr>
    </table>
</xsl:template>

<xsl:template match="dialog">
    <table xsl:use-attribute-sets="table-attribs">
            <tr><td class="header">classic dialog</td></tr>
```

```
            <tr><td><xsl:apply-templates/></td></tr></table>
</xsl:template>

</xsl:stylesheet>
```

CSS2 Stylesheet

Finally, there's this: a CSS2 stylesheet, expressly designed for use with the above XSLT stylesheet. (Note that it's specified in the template for the `flixinfo` element, appearing as an attribute to the `link` element in the result tree.)

flixml_in_html.css

```
*  {
            font-family: Verdana,Helvetica,Univers,sans-serif;
}

.primary {
            font-family: Verdana,Helvetica,Univers,sans-serif;
            font-size: 24pt;
            font-weight: bold;
            background: teal;
            text-transform: none;
            text-align: left;
            line-height: 26pt;
            margin-top: .125in;
            margin-bottom: .125in;
            margin-left: .125in;
            margin-right: .125in;
            padding: 0in;
            border-top: double;
            border-bottom: double;
            position: static;
            width: 640px;
            height: 1in;
}
.menu {
            font-family: Courier,Courier New,monospace;
            font-size: 8pt;
            font-weight: bold;
            background: silver;
            text-align: center;
```

```
}
.alttitle {
        font-family: Verdana,Helvetica,Univers,sans-serif;
        font-size: 18pt;
        font-weight: bold;
        background: #2D9696;
        text-transform: none;
        text-align: right;
        line-height: 26pt;
        margin-top: .125in;
        margin-bottom: .125in;
        margin-left: .125in;
        margin-right: .125in;
        padding: 0in;
        border-top: double;
        border-bottom: double;
        position: static;
        width: 640px;
}
.header {
        font-family: Verdana,Helvetica,Univers,sans-serif;
        font-size: 18pt;
        font-weight: bold;
        background: silver;
        text-align: left;
        text-transform: lowercase;
}
.subheader {
        font-family: Verdana,Helvetica,Univers,sans-serif;
        font-size: 12pt;
        font-weight: bold;
        background: silver;
        text-align: right;
}
.callout {
        font-family: Verdana,Helvetica,Univers,sans-serif;
        font-size: 12pt;
        font-style: italic;
        background: #ADBFD3;
        padding: 8;
        text-align: right;
        border-top: double;
        border-bottom: double;
        width: 200;
        float: right;
}
```

Other Resources

I'm sorry, I just couldn't tell you *everything* about XML in *Just XML*—or about B movies, for that matter. This appendix will point you in the direction of some fairly authoritative resources for further reference.

XML-related W3C Specifications/Proposals

XML 1.0 Recommendation:

> http://www.w3.org/TR/1998/REC-xml-19980210

There's also a wonderful annotated version of this, by Tim Bray (co-editor of the spec), which is one of my most oft-consulted XML resources; find it at:

> http://www.xml.com/axml/axml.html

Namespaces in XML Recommendation:

> http://www.w3.org/TR/1999/REC-xml-names-19990114

XLink Working Draft:

> http://www.w3.org/TR/xlink

XPointer Recommendation:

> http://www.w3.org/TR/xptr

XPath Recommendation:

> http://www.w3.org/TR/xpath

CSS2 Recommendation:

> http://www.w3.org/TR/REC-CSS2

XSLT Recommendation:

> http://www.w3.org/TR/xslt

XSL Formatting Objects (FO) Working Draft:

> http://www.w3.org/TR/xsl

DOM Level 1 Recommendation:

> http://www.w3.org/TR/REC-DOM-Level-1

RDF Model and Syntax Recommendation:

> http://www.w3.org/TR/REC-rdf-syntax

Other Web resources

Robin Cover's SGML/XML page: In many respects, this is the "master site." Frequently updated, it includes pointers to all the XML software covered in Chapter 10, to current versions of all XML-related specs, and to just about anything else XML-related, as well as cross-references to other links within the site itself.

> http://www.oasis-open.org/cover/

The XML FAQ:

> http://www.ucc.ie/xml/

James Tauber's XML sites: Tauber has set up three excellent sites that can be the starting point for just about any XML exploration. Respectively, they provide general XML information, links to XML software sites, and links to schemas and DTDs of all sorts:

> http://www.xmlinfo.com
> http://www.xmlsoftware.com
> http://www.schema.net

Lars Marius Garshol's page of links to free XML software:

> http://www.stud.ifi.uio.no/~larsga/linker/XMLtools.html

W3C page of links to information about encoding:

> http://www.w3.org/International/O-charset.html

Mailing lists and newsgroups

XML-DEV: Primarily for *developers* of XML software, rather than for user or other general discussion. Archive at:

```
http://xml.org/archives/xml-dev/threads.html
```

To subscribe, send an e-mail to: majordomo@xml.org. The message body should simply say:

```
subscribe xml-dev
```

XML-L: General discussion of XML and related technologies, for users as well as developers. To subscribe, send an e-mail to: listserv@listserv.hea.ie. The message body should simply say:

```
subscribe xml-l "yourname"
```

XSL-List: Discussion of XSLT (including XPath) and XSL FOs. Archive and general information (including subscription info) at:

```
http://www.mulberrytech.com/xsl/xsl-list
```

XLXP-DEV: Discussion of XLink, XPointer, XPath, and related subjects. To subscribe, send an e-mail to: majordomo@fsc.fujitsu.com. The message body should simply say:

```
subscribe xlxp-dev "yourname"
```

Microsoft XML discussion forum:

```
news://msnews.microsoft.com/microsoft.public.xml
```

For other mailing lists and newsgroups, see the list at:

```
http://www.oasis-open.org/cover/xml.html#discussionLists
```

B movie information

As I've said, I can't possibly cover everything you might want to know about the Bs. Here are some places to check if you're interested in more information.

Web resources

I'm collecting a page of links on this subject. It's at:

```
http://www.flixml.org/bmovies.html
```

Let me know if you've got additions or corrections, at: simpson@flixml.org. For now, here are a couple of sites to get you started:

- **The B-Film Webring:** A collection of sites dedicated to the Bs; complete lists of member sites at:

      http://www.webring.org/cgi-bin/webring?ring=bfilm;list

- **MonsterVision with Joe Bob Briggs:** Briggs (certainly one of the funniest people on the planet) hosts the Saturday late-night "MonsterVision" program on the TNT cable channel. As the name implies, many of the films are of the horror or science-fiction genres... not all of them, though.

Books

- **Second Feature: The Best of the Bs:** John Cocchi; 1991. A Citadel Press Book, Published by Carol Publishing Group. ISBN 0-8065-1186-9. ($16.95)
- **A Girl and a Gun: The Complete Guide to Film Noir on Video:** David N. Meyer; 1998. Avon Books. ISBN 0-380-79067-X. ($14.00)
- **The Devil Thumbs a Ride (and Other Unforgettable Films):** Barry Gifford; 1988. Grove Press. ISBN 0-8021-3078-X. (Now out of print, sadly; price according to the jacket is $7.98. I found my copy via Amazon.com's out-of-print book search; it took them four months to come up with it!)
- **Mondo Macabro: Weird & Wonderful Cinema Around the World:** Pete Tombs; 1998. ST. Martin's/Griffin. ISBN 0-312-18748-3. ($18.95)
- **VideoHound's Golden Movie Retriever (1998 ed.):** Various contributors; 1998. Visible Ink Press, a division of Gale Research. ISBN 1-57859-024-8. ($19.95 for nearly 1800 pages—a bargain)
- Also see **VideoHound's Complete Guide to Cult Flicks and Trash Pics:** Various contributors; 1996. Visible Ink Press, a division of Gale Research. ISBN 0-7876-0616-2. ($16.95)

Videotape/DVD distributors

- By far, the one catalog you must have is the one for **Movies Unlimited** (70,000+ titles!). Call 1-800-4-MOVIES, contact via e-mail at movies@moviesunlimited.com, or visit their Web site at:

      http://www.moviesunlimited.com

(Note that the Movies Unlimited catalog is not free—it costs $19.95.)

• Another good source is **Facets Multimedia** (35,000 titles), not just a film distributor but more like a complete film *experience*. It may be a little hard to believe that Movies Unlimited, above, doesn't carry *everything*. Nevertheless, for one instance, they didn't have *Ms. .45*—I got my copy from Facets instead. (When you're skulking about in the dark alleyways of B films, I guess you can expect to run into some snags.) Rentals by mail available, too. Call them at 1-800-331-6197, send e-mail to sales@facets.org, or visit the Web site at:

```
http://www.facets.org
```

• Of course, there's always **Amazon.com**:

```
http://www.amazon.com
```

• ...as well as **Reel.com**:

```
http://www.reel.com
```

INDEX

E

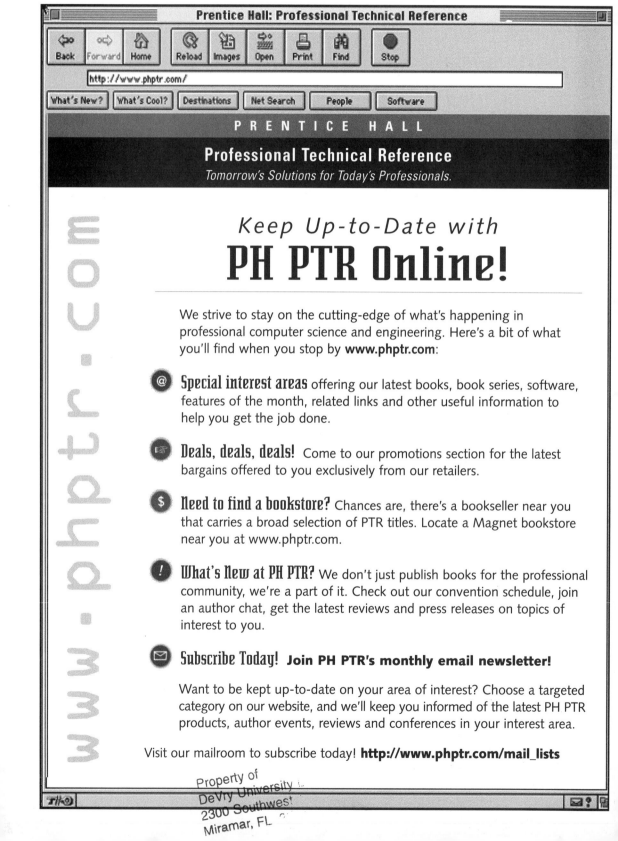
Property of
DeVry University
2300 Southwest
Miramar, FL